WORKFLOW
HANDBOOK 1997

WORKFLOW HANDBOOK 1997

Edited by Peter Lawrence

Published in association
with the Workflow Management Coalition

JOHN WILEY & SONS LTD
Chichester • New York • Weinheim • Brisbane • Singapore • Toronto

Other Wiley Editorial Offices

John Wiley & Sons, Inc., 605 Third Avenue,
New York, NY 10158-0012, USA

VCH Verlagsgesellschaft mbH,
Pappelallee 3, D-69469 Weinheim, Germany

Jacaranda Wiley Ltd, 33 Park Road, Milton,
Queensland 4064, Australia

John Wiley & Sons (Canada) Ltd, 22 Worcester Road,
Rexdale, Ontario M9W 1L1, Canada

John Wiley & Sons (Asia) Pte Ltd, 2 Clementi Loop #02-01,
Jin Xing Distripark, Singapore 0512

British Library Cataloguing in Publication Data

A catalogue record for this book is available from the British Library

ISBN 0 471 96947 8

Typeset by the Publishing Technology Dept, John Wiley & Sons
Printed and bound in Great Britain by Biddles Ltd, Guildford and King's Lynn
This book is printed on acid-free paper responsibly manufactured from sustainable forestation,
for which at least two trees are planted for each one used for paper production.

Contents List

APPENDICES   493

Foreword

The Workflow Handbook has been created for you by the Workflow Management Coalition (WfMC). Founded in 1993, WfMC is an organization of more than 170 members located in 24 countries around the world. Its focus is on the advancement of the workflow management technology and its use in industry.

The Workflow Handbook will provide you with valuable information concerning the management of business processes and the attendant benefits.

In the physical world, it would be difficult to identify an action that did not interact in some way with other activities which combine to make up one or more processes. A great amount of research goes into the discovery of what activities make up a physical process and the determination of what rules govern particular processes. Business processes bear a close resemblance to those in the physical world in that business processes comprise discrete activities operating under a set of rules to achieve one or more results. However, unlike naturally occurring physical processes, business processes with their associated activities and rules of operation are defined by humans. Workflow Management is all about the definition and management of business processes through the use of computer technology.

Today, the use of Information Technology is dominating all aspects of business. So, too, is Workflow Management applicable to and becoming pervasive in all industries. Within this context, Workflow Management is experiencing evolution in three areas; 1) in the way it is increasingly being exploited by the industry; 2) in the advances of the workflow technology itself, and; 3) in its interaction with the myriad facets of new computer technologies. The accelerating adoption of new technologies such as the Internet, multimedia, and others is causing shifts in the way people work and in their work environment. The Workflow Management Coalition is chartered with keeping pace with these advances. You will see some of these topics addressed in this book. WfMC's initial activities centred around groundwork for the definition of a universal Reference Model for workflow systems together with a Glossary of workflow terminology to be used in developing subsequent specifications of WfMC's reference model APIs. The first of these API specifications (Interface 2) was formally released in late 1995.

With such a broad range of applicability, it is easy to understand why the Workflow Management Coalition membership comprises a highly diverse group of workflow product vendors, analysts, universities, government organizations, and corporations all touched by workflow technology. For the same reasons, it should not be surprising that different approaches are chosen for managing workflow. All this combines to make workflow management a diverse and rich technology.

The members of the Workflow Management Coalition hope you enjoy the Workflow Handbook and find it useful as you explore workflow technology and its many diverse benefits.

The Workflow Management Coalition
May 1996

Introduction

Workflow - Technology for Business Change

From time to time a key new technology emerges with the potential to change the way in which we look at much of computer system development. When that technology is in tune with business thinking, *and* has an active standards body which enjoys widespread support as well, then it must be something to shout about.

We are talking, of course, about *Workflow*. Workflow Management (or "Workflow Automation" as some prefer) has been gradually creeping up the awareness scale of corporate information technology – IT – developers for a number of years. As a result, in addition to spawning a host of specialist product suppliers, workflow functionality is being added to other types of product, and the market is well supported by regular conferences, training courses and seminars, and by periodicals which focus on the technology.

But workflow is more than just a technology. Other technologies can claim, with justification, to change system development methods. They include object orientation, client-server architectures, and visual programming. While these have all had a large and irreversible impact on the way in which systems are developed, they have not been quite so closely associated with current business management thinking as workflow is. In particular, as organisations seek to evolve or to re-invent themselves to accommodate the demands of their particular markets, there is a new focus on the *processes* by which business is performed. While some would claim that Business Process Reengineering – BPR – is a passing fad, there can be no doubt that it encapsulates much of what is consuming management attention in these fast changing times.

At the end of a BPR exercise (at least, at the end of a particular phase, since BPR should be an ongoing activity), after a radical look has been taken at an organisation, the question must be 'how do we implement what we know needs to be done?' Very often, workflow is standing in the wings as an ideal way for the organisation to put the new processes into motion.

Of course, BPR and workflow do not always go together - a topic explored in some of the articles contained in this Handbook in *Section 1–The World of Workflow*. It is quite possible that BPR will result in a set of changes which do not include the implementation of workflow. Conversely, workflow may be applied to *existing* business processes to make them more efficient or more effective.

Whatever the driving force for implementing workflow, *integration* will be a key concept to be addressed. In most cases, workflow systems will be used to link the "islands of automation" represented by existing IT systems. Such systems are likely to pre-date the roll-out of workflow; but even in a green-field site, software which is separate from the workflow system will be used to implement line-of-business applications, desktop applications, database management systems, and so on. Workflow software needs to link with these, imposing a business process orientation onto their usage. As a result, such software systems cease to be isolated stores of information and of processing capability, since they are put into the overall context of what the organisation is seeking to achieve.

In addition, business is not done in isolation. All organisations work within a framework of suppliers and customers. Where a relationship is of sufficient value, it increasingly makes sense to integrate the business process *across* the organisations.

All of these integration requirements – both with other software systems, and across organisations – point to the need for standards. The Workflow Management Coalition started the standards ball rolling early enough to achieve widespread support, almost universal among suppliers. As a result, even though there is much yet to be done, users and potential users of workflow technology can have a realistic expectation that workflow systems from different vendors will be capable of working together.

So this Handbook comes at a significant time in the life of workflow. It represents the end of the introductory phase of workflow's life, since it has now been proved beyond any doubt to have real business benefit. It comes at a time when standards are beginning to bite – to the benefit of all – and there is increasing awareness of the right and wrong way to apply the technology.

What are you waiting for? Read on to find out how you can be a part of a significant change in business and IT thinking. Look out for future editions of this Handbook, too, since the world of workflow in 1998 will be somewhat different to that in 1997.

How to Use this Handbook

This Handbook can be approached in a number of ways, depending on the type of interest which you have. Of course, in practice, nobody conforms exactly to a type! So you will just pick and mix the best approach for you. But this section should provide some guidelines.

For all types of user, consult *Section 3–The Directory* to find out who the players are, and to discover if *your* supplier is represented in the Workflow Management Coalition.

To help you find the information you want there are three indexes. As well as the main Subject Index, there are Product and Organization indexes.

Starting out with Workflow

Whether you have a business or an IT focus, if you are starting out with workflow, the articles in *Section 1–The World of Workflow* will have something for you. The article on *Understanding Workflow* provides an excellent introduction which is applicable to anyone. It includes an overview of the technology aspects, and of the business benefits, as well as of the direction of the workflow market. This is reinforced by *Workflow in Context* which provides help in seeing what the problems are which might be addressed by workflow, and what the benefits are likely to be once implemented.

You might then to choose to dip into articles in *The Business Impact of Workflow*. This contains articles which relate workflow to Business Process Reengineering, to Quality initiatives in organisations, and to other technology focuses like business process modelling, and groupware.

Articles in *Applications of Workflow* illustrate that workflow has provided real benefit to real businesses, so you might choose an article or two here which most closely match your situation.

Articles in *Implementing Workflow* and *The Future of Workflow* may tempt you once you have grasped the basics.

If you have a strong technical inclination, you might find it worthwhile to look at the scope of the documents in *Section 2–Workflow Standards*. In particular, you may find *The WfMC Glossary* helpful in understanding the terms which suppliers use.

Building Workflow Application Knowledge

If you already know something of workflow, but need to see how it is being used to advantage by other people, you can do no better than go straight to the articles in *Applications of Workflow*. Here you will find various areas of business and government addressed. *Workflow in Insurance* represents that sector, while there are other articles representing specific users of workflow in Finance, Government, and Healthcare.

The documents in *Section 2–Workflow Standards* will tell you more about workflow systems. In particular *The Workflow Reference Model* shows the components of typical workflow products, and how they interact. *The WfMC Glossary*, too, should prove useful in extending knowledge.

Planning a Workflow Implementation

If your interest in workflow is because you will be implementing such a system, then there is much to help you, and to ensure that you build on the accumulated knowledge in the workflow arena. In *Section 1–The World of Workflow* articles in *Introducing Workflow* will provide a good foundation, while those in *Applications of Workflow* will give you some information on what other users have done.

Some more practical information can be found in articles in *Implementing Workflow*, including *Workflow Success Starts with Application Understanding* which helps you to know the right questions to ask about your project. Workflow enabling existing software systems is also likely to be relevant, so *What is Workflow Enabling?* will start you off in the right direction. Various other aspects of workflow projects are also covered there, including the World Wide Web, and considerations of roles within workflow systems. The workflow project itself is addressed in *Learning from Experience in Workflow Projects* which takes a realistic look at what happens in many projects, so you can avoid the same mistakes in yours!

Your attitude to workflow standards needs to be considered, so *Section 2– Workflow Standards* is likely to deserve some basic attention, particularly *The Workflow Reference Model* which will enable you to see which of the areas of workflow standards may be relevant to you, and so that you can address this with your supplier. Depending on the scope of your workflow implementation, you may need to consider *The WAPI Specification* in more detail. If you are providing the entire front end (user interface) of the workflow system, then writing it to conform to WAPI is likely to be a good thing. However, for the detailed implementation you will still need the supplier's information.

Talking of suppliers, *Section 3–The Directory* will provide useful source information. It may even encourage you to become part of the Workflow Management Coalition.

Supplying Workflow Technology

For those in the software industry involved with supplying workflow technology – a workflow product, or perhaps implementation, consultancy or training services – your starting point in **The Workflow Handbook** is likely to be different. On a technical level, the specifications in *Section 2–Workflow Standards* will show what needs to be done to conform to the published standards - particularly from workflow client applications.

Other people's experiences are always useful, as well, so many of the articles in *Section 1–The World of Workflow* will be of benefit – especially, perhaps, articles in *Applications of Workflow*.

Since workflow technology is certainly not standing still, suppliers need to be working on the future now; so articles in *The Future of Workflow* will have value in identifying some of the major issues which are just around the corner. In particular, extending the scope of workflow systems across distributed organizations and between organizations is a strong focus. *Planning for the Clustered Corporation* and *Workflow Interoperability Between Businesses* both address this key issue.

The World of Workflow

Those in the habit of visiting any of the large computing exhibitions around the world will no doubt have noticed how the latest technology appears on a good proportion of the stands – in words if not in product. While this is certainly a good thing to raise the profile of the technology, it can lead to some confusion in the minds of those who are less *au fait* with the week by week machinations of the industry, since initially there is no real consensus about what that technology really is.

As far as workflow is concerned we are past the introductory phase and there is now a good degree of consensus - witness the very existence of the Workflow Management Coalition and its ability to produce standards. What needs to happen now is that the consensus needs to be made known so that suppliers and users can be sure they are trading in the same commodity.

Introducing Workflow

This Handbook contains three main sections, the largest of which – *Section 1-The World of Workflow* – consists of articles from a wide spectrum of contributors. As a decisive step towards making known the consensus, the section starts with two articles giving an introduction to workflow.

Ovum is a research and consulting company who have been active in understanding workflow and making it known for some time. In the first article: *Understanding Workflow*, Ovum's Heather Stark provides us with a solid foundation for the rest of the Handbook by introducing the benefits and the concepts. In addition, a helpful distinction is made between different *types* of workflow product: Forms-based, and Engine-based. While this is one of a number of possible ways of cutting the workflow cake, it nevertheless shows how the market is maturing and how understanding is being refined further. The future of the workflow market is a subject of interest both to users – who need to ensure that they are not going out on a limb – and to suppliers – whose future existence depends on going in the same direction as market demand. Heather includes Ovum's forecasts for the technology, and for workflow expenditure.

Understanding Workflow is reinforced by Keith Hales' *Workflow in Context* which highlights the business problems which can be addressed by workflow, and the benefits which can be derived. Productivity improvements quoted by workflow suppliers can be misleading since the nature of workflow implementations is such that it is rare simply to be automating what was already there. Keith quotes a realistic productivity gain of 30-50% after the initial introduction of workflow; it will be interesting in future editions of this Handbook to monitor user experiences of this.

The Business Impact of Workflow

Workflow has a non-technology cousin in Business Process Reengineering. The relationship has benefits on both sides: BPR often requires technological support during the implementation phase, and the scale of organizational change required for effective workflow implementation is more readily recognised once the fundamentals of reengineering have been addressed.

Thomas Koulopoulos explicitly considers the relationship in *Reengineering and Workflow*. He claims that one of workflow's key advantages is the ability to respond to organizational change – initiated by reengineering – on an ongoing basis.

For this approach to be successful, it is necessary for an organization to change its thinking, and become much more process-aware. Instead of focusing on how the organizational structure satisfies customer requirements, the focus shifts to business processes. This change in thinking is the subject of *Workflow Applications within Business Organizations* by Nikolaos Vlachantonis, who shows how workflow can be used to achieve this.

Clearly it is no simple task to move from BPR to automated business process. Generally, the emphasis with BPR is on the organization, while the emphasis in workflow is much more on IT. *From BPR Model to Workflow Applications* outlines a method to support the transformation of reengineered business processes into workflow applications. Marc Derungs and the other authors propose a three stage approach to achieve this.

The Benefits of Business Process Modeling for Workflow Systems by Michael Amberg also addresses a business process question. It recognises that there is advantage to modeling the business process before committing to an executable workflow model.

When considering the business benefits of workflow systems, one of the first to arise will be quality, in one form or another. By facilitating consistency, and enforcing standards, workflow can certainly be said to contribute to quality in an organization, an issue addressed by Monique Attinger in *Is Quality an Art Form?*.

"To the man with a hammer, everything looks like a nail". While workflow technology undoubtedly has many feasible application areas, one potential point of failure of any new technology is applying it in an application where there is something more appropriate. Workflow's relationship to groupware has been the subject of many discussions. Whatever view is taken, there is certainly a class of workflow-type applications which benefit from recognising that they have a less structured process at their heart – called "groupware" applications by some. Without becoming embroiled in pointless definitions, Fred van Leeuwen addresses these issues in *Relating Groupware and Workflow*. He looks at various types of work coordination, with a view to guiding towards the most appropriate solution in a particular case.

Applications of Workflow

As Oscar Wilde said: *"Experience is the name everyone gives to their mistakes"*. Part of the objective of this Handbook is to enable future users of workflow technology to build on other people's experience. We include a group of articles relating to more specific application areas. Insurance, for example, has long been cited as fertile ground for workflow management. Nick Kingsbury reinforces this view, and points out in *Workflow in Insurance* that what the workflow handles is the business - there is nothing else (for example, a manufactured component).

The finance sector is in a similar situation, given that most financial transactions involve nothing more or less than information. *Complex User-Modifiable Workflow* considers one small part of this sector; Jesse T. Quatse addresses an application where more control needs to be handed to users than in many finance workflow applications.

By using an example application *Workflow Enabled Applications for Dresdner Bank* shows how the focus of individual users may well be different from that of the business process owner. They need to have a list of tasks to be performed, and may want to be able to handle all tasks of a similar type at the same time. A consistent user interface with other applications is also a significant point for many users, easily overlooked, contend Jürgen Edelmann and Michele Rochefort.

A Workflow Recipe for Healthy Customer Service – takes us through the implementation of workflow in a healthcare organisation. The particular application area is a common one for workflow: that of customer services. The requirement to provide electronic access to documentation relating to customers was an important part of the system as described by Dave Ruiz.

One way or another, government, whether central or local, has been a target for workflow systems for a long time. High volumes, and much bureaucracy lend themselves to automation with workflow. A second case study – *IT-Supported Process Management in a Public Agency* – illustrates the sequence of events, from recognising the requirement (due in this case to political change - the reunification of Germany), through the call for bids, and on to a description of the solution. Particularly interesting in Nicole Koerber's description is the consideration given to ensuring that the system was well accepted by its users.

Also related to government is the Dutch Defence Computer Centre which is described in *Using Workflow and BPR for 45-fold Improvement*. Its move to being a semi-autonomous agency precipitated an in-depth look at its business processes, leading to the implementation of workflow for one of them. While the authors are not claiming that all the improvement was down to workflow, in combination with BPR significant improvements have been made in the "first time right score", the overall time taken for the process, and the overall accuracy of work.

Implementing Workflow

Of course, other people's experiences are only helpful up to a point. There comes a time when you have to start making your own mistakes. Increasingly there is a body of knowledge which will help you avoid some of them, and this group of articles starts with *Workflow Success starts with Application Understanding* in which Peter Lawrence outlines a dozen characteristics which need to be considered in applications which will potentially be implemented with workflow. While there is undoubtedly a degree of commonality between workflow projects and any other IT project, there are also some unique aspects, including some which do not necessarily come to mind at all in other contexts.

One such aspect is the degree of integration between workflow systems and other software systems. Typically this is very high, and Jon Pyke asks the question *What is Workflow Enabling?* to address this key point. He contends that existing applications can be fully integrated into the workflow environment, and outlines a number of techniques to achieve this.

A software environment which is receiving ever-increasing interest is the World Wide Web. It has a number of characteristics which make it suitable for certain workflow applications. Herbert Groiss and Johann Eder address *Integrating Workflow Systems and the World Wide Web* by presenting a prototype system which is illustrative of imminent commercially available extensions to workflow products.

In planning a workflow application, one of the first questions to be contemplated is how the work is to be assigned to users. Essentially, there has to be a mapping between the workflow model and an organizational model. In *Organization and Role Models for Workflow Processes*, Walter Rupietta outlines a framework for organizational modelling which can be used in defining the allocation of work in the workflow system. As well as considerations of position in the hierarchy, questions about authority levels for sign-offs are addressed.

Another activity which forms part of a workflow project is the development of the software to take care of the tasks to be performed at each step of the process. Since there will be elements of commonality between different processes, and at different points in a single process, there must be scope to enhance productivity be re-using such developments. *Reusing Tasks Between Workflow Applications* proposes a method of cataloguing common tasks to facilitate their reuse across processes. Thomas Magg uses some real world statistics to show the benefits of his approach.

On the other hand, Fred van Leeuwen looks at the overall approach to a workflow project, and points out some of the potential pitfalls. In *Learning from Experience in Workflow Projects* he draws on experiences to caricature projects so that we can indeed learn. *"Between the idea and the reality there falls a shadow"* said T.S.Eliot; Fred's objective is to minimise that shadow.

Any technology which is going to be useful over the long term must have a sound technical base on which to build. In more established system developments involving distributed and fault-tolerant databases, the idea of transactions is well established. In particular, the so-called "ACID" transaction concepts are well understood. This is not the case for the longer duration "transactions" in workflow systems. *Workflow Transactions* makes some progress in redressing this situation; Johann Eder and Walter Liebhart propose the concept of the Workflow Transaction.

The Future of Workflow

Even if the world stayed still, there would be plenty of opportunity to move workflow technology forward. Product suppliers in particular have their work cut out to satisfy the greater understanding of requirements which their users are bringing them. But of course the world does not stay still, and there are a number of key areas in which workflow will change in response to external pressures. All of that is the subject of this set of articles.

One such area of change is the location of work. As networking and communications technology improves so it becomes increasingly feasible for an organization to distribute work across its various offices. And with groups of companies working more closely in "virtual corporations" there is a need to integrate the business processes. John Williams puts forward his views on this area in *Planning for the Clustered Corporation*, which recognises, among other things, the importance of the Workflow Management Coalition standards in this area – still being developed.

The theme is also taken up by Thomas Adams and Steve Dworkin in *Workflow Interoperability Between Businesses*. Beyond the requirement for workflow engines to talk to each other, they discuss the need – originally recognised in the artificial intelligence community – to communicate at a deeper level.

As well as physical distribution of processes within and across organizations, in *Growth and Challenges in Enterprise Workflow*, Dave Ruiz considers other aspects of large scale workflow usage, such as concurrency, scaleability, and systems management issues. All vitally important in the successful implementation of workflow systems.

Martin Ader takes a different angle on the future, and contends that *Workflow Engines as Transaction Monitors*. The pervasiveness of traditional transaction monitors will be mirrored by the roles which workflow engines take, when used together with document management systems.

Other aspects of the future of workflow have been addressed in other articles, too. As we have seen the World Wide Web is going to have an increasingly significant impact on certain types of workflow system. *Integrating Workflow Systems and the World Wide Web* gives a taste of the future here, while the developing relationship between business process modelling and workflow has been explored elsewhere, such as in *The Benefits of Business Process Modelling for Workflow Systems*. All in all, there will be plenty of development of workflow technology in the years to come, ensuring that the subject will remain on our agendas.

Workflow Standards

Not all of life's endeavours have the potential for benefiting all concerned. The production of standards is, happily, one of those. And while there is always the potential for conflict in the development of standards, the Workflow Management Coalition has started the ball rolling early enough in the life of workflow technology to avoid this in any major way. As a result, even though interest in the standards work of the Coalition has been wide, there are few interests which are entrenched enough to want to raise their voices attempting to dominate the proceedings. Having said that, the chair persons of the various working groups will undoubtedly confirm that the work is not always plain sailing. And the existence of a number of standards in their first versions, and a number of others in draft form, bear testimony to the dedication of the working groups.

So the Coalition is pleased to be able to publish the standards which are included in this Handbook as the first fruits of its standards work. In many areas work continues, and we include information below on the likely impact of that work on the published standards, as well as a general idea of the direction of work in other areas which are yet to be published.

The latest generally available versions of the standards are available on the Internet; the necessary address information may be found in *Further Reading and Sources of Information.*

As workflow systems became recognised as a category of computer system in their own right, it was recognised that all workflow management products have some common characteristics, giving them the potential to achieve a level of interoperability through the adoption of standards for various functions. The Coalition intend that such standards will enable interoperability between heterogeneous workflow products and improved integration of workflow applications with other IT services such as electronic mail and document management. By doing this, the opportunities for the effective use of workflow technology within the IT market are improved, to the benefit of both vendors and users of such technology. Hence the standards included in this Handbook, along with the others still under development.

The Workflow Reference Model

In order to develop standards which different workflow products could adhere to, there was a need to start talking a common language. Thus an early part of the technical work of the Workflow Management Coalition was to define terminology – now consolidated into *The WfMC Glossary* – and to provide a framework to support the development of the various specifications; hence *The Workflow Reference Model.* The purpose of this is to identify the characteristics, terminology and components of workflow management systems, enabling the individual specifications to be developed within the context of an overall model.

As part of this, *The Workflow Reference Model* identifies the interfaces and information flows between the major functional components, leading to the identification of the areas appropriate for standardisation. Within the Reference Model, these interfaces are referred to simply by number: Interface 1 to Interface 5.

While it is written as the foundation of the technical standards, it also provides a readable introduction to the generic structure of workflow systems, and no particular prior knowledge of workflow systems is assumed. Chapter 1 of *The Workflow Reference Model* includes an introduction to workflow, couched in terms which form the basis of the rest of the document. Alternatively, it may well aid the reader if an introductory article or two in **Section 1–The World of Workflow** have been read.

Once familiar with the basics of workflow systems, Chapter 2 discusses the internal structure of workflow systems, the major functional components and the nature of their interactions. It introduces the top level architecture and identifies the various interfaces which may be used to support interoperability between different system components and integration with other major IT infrastructure components.

Chapter 3 provides a general overview of the Workflow Application Programming Interface (WAPI), comments on the necessary protocol support for open interworking and discusses the principles of conformance to the specifications. It identifies those aspects of the specifications which are required to support various classes of interoperability. The full WAPI Specifications is included in this Handbook in its own right (see next section).

WAPI Specification

Having built the foundation, the WAPI Specification is the first of the standards themselves. This represents Interface 2 in the Workflow Reference Model. Its purpose is to specify standard workflow management Application Programming Interfaces (API) which can be supported by workflow management products. The support of these interfaces in workflow management products means that front-end applications – typically written by those implementing a workflow system, such as the systems integrator or the user's IT department – can have access to workflow facilities provided by the workflow engine. By defining a standard, it means that workflow applications can be made to work with different workflow engines from different vendors.

The WAPI calls are for use at run-time. That is, when processes are executing or are to be executed. They would normally be used by applications with user interfaces such as worklist handlers, but may also be used by a workflow engine when it wishes to interact with another workflow management product within the scope of the API functions.

There is no constraint on the programming language used. WAPI calls may be implemented in a number of languages. However, the current specification is for the 'C' language.

WAPI Naming Conventions

The Naming Conventions standard supports the WAPI Specification by specifying guidelines for naming such entities as functions and variables. It also includes the

common header files for the 'C' programming language. As such, it is particularly
suited for vendors involved in developing 'C' language bindings for the APIs they
are developing. It is also intended to serve as a reference for 'C' programmers
making use of Coalition APIs.

The WfMC Glossary

The terms and definitions given in this section are there to help in establishing a
consistency in the use of terminology across the industry. However, recognising that
in practice there are different terms for similar concepts, it also provides a list of
synonyms variously used as alternative terms to the preferred WfMC terminology.

Other Standards Work

By no means all of the work of the Coalition is represented by currently available
standards. As well as ongoing activity in the area of the WAPI, other work in
progress relates to exchange of workflow process definitions between products
(Interface 1), interoperability between workflow engines (Interface 4), to workflow
auditing standards (Interface 5), and to a general approach to conformance to
standards (the Conformance Working Group). In addition, a further working group
is addressing questions of consistency of architecture, terminology, and approach
across other working groups.

The ability to exchange workflow process definitions between products is a key
one to protect users' investment in their workflow systems. *Working Group 1B* is
defining the "Workflow Process Definition Language" – WPDL – to achieve this.

Although the *WAPI* itself is stable as a standard, work has been going on to be
able to 'wrap' WAPI within an OLE automation binding.

Working Group 4 is responsible for workflow interoperability. The objective of
this Working Group is to define standards to support the enactment of business
processes that span multiple workflow systems. By permitting workflow systems to
pass work items seamlessly between one another, such interoperability will enable
organizations to manage processes across departments that may have purchased
different workflow products based on their individual needs. This benefit also
extends to electronic commerce and other inter-organizational workflow processes,
such as between a company and its customers, suppliers, and partners.

Current efforts of Working Group 4 address interoperability at two levels. First,
the information content of messages that need to be exchanged between workflow
systems, in order to achieve the desired interoperability, is specified. This
specification is at an abstract level that permits a variety of concrete
implementations, such as electronic mail, remote procedure calls, object request
brokers, EDI, World Wide Web, or shared file exchange.

Based on this abstract specification, work is proceeding on concrete implementation bindings and on interoperability demonstrations that use these bindings. Two concrete implementation and demonstration efforts are being addressed, using Internet (SMTP) electronic mail and using Microsoft's MAPI Workflow Command Message Interface. It is expected that the Workflow Interoperability Specification, with at least two concrete implementation specifications, will be released as a Coalition standard in late 1996.

One of the key aspects of standardisation between workflow products is being able to manage in a coherent way across different products. *Working Group 5* has an objective to address this area. In particular, to define auditability and status monitoring standards. Their work includes defining a consistent syntax and semantics for workflow audit information. This will enable events from different products to be consolidated into a single view.

The objective of the *Conformance Working Group* is to guide the creation of appropriate policy and procedure for defining and measuring vendor conformance with the published specifications of the Workflow Management Coalition. The aim is to have a general set of policies and procedures, as well as tests and procedures that are specific to the different functional areas. Conformance measurement matters to workflow system users because they need assurances that the vendor's implementation of the WfMC specification performs as expected. Rather than rely on undocumented (even if well intended) claims by a vendor, they want some assurance that there is an objective basis for such a claim. A well-crafted conformance policy provides this objective measure that users seek.

The working definition of conformance is that it is "a measure of adherence between a published WfMC standard and a particular vendor's implementation of that published standard." Conformance measurements will provide vendors with the means to test the quality of their implementation of the WfMC specification, and provide some assurance to each vendor that their competitors are playing by the same "rules" as they do. To achieve this measurement a set of test suites are planned.

Section 1

The World of Workflow

Introducing Workflow

Understanding Workflow
Heather Stark

Workflow in Context
Keith Hales

Understanding Workflow

Heather Stark
Ovum Ltd

This article is designed to give you an understanding of the uses and benefits of workflow and of the relationship between workflow and other business technologies. It introduces the fundamental concepts of workflow and gives Ovum's view of the future prospects and evolution of the technology.

Introduction to Workflow

This section explains:

- What workflow systems do
- How organizations are using workflow

What is Workflow?

Workflow promises a new solution to an age-old problem: managing and supporting business processes. What is new about workflow is the way it harnesses the power of information technology to support structured work. Workflow systems offer a new model for the division of labor between people and computers.

As shown in Figure 1, workflow systems support business processes by:

- Enforcing the logic that governs transitions between tasks in a process, ensuring that all the tasks appropriate to a particular case or instance of a process are performed
- Supporting the individual tasks in a process, bringing together the human and/or information resources needed to complete each task

Workflow systems provide a *process control backbone* for business processes: they mediate the flow of responsibility in a process from person to person and from task

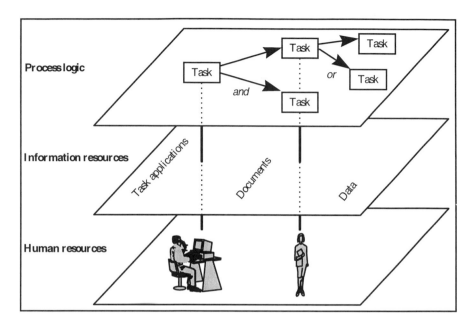

Figure 1   Workflow Enforces Process Logic and Delivers Task Resources

to task. They differ from ordinary computer programs because of the way that they "cut" the world. Instead of hardwiring a process, and making it implicit (and hard to change), they enable you to design with process in focus, and make the right abstractions in your design.

Benefits of Workflow

Motivations For Using Workflow

Most organizations using workflow are motivated by three factors:

- Improved efficiency, leading to lower costs or higher workload capacity
- Improved control, resulting from standardization of procedures
- Improved ability to manage processes: performance problems are made explicit and understood

For many organizations, the real driver for their workflow decision is:

- Pressure for cost reduction, where "cost" is a euphemism for staff
- Pressure for increased quality or capacity while controlling costs

However, it is important to remember that balance-sheet improvement is not an inevitable consequence of introducing workflow. Process improvements happen as a result of less abstract changes:

- Process standardization
- Process management
- Efficient delivery of information-based tasks to workers
- Explicit focus on process design

In considering whether workflow can help improve your processes, it is important to focus on these effects: they summarize what workflow actually does. Process improvement, if it occurs, will occur by means of these more concrete effects.

Who Uses Workflow?

Workflow systems are being used by many different types of organizations, in many different ways. For example:

- Insurance companies are using workflow to speed up claims management while maintaining control over it
- Government departments are using workflow to improve efficiency in making decisions about paying social security benefits
- Organizations of all types are using workflow to improve the effectiveness of their customer service operations and order processing
- Workflow is being used to support routine internal administrative processes, such as personnel reporting and expense-claims management
- Workflow is being used to enable people to construct their own, customised, workflow processes to deal with their own specialised process responsibilities
- Even very complex processes, such as extremely large software development projects, are being supported by workflow systems

More and more organizations are adopting workflow: the market is growing strongly.

Fundamental Concepts

This section explains the basic concepts of workflow. It also gives Ovum's view of differences between the philosophies of different styles of workflow products, and gives an overview of the different types of product architecture on offer.

There are four basic concepts in workflow:

- Process logic
- Match-making people and tasks

- Providing information resources for tasks
- Process management

Once you understand these fundamentals, you will be able to understand the most important aspects of the workflow systems available on the market today.

Process Logic

A workflow system provides computer-based support for business process logic. Using a workflow system, a business can both enforce and document the business process rules it uses.

Workflow systems provide a *process control backbone* for business processes: they mediate the flow of responsibility in a process from person to person and from task to task, by:

- Representing the definition of each process
- Keeping track of the state of each instance of the process as it progresses through its defined task stages
- Pushing the process along to the next task that needs to be performed, according to the logic that is defined for the process

The workflow designer uses the workflow system's design tools to define which actions should be taken, by whom, under what circumstances. The workflow system provides run-time software support for the flow of control from one task in a process to the next, and from one worker to the next, following this design.

Depending on the workflow system you choose, a workflow designer may be an "ordinary" end-user, or a specialist. Different products have different assumptions:

- Some products assume that workflow design must be done by a specialist; others allow end-users to define their own workflows
- Some processes do not require complex integration with information resources: they are essentially ready to run after their logic has been defined. For other processes, process design is just a precursor to specialized system integration which knits together the workflow's process definition and the applications which people use to perform tasks.
- Most products assume that a complete definition of process logic must occur before the process executes, and each instance of the process must follow this path; others take a more dynamic approach, and allow the logic of process instances to be modified (or even determined) "on the fly"

Match-Making between People and Tasks

Workflow systems take responsibility for ensuring that the tasks that need to be done are matched up with the resources needed to perform them. When a task needs a person in order to be completed, the workflow system will support the necessary match-making between people and tasks.

Workflow systems differ in their approach to matching people with the tasks in a process. In most cases, the workflow system matches people with whatever tasks are ready to be done right away, because their logically preceding tasks have already been completed.

The protocol by which the system does this match-making varies. Some workflow products just deliver tasks to individuals who were named during process definition, when it is their turn to do something that moves the process forward. (This is frequently the easiest protocol to implement using forms routing packages. See "Product Architectures" below.)

Other types of systems offer a more sophisticated protocol which enables just-in-time matching (also called late binding) between people and tasks. In this scenario, the workflow engine offers a task that needs to be done to a group of people, each of whom is capable of doing that particular task. The person who is able to take the task on accepts the task, which is then withdrawn from the task lists of the other workers who have been offered the task. We call this the *system-offer protocol*. The ability to use a system-offer protocol is a highly significant capability, especially when it is used in combination with roles.

Roles are a very powerful design construct which can enable a workflow environment to exhibit a degree of *automatic load balancing*. Rather than "hard-wiring" the relationship between specific individuals and tasks, at design time the designer merely specifies the role of the person who should perform a task. At run-time, the workflow system does a lookup of the individuals who are listed as being able to take that role.

Either the system or the end-users themselves can help ensure that the right person from this list takes on the task:

- The system can sort out who it will assign responsibility to, perhaps based on a rota, or data about previous performance and current commitments
- The system can uses a *system-offer* protocol, in which the first person to grab an offered task takes responsibility

Using a role is not the same thing as broadcasting to a group of people. If you broadcast a task to a group of people, what happens next? Role-based reference implies some mechanism for turning the reference to a role into a definite matching between a task and the individual who becomes responsible for the task.

The use of roles requires correspondingly strong reporting and management capabilities in the workflow system: what if nobody takes responsibility for a task, and it languishes unattended?

All workflow systems help to match people and tasks for the processes they control, but there are some significant differences in how they go about it:

- Some systems use clever techniques for matching people with tasks; others allow the end-users to apply their own intelligence to this problem
- Systems also differ in their attitude to users' control over the tasks they have responsibility for: some allow users to reassign responsibility, but others don't

Providing Information Resources for Tasks

Tasks may require both human resources and information resources. When these information resources are computer-based, the workflow system can make sure that the tasks which need to be done are matched up with the information resources that are needed to help complete the task.

There are many types of computer-based information resources. We distinguish between *task application* resources, and *content* resources.

Task application resources are used in workflow tasks. They display, create and change content resources. Task applications include:

- Personal-productivity applications, such as word processors
- Line-of-business applications, such as sales-order support systems
- Electronic forms

Unlike the matching between people and tasks, which is usually dynamic, the association between tasks and application resources is usually determined at design time, by hard-coding.

Content resources contain the information which is used, changed and even created by application resources in the workflow process. They include:

- Data
- Documents

Most workflow systems go some way towards matching tasks with content resources. However, tools have a variety of approaches to this issue. Some take a very "hands-off" approach: they do nothing in particular to support the designer's mapping between tasks and content resources. Other systems make the association between content resources and tasks an integral aspect of task definition.

All workflow systems enable you to do something about providing information resources for tasks. However, as ever, there are significant differences in approach:

- Some products provide a way for you to build task application resources, using a forms design capability in the workflow tool itself; others provide the means for you to integrate external task applications with the processes that the workflow system controls. *Few products are equally good at both*
- Some products provide special design and execution support for particular types of content resources, such as images; others don't

- Some products take a very concrete approach to the mapping between tasks and the content resources they use; others use a more general model in which different content resources may be freely associated with different tasks
- Products which have a very concrete model of the relation between tasks and information resources are less flexible, and may have problems dealing with parallelism in process design

Process Management

Process management is a key concept in workflow systems: organizations are under constant pressure to make better use of resources. The ability to manage processes effectively is even more critical than the ability to implement them efficiently.

Workflow systems have obvious strengths in controlling processes. However, workflow systems also hold out the promise of being able to help manage as well as control business processes. Proper process management means more than just process control. Workflow systems help process management by:

- Making process logic an explicit, discrete layer of the design representation, which can be reasoned about independently and – within limits – altered independently
- Allowing designers to create, collect and evaluate metrics relating to the time, cost or quality of performing a process and its constituent tasks – thus enabling intelligent improvements to be made to process design and process resourcing

Process management also involves the ability to change processes when necessary, either to make best use of available resources or to respond to changing needs. For example:

- In order to clear a bottleneck in the process environment, it may be necessary to allocate more people to specific tasks
- Regulatory changes or internal events (such as the introduction of new products and services) may mean that process definitions currently in force must be changed quickly, to apply to existing instances

While most workflow products are, at least in theory, committed to helping process management, there are some striking differences in what they actually do:

- Some products provide full auditing and tracking capabilities that help you determine when your process environment is having problems – but others don't
- Some systems also allow the designer to specify rules for dynamic optimization of the process-execution environment – but most don't
- At its most sophisticated (i.e. complex), a workflow system might perform load balancing between the workloads of different groups of people within an organization. It might also dynamically adjust the process to be followed,

depending on the availability of resources and the performance of the process environment

Product Architectures

Most of the workflow products available on the market today fall into one of two categories:

- Those which use forms and messages, routing electronic forms to users' email in-boxes
- Those which use a centralized "workflow engine", which communicates with workers via specialised client software and is integrated with external task applications.

The distinction between the two, though clear enough at the moment, will blur in time.

A new architecture for workflow is also appearing – using the Web. At present, a typical Web architecture for workflow is close to the centralized "engine" paradigm. Where it differs from older-style engine implementations is in its use of a super-thin client (i.e. a Web browser), with the end-user functionality resident and executing on the server (coded into HTML forms and CGI gateway scripts which invoke other server applications).

Forms and Messages

The typical forms-based workflow product works through a combination of the following processes:

- A messaging service is used to route a process instance through its predefined tasks
- The logic of the process is not executed centrally, but is handled at the worker's desktop via interaction between the forms package and the worker's mail system
- People are matched with tasks by being named at the start of a process instance and being delivered tasks as appropriate to the sequence
- The user interface for each task is a form (or a view of a form, or a set of linked forms)
- Forms may be linked to a database which stores information which is displayed in form fields

Typically, the logic of the process is bundled with the form, which is transmitted between users. Definition of process logic and task logic uses a script language. There is rarely a clean separation between task logic and process logic in the design.

Figure 2 shows how the elements of a typical forms-based product fit together.

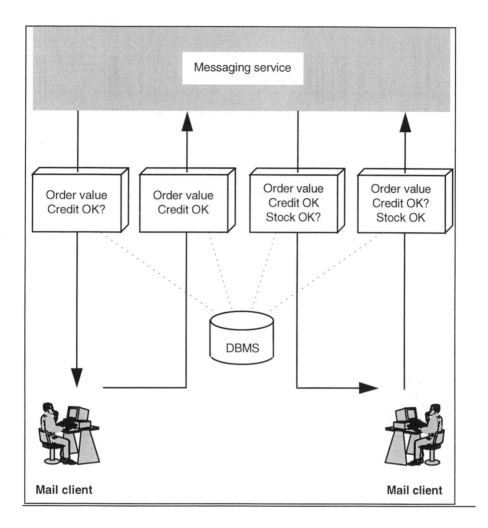

Figure 2   A Typical Forms-based Product

Workflow Engines

By contrast, the typical "engine-based" workflow product works through a combination of:

- A database which stores process definitions
- A database which stores the state of all process instances in the process environment
- A server-based enactment service, or "engine"

- Client software at the worker's desktop which communicates with the server engine

Typically, the engine is responsible for:

- Implementing the rules that govern transitions between tasks
- Updating the state of each process instance as tasks are completed and rules are evaluated
- Offering or delivering the tasks which need to be done to the workers who can do them, via communication with the users' desktops
- Taking appropriate action (for example, alerting) on deadline overrun for tasks or processes

The desktop component of the system, on the other hand, acts as a local "task controller". It usually:

- Receives notifications of the tasks which need to be done from the server engine
- Offers a display of tasks to the worker
- Invokes the task application which is associated with a particular task, when the worker selects it
- Updates the server engine when a task is selected to work on, so that it is withdrawn from the central list of tasks which need to be done
- Updates the server engine when a task is complete, so that the server engine can update the state of the process instance

At present, most "engine-based" products communicate between the worker's desktop machine and the server engine using a form of remote procedure call.

A basic scenario for how these elements work together is shown in Figure 3.

Trade-Offs

What does it matter which product architecture you choose? Table 1 gives a stereotype summary of the strengths of each type of product. Of course, individual products within each category vary, sometimes considerably, so it is well worth considering a broad selection of products of each type before honing down your choice.

Workflow in Context: Related Concepts

In this section, we discuss:

- The relationship between workflow and BPR (business process reengineering)
- The relationship between workflow and related technologies such as groupware and document management

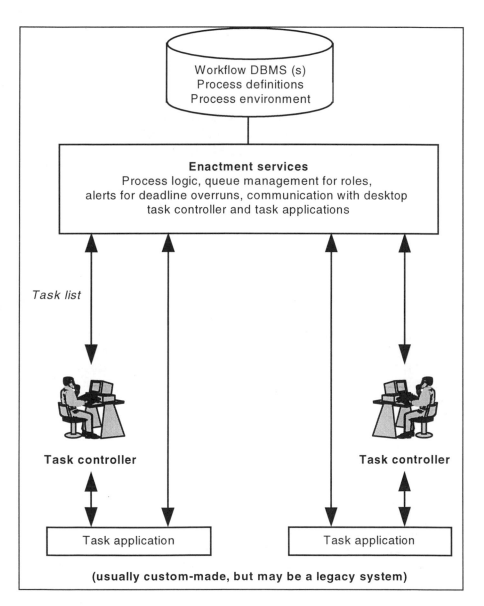

Figure 3   A Typical Engine-based Product

Table 1   Trade-offs between Product Architectures

Advantages of forms-based products	Advantages of engine-based products
Low cost per end-user seat*	Designed for close integration with external task applications
Task applications may be built using the workflow tool	Powerful tracking and management facilities
Quick prototyping of task applications	Good visual design support for complex topologies such as multiple parallel processes
Many use existing messaging infrastructure	Use of role-based matching between people and tasks

*   *Note: for very large orders, suppliers of engine-based workflow products may offer substantial discounts. The classic response is "ask me".*

Workflow and BPR

In some markets, workflow's popularity has been a direct consequence of its affinity with the recent craze for BPR. However, BPR, like any fashionable management practice, is now falling from favor. In due course, it will undoubtedly undergo a revival.

This doesn't mean that workflow will necessarily follow the same boom and bust trend. The relationship between workflow and business process reengineering is terribly straightforward:

It is possible to do one without the other – and it is also possible to do both.

Enabling BPR

There are several capabilities of workflow systems which are synergistic with the aims of BPR, as espoused by management gurus. In particular, many workflow systems are capable of supporting:

* Effective triage – workflow systems provide good support for providing alternative process paths and automating the choice between them
* Parallelism – some (but not all!) workflow systems are very good at supporting parallel flows
* End-to-end responsibility – workflow systems, provided they are appropriately designed, can be very good at supporting processes which cross functional boundaries
* Event-driven processes – workflow systems can support processes which are triggered by events (although they are typically not too nimble at responding to events once a process has been initiated)

Inhibiting BPR

Pitting the wisdom of management gurus against the capabilities of the technology, there are pitfalls to watch out for if you want to use workflow to reengineer processes:

- *Paving the cowpath*. The process you implement with workflow need not be effective or efficient
- *Over-linearization*. Workflow's "Tayloristic" white-collar assembly line may be less effective than a more open, flexible system which supports team work, or empowers a single person to cope with a range of tasks
- *Dynamic processes*. Many workflow systems do not support dynamic delegation of work, or dynamic task refinement
- *Inflexibility*. If major systems integration is done to encapsulate existing legacy systems with a workflow shell, then these basic building blocks may prove to be a fundamental limitation on redesign

Beyond BPR

The focus of management thinking is now undergoing a pendulum swing from cost reduction to revenue generation. In theory, BPR is about more than just cost reduction; in practice, though, this is often the prime motivation for undertaking a BPR exercise. Workflow can be of use here, too: its capabilities may be used to help provide new services and products.

Related Technologies

There are several software technologies which are often used in workflow implementations or which share some common goals. This section gives a brief overview of these related software technologies, comparing and contrasting them with workflow:

- Groupware
- Workgroup
- Imaging
- Document management
- 4GLs and GUI builders
- Project management
- Integrated project support environments

The figure below summarises Ovum's view of how workflow compares with several of these other solutions.

Groupware

Groupware is a general term for software which is specifically designed to improve collaboration and co-ordination between groups of people. It includes:

Workflow and Related Technologies

	Groupshare*	Workflow	Doc mgt	4GLs	Project mgt	IPSE
Shared access to content resources	●					
Controlled access to content resources	○	●				●
Communication	●	○				
Management of complex content relationships			●			●
Explicit design representation of structured work process		●			●	○
Process tracking		●			●	
Resource planning					●	
Live support for flow of process control		●				○
Flexible choice of process models		●				○
Dynamic process control		○				
Building applications for process tasks	○	○		●		
Integrating external resources into process		●		○		

●   Core capability
○   Sometimes present

*'Groupshare': groupware which supports communication and shared access to content resources, but is not explicitly focused on supporting specific tasks and processes

- Team productivity tools (electronic meetings, desktop video conferencing, collaborative writing, shared whiteboards)
- Information-sharing systems (object stores, document databases, group calendars)
- Messaging
- Workflow

The simplest story to tell about workflow and groupware is that workflow is a type of groupware.

Groupware is not about the organizational 'groups' known as departments. Its focus is much wider. It tries to enable people, as members of *multiple virtual teams* within an organization, to overcome boundaries of distance by improving access and sharing of 'human-format' information: documents, forms and messages.

Many groupware products support communication and collaboration between people by providing a shared means of creating and accessing information resources. In this style of groupware, the communication which groupware supports can itself become the object of shared knowledge. There is indirect support for a variety of business processes, by supporting the communication and collaboration that underpins those processes. The specific means and methods by which business process goals are achieved need not be specified in advance as part of the design: the strength of these products is their ability to support open structure processes.

In contrast, workflow is a type of groupware which aims to provide very explicit support for business processes with a defined structure. Typically, there is little emphasis on general support for communication between people: it is the workflow system which communicates with people about the tasks which need to be done.

Imaging

'Imaging' refers to the assemblage of hardware and software used for the capture, storage, compression, access and transport of digital images – usually, but not necessarily, still images – and their interpretation via optical character recognition (OCR).

There is a strong relationship between the workflow and imaging markets. Many workflow suppliers started out as suppliers of imaging solutions, and only later added workflow capabilities.

When workflow is used to automate a process which uses information held in a paper document, imaging may be used as a supporting technology. Using imaging in conjunction with workflow enables a scanned image to become one of the information resources used by the tasks in a process.

However, imaging does not need to be built into a workflow product in order to be used in a workflow process. You can select a supplier which supplies both technologies under one umbrella, but it is often also possible to mix and match.

Document Management

Like imaging solutions, document management systems are a companion product to workflow. A document management system provides controlled location-transparent access to documents. The content resources managed by a document management system may include images, but may also include other information formats, such as word processor files, graphics, source code, multimedia hypertexts, electronic forms, video clips, audio clips and even databases.

This rich view of documents also includes the notion that documents change over time, and have a history. These relationships can also be tracked and managed by document management systems through versioning – which maintains a history of a document's lifecycle – and check in/check out facilities. More sophisticated document management systems also take account of the fact that documents have internal structure, and may contain other documents.

Application Development Tools

Application development tools such as fourth-generation languages (4GLs) and graphical user-interface (GUI) builders are aids to software development. So are workflow tools. However, each type of tool offers different abstractions to the developer.

For example, the goal of 4GLs is to insulate the developer from the nitty-gritty of the operating environment: operating systems, databases, communications, and client-server partitioning. However, unlike workflow systems, neither 4GLs nor GUI builders

- Represent tasks explicitly
- Make a meaningful distinction between tasks and processes
- Take account of how processes involve the participation of many different people
- Provide either design-time or run-time support for matching people with the work that needs to be done

There is a complementary relationship between 4GLs/GUI builders and workflow tools. Both 4GLs and GUI builders may be used to provide application resources which are used to support tasks in a process defined within the workflow tool and supported by the workflow run-time environment.

Project Management

Project management software shares many concerns with workflow systems. It is also used to track the time, cost, and other resource demands of projects. Unlike most workflow systems, project management software enables managers to plan and forecast utilization of project resources and to observe how this affects process completion time and project costs.

The crucial difference between the two is that project management software is not "live": it does not provide online software support for either the tasks which are required to complete the processes, or the flow of control between tasks in a process.

Project management systems are concerned with models of processes rather than with direct run-time support for the process itself.

Integrated Project Support Environments

Unlike project management software, an integrated project support environment (IPSE) aims to support the tracking and management of projects, as well as the information resources needed to get the projects done. The development of these products has been seeded by government-sponsored R&D work, most of it aimed at controlling and improving processes in large software development projects, particularly in the military sector.

Most systems developed in the various IPSE initiatives emphasised support for the "waterfall" model of software development and did not integrate project management features. Perhaps for this reason, few IPSEs have been fully commercialised.

However, there are several workflow tools which come from an R&D background which are closely related to IPSEs.

The Workflow Market – Present and Future

Market Dynamics

Although the workflow market has grown substantially over the past year, the market penetration of workflow is still relatively modest: most people who work with computers do not use workflow. Workflow's ability to grow further relies on several other factors.

The first, and most important, is demand. There are many business processes workflow is *not* suitable for: this places a natural limit on the extent to which workflow will dominate organizational processes. However, Ovum's view is that most workers, whether they are computer-based or not, partake in *some* organizational processes which workflow could facilitate. Adoption of the technology is nowhere near ceiling levels: workflow is far from becoming a mature, saturated, replacement market.

Workflow's ability to realize its potential relies primarily on:

- Cost
- Supply-side dynamics
- Standards
- Technological developments

The cost of workflow is, at present, mostly value-priced, where *value = a large number*. This limits its adoption to processes which are known to be broken, or in need of urgent fixes. Cost to customers is further aggravated by the fact that the workflow market is extremely fragmented. AIIM (the Association for Information and Image Management) lists over 240 workflow suppliers in its membership directory. Volume-based pricing in a serious sense cannot begin to percolate through the market until there has been some serious consolidation in the number of suppliers.

Since not all suppliers are making money out of their products, Ovum predicts that consolidation will indeed happen over the next five years. However, at present, the large number of suppliers acts as an inhibitor on market development. Customer choice is more difficult, more risky, and more expensive.

Therefore, the development of standards is critical to the success of the industry. The Workflow Management Coalition is the leading organization in this field. Interestingly, the urgency of this effort is underlined by the increasing maturity of the market. Increasingly, customers are being faced with tough choices about whether they will need to adopt several workflow products, suited to the needs of different applications (i.e. processes). Uncertainty about these choices is acting as an inhibitor to the market. The development of interoperability standards, even minimal ones, will give a comfort factor to organizations which are experiencing internal conflict between:

- Developing proprietary, special-purpose systems that don't inter-work, and
- Deferring investment

On the technology front, the most significant influences on the supply side of the market are:

- The packaging of workflow with other software technologies
- The use of the Web for deploying workflow in corporate intranets

By its very nature, workflow is most easily thought of as "workflow and": it is, by nature, an integration technology. One of the most critical power struggles in the industry at present is the tug-of-war between suppliers of general-purpose workflow systems, versus workflow systems which come pre-integrated with other functions.

The close alliance between workflow and imaging systems has played a role in shaping the initial development of the workflow market; a similar trend is seen today in the relationship between workflow and document management systems. However, the future of the market will be strongly shaped by the interplay between "pure" general-purpose workflow and workflow which is embedded in business applications. Business application suppliers such as CA, CGI, D&B, QSP and SAP have already included workflow into their product sets. Ovum believes that over the next five years, all leading edge business application suppliers will follow suit.

The other technology trend which will shape the future of the market is the use of corporate intranets for software deployment. Over the past year, both new and existing suppliers have jumped on the both the Web and workflow bandwagons at the same time, by offering workflow systems which can be deployed over the Web.

Using an "internal Web" (if that isn't too much of a contradiction in terms) to deploy workflow offers manifest advantages, not least of which is the reduction in complexity and expense of deployment. Security permitting, using workflow over the Web also enables you to apply workflow design and control techniques to processes which extend outside the boundaries of an individual organization, to include partnerships, suppliers, and even customers. It is this last area which holds the most promise for enlarging the scope of workflow in business processes.

The impending integration of messaging and HTML forms will also have an impact on workflow architectures. This will enable more effective "push" delivery of task notifications, combined seamlessly with centralized tracking facilities.

However, Ovum's view is that the success – or otherwise – of the many and various vendor ventures onto the Web will not be fundamentally linked to the Web. Web-ableness is fated to become another checkbox item in vendors' marketing literature. The real differentiators between products will remain.

Market Forecast

Ovum predicts continued growth for the workflow industry over the next five years. However, there will be pressure on prices due to the impending overlap between high-end, engine-based products and low-end, forms-based products. There will be consolidation in the market and the number of suppliers will fall: the supply side of the market is tremendously volatile and will continue to be so. These factors, coupled with standards uncertainty, will act as inhibitors to revenue growth for suppliers. Against these negative influences, we set the importance and value of workflow as a solution to business problems. The net effect of these factors is summarized in Table 2, which forecasts worldwide expenditure on workflow products and services to the year 2000. Market growth is set for a "spike" in 1996 and 1997, as pilot programs roll out into production.

Table 2   Worldwide Workflow Expenditure ($m) (Ovum estimate)

	1995	1996	1997	1998	1999	2000	Growth (% p.a.)
Products	206	464	830	1,080	1,240	1,340	45
Services	930	1,855	2,905	3,564	3,844	4,020	34
Total expenditure	**1,136**	**2,318**	**3,735**	**4,644**	**5,084**	**5,360**	**36**

Amidst all the changes that the market is undergoing, one factor will remain more or less constant: the real cost of deploying workflow will continue to be the services associated with the development, and not the software itself. However, Ovum predicts that the ratio between service and software costs will drift downwards slightly over the forecast period.

There will also be changes in the relationship of workflow with established technologies such as business applications. The relative values of these markets are difficult to establish. Clearly, not all the revenue from workflow-enabled business applications is attributable to workflow. However, taking the conservative view that workflow functionality could eventually constitute around 5% of the value of business application software, Ovum predicts that uptake of workflow technology by business applications vendors ("embedded workflow") will contribute to market growth, accounting for 20% of the value of workflow software by 2000 (see Table 3).

Table 3   Worldwide Product Expenditure by Type ($m) (Ovum estimate)

	1995	1996	1997	1998	1999	2000	Growth (% p.a.)
General purpose workflow	201	359	626	825	960	1021	38%
Embedded workflow	5	105	204	255	280	319	130%
Total expenditure	**206**	**464**	**830**	**1,080**	**1,240**	**1,340**	**30%**

Challenges for the Future

Vendors of workflow, individually and collectively, face several challenges in the years ahead:

• Keep the standards story quick and simple

Competing standards add confusion.

• Scaleability

   Workflow systems risk becoming victims of their own success – vendors must accelerate their efforts to deliver scaleable systems that don't sacrifice control.

• Improve workflow development environments by encouraging "pessimistic" design using error handling, and encouraging design for reuse

Workflow systems typically do not have much in the way of event-handling capabilities, and copying is often the only way to reuse scripts and definitions. This is well behind the state of the art.

- Introduce second-order process control

Products may be able to report on the state of the environment, but they are rarely able to do anything constructive about it, besides complain.

- Widen the notion of 'task'
The present, rather narrow, scenario for workflow tasks is that a task is something done by one person, using one task application, at one time.
- Bridge the gaps between the different styles of workflow products

This is not just a standards issue, it is a design challenge. If vendors can combine the advantages of a process control backbone with ad-hoc flexibility about design and actual methods, their systems will have wider uptake.

Workflow will be with us for the foreseeable future, whether or not these challenges are met. However, the next generation of workflow products will be worth watching for.

Workflow in Context

Keith Hales
SODAN

In this article you will see where workflow management fits in the context of the business problems faced today. Motivations for using workflow and the likely benefits resulting from its implementation are suggested.

The increased wealth of the industrialized world during the twentieth century is due to ever-improving productivity in the manufacturing sector. This process has now reached the point where further enhancements to manufacturing processes are becoming less significant.

To continue economic growth, it is now the turn of the service sectors to improve their efficiencies. In contrast to manufacturing, productivity in offices has barely changed in recent years, despite the widespread introduction of computers.

Business Problems

If we compare the situation in the office today with manufacturing, most offices are still at the "village forge" stage. Staff react to immediate demands, and base their actions on experience rather than any written plans of action. Some larger offices have progressed to the "workshop" phase, whereby business processes are broken down into stages and cases dealt with in batches. However, this leads to buffer stocks of work between stages, thus slowing down the overall process. Other problems include:

- Frequent mislaying or loss of documents
- Inability to respond promptly to customer enquiries, because particular cases cannot readily be located
- Difficulty in monitoring workloads and throughput due to lack of data

Organizations are also faced with other problems connected with the way in which business is conducted:

- Difficulty in measuring the performance and efficiency of work groups and departments
- Inadequate integration among different computer systems and applications
- Poor return on investments in information technology

Perhaps most significantly, the introduction of changes to the organization is often the greatest problem facing senior management. Changes which management might want to make are:

- Decentralization of functions, to take them closer to customers or reduce operating costs
- More flexible staffing, using more part-time staff, job-sharing, or the introduction of home-based working for selected functions
- Wider and better controlled use of information technology
- Faster introduction of new products and services in response to changing markets
- Merging of businesses following major reorganizations or take-overs.

Introduction of such changes is often traumatic for the staff at all levels. Most organizations function largely because individuals have learned only from experience how to perform their various duties. When large changes occur, they no longer have a sound basis for fulfilling their roles, and it can take the organization a long time to adapt and recover.

The Solution

Workflow Management (WFM) is the key to solving these problems. WFM is to business process what the production line is to manufacturing. It has already been proved by pioneer users to yield not only increases in productivity (typically between 30 and 50%), but also enhanced service to customers. In many cases, the latter has proved to be even more advantageous than the productivity gains, because it provides a competitive edge, attracting additional business.

Everyone seems to have their own definition of what workflow management is, so here is SODAN's:

Workflow Management is a pro-active system for managing a series of tasks defined in one or more procedures. The system ensures that the tasks are passed among the appropriate participants in the correct sequence, and completed within set times (default actions being taken where necessary).

Participants may be people or other systems. People interact through workstations, while other systems are accessed over a communications network.

This definition excludes various products generally known as "groupware", because such products are not pro-active, but leave the initiative with users. The best-known example is probably **Lotus Notes**. Groupware products are usually only capable of processing single cases, and not multiple transactions of similar type.

How it Works

A business process is defined to WFM as a procedure. Each time the procedure is invoked, a case is created. Thus, at any given time, there are a number of cases being processed, each case being at its own point in the procedure.

A procedure consists of a series of tasks, which are processed in a logical sequence. Branching may occur within a procedure, with decisions made by the procedure and based on information within each case. All case forwarding from task to task is executed by WFM, by means of an electronic mail system. Where there are parallel tasks, WFM collects the output from each task together at a rendezvous point in the procedure, before forwarding the case to the next task.

Each task has a set time allowed for the task to be completed, from which a deadline is calculated and given to participants on their task lists. If any task is not completed within a deadline, an alarm is raised.

Data is input by participants, collected from other systems or databases, or derived within tasks. Data can be of any type, including text, numeric, image or voice. Data is stored within documents, and each case has a folder containing one or more documents. Although documents are normally stored within the WFM system, documents stored elsewhere may also be referred to, including off-line media such as paper.

The Immediate Benefits of Workflow Management

A major benefit is the reduction in use of paper, since most documents can be stored and processed electronically. This in turn leads to further advantages:

- There is just one master copy of each document, avoiding the use of extra copies which may form a security risk
- Documents do not have to be physically transported from person to person, so that the staff involved in any one procedure no longer have to be located close together to minimize transport costs and times
- Documents are always traceable and available, to allow immediate response to enquiries
- Data entered to documents can be validated on entry, reducing errors and consequent delays
- Accurate information on work-in-progress is instantly available, including the content of documents; for example, summaries of the value of work in progress

A major benefit is that the speed of processing is greatly increased, due to the elimination of hidden delays in manual procedures. Processing work more quickly not only reduces costs, but also improves service to customers, which provides a major competitive advantage for commercial organizations.

Further Benefits

Staff not only no longer need to be located close together for efficiency, but can be located anywhere with access to the computer network; they do not even have to be based at a fixed location. This opens up the possibilities for:

* Decentralization of functions and staff, to reduce the costs of having large, centrally located offices, or siting key staff at customer contact points
* Making staff more mobile, working out of multiple locations
* Including mobile staff, such as traveling sales representatives, in business procedures to eliminate intermediate processing
* Allowing the use of home-based staff, to reduce traveling times and costs, make use of permanently or temporarily disabled staff, or simply reduce office costs

Other benefits arise from having business procedures inherently well defined and enforced:

* Errors are reduced, and the quality of work enhanced; compliance with quality standards such as BS 5750 and ISO 9000 is much more readily attained
* Changes are easier to introduce, because they can be better defined and implemented
* Staff training times are reduced, because the WFM system itself leads staff precisely through procedures
* New procedures can be developed and introduced very rapidly, enabling fast responses to changing markets

From a data processing viewpoint, WFM is an efficient means of integrating existing and new applications across multiple platforms. The WFM system acts as a flexible user interface layer over the application software packages, automatically carrying the necessary data forward from package to package.

Users' Experiences

Workflow Management (WFM) has gained greatest acceptance so far in the government and finance sectors. However, WFM is applicable to every sector, including manufacturing, which has many back-office functions.

Any service-oriented activity can take good advantage of WFM, because of the greater speed of processing, and this has proved to be of greater significance to many users than even the high productivity gains. The latter are typically of the order of 30 to 50% after the initial introduction, and continue to increase as organizations become more familiar with the techniques.

Since faster processing offers a real competitive advantage to commercial organizations, business levels are often increased, to the extent that no staff need be made redundant due to the greater efficiencies. The same number of staff simply process more business.

The staff themselves may initially be wary of WFM, seeing it as a threat both to jobs and to their individual freedom. However, WFM can relieve staff of the tedious elements of their duties, such as retrieving and storing files, and so allow more time for the creative aspects. Furthermore, rewards for good performance can be given on a more objective basis. Staff of organizations using WFM generally become very enthusiastic once they see what it can do for them.

An important factor in the successful introduction of WFM is the commitment and full support of senior management. Because WFM can have a profound effect on the way in which an organization works, introducing it at a low level can lead to conflicts of interest.

Applying Workflow Management

Workflow Management (WFM) can be introduced into an organization in one of two ways:

- For a particular application within one department of an organization
- As part of business process reengineering

The first method of introduction usually occurs when there is a recognised problem which needs to be solved. In such cases, a WFM solution is often competing with "conventional" computer systems.

WFM will yield the greatest benefits to an organization that makes it part of its business development strategy, and is a powerful means of implementing reengineered processes.

Implementation

Having decided to implement WFM, the introduction has to be planned in distinct stages:

- Identification of suitable applications
- Selection of a Workflow Management system
- Preparation, including staff training
- Application development

These early stages are where the services of an outside consultancy can be of greatest benefit. Its experience of WFM can help avoid potential pitfalls, and get WFM up and running in the shortest possible time. The organization should use this time to learn about WFM itself, so that it can maintain its own applications, and progress towards development of new applications unaided.

The Business Impact of Workflow

Reengineering and Workflow

Thomas M. Koulopoulos
Delphi Consulting Group

Unlike reengineering, workflow does not require radical change and exceptional sponsorship in the organization. This article looks at the links between reengineering and workflow, the way in which workflow supports reengineering and BPR efforts, and the importance of workflow in any ongoing change effort.

Responding to Change

The cry for reengineering ringing out through the hallowed hallways of corporations around the globe is an attempt to begin a fundamental shift in the way enterprises respond to the increasing rate of change. But of itself reengineering is a noble but feeble effort that will, in the words of Tom Peters, "Replace old sterile organizations, with new sterile organizations".

In reality, no reengineering effort can cause an organization to change as fast as today's market forces demand. Success and growth in today's world demands the ability to innovate at rates that were unimaginable during the age of factory automation. Organizations making the transformation to mass customization and mass innovation couple workflow with reengineering and BPR to create adaptive organizations that are able to constantly change. This ability to quickly identify and respond to change is the fundamental benefit and the enduring advantage of workflow, and its most critical link to reengineering.

Using Workflow as a Metric for the Reengineering Process

The popular view of reengineering as the "obliteration" of existing process and systems has its own set of issues and risks. For one, few of us have the level of sponsorship required to cause such drastic change to occur within large organizations. Second, even sponsorship requires some direction. Where should reengineering begin? Which business processes and information systems are least efficient? What is the measure of efficiency?

Without answers to these questions, any reengineering exercise is no more than a roll of the dice. Workflow can provide these answers and in the process establish the foundation for a sound reengineering effort. But to do this, workflow must be used as more than an automation tool. It must also provide the analytical and reporting tools that help change-managers better understand their organization's business processes. In this light, workflow becomes an overall discipline for restructuring information systems, and not another competing technology.

Make no mistake, however, although workflow is part methodology, it is not always synonymous with reengineering. The two are complementary methods. Reengineering proposes the obliteration of existing work processes and the establishment of new business methods based on new sets of assumptions regarding desired business objectives. It is a comprehensive approach to redefining the organization. Workflow is the analysis, compression, and automation of information-based process models that make up a business. In short, workflow provides the metrics for reengineering.

Although workflow appears to represent only one component of total reengineering, no reengineering project should proceed without the use of workflow, at the very least as an analytical tool. The reason? How can you undertake a redefinition of an organization if there is no benchmark against which to measure the efficiency of its business processes? Workflow offers the means by which to establish these benchmarks within your organization.

But measurement alone will not foster change without the application of some form of sponsorship to the reengineering effort. The specific form of sponsorship, and the motivation behind it, determines one of three methods of reengineering with workflow. Although each may have its place in an organization, they should not be regarded as interchangeable. Once again, an understanding of each approach is necessary to determine which is appropriate for your organization.

The Dimensions of Reengineering

Three models of reengineering are commonly used: the lifecycle model, the crisis model, and the goal-oriented model.

Lifecycle reengineering results from a strategic initiative to constantly reevaluate existing processes. Change is incremental and basic processes remain essentially intact, modified slightly to accommodate new requirements. Modification is usually aligned with the critical success factors of the organization. Automation is often applied, but the primary emphasis is on enhancing and streamlining the process. The sponsorship must be cultural, not mandated. In lifecycle reengineering, workflow is a necessity for identifying the ongoing metrics that lead to change.

Crisis reengineering is a response to systems crumbling under the weight of user demands or organizational pressure. For example, a service firm with a cumbersome billing process had a high percentage of fee-earned-not-billed. The prolonged billing cycle resulted in a negative cash flow and led directly to a crisis reengineering of the billing process with the objective of speeding client invoicing. Sponsorship is almost always present, although, ironically, you could easily make a claim that it is not necessary since change must occur regardless of the solution chosen. In reality, however, the sponsor fills the vital role of defining the problem to the enterprise. Workflow may not be required to begin a crisis reengineering exercise. But without workflow such an organization is likely to face crisis after crisis since ongoing process metrics are mostly absent.

Goal-oriented reengineering has defined objectives which may differ substantially from the objectives in place when the system was first developed. This is a deliberate attempt to bring an existing process in line with business objectives. Business processes are totally redesigned with new goals and objectives in mind. Sponsorship is inherent. The sponsors must have the clout to drive the application through the organization, often without cost justification. A reengineering methodology and a corresponding tool, such as workflow, is almost always used in this case, since the emphasis is on a strategic, long-term implementation with an extended measurable payback.

Of the three reengineering methods lifecycle reengineering is the least disruptive approach and the most compatible with workflow because it fosters an opportunistic attitude towards change and an incremental, ongoing approach to modifying information systems. Another way to look at this is to ask the fundamental question, " Does my organization budget a certain amount of money each year for reengineering?". Without that type of commitment – let's say a few hundred dollars for each technology-enabled desktop – reengineering will always be overdue by the time its mandate arrives.

In a lifecycle reengineering effort customization will be minimal since it is spread out over time. The risk is that significant inefficiencies may be overlooked because of the effort required to reengineer them. Also, it can only be used if organizational critical success factors (CSFs) are well stated and supported among management and users. Workflow is best applied in this type of a reengineering mode since the workflow will provide an ongoing measure by which to constantly modify and refine the business processes.

To support the lifecycle model a good workflow tool will generate online reports that offer insight to the workloads, bottlenecks, resource allocation, throughput, productivity, and overall business cycle. By analyzing these, immediate decisions can be made to alter a process by reallocating resources, changing task relationships, eliminating redundancy, or altering priorities of work. The result is a highly adaptive and responsive organization – not unlike the model used to retool factory assembly lines for the purpose of mass customization.

The approach that is most often touted by the high priests of reengineering, crisis reengineering, is thrust upon an organization with no other choice. The decision is not "Should we reengineer?" but rather "Can we afford not to?". Organizations that rely on crisis reengineering are doomed to encounter a reengineering crisis regularly. Ironically, the prevailing attitude in these organizations is "well enough is best left alone", until a major crisis looms. In such an organization, process entropy increases regularly until action must be taken. Since the reengineering is forced by a particular scenario, the analysis is often biased and rushed.

During the industrial revolution and the decades leading up to the present day, technology obsolescence occurred at regular, planned intervals measured in decades. In that environment, it was possible to retool and reengineer once or twice each decade. Today, technology is obsolete in months, not years. Reengineering can no longer be a decade-interval activity – if it is, it will always be too late to do any good.

The least common approach, goal-oriented reengineering, requires high-level corporate sponsorship for change in the absence of a clear and pending crisis. It is driven by the anticipation of future benefits resulting from reengineering rather than the cost of an old or inefficient solution.

Workflow is compatible with goal-oriented reengineering as long as sponsors demonstrate a quantifiable measure of business process improvement. Workflow assists in reengineering through its ability to monitor and report on changing business cycles. Unfortunately, technology is often separated from business process redesign in most reengineering approaches. For many, that has meant that workflow should be left out of the reengineering effort, in order to avoid compromising business goals. That need not be the case. Since workflow does not impose a specific technology toolset of its own for the actual performance of work – office automation tools, such as word processing, database, spreadsheets, email, and EDI should all work within the workflow environment – it does not alter, impede, or compromise the reengineering effort.

It is safe to say that not only can multiple reengineering approaches exist in a single organization, but there may be elements of any two or all three approaches applied simultaneously to a single reengineering effort. In practice, the most likely case is that all three will come into play over time. For example: a crisis may initiate the reengineering effort; management then identifies a long-term goal that provides a context for the initial project and a series of subsequent reengineering efforts intended to achieve a strategic vision; finally, the vision itself is tested repeatedly in a lifecycle approach that continuously validates the vision against the reality.

A striking analogy is weight loss. Most people struggle their entire lives with weight gain and loss. An endless roller coaster for most of us. On occasion, however, a crisis will occur, perhaps a physician's warning of health risks, an actual health crisis, or something as subtle as seeing themselves in a family photo. Whatever the impetus, it is strong enough to cause them to take action. In some cases that action, and a bit of success, turns into a vision of themselves on a regimen. That vision needs to be reinforced with success, since it is not of itself a pleasing experience – what drives the vision at this stage are results. Over time, however, the only successful weight loss program is that which not only reinforces the vision of a regimen but that of a person and a lifestyle. At that stage every decision and future action taken by an individual will have a bearing not on their weight but instead on their lifestyle. By this time there is no regimen, only an ongoing process of checks and balances that act as the measure and countermeasure of success. That is the essence of workflow.

Workflow Applications within Business Organizations

Nikolaos Vlachantonis
LION GmbH, Köln/Bochum, Germany

This article is about the implications which workflow-oriented applications have on business organizations. The characteristics of workflow applications and how they fit into changing organizations are described. The complexity and the consequences when a workflow application is adapted to a company are shown and vice versa.

Introduction

Workflow-oriented applications are increasingly becoming a key factor within companies which have to successfully face fast-changing markets. The constantly changing behavior of today's customers is one reason. Customers expect low-priced products which are more specialized and better adapted to their needs. Another reason is a surplus of goods, which leads to a pressure on prices. As a result, companies are facing new and rapidly changing challenges. They can no longer rely simply on optimizing their production processes as in past decades. They are searching for new opportunities to minimize costs. Outsourcing of certain divisions – e.g. R&D, customer care, clearing center, etc. – is one such possibility. This is a means to set external organizations under pressure and to get lower prices for services. But experience shows that this way is not always successful.

Many companies are looking more closely at their own administration in order to find ways to optimize their internal and external processes. Often this leads to a restructuring: "Business Process Reengineering" (BPR) [HC 1993] which has become more and more popular in recent years.

BPR, however, has implications on IT systems. They have to adequately support the new structure of the company. In particular the newly defined business processes must be implemented by the IT applications.

This has led to the development of different kinds of "Workflow Management Systems". They are integrated within IT systems with the objective of controlling the flow of work, i.e. the sequence of tasks performed. The idea is to define the processes independently of the IT application. This leads to higher flexibility in the IT application. Moreover, management can understand the processes because they are defined explicitly.

In the following section the notion of process orientation within companies is explained. A process orientation leads on to IT systems, i.e. workflow applications, with characteristics which are explained in section 3. In a later section the consequences for companies installing workflow applications are described.

Process Orientation

Process orientation means radically rethinking the way work is done within a business. The hierarchical structuring of organizations into functional units and sub-units has historically been the main focus when organizing businesses. Each unit in each level has a defined function within the company, is responsible for this function and has directly assigned resources for accomplishing it.

One effect of this is that people belonging to one unit start thinking in a narrow way concerning only their own functions. They no longer have the company as a whole in mind and therefore build organizational barriers between them and other units. This leads to a lack of communication between units and people, slower working and more intensive administration. Adding more people and resources to units in order to make them more efficient has exactly the reverse effect.

Process orientation is a means of solving this problem. The functional unit of a company is no longer the most important means of structuring. Starting from the company's goals the flow of work, i.e. the business processes, within the company are described in order to achieve the targets. This is a basis for setting the different units and divisions within a company into working relationships and for defining how they have to work together to exchange information. This is also a prerequisite for "Lean Management".

Figure 1 depicts the idea of process orientation within a company in a schematic way. The flow of work is described explicitly by a process definition, which, along with further information, describes in which unit and by which user the sub-processes must be performed. Later this is a basis for the construction of the IT system supporting the defined business processes.

Process orientation is also a means for measuring the working effectiveness of administrations. The defined business processes are now the main objects of interest for management. The work items and sub-processes, for instance, may be checked in such a way that they add value to the product resulting from the business process they are a part of. The business processes can be analyzed and gradually optimized when the company, its products or the customers change.

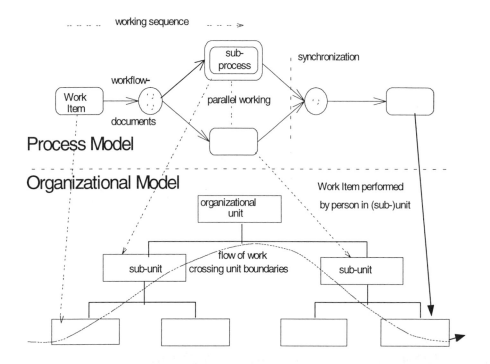

Figure 1 Abstract Business Process Model

Another positive effect of process orientation is the fact that the business process model is the input for the workflow management system. These data are used to steer and control the flow of work, i.e. to control the IT application. But this is not the whole truth. It is far more difficult to build a process-oriented application (workflow application) owing to the fact that the type of handling for such a system radically changes when compared to classical function-oriented ones. Another point is that the user desktop looks different. These aspects are more closely explained in the following two sections.

Characteristics of Workflow Applications

The nature of a workflow application results from the fact that not all functionality of the underlying software system is directly accessible; this means that a user cannot directly start any dialog or batch procedure. All functionality is associated with the defined business process model. Certain dialogs or batches are started directly by the workflow engine if and only if all defined prerequisites are met.

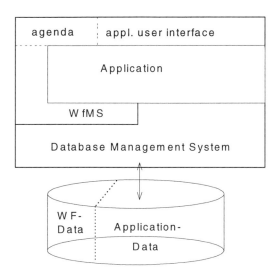

Figure 2   Architecture of a Workflow Application

Architecture of a Workflow Application

A workflow application generally consist of a database application, an interface system and a workflow engine, that controls all other components. Figure 2 depicts the technical structure of a workflow application.

The task of the workflow engine is to run the defined business processes. Many workflow management systems store data within a repository and interpret them during execution. This has many advantages because part of the repository data may be changed dynamically to affect the behavior of the whole system. For instance, changing the authorization data for a user changes the list of possible activities and data that the user may execute or access. This holds true (with some constraints) also for the process models themselves. For this no programming code must be changed.

Objects of Interest

Besides the normal data that a classical database application manages, for each instance of a process type (from here on, a "case") a workflow application adds the associated workflow data to the database. Each case is therefore represented by a process instance and some workflow data. This data comprises on the one hand data from the underlying application, and on the other hand added workflow control data, e.g. case number, process status, etc. The workflow control data is irrelevant for the application itself. It exists only during the execution of the case. Afterwards it is deleted.

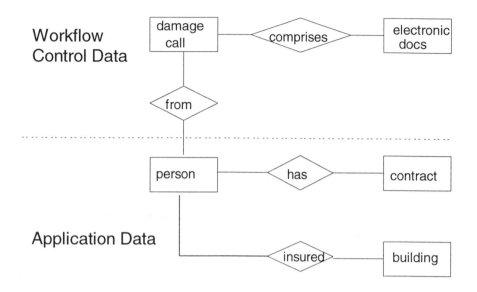

Figure 3   Association between Application and Workflow Control Data

Viewing a workflow management system as an independent but deeply integrated component of a workflow application requires the integrated storage of workflow control and application data within one database. One way to do this is to extend the data model of the application by those entities which will represent the structure of the workflow data later on and to set them into relationship with the internal ones. This makes it easier to ensure the integrity of data updates by one transaction control system. Figure 3 shows as an abstract example the association of application and workflow control data within one data model.

The workflow data is also a means of getting a historical, accumulated view on the organization. Management, for instance, may gain more information about a working administration, for example:

- How many cases are being processed at the moment?
- How many cases have been processed in a previous time frame?
- Which type of cases are processed more often than others and which ones are never processed? (what is our main business?)
- Which units/people are involved with which cases?
- Which units/people are over- or under-loaded (resource planning)?

It should be clear that a workflow management system adds much to an application and to the controlling ability of management.

Desktop Structure

The desktop of a workflow application is very important to the users because it reflects on one side the process-orientation and on the other side the way users organize their own work and exchange information and tasks with colleagues.

The process-orientation is represented as an electronic agenda or work list showing all current cases assigned to a certain user. The user may then select one of the offered activities, i.e. a work item, and work further on the selected case.

The electronic agenda is automatically filled with data from the workflow engine. Many workflow management systems generate a standard agenda which in most cases is shown to be unacceptable by users. In order to be accepted, the electronic agenda must be adapted to the type of application it is integrated in.

It should be determined from the business process models and from the type of application what data to show, and how to show it in the agenda. Often, different views for different types of processes are necessary for fulfilling the ergonomic and organizational requirements.

The user should be able to define sorting and filtering criteria for the agenda. The actual status for each case should be displayed from an application point of view.

These characteristics are particularly important when physical paper is replaced by electronic documents. Paper is not only an information carrier but also a means for organizing work. Clerks have always used paper to structure their own work. How does a clerk know what to do next if he or she is not holding the physical paper? And how should he or she pass on tasks to colleagues?

These important features of physical paper must be replaced by the workflow application. Some important functions are listed in the following.

The electronic agenda of a WF application should

- Represent case data in an application specific way
- Allow sorting and filtering of cases (the clerk customizes the agenda to his or her needs)
- Allow the exchange of cases between clerks for different reasons (deputy management, work balance, etc.)
- Display the status of cases in an application specific way (not in a way which is pre-defined by the workflow management system)
- Allow the clerk to retrieve information about current cases in order to answer questions from calling customers or for other reasons

There are many more required functions which stem from the application and the kind of organization. It should be emphasized that the electronic agenda is not only a work list, as positioned by many workflow management systems, but much more: it is an important means for structuring the clerk's desktop, and therefore a main factor in the clerk's acceptance of a workflow application.

Implications on the Organization

Organizations installing workflow applications have to adjust themselves to this new paradigm of working in different ways.

One aspect is that BPR should lead to a process-orientation within the company. As stated before, functionality of the workflow application is not directly accessible to the users because it is only associated with business processes. It is therefore necessary for the organization to thoroughly define all possible triggers – internal or external – which start instances of the defined business processes.

These triggers could be physical letters from customers, electronic mail, telephone calls, internal time triggers, etc. Defining such triggers includes making clear how they are to be processed by the workflow application. For instance, physical letters have to be scanned first, indexed manually and forwarded electronically on certain criteria to the right clerk, i.e. into his or her electronic agenda, starting an instance of a business process. A telephone call is also a trigger. But telephone calls cannot be scanned. The called clerk must start a dialog in which the call is registered, assigned to a business process and then forwarded to the workflow application.

Reflecting further on this, it becomes clear that the necessary infrastructure must be installed as a prerequisite for the workflow application. This also means that some job profiles – like post clerks, customer service clerks, etc. – change and require newly trained or educated personnel.

Another aspect is that the workflow application provides a technical basis for measuring the effectiveness of the administration and therefore of the company itself. A side-effect is that it becomes a Management Information System (MIS) which allows a deeper and more detailed view of the company.

The training of new users can become easier, because they do not have to learn which dialog or batch process to use in which situations, since this is done automatically by the workflow application. They have to learn about the business processes, their work items and sub-processes and how to handle them within the workflow application.

The implications of BPR and Workflow Management on organizations are more closely described in [Kou 1995]. How to develop software from defined business processes is described in [GW 1995; JEJ 1994].

Conclusions

This paper tries to give an overview of the complexities that come with workflow applications and which have to be considered within organizations.

It is highlighted that it is not sufficient to install a workflow management system on top of an existing application. A workflow application leads to a radical changing of the user interface, desktop structure and the work handling paradigm.

Different aspects change, e.g. the clerk's desktop, the organizational structure, the infrastructure, etc. The changes are even greater when paper is replaced by electronic documents.

One important prerequisite for the success of a workflow application is an open attitude by company staff toward such new ideas. Not only must the company change, but also the employees.

References

[GW 1995]
> Gruhn, V. and Wolf, S. Software process improvement by business process orientation, *Software Process Improvement and Practice*, 1, August 1995, pp. 49–57.

[HC 1993]
> Hammer, M. and Champy, J. *Reengineering the Corporation: A Manifesto for Business Revolution*. Harper Collins, New York, 1993.

[JEJ 1994]
> Jacobson, I., Ericsson, M. and Jacobson, A. *The Object Advantage – Business Process Reengineering with Object Technology,* Addison-Wesley, New York, 1994.

[Kou 1995]
> Koulopoulos, T. M., *The Workflow Imperative: Building Real World Solutions,* Van Nostrand Reinhold, New York, 1995.

From BPR Models to Workflow Applications

Marc Derungs, Dr Petra Vogler, Prof. Dr Hubert Österle
Institute for Information Management
University of St Gallen, Switzerland

This article outlines a method to support the transformation of business processes into workflow applications. The basis for the implementation is a reengineered process but it recognises that organisations are usually saddled with legacy systems. This article concentrate on workflow-specific topics, giving an overview of the three central steps of the method: Requirements Specifications, Conceptual Design and Realisation.

Statement of Problem

Several companies have over the last few years carried out Business Process Reengineering (BPR) projects. These projects promise radical improvements in respect of cycle time, production costs and error rates [Dav 1993; HC 1993]. Suppliers of workflow systems offer their systems as a means of transforming the BPR outcome into an information system. The large number of tools available is influencing the workflow market which is undergoing immense changes. Initial experiences from projects have shown that workflow projects do not only involve the drawing of process flows and the specification of graphical user interfaces. Rather, workflow is a significant and complex subject.

The transformation of these BPR results into applications often turns out to be a problem. Many companies already have an information system whose applications are based on business function areas (e.g. personnel, logistics, and finance) and not arranged according to processes. These firms must consider their legacy systems during the process implementation since these systems bind substantial resources and contain business knowledge [JAD+ 1994, p. 113ff]. An implementation from scratch, i.e. development of a new information system based on the process design, is not realistic due to cost and time constraints [GGÖV 1995]. For that reason, this article sets out to accomplish the following goal:

- Outline a methodology for the implementation of a process using a workflow management system

Methodology

For the implementation of a process various alternatives are available such as

- Packaged software
- Self-developed software
- Further development of the As-Is-System
- Workflow systems

For example, in many businesses packaged software is the most attractive choice since packages entail high quality and ensure quick implementation. The decision relating to packaged software often means that not all requirements of BPR projects can be addressed since this type of software provides limited flexibility. Additionally, the introduction of packaged software entails total or partial removal of existing information systems. The other alternatives have their advantages and disadvantages which are not the subject of this paper; a solution which can be assigned exclusively to one of the alternatives will seldom arise. This statement also applies to current views held on workflow.

The use of a workflow system pursues the goal of incorporating available applications in the new process in order to reuse them. The workflow system steers the work between the participating positions (user and system) in accordance with its specifications. It should ascertain the next processing step as well as the people responsible. In addition it should prepare the necessary information, initiate automatic programs for the execution of individual steps and carry out their timely monitoring [HL 1991, p. 24; Mar 1994; WfMC 1994; Jab 1995, p. 5ff].

Workflow assumes a detailed specification. However, BPR projects do not reach the necessary depth and give too little consideration to the aspect of integration [HBÖ 1995, p. 11]. The following sections describe the stages of the implementation process which should mitigate this weakness (see Figure 1). This description relates to the specification of workflow applications; the organisational transformation is not included.

The sequential representation in Figure 1 and in later sections does not characterize such a method in projects. Projects are much more influenced by iteration and feedback which in this article, for reasons of clarity and size restrictions, will not be further analyzed.

The proposed solution assumes that the process has been reengineered and that it will be implemented with a workflow system using new and legacy systems.

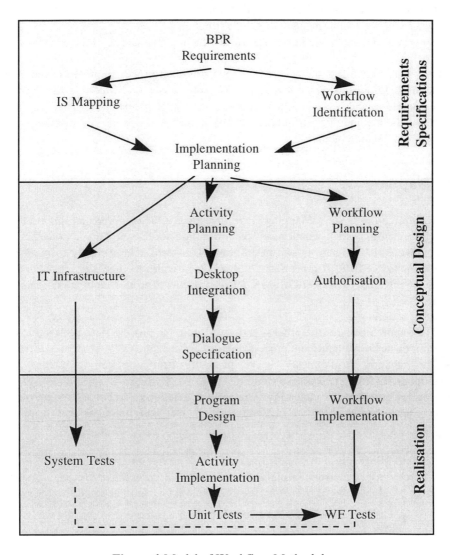

Figure 1 Model of Workflow Methodology

Requirements Specifications

The specification of requirements in the workflow procedure methodology has the following goals:

- Investigate the data and function requirement gaps between the process design and the As-Is-System

- Identify and outline the relevant workflows
- Determine the requirements for the infrastructure
- Determine a plan for the infrastructure and the implementation of the workflow

These goals only differ slightly from the goals of other procedure models. The main task of Requirements Specifications is to estimate the magnitude of the process transformation and, based on this estimate, develop implementation plans. Central parts of the methodology are the IS Mapping, the identification of workflows and the implementation plan.

IS Mapping

The Information System Mapping stage investigates the requirements imposed on the information system which result from the process design. This is done first to recognize early deficiencies on the information system, and secondly to mark out the boundary of BPR. A profile of requirements provides the necessary basis for the IS Mapping [JEJ 1994, p. 285ff; MK 1994, p. 136ff]. The IS Mapping is organized as follows:

- The required data for the process is derived from the process design, in particular from the activity chains and process outputs
- The function requirements derive primarily from the activity chains and secondarily from the process vision
- Beside the aspects concerning data and functions, technical requirements originate predominately from the identified data and functions and from the process vision

To enable IS Mapping, the method must not only derive the requirements from the process, it must also provide techniques in order to describe the existing information system. A description of the As-Is-Information System must include the following points:

- Application scenarios and application directory
- Description of interfaces
- Description of transactions and service programs
- Description of data structures

The basis for the description of the As-Is-Information System is not the current situation; rather it is a realistic scenario which represents the image of an application structure at the time of the planned introduction. For example, the application scenario describes the situation which will pertain when the process is implemented. It reflects neither the actual nor the ideal situation. It is usually the situation in six to eighteen months' time.

The IS Mapping operates within the domain of data and functions to see if the available applications satisfy the needs of BPR in respect of content, structure, integration, etc. In respect of IT, it is necessary to check whether the existing capacity (e.g. network, memory, hardware) is sufficient as well as to match the measures to be taken with the IT strategy.

Workflow Identification

BPR projects involve a specific view of processes. They break down processes into tasks to such a level that all process members fully understand the sequence. The approach to the implementation is not determinate [see Öst 1995, p. 91f; JAD+ 1994, p. 195ff]. The Requirements Specifications must illustrate how complex the implementation of the process is and at which positions the use of workflow makes sense. In addition, we must refine the tasks derived from the process design:

- The process design describes tasks comprising objects and actions [Öst 1995, p. 87]. With the decomposition of objects and actions based on class and complex principles, we obtain the elementary units of work which enable the description of tasks and provide references for workflow candidates
- To use a workflow system which can be purchased today, a high standardization of the sequence of tasks is required [Sil 1994]. This effort in the specifications involves a great deal of work which can only be justified when the processes are carried out in a similar and frequent manner and the information is structured and formalized [Kou 1994]

This approach solves the problem of how much detail a BPR project must specify for the process. If the outcome derived from BPR is only defined roughly, then this step delivers detailed information. Otherwise if the BPR project has refined the process and analyzed it in detail, then the expenditure for the decomposition based on class and complex principles will be easy. In this way, the gap between BPR and workflow is filled.

Implementation Plan

On completion of the Requirements Specifications, the Implementation Plan collects the results from the IS Mapping and the Workflow Identification stages. It must co-ordinate the planned workflows with the preparation of the required technical infrastructure and applications.

Conceptual Design

Based on the results of the Requirements Specifications, the Conceptual Design has the central aim of specifying the workflow from a conceptual viewpoint, independently of implementation tools. The Conceptual Design stage has the following objectives:

- Identify activities and assign them to work steps
- Describe activities for the program design from the business viewpoint
- Determine the integration mechanism for applications
- Specify the dialog for the user
- Summarize the sequence of activities in a workflow
- Design and implement the organizational structure
- Prepare the required infrastructure

In respect of workflow, activity planning, workflow planning and desktop integration are important elements of the Conceptual Design. (Organizational structure – roles, authorization, degree of use, etc. – dialog specification and infrastructure preparation will not be covered further in this paper.)

Activity Planning

Based on decomposition, activity planning has the objective of creating units of work for the user. Such units of work are described in the literature dealing with workflow as "activities" [WfMC 1994]. An activity is a self-contained unit of work found in a workflow. It summarizes the work steps which the user applies in the same business and time context and carries out in one step [RS 1994; DSW 1994; HL 1991, p. 24f; JAD+ 1994, p. 6; SL 1995, p. 30ff]. Work steps are elementary units of work for an activity. They are either supported by IT or carried out manually.

Workflow Planning

A workflow is the precise description of a process from the viewpoint of an information system. In contrast to the process design, it contains detailed aspects of the realization. Decomposition in the requirements specifications as well as in the activity planning for the conceptual design have defined activities and work steps, which are not embedded in the entire flow. Workflow planning includes the following tasks:

- Arrange the activities in a sequence – the activity chain of the process design serves as the means to achieve this
- In addition to process design, the workflow describes special cases, e.g. exception handling, error handling, deadlines, and alarms

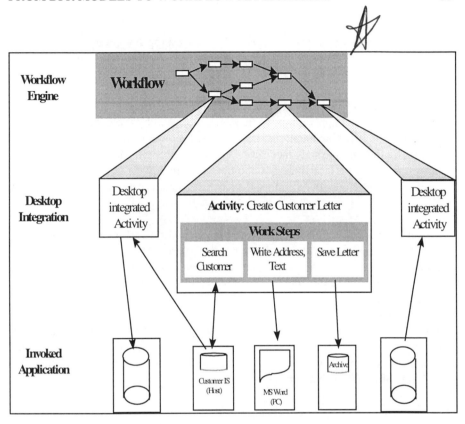

Figure 2   Workflow - Desktop Integration - Legacy Systems

A point of special interest for workflow planning concerns the flexibility of workflows. Current workflow systems provide rigid structures for the flow; they permit no flexibility during run-time. Therefore, ways for creating flexibility need to be incorporated into the specifications; this can be accomplished with skillful workflow planning. The approach is that an employee can freely configure individual processes within the constraints of a given framework. Workflow provides both mandatory and optional activities. Consequently, the user is able to add or delete optional activities within a workflow in accordance with the business context.

Desktop Integration

Activities bundle work steps which provide the necessary applications for the execution of an activity (see Figure 2). A work step supported by IT integrates all kinds of applications, such as logical transactions, office programs and service programs (dialog-free transactions) [DVÖ 1995]. Desktop Integration describes the combination of various applications at the user's workstation. The following integration mechanisms [HH 1994; CLH 1994, p. 19ff] are possible:

- User Interface Integration is often given the buzzword "screen scraping" – it uses screen masks of the applications to be integrated whereby it can emulate the user by reading and inserting data (e.g. the EHLLAPI protocol from IBM)
- Middleware Integration uses mechanisms such as RPC and Message Queuing – in contrast to User Interface Integration, it does not employ the user interfaces of the applications to be integrated; rather it exchanges data directly during the program call

In respect of workflow, both User Interface and Middleware Integration can be realised interactively or in the background. Aside from the variety of integration techniques (including the respective advantages and disadvantages), the design of the data flow between applications using input and output interfaces of work steps is an issue of great importance.

Between work steps a flow of business data (e.g. customer number, customer address, order data) takes place, data which is required by the work steps for its processing. On the other hand, activities exclusively exchange control data (e.g. order number, document number), which the workflow system uses to regulate the flow. A rule of thumb is that control data consists of key variables.

Realization

The goal of Realization is to carry the results from Conceptual Design over into software. This can be done in three steps:

- Design and develop programs for activities as well as integration of applications
- Implement the workflow within a workflow system
- Test individual activities as well as the entire workflow

Most workflow systems provide a graphical editor to model the sequence of activities. Opportunities for the use of graphics are strongly dependent on the workflow system [HL 1991; SL 1995]. The use of a graphical editor during Conceptual Design, for example for prototyping, has both disadvantages and advantages which will not be included in this paper. The implementation of individual activities (a bundle of work steps) must not be subject to a workflow system. This problem is addressed by a client/server development environment which provides the necessary mechanisms for Desktop Integration [SL 1995, p. 126f].

The testing of workflows orientates itself to conventional methods: modular, single activities, chain and system test.

Outlook

This report has provided a general overview of a workflow methodology which is helping to specify workflow applications for reengineered processes. It has considered most of the aspects, although some individual steps have been neglected (e.g. evaluation, introduction, training, and maintenance). They are the subject of current research on workflow methodology being carried out by the CC PSI, which taps the experience gained through pilot projects with business partners.

Acknowledgments

This paper is result of the current work being carried out by the Competence Centre for Process and Systems Integration (CC PSI) at the Institute for Information Management at the University of St. Gallen. The focus of the research activities at CC PSI is to design an extensive methodology for the planning and realization of integrated heterogeneous applications within a company.

We are grateful for the contributions made by the business partners of the Institute for Information Management: Aktiengesellschaft für Informatik, Ciba-Geigy, Information Technology PTT (ERZ), Union Bank of Switzerland, Swiss Bank Corporation and Winterthur Insurance.

References

[CLH 1994]
    Chappell, C., Lachal, L., Hewett, J., *Client-server Markets: Strategies for Success*, Ovum, London, 1994.
[Dav 1993]
    Davenport, T., *Process Innovation, Reengineering Work through Information Technology*, Harvard Business School Press, Boston, MA, 1993.
[DSW 1994]
    Deacon, A., Schek, H., Weikum, G., Semantics-based multilevel transaction management in federated systems, in: *Proc. 10th Int. Conf. of Data Engineering (ICDE-94)*, Houston, TX, 14–18 February 1994
[DVÖ 1995]
    Derungs, M., Vogler, P., Österle, H., *Metamodell Workflow*, Arbeitsbericht IM HSG/CC PSI/3, Institut für Wirtschaftsinformatik an der Hochschule St Gallen, St. Gallen, 1995.

[GGÖV 1995]
   Gassner, C., Gutzwiller, T., Österle, H., Vogler, P., *Bestandteile einer Ist-Informationssystembeschreibung für die Systemintegration*, Arbeitsbericht IM HSG/CC PSI/2, Institut für Wirtschaftsinformatik an der Hochschule St Gallen, St Gallen, 1995
[HL 1991]
   Hales, K., Lavery, M., *Workflow Management Software, the Business Opportunity*, Ovum, London, 1991.
[HC 1993]
   Hammer, M., Champy, J., *Reengineering the Corporation*, Harper Business, New York, 1993.
[HBÖ 1995]
   Hess, T., Brecht, L., Österle, H., *BPR-Projekte im deutschsprachigen Raum, Erfolg, Vorgehen und methodische Unterstützung*, Arbeitsbericht IM HSG/CC PRO/17, Institut für Wirtschaftsinformatik an der Hochschule St Gallen, St Gallen, 1995.
[HH 1994]
   Hsu, M., Howard, M., Work-flow and legacy systems, *Byte*, 19(7), 1994, pp. 109–116
[Jab 1995]
   Jablonski, S., *Workflow-Management-Systeme, Modellierung und Architektur*, Thomson, Bonn, 1995.
[JEJ 1994]
   Jacobson, I., Ericsson, M., Jacobson, A., *The Object Advantage, Business Process Reengineering with Object Technology*, Addison-Wesley, New York, 1994.
[JAD+ 1994]
   Joosten, S., Aussems, G., Duitshof, M., Huffmeijer, R., Mulder, E., *WA-12, an Empirical Study about the Practice of Workflow-Management*, S. Joosten, University of Twente, Enschede, 1994.
[Kou 1994]
   Koulopoulos, T., The workflow food chain, *The Delphi Report*, 1(2), 1994, pp. 1–3.
[MK 1994]
   Manganelli, R., Klein, M., *The Reengineering Handbook*, AMACOM, New York, 1994.
[Mar 1994]
   Marshak, R., Perspectives on workflow, in: White, T., Fischer, L. (Eds), *New Tools for New Times, The Workflow Paradigm*, Future Strategies Inc., Alameda, 1994, pp. 165-176.
[Mut 1995]
   Muth, M., Workflow budgets, experience is not the best teacher, *The Delphi Report*, 1(10), 1995, pp. 1–3.
[Öst 1995]
   Österle, H., *Business in the Information Age, Heading for New Processes*, Springer, Berlin, 1995.

[RS 1994]

Rusinkiewicz, M., Sheth, A., Specification and execution of transactional workflow, in: Kim, W. (Ed.),*The Modern Database Systems, The Object Model, Interoperability and Beyond*, Addison-Wesley, New York, 1994.

[Sil 1994]

Silver, B., Automating the business environment, in: White, T., Fischer, L. (Eds), *New Tools for New Times, The Workflow Paradigm*, Future Strategies Inc., Alameda, 1994, pp. 129-154.

[SL 1995]

Stark, H., Lachal, L., *Workflow*, Ovum, London, 1995

[WfMC 1994]

WfMC, *Glossary*, Workflow Management Coalition, Brussels, November 1994.

The Benefits of Business Process Modeling for Workflow Systems

Dr. Michael Amberg
Business Information Systems
University of Bamberg

What is the relationship between workflow modeling and business systems? How is workflow modeling related to business process reengineering? What are the benefits of a workflow modeling approach based on business process modeling? This article considers the link between the two levels of modeling.

Positioning Workflow Modeling

We embed workflow modeling into the overall framework shown in Figure 1. We differentiate between a "Workflow Specification Layer" and a "Workflow Meta Layer". The Workflow Specification Layer focuses on the development of workflow-oriented application systems for specific business tasks. The Workflow Meta Layer defines the underlying modeling characteristics and provides computerized support.

In the Workflow Meta Layer a Workflow Process Definition Language (WPDL) defines the modeling characteristics that are relevant for defining, managing and executing workflows. Workflow Management Systems (WFMS) provide computerized support for the build-time and run-time. The build-time components of a WFMS are CASE tools for the workflow specification. The WFMS run-time components serve as middleware for workflow-oriented application systems analogous to database management systems for database-oriented application systems. Looking at the Workflow Reference Model of the Workflow Management

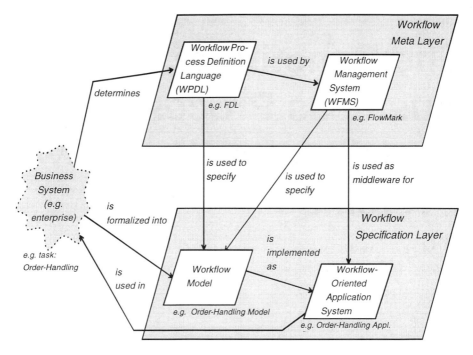

Figure 1   Positioning the Specification of Workflow-Oriented Application Systems

Coalition [WfMC 1994], "process definition tools" are build-time components whereas all the other components primarily support the run-time.

In the Workflow Specification Layer a workflow model depicts the relevant parts of the underlying business systems. A business system here is an enterprise, some organizational units of an enterprise, or an alliance of enterprises (a virtual corporation). The WPDL determines the structure and the conceivable contents of the workflow model. The WFMS build-time components provide a computerized support for the modeling procedure. Based on the workflow model the implementation of the workflow-oriented application system follows.

The example in Figure 1 illustrates the overall context. The WFMS **FlowMark (IBM)** provides the workflow definition language FDL (**FlowMark** Definition Language) [LA 1994]. For the business task "Order Handling", the workflow model Order-Handling Model is specified using FDL (directly or by using the graphical editor of **FlowMark**). Afterwards an Order Handling application system is implemented as a **FlowMark** application.

Already on this level of abstraction, the framework helps to identify issues that are relevant to workflow modeling. Which WPDL and WFMS exist? How do they differ? Which WPDL are used by which WFMS? How can different WFMS be linked together?

For some frequently occurring scenarios the framework can be further refined. For instance, to combine a workflow and a business process modelling approach the WPDL and the workflow model could be subdivided. Then, a business process definition language is used to define a business process model. After that, a WFMS-specific definition language is used for the specification of the workflow model.

The Workflow Modeling Perspective

Meanwhile numerous WFMS and corresponding WPDL exist. Today, they differ significantly in the modeling characteristics that are regarded as relevant for workflow modeling. Thus, they affect the manner and capabilities of workflow-oriented application systems. When abstracting from the details and maturity of individual WFMS and WPDL, we come to the overall point of view shown in Figure 2.

Workflow modeling concentrates on the (workflow) processes that are to be performed. Workflow processes are defined as a coordinated set of activities that are connected in a specific order to achieve a common goal. Basic concepts for workflow modeling are (Figure 2):

- **Activities:** Activities are the smallest items of work. They have an implementation. The activities can be directly performed by actors. They are not necessarily bound to be performed by a particular actor. Regarding their degree of automation, activities are separated into automated activities (workflow activities) and manual activities. Workflow modeling considers both types of activity.
- **Flow of work:** The flow of work determines the control and data flow between activities. The basic idea is that changes in the flow of work are mostly independent of changes concerning individual activities. For instance, using additional or alternative paths as well as changing the order does not necessarily affect the set of activities.
- **Actors:** Actors perform activities. They are further differentiated, e.g. into human actors and computers. Human actors perform manual activities. Computers perform workflow activities. Allocation strategies help to find an appropriate actor during run-time. For instance roles and competencies of human actors are relevant characteristics that influence allocation strategies.

This point of view leads to a workflow-specific architecture of application systems. The components of an application system are separated into workflow management components and activity-based components. Workflow management components deal with the flow of work of one or more workflows. They have to include invocation capabilities and allocation strategies. Activity-based components provide the implementations of one or more automated activities. The workflow management components can be provided by WFMS or be reimplemented.

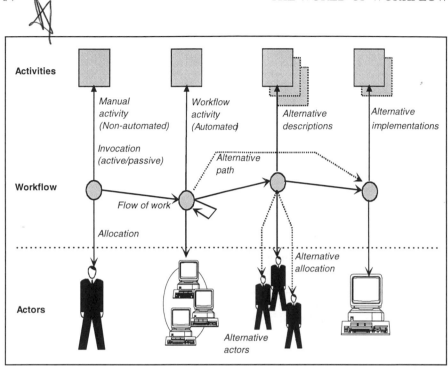

Figure 2   The Workflow Modeling Perspective

Workflow-oriented application systems have two main benefits. First, workflow-oriented application systems shift the automation border further. They consider manual activities in the workflows as well as the allocation of manual activities to human actors. Automated activities are directly invoked. Second, changes in the flow of work and in the available actors are more easily adapted to workflow-oriented application systems than to "conventional" application systems.

The Relationship of Workflow Modeling and Business Process Reengineering

Workflow modeling and business process reengineering came up independently. However, "workflow" and "business process" are often used synonymously. A distinct separation is indeed not possible. Both approaches overlap in the object of investigation, in the goals that are pursued as well as in the techniques used and in the methodical concepts. But there are still a number of characteristics that justify a differentiation on a higher level.

Business process reengineering has an overall objective to analyze and design business systems and their parts. For this, the business processes are analyzed and variants as well as alternatives are revealed, investigated and evaluated. Process reengineering focuses primarily on planning "better" business systems (the build-time). The run-time is considered only as far as it provides feedback about the effects of reengineering. Business process reengineering should be based on business process modeling.

Workflow modeling instead primarily aims at the execution of the business and of the business processes. The analysis and design (build-time) are directly targeted at the run-time. For instance, the discarded variants and alternatives as well as the underlying reasons are not relevant for the execution.

The different objectives have led to a number of consequences. Some fundamental consequences are:

- **Modeling characteristic:** Business process modeling typically results in "modeling in the width". The questions used, e.g. begin with "what" (higher level), "why", "what else" and "what if". Workflow modeling, used begin, for example, on the other hand, results in "modeling in the depth". The questions used begin with "what" (detailed level), "how" and "who".
- **Identification of workflows:** Workflow modeling focuses directly on the business tasks and the workflows. This can be done with business process reengineering, too. Additionally, business process reengineering identifies business tasks and workflows by examining the business services, the cooperation of services, the value of services and the coordination when exchanging services.
- **Scope of investigation:** To computerize the run-time, workflow modeling has to analyze in detail the business tasks as well as the actors that perform these tasks. For reengineering, it is also acceptable to gain an efficient analysis and design procedure by exclusively focusing on the business services and business tasks. Then the design potential is identified independently from the various aspects concerning actors.
- **Model characteristic:** A stepwise and hierarchical procedure of modeling can be used for a method based business process reengineering. Then, the result is a hierarchical process model comprising multiple levels of abstraction. Starting with the main processes of a business system each level of refinement reveals some more detail. A reengineering decision on an abstract level makes detailed modeling and multiple detailed reengineering decisions in that area obsolete. On the other hand, the workflow execution only needs a "flat" workflow model existing on one level of abstraction.

Benefits of a Business Process Model-based Approach to Workflow Modeling

Already on this level of abstraction, the characteristics of business process reengineering and workflow modeling described above suggest a two-stage modeling procedure. We call it a "business process model-based approach to workflow modeling" (Figure 3). In the first stage you specify an overall business

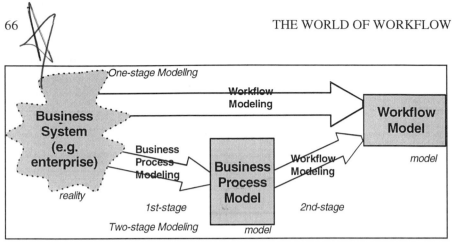

Figure 3   A Business Process Model-based Approach to Workflow Modeling

process model. In the second stage you specify one or more workflow models. Each workflow model is based on the overall process model. Compared to each other the business process model then represents a "macro view" whereas the workflow models define "micro views" towards business systems.

The specification of a process model in the first stage has several benefits for the succeeding workflow modeling. Some essential benefits are [Amb 1995]:

- **Modeling confidence**: The process model provides an overall design. It ties up the objectives, strategies, markets, products and services pursued by the business system. Other conceivable alternatives and opportunities were already taken into consideration, examined and declined. This determines the borderline and guarantees an overall understanding.
- **Controlling complexity**: It is very complex, time-consuming and susceptible to errors to develop and maintain an enterprise-wide workflow model. An alternative is to use the business process model to combine a set of local workflow models. Each local workflow model could describe in detail the flow of work for one or more business processes. The process model helps to classify the workflow models and to differentiate between workflows.
- **Flexibility concerning computerized support**: The decision on what business task should be supported by which (workflow-oriented) application system can take place behind the first stage. The consequences (e.g. interfaces, media breaks) become visible in the process model. Business-wide business process models help to classify application systems, to expose the need of interfaces between different application systems and to discover the areas which are not sufficiently covered by any application system. The demarcation of the areas with computerized support leads to a business-wide application systems map. Such a map is suitable to take legacy systems as well as standard application systems into consideration, e.g. serving as a basis for integration.

postpone model selection

- **Flexibility concerning alternative WPDL and WFMS**: Today, there are numerous WFMS and WPDL that differ considerably in detail. You can postpone the selection of the appropriate WFMS and WPDL until after process modeling. In this case you have already formalized essential requirements. A later migration does not necessarily mean that you have to redo all the work. The process model may provide the stable platform. Additionally, the relevant parts of the process model can be transformed into the workflow model on a broad level and using the specific WPDL syntax. If you have undertaken process modeling to reengineer your business, the transformation saves a lot of work.
- **Improving reusability**: Detailed workflow models are not very suitable to act as reference models. The reusability and the efforts for extensions and adaptations depend strongly on the level of abstraction. Process models represent business systems on a more abstract level. They are much more promising for consideration as an extendible and reusable reference model in regard to workflow-oriented application systems.

Conclusions

The benefits of computerized support are sufficiently known and well accepted. Still outstanding is the development of business-wide application systems in such a way that the benefits can take effect.

In this paper we have discussed a two-stage modeling procedure for the development of workflow-oriented application systems. The first stage uses method-based business process modeling to identify the relevant business tasks to be supported. The second stage uses workflow modeling to specify in detail the domain-related requirements for workflow-oriented application systems. This helps to gain the above-mentioned benefits. To summarize, the modeling results are better in quality, more reproducible and reusable. Therefore, the combination of the business process reengineering and the workflow modeling is better able to deal with change and evolution. Naturally there is a price to pay.

On a high level of abstraction the potential benefits are overwhelming. Particular approaches to workflow modeling and business process modeling lead to a divergent picture. Today, the different approaches vary visibly in their point of view. When selecting specific modeling approaches the overall criteria mentioned in this paper should be considered. The demand for standardization is clearly recognizable as well.

References

[Amb 1995]
    Amberg, M., Ableitung von Spezifikationen für Workflow-Management-Systeme aus Geschäftsprozeßmodellen, in: *Informationssystem-Architekturen*, Vol. 2, Rundbrief des GI-Fachausschusses 5.2, 1995.

[LA 1994]
    Leymann, F., Altenhuber, W., Managing business processes as an information
    resource, *IBM Systems Journal*, 33(2), 1994, pp. 326-348.
[WfMC 1994]
    Workflow Management Coalition (WfMC), *The Workflow Reference Model*,
    TC00-1003 (Draft 1.1) 29 Nov. 1994.

Is Quality an Art Form?

Monique Attinger
Workflow Solutions Group

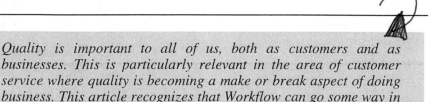

Quality is important to all of us, both as customers and as businesses. This is particularly relevant in the area of customer service where quality is becoming a make or break aspect of doing business. This article recognizes that Workflow can go some way in delivering "Quality" by ensuring process consistency.

For business, quality is its lifeblood. Quality is essential to both the attraction of customers and the retention of customers. For customers, quality means getting what they paid for, being able to predict with some assurance what they are getting, and potentially, if an organization really wants to impress, getting an additional value which addresses the customer's specific needs.

Quality is not a one-time event, however; it is determined over time, in the pattern of service provision, and in consistency of good results. Workflow technology supports the provision of quality services and products, particularly in that it aids both consistency and adherence to standards.

Workflow and Quality

Automated workflow is a technology which helps an organization to manage business processes. For the first time, organizations can now manage their business processes separately from the tools used to complete the tasks in a process. As such, automated workflow is an exciting new technology. Automated workflow, as a result of this approach, can potentially provide an organization with a large range of benefits:

- Improved efficiency and lower unit cost
- Improved change management, with a "plug and play" approach to new tools and technologies
- Improved information distribution, with the elimination of the delays caused by the need to move hard copy around the organization (this being true when workflow technology is combined with other enabling technologies, like imaging)
- Improved customer service, with the potential ability to answer a question first time while the customer is still on the phone
- Improved quality of the product or service

"Quality", in particular, has been a buzzword in business literature over the past few years, particularly in the late eighties. Quality management programs have had much popularity. "Total Quality Management" and "Quality Circles" are two types of program which some organizations have implemented. However, the results were not always as good as one would hope, and many people involved in quality programs began to pay them no more than lip service. It is true that most organizations want to have quality in their products and services (and would be foolish to admit that they did not, if such is the case!). However, how does an organization create quality? And for that matter, what defines quality services or products?

Assuming that quality can be achieved (and be recognized by one's consumers and clients), good quality can be a long-term marketing and sales strategy. Quality services and products can be a vital component in distinguishing a company from its competitors. So the benefits of quality are not insignificant, although those benefits may not be easily quantified. Better quality is an intangible. As such it is a difficult sell even though we all want it.

Quality is one of the greatest concerns when one talks about line of business processes. It is particularly in line of business processes that an organization must succeed; it is a matter of continued viability. As a result, these processes are most likely to be targeted for automated workflow installations, as an organization strives to achieve greater efficiency and effectiveness in its core business. Line of business processes are often supported by "knowledge workers". Knowledge workers are professionally trained, highly skilled staff with highly paid resources.

Organizations hire these professionals specifically for their specialized skills. Therefore, knowledge work processes are often more expensive than other types of process, in part because of the higher-cost professionals who do the work. Why is this important? Because automated workflow is ideal in this environment; it creates a fully enabled work environment, by ensuring that all the information required is provided to the knowledge worker's desktop. It supports the knowledge worker and helps make these workers more effective and efficient.

This is a new approach in the technology arena, since knowledge work has been largely overlooked previously. As a result, the knowledge worker has not had the same support from technology resources as have other types of workers. The knowledge worker has often had to spend considerable time on tasks not related to their specialized skill set, like finding files or chasing information, which reduces their productivity and takes their attention away from the true focus of their work.

Given that, automated workflow can now be joined to other enabling technologies (like imaging) in order to create a comprehensive, automated work environment for the knowledge worker. This approach leverages both the knowledge and time of the professional, by eliminating activities which do not add value to the process (like looking for missing files or performing other manual and administrative tasks which could be handled by a workflow system). The value of this reallocation of work cannot be underestimated, since eliminating no- or low-value tasks then frees up additional time for the knowledge worker to be applying their specialized skills.

Therefore, knowledge work is also one of the areas which is likely to experience very good benefits from workflow.

work & art not synonomous.

Professional Activities as "Black Boxes"

−replicate common activities   −fairness of workload
−consistency of work activities   −prof. activities= unique & individua

Given that knowledge workers are hired for specialized skills, and that these skills are often viewed as somewhat of a mystery to their co-workers, a mythology has arisen concerning professional activities as "black boxes". Let's look at an example.

Recently, while working with an insurance company in their New Business area, I had a detailed discussion with the manager about the flow of work through his department. After discussing each step in detail, we reached the discussion of the underwriting process, at which point this articulate and educated manager said, "And then, underwriting happens". I was intrigued that underwriting was considered such a mysterious process. I probed with more questions. The first response to my request for additional detail was that anything could happen once the underwriter got the file, and that it was imperative that all options be left open. I was horrified. I asked if there were any standards for how underwriting was completed. I was told that all was left up to the discretion of the underwriter. To which I replied, "How does the underwriter know what to do? What rules are in their heads?". I was assured that those rules were beyond the ken of mere mortals, and that to imply that underwriters should follow any sort of standards was to reduce the whole process to a merely mechanical approach, which was surely unacceptable.

The underwriters had maximum flexibility to address what they perceived to be the client's needs, which is admirable. However, what I eventually pointed out to all concerned was that if this insurance company could not be sure that similar underwriting cases were being approached in a consistent way, then they could be at risk. I assured them that they wanted some consistency in how cases were underwritten, otherwise the mistakes would surface, but only after a long period of time, at which point they also become expensive.

How do I verify that my underwriters are doing a good job? How do I ensure consistent, "quality" underwriting? How do I enforce standards if a business process is a "black box"? It is true that we all want to view what we do as "arty". We definitely want to believe that the work we do is unique, and that we ourselves are invaluable. However, "art" and "quality" are not necessarily synonymous, and the idea of work as art may actually be counter-productive to quality unless combined appropriately.

Thinking of professional work as a mysterious activity tends to promote the black box approach to understanding business processes. It seems that most of us feel comfortable that we know what happens when administrative processes take place; but when we begin to discuss the activities done by professionals we often lose this sense. When professional activities begin to be discussed, the adherence to standards, the recognition of steps in the process, and the predictability of the tasks appear to go down. It is true that we need the specialized skills and knowledge of

Art belies consistency
processes not black boxes
quality essential — whatever world demands
quality part standards, part art.

the professional in order to get the job done, but does this in turn mean that we cannot expect that certain tasks will be completed in a particular, predictable order to ensure that the work is properly addressed? This is contrary to the concept of quality.

Business Process as an Art Form

Business processes, similarly, are not "art". If the only way to ensure that work gets done properly is to ensure that Shirley is around to check it, because Shirley has worked here for 17 years and knows what needs to be done, then the organization has a problem. Certainly, the risk is that something happens to Shirley, or that Shirley leaves our company and goes to a competitor. Without standards which become part of the "corporate memory" (and which have been documented as rules and procedure manuals in the past), then the outcome of a process is not predictable.

Just as professional activities are not "black boxes", neither should the business processes within an organization be black boxes. Quality requires consistency. If I cannot ensure that the outcome of a process is the same every time, then I cannot guarantee quality. For customers, this is problematic. Of course, consistency alone does not make quality. (Anyone who has ever eaten more than one hamburger from a fast food chain can verify that statement.) However, being able to predict a good outcome from a process is an essential building block to being able to provide quality service.

Art, at its best, is creative and unique. Art forms do not promote standards. Often the best art is a result of breaking the rules. Art is not a business of consistency; art is conceived of as dramatic, intense, without category. Viewing quality as an art form can create an unrealistic approach to quality which says that it cannot be controlled, cannot be legislated for, and cannot be achieved without the unpredictability of "art". Quality then becomes a nebulous concept that differentiates the very successful organization from the mildly successful one but we do not quite know why, even though we all believe that we know quality when we see it, much as we believe that we know art when we see it.

Having said that, quality is essential to good business. Lack of quality has meant the downfall of empires, and provision of quality has meant the meteoric rise of virtual unknowns. Quality is what we all want to buy, what most of us want to sell, and what everyone claims they have. How does one decide what is quality and what is not? Quality is not a one-time event. Quality is not just what I did today. Quality is not just what the organization did today. Quality is more than delivering good service, at this particular point in time. Quality is delivering good service every time. This is a large undertaking. No organization is going to be able to do this 100% of the time. Therefore, the intent is that the organization works towards quality service delivered 100% of the time, and that an overall pattern of quality develops.

This means consistency is required. This also means that standards are necessary. Therefore, not being able to predict what will happen in any process or professional activity is unacceptable. Automated workflow supports consistency, standards and predictability by automating the rules for completing work. A workflow system can be as rigid as enforcing those rules or as flexible as specifying the rules as a default and permitting the user to bypass those rules (either by choice or under certain conditions).

In this way, over time, a habit for completing work in a predictable way will develop. And this habit will help support quality. Further, automated workflow tools provide metrics on the work performed. These metrics detail who, what, when and where regarding the work in the process. As a result, the organization can measure success. The organization can analyze how work has been handled, and whether or not the outcome was positive. This is also critical to the development of quality.

Quality: One Part Standards, One Part Art

So, once a workflow system has been implemented to guarantee consistency, does this mean that the organization will automatically produce a quality output? Unfortunately, no. One part of quality is consistency. The other part of quality is the true art, the ability to decide when to go that extra mile in order to best meet the needs of the customer. Enforcing a minimum standard guarantees a minimum acceptable level. Quality also means being able to exceed this minimum and win a loyal customer. And the knowledge worker will have the skills and experience to decide when to exceed the minimum. Therefore, the bottom line is that automated workflow can ensure that work is completed according to a standard (provide a checklist, if you will).

This approach frees the knowledge workers to focus on those specialized tasks which are their expertise, and to make decisions about "going the extra mile" to achieve the quality that most organizations desire. Quality is important to all of us, both as customers and as businesses. Customer service is becoming a make or break aspect of doing business. Ensuring quality means being able to provide consistently better service. Automated workflow is part of the tool suite to get there.

Relating Groupware and Workflow

Fred van Leeuwen
Managing Consultant
DCE Nederland b.v.

Groupware and workflow are opening up new horizons in process organization and control. They come in many forms and we need to see how the two concepts relate to each other. If we break down collaboration (the basis of both) into its component parts, we can understand something more about the dynamics of collaboration.

In recent years publications and conferences on groupware and workflow have burgeoned but implementation has trailed behind (even though applications appeared at an early stage and brought definite benefits). Now we are witnessing the breakthrough we were waiting for – and it has been set in motion by the emphasis which management is now placing on radical improvements in external performance (by using Business Process Reengineering to improve process organization and control, by streamlining the work processes and implementing process control).

What is What?

Given that groupware and workflow often go hand in hand with documentary information systems (DIS) and imaging, it may help us get things clear in our mind if we take a brief look at all four (Figure 1).

DIS

DIS stands for Documentary Information System. It is a database management system for textual information indexed so that it can be consulted using predefined searching criteria and/or with the option of searching the text for specially selected words. Here synonyms, homonyms, etc., are relevant. Ideally, the system should gradually learn the idiosyncrasies of the user and anticipate them.

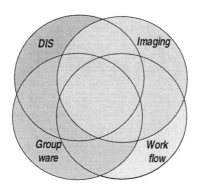

Figure 1   Overlapping Technologies

Imaging

Imaging is the scanning of documents (usually forms, letters, etc., from outside the organization). The information can then be stored as an image (in this form the computer does not recognize text as such). This makes it possible to store multimedia information (pictures, sound and even moving images). The number one challenge is to be able to index *and* keep information accessible.

Text that is contained in a document can be interpreted while it is being read by the computer (Optical Character Recognition – OCR). This text can then be made accessible and maintainable with the aid of a DIS.

Imaging is a transitional technology: we want information to be manipulable. More and more information will come directly from electronic sources and the exchange between parties will become more and more electronically controlled. Forms will disappear, even in the private market; the customer uses the ubiquitous telephone to gain direct access to the call center (telephone–computer integration) of the service provider. For more complicated interactions there is the PC/TV combination and the electronic superhighway. Book clubs, mail order companies and some financial services have already made considerable headway in this area.

Groupware

Groupware is the most difficult concept of the four to define. The most logical interpretation is the literal one: all hardware and software facilities that support collaboration. It begins with electronic mail and telephone conferencing and is followed by shared and perhaps distributed databases (data, text or multimedia), computer conferencing, video conferencing, multimedia meeting facilities (face to face or remote) and finally workflow management (for *ad hoc* as well as structured workflow).

The logical interpretation of groupware is used in practice, but not generally. Some suppliers offer a specialized support tool for *ad hoc* workflow under the name of "groupware" to distinguish it from the far larger group that supplies "workflow".

Workflow

Workflow is the automated control of business processes that are more or less structured. (Here "structured" means that the sequence of activities in the process is determined beforehand or, at any rate, that the rules which dictate this sequence for specific cases can be programmed in advance.)

Groupware and Workflow

Figure 2 summarizes the relationship between groupware and workflow. It seems then that groupware in the more restricted sense can overlap with workflow. Anyone who can draw a clear line between the *ad hoc* and the structured process is welcome to do so. This applies equally to anyone who can point to a process that is 100% structured.

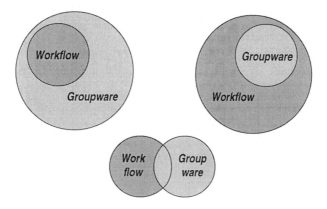

Figure 2 Relating Groupware and Workflow

Analysis of Collaboration

An analysis of the application environment, of collaboration in general, will clarify the functional requirements for automation products that are intended to support collaboration, in this case groupware and workflow (see Figure 3).

Let's say that you have a one-man business. Suppose you're a freelance journalist who spends all his time writing articles or books that have been commissioned by a publisher. The situation gets more complicated if you are working with a partner, if you are writing other articles at the same time, and if you have to take care of the graphics as well.

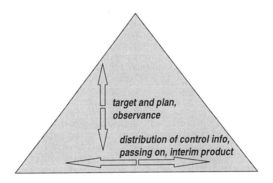

target and plan, observance

distribution of control info, passing on, interim product

Figure 3   Supporting Collaboration

Management Process, Production Process and General Policy

If group work is to run smoothly, it needs a management process that:

- Sets objectives – an article has to meet its deadline
- Plans actions and resources – responsibility for each article, interim products, research, paperwork, images, aids
- Monitors the timetable and, if necessary, intervenes to redirect the production process (or to review the agreement with the publisher)

The tangible results (interim products) will be passed on in the production process. The control data (delivery date, man-hours, status of the interim product etc.) will also be registered and passed on.

If the production process is more or less predictable, the management process is facilitated when production structures are organized in advance (policy creating process design):

- General policy – responsibility for articles depending on specialisation and subject, authority to approve quality, percentage of extra time in each timetable to absorb setbacks
- Organization of the production process – sequence: research, draft conclusions, main thread of article, text and figures, evaluate and adjust draft conclusions
- Norms for steering the production process – time per activity, monitoring method, escalation, especially with respect to deadlines

Elements In and Around the Work Process

Here it might be worthwhile to take a closer look at the concept of coherence. The process establishes the connection between the activities. Each activity (e.g. graphic design) creates an interim product (say, one of the figures) and thus contributes to the final product. An activity can also be restricted to changing the status of an interim product (this applies, for example, to quality control). The final product, the output, can be tangible (such as the magazine article) but it can also be a service to an internal or external customer. It then becomes the input for the customer's own business process (the production of the magazine).

The control from upper management is depicted in Figure 4. Lastly, the connection is laid with the resources. Each activity draws upon certain resources (employees, means of production) which are made available to a number of "cases" in the same process (one journalist who writes various articles) or even contribute to multiple processes (one journalist who writes articles, produces courses and manuals and also offers his services as a consultant).

Coordination Possibilities

Coordination in and around the work process can be set up in a number of ways:

- Output Coordination

Standards of quality, time and place have to be fixed in advance for interim products. For instance, if a WordPerfect text is to be registered on the central database server, this should be done in a standard format and layout, and the spelling should be checked. The date upon which the text is to become available must also be set.

- Process Coordination

The process structure has to be determined. Which activities are to run parallel, which are to run in sequence and which are optional? There should also be coherence with any other processes that may play a role.

- Control Coordination

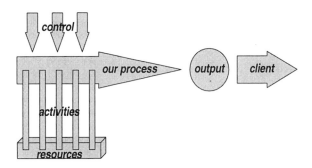

Figure 4   Linking into the Process

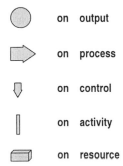

Figure 5   Coordination Possibilities

Decide when progress is to be monitored and by whom, which norms to apply and what action can be taken in the event of escalation (strictly speaking, this is coordination of elements in the management process).

• Activity Coordination

With this type of coordination, an activity is not seen as a black box; it has to be determined and standardized in advance. A pilot, for example, controls his or her aircraft by following a strictly prescribed procedure.

• Resource Coordination

Paul Henderson always writes the articles on subject X. In a larger organisation this would be less dependent on one person. It might be "a graduate in the relevant field". In this kind of situation, management has to establish who does what in terms of role, authorization and qualifications.

- Element Coordination

The process links the activities. An activity is linked to a resource. If this resource is an employee, it relates to a role or a person. When one activity ends the process dictates the next one. This can be done by placing the case directly in the "mailbox" of the following handler. We could use a role-linked mailbox and leave it to the group manager to decide which case is to be assigned to whom. Or we could leave the employee free to select a new case from the role-linked mailbox. The manager then concentrates on the exceptions, such as cases that have been lying for too long. Lastly, we can set priorities within the mailboxes. Here too, important choices need to be made. The system can set or propose priority but so can the manager or the employees.

Coordination in Practice

Although there are many coordination possibilities (Figure 6), they hardly ever exist all at the same time. This would kill off all employee initiative (the pilot with his detailed safety procedure is in an exceptional situation). Normally, a selection is used. Computerized aids must offer the right function for the coordination mechanisms which are most relevant to the organization.

This brings us to the next angle: when should we apply coordination? Given that the work process usually involves people who function best when they have some measure of freedom, we propose the following approach.

The Need for Coordination

First we have to determine the nature of our need, assuming that we want to achieve our aim within a particular situation. In practice it is very helpful to start from a zero situation ("what will go wrong if there is no coordination at all and how bad would this be?") and then determine step by step the minimum level of coordination needed to prevent mishaps. Coordination is less restrictive for some elements than for others. Agreements on an interim product can prevent hitches when work is to be passed on from one person to another. This gives people plenty of space to determine how their own activity is to be organized (what does it matter if the journalist produces his best work between 0.00 and 4.00 in his favourite pub, as long as it gives results).

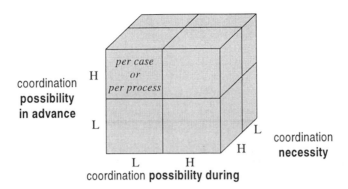

Figure 6   Understanding Coordination

Coordination During Production or Policy in Advance?

Let's then see if it is possible to take decisions when the need arises – in other words, coordination during production. If this involves risks or drawbacks (as in the situation of the pilot), decisions must be made beforehand (policy and implementation). Here we need to differentiate between two situations:

• Case-oriented situations

We take the decision when the case arises. This is the approach that is usually employed in projects. The first activity is setting up the rest of the process in line with the requirements. This is strongly influenced by the nature of the case.

• Process-oriented situations

We make a one-off decision in advance for this process which is subject to organizational variations, depending on the types of cases that we expect to handle. This approach may be appropriate if we are dealing with the processing of mortgage tenders.

Freedom and Corporate Culture

We should not overlook the fact that the above description is subjective (i.e. not free of value judgements). The argument was based on a specific premise: give the employees plenty of freedom if you want to get the best results. Only apply coordination when you can see that serious difficulties will arise if you don't (difficulties that weigh heavier in the balance than the benefits of motivated, self-sufficient individuals). It is quite possible to use other departure points. The choice is tightly bound up with the (organizational) culture and the styles of individual managers.

We can now draw the following conclusions on automated support for process management:

1. If there is only a minor need for coordination, there will be relatively little scope for (automated) process management. There might be a need for electronic communication to transfer interim products.
2. If coordination takes place mainly at production time, there will be a market for a flexible form of (last-minute) process management, say, aids for planning the following activity and monitoring the timetable.

Coordination in advance calls for highly automated process management. Case orientation (see above) needs a tool for organizing and monitoring a specific process (project management for "heavy" cases or case management for more routine instances). The needs of process orientation (see above) are far deeper: support is required for organizing a process that has to meet complex demands. This kind of process must, for instance, be optimized for processing various types of cases in large quantities (which could vary sharply). A balance has to be struck between rapid response and high productivity.

Collaboration in Time and Place

When group activities are involved, we must take account of two other dimensions which can strongly influence (severely restrict, in traditional organization designs) the demands that are made on the coordination: time and place (see Figure 7). This angle is particularly interesting because electronic aids have the capability *par excellence* to make time and place transparent. It presents unprecedented opportunities, such as brainstorming at different times and places (computer conferencing) and home-based office activities. But it also offers the possibility of bringing together expertise from anywhere in the world in a process with critical response requirements.

Functionality of Products that Support Collaboration

Looking at the market supply, we can categorize products according to the functions they provide (note that these categories are only indicative and are neither comprehensive nor definitive).

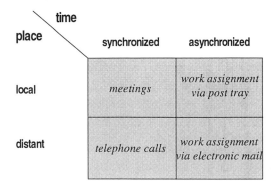

Figure 7   Collaboration in Time and Place

There are products for electronic conferencing; these help when meetings are being held. The specific functions range from electronic whiteboard via video/multimedia conferencing (synchronous) to computer-supported brainstorming (asynchronous with specific support for the brainstorming process). Examples are (components from) **Collabra Share**, **Oracle Office**, **Microsoft Exchange**, **Novell Groupwise** and **Teamtalk** from **Trax Softworks**. But Internet (and Intranet) also offers services in this category.

There are other products which focus more on scheduling: they support timetable and facility/resource planning. For example, **CaLANdar (Microsystems)**, **Microsoft Exchange**, **Russell Calendar Manager** and **Time and Place/2 (IBM)**.

The groupware tools support work processes with an open (loosely structured) character. They range from electronic mail with prestructured address lists, through shared database (multimedia or otherwise) to "case handling" with *ad hoc* planning of process steps and an alarm if time limits are exceeded. **Lotus Notes** has won itself a reputation as the archetype of the groupware tool; in practice it is primarily a development platform with a clever management mechanism for replicated files. **Link Works** from **DEC** is another early example.

There is nothing new about the groupware concept. The path was cleared by the integrated office systems that were marketed in the eighties by minicomputer suppliers, such as **Data General**, **DEC**, **Four-Phase**, **HP** and **Prime**. They were unfortunate in that the infrastructure of user organizations was not sufficiently well developed for low-threshold use. Furthermore, management was not aware at this time that drastic streamlining of office work would be feasible. Now conditions are more favorable for marketing groupware solutions; e.g. **Microsoft**, **Novell** and **Oracle** are profiling themselves as suppliers of integrated solutions. **IBM** is joining in as well, via **Notes** of course, but also with a mixture of old and new from its own development.

Our last product category consists of the real workflow tools. These represent real specialization in the "coordination in advance, process orientation variation" principle. This is an extensive category with product examples such as **Action Workflow**, **Business Review**, **Cosa (Software Ley)**, **Filenet Workflo**, **FlowMark (IBM)**, **InConcert (Xsoft)**, **Open/Workflow (Wang)**, **Plexus (Recognition)**, **Staffware** and **Workparty (SNI)**.

Cultural Differences between Nations

If we wish to select from this market we must go farther than the usual considerations such as functionality, technological suitability, continuity, etc. We must realize that we are talking about products that make certain assumptions on the way people work together. We touched on this earlier.

The (native) culture of the designers is discernible in many products. In the US the employee starts out by assuming that the boss really is the boss, with a natural right to be in control. Also, many US companies operate within tight corporate regulations. Finally, people in the US do not really mind adapting their own lifestyle to suit the technology; they are often even proud to do so.

European employees are a different kettle of fish altogether. Vastly different company cultures exist in France, the Netherlands, Scandinavia, Belgium, Germany, the Mediterranean countries and Great Britain. In this area of groupware and workflow, Europe is certainly not trailing behind the US: many outstanding (even leading) tools originated in Europe. We do not intend to select tools on the basis of national prejudice, but clearly we should take note of how collaboration is viewed within our own organization. Products must be tested for this as well in order to avoid strait-jacketing the organization.

Work + Group + Flow + Ware

The nub of this argument is that there is no sharp division between groupware and workflow and that both are based on collaboration. When sharp differentiation is applied to create separate tool categories of groupware and workflow, chances are that we will fail to recognize important functional differences within each category. One workflow tool may have difficulty deviating from a predefined process organization, while another offers outstanding flexibility: structure where required, freedom where desirable.

A recent and interesting example is **TeamWARE Flow** (producer: **Fujitsu**, obtainable from 1995). The principle of "collaborative workflow" was central in the design of this product: it offers excellent support for incremental innovations in a team context. This tool represents a new trend: functionality highly focused on facilitating the learning organization.

Functional Layers of Groupware and Workflow

Analysis and formulation of the function requirements of groupware and workflow may be facilitated by distinguishing three levels (Figure 8).

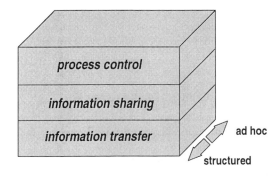

Figure 8   The Three Levels of Collaboration

Communication is the basic function for supporting collaboration: transferring information in a free form (this may be an interim product but also process control information) from one employee to another. A tool that offers this has high flexibility, but its functionality is restricted.

The second level goes further; functionality is offered to the team so that they can make use of information together: multi-user access and update is supported. The system guarantees integrity.

The third level offers systematic support for all aspects of the process planning and control. The management process and the connection between the management and the production process are supported in such a way that the employees have a complete overview and can manage themselves as a team.

The Learning Organization

One very important phenomenon has only been mentioned in passing: the learning organization. We have thrown ourselves into "coordination during production" and "coordination in advance" and have pretended that the choice between the two is made rationally and immediately. This rarely happens in reality. There are many organizations where no thought is given to processes: they have developed "organically". There are all sorts of possibilities for more coordination in advance, for replacing unnecessary improvisation and human stress with quality and attention for the customer. The suggestions for improvement come in bilaterals and continue to surface during department meetings.

To a Higher Plan through Ongoing Improvement

Up to now all that the rigid organization of the work process (and the automation around it) allowed us to do was to make note of where improvements could be made. With any luck they were included in a project once in so many years. The flexibility that is offered by groupware/workflow tools can realize its full potential if improvements are implemented rapidly and incrementally. This is ideally suited to the turbulence of the present external environment which demands that we effect improvements immediately. What is more, an incremental approach fits in naturally with the way people work, think and learn. Each improvement leads to a new implementation. We arrive at a higher platform and are able to identify the next phase. But the greatest advantage is this: when we realize improvements quickly we reward people for good ideas and encourage them to contribute further improvements. In the past, technology tended to be constricting; it forced us to cast functionality in concrete and made us rack our brains beforehand ("waterfall approach" for the system development lifecycle). Nowadays technology can make our life easier provided we renew our approach to projects.

Ongoing Improvement

The concept of the "improvement project" is being superseded. A project is, by definition, finite. It takes us from the one (unsatisfactory) static situation to the other (more attuned to our requirements). There is no place nowadays for static situations. Now the real challenge is to equip the organization in such a way that improvement is ongoing. Technology offers the opportunities. Admittedly, it makes new demands on everyone involved: the team specialist, the user and the management. Nowadays projects not only have to deliver specific results, they have to set off the flywheel of ongoing improvement.

The New Automation Practices

Every project has its sights set on improvement. Nowadays this means responding decisively to the customer, getting things done quickly and right first time, raising productivity and delivering tailor-made products for the same price as off-the-peg. If all these aims are to be realized in a new business situation, the project has to reflect them. The team members of this new-style project are also customer-oriented, quick, efficient and effective.

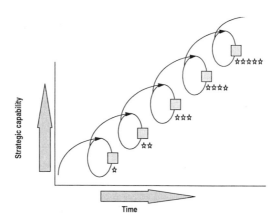

Figure 9   Ongoing Improvement

The working methods which are implied by this will, at first, be a threat to the safe world in which company specialists, including the information technologists, think they operate. The automation expert will not only have to keep abreast of new methods and techniques (the usual training courses are already available to help us "learn workflow"). More importantly, he or she will have to develop new attitudes and skills. Only then will he be able to play the appropriate role: no longer entrenched behind the monitor and with a functional specification as long as his arm, but open and interactive in an interdisciplinary team where he can make a valuable contribution to company improvements in short consecutive steps. Practice already proves that he can learn this, but only if he is being motivated by a new management approach supplemented by coaching and training – not in the form of isolated courses, but as an integral part of the project activities.

Modern process management tools offer users the option to carry out coordination in advance (process design, where necessary) as well as adjusted or even organised during actual execution. Thus they perfectly support the concept of the learning organization.

The first version of this article appeared in the groupware issue of Informatie, a leading IT magazine in the Netherlands and Belgium (Informatie, March Edition, 1996, Kluwer Bedrijfswetenschappen).

Applications of Workflow

Workflow in Insurance

Nick Kingsbury
International Marketing Director
Staffware plc

Insurance claim processing is an oft-quoted example of a workflow application. Dramatic improvements in productivity, claim payment and customer service are features of most case studies. But what are the real benefits? This article looks first at the factors making implementation of workflow technology a top priority for many insurance companies. Once the purpose is understood, the real job of implementing the vision begins. The second section looks at the issues that are faced when implementing workflow.

Introduction

The growing evidence on the ground supports the notion that insurance companies believe workflow to be powerful technology for improving their businesses. Analysts are predicting that by the end of 1996 over 80% of organizations will have some sort of practical workflow initiative underway, and that the workflow market will continue growing by 60% per year for at least the next couple of years. The Workflow Management Coalition has delivered its first clutch of standards – a clear sign of a maturing industry – which should help reduce risk and increase the value of customers' investment in workflow technology.

Dramatic productivity improvements, reduced claim payment and improved customer service are factors often quoted in case studies. What really are the benefits? Furthermore, opportunities arise for changing the ways that businesses operate, whether through the removal of geography as a problem in deploying resources or even the potential for taking a different view on the nature of the business itself; as one company said "Are we in the insurance business or in the insurance process business?".

And the world is changing. One **Staffware** site, a Life and Pensions start-up company, created history in October 1995 by being the first insurance company to set up shop on the basis of having all significant processes automated using workflow; most other workflow users would be green with envy at the opportunity of starting with a clean sheet of paper!

The theory seems good, but large-scale implementations are not commonplace, and tales in the industry abound of drawn-out product analysis by the potential buyers and of delayed roll-outs. Surely by now we should have a reliable approach.

This article looks first at the factors that are causing the implementation of workflow technology to be a top priority for many insurance companies. Once the purpose is understood, the real job of implementing the vision begins. The second section looks at the issues that are faced when implementing workflow.

One is often struck with the enormity of the possibilities and the profound impact workflow could have on the way we work on a day-to-day basis and on the economy in general. A friend in a senior position in a well-known insurance company summed it up rather well with the reflection that ..

"We are on the verge of the clerical equivalent of the industrial revolution"

A dramatic and somewhat forbidding statement: can it be true?

The Business Imperative (or Why Bother?!)

Much has been written and spoken concerning the benefits of workflow generally; however, little authoritative work exists that is specific to the insurance business.

One exception is a survey published in April 1995 (by M. A.Geraghty, Derbyshire University, 1995) which showed the benefits derived by companies from the introduction of workflow technology (see Figure 1). It can be seen that around 40% put productivity as the key reason (efficiency plus headcount reduction), with customer service being the next most significant reason. Somewhat surprising was the small percentage expecting to gain business or achieve some sort of radical change.

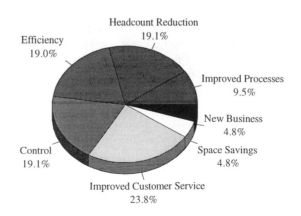

Figure 1   Benefits of Workflow

Broadly speaking the benefits of workflow can be put in four categories:

- Productivity gains
- Control
- Responsiveness / Customer service
- Flexibility / The power to change

These benefits apply to any market sector – manufacturing, government or whoever. Why is the insurance market different? There are some factors that make this particularly fertile ground for workflow technology.

Firstly, insurance companies are basically (at the moment) paper factories: what the workflow handles *is* the business; there is nothing else (like a manufactured component). Secondly, there are large numbers of personnel all performing the same, reasonably repeatable process, which is where "Production" style workflow products are best used. Thirdly, there is an increasing burden of legislation and self-regulation (particularly in the Life and Pensions sector) which requires a standardized, auditable process to demonstrate conformance.

These are the more mundane reasons. The more imaginative companies are looking at some more profound consequences of the digital capture of work. Typically a large insurance company will have a number of offices scattered geographically across the land. Each will have its own complement of staff, designed to handle peaks of work in up to say 90% of situations. If one office is overloaded there is not much another can do other than physically move people or paper, and even then there are often insurmountable management problems. Few companies do it. Workflow can allow the whole organization to be viewed as one resource pool and consequently staffing levels can be set accordingly lower.

Whilst it is not yet happening in the insurance industry, some financial institutions are already implementing "Follow The Sun" working where a job is initiated in one country and is worked on until close of day when it is passed to another office to the west in a different time zone where the day is just starting.

What is becoming more common is the transfer of clerical work to areas in the world where employment costs are lower. British Airways' ticket reservations are now handled in India, and there are low cost areas closer to the UK's time zone such as Eastern Europe. Insurance companies are also starting to catch onto this idea.

The scenario described above can be termed as intra-organizational workflow (i.e. within the organization). The opportunities for radically improving the efficiency and effectiveness of a process are an order of magnitude greater when one looks at inter-organizational processes. The electronic connection of the participants in a process (IFA, broker, insurance company, repairer, doctors, loss adjuster, for example) profoundly changes the scale of effort and cost associated with an activity. Whilst the idea of all the parties being part of an electronic workflow infrastructure may have seemed far fetched, the explosion in usage of the Internet and World Wide Web brings this into the realm of the implementable. The financial incentive is present, so it will happen.

One workflow user, a motor insurer, already receives notification of claims via Internet-style email (CompuServe, in fact) from an agent that operates a 24-hour telephone service. The workflow system checks the basic details of the claim and if OK a repairer is instructed to quote (by fax automatically). The repairer faxes back the quote on a standard form (a limited number of repairers are used) and the workflow/image system auto-OCRs the fax, firstly to find the claim reference and secondly to pick out the estimated repair price. Only then is someone in the insurance company involved; up until this point everything happened automatically.

When looking at the relevance of the categories of benefits listed above one should look at the key processes within insurance companies to assess the benefit yield. These (broadly speaking) are:

(a) Quotations

(b) New business processing

(c) Underwriting

(d) Adjustments / policy administration

(e) Claims

(f) Technical claims processing

(g) Reinsurance

(h) Investments

(i) Product development

(j) Marketing

(k) Analysis and reporting

Processes (g) to (k) tend not to be mainstream candidates for automation, though there are strong arguments for automating product development – the reduction in time to market can give crucial competitive advantage.

Processes (a) to (f) usually involve the vast majority of an insurance company's staff. Preparing quotations is a key customer-facing activity where the priority is reducing the elapsed time whilst maintaining the necessary checks, and conforming to the regulatory authority's standards. Processing new business involves much resource and the priority is in reducing the person-hours of effort.

In claim processing the greatest benefit is probably derived by employing best-practice claims handling such that exaggerated claims or payouts on risks not covered are minimized. Since a large proportion of an insurance company's income is (quite rightly!) paid out to claimants, a small reduction in the Net Claims figure yields substantial savings. Furthermore, experience has shown that the customers are not disenchanted with the stricter processes; claims are settled quicker and, as one insurance company put it,

"I am ashamed to say that we used to lose claim files – particularly the more difficult ones! Now we do not lose files, and when a claimant telephones us we know exactly where the case is in the process and why."

Efficiency gains can often cost-justify a workflow system on their own. These have ranged from 30% to eight-fold! A health insurer reported an 80% increase in throughput following implementation – this was over 2000 users! The "minimum" one can expect – where efficiency is one of the goals – is around 30%, according to Price Waterhouse in a report they produced in 1994. In practice 50%+ is not untypical.

Reduction in process times is key. Typically a claim might take an average of four weeks to process. The time spent actually working on the case is remarkably low – perhaps as little as 20 minutes. Workflow can help to reduce the other elements: the task transfer time, the time taken to organize and prioritize tasks, the time to produce outbound documents, and being more efficient with chase-ups when a participant (underwriter, doctor, motor engineer, etc.) fails to complete their task in a timely manner.

The fourth benefit listed above – "flexibility and the power to change" – is not generally listed in the business case, or even discussed much in the early days of a workflow initiative. However, over time it could yield a competitive edge by opening new opportunities for a company to exploit.

Increasingly organizations are gaining competitive advantage through better processes rather than product; indeed in many sectors (not just insurance) it is the process that differentiates, or at least more efficient processes can lead to reduced costs and therefore a price advantage. Given this emphasis it follows that the organization's processes should be viewed as assets (though in some cases they are liabilities!). The trouble is that the environment in which the company operates (and hopefully internal innovation) should mean that change is the norm.

And it is unsurprising (certainly in the context of this article) where the level of change is greatest.

If one looks at an organisation as the classic pyramid (Figure 2) one sees that there is little change in the mission over the medium term. The greatest level of change comes at the tactics/process level. It is in this area that workflow is applied, and therefore it is necessary for workflow systems to be more flexible than conventional transaction and data based systems.

Having said all this, the business case for workflow is solid without the more futuristic and far-reaching strategies. Focusing purely on efficiency and control of the claims process it is not uncommon for the business case to suggest that a return of three times the investment is possible – per annum.

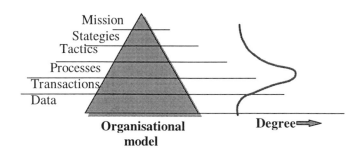

Figure 2   Vulnerability to Change

So it's a Good Idea – How Do We Do it ?

One of the greatest hurdles to overcome, for the vendor community, for the users and the for users' IT support staff, is to understand the difference between a workflow system implementation and a conventional database/transaction system.

We have been building the latter (with varying degrees of success) for many years and developed and argued about methodologies for the design and construction of such systems. This article is not setting out to solve the Workflow Methodology problem, but hopes to provide some enlightenment by reflecting on some of the issues.

Issue One: Change

involve people & uncertainty
style of WF project = interative prototyping
exercise - due to ∆ business initiativ

Database systems have some major points of certainty, specifically the data model. Workflow systems are not so lucky. The process suffers from being concerned largely with what people do and therefore from being vulnerable, you guessed it, to change. Change during design; change during testing and implementation; change when running live.

In one (bitterly memorable) project the process was subject to six major business initiated changes in the course of as many months and was still implemented a mere two months late. One of the options had been to build the system using conventional 4GL/database technology; had this been the case the project manager would have surely been a regular customer of the Samaritans by the end of the project (if it had ever ended). Because of this, the style of a workflow project has to be that of an iterative prototyping exercise.

Issue Two: Depth of Automation

Control over scope of automation
depth of automation
combination leads to more
effective processes.

The up-side is that one has more control over the scope of what is to be automated and the "depth" of automation. This is worthy of more explanation. A very high-level claims process might consist of two steps: handle claim, make payment. In fact each consists of many steps, and what we regard as a step (for example "check estimate") can be implemented at a number of levels, the highest being a note to the claims handler saying "Now check the estimate and select one of the following actions". Or the step can prompt the claims handler to capture all the relevant information, estimates, claim details, data from the mainframe system – and then decide what to do next.

Issue Three: Whose Process is it Anyway?

With modern graphical workflow definition tools it is possible (and highly desirable) for people from the business area to define and build the processes. It is at this point when presenting these ideas to an audience that the countenance of some of the IT personnel would suggest that a vote for heretics to be burnt at the stake might just get passed!

View the process in the same way as you would view a spreadsheet template or a standard form designed using a word processor. Yes, workflow *implementations* are complex and need the rigors of IT project management, but put the process *definition* into the hands of the people who really know the process – the user.

A workflow application must be built in such a way as to create a clear distinction between the Process and the Integration components (Figure 3). The former should be under the control of the business; the latter comprises a series of functions or objects that link the workflow with other applications, such as databases, email systems, image and document management systems.

The motor insurer referred to earlier was a shining example of this. After two days' training, the claims supervisors went on to build the process; IT professionals were needed to integrate the workflow with the other applications, and to manage the overall project.

Issue Four: Integration

A good workflow product should have been designed from the very beginning to provide the maximum opportunities for integration with other applications and systems. The nature of workflow is to automate processes that span different parts of an organization and therefore (not surprisingly) different systems. Virtually any combination can and probably has been implemented: the workflow accessing existing databases; the workflow accessing existing applications; applications invoking workflow functions; the workflow invoking standard applications (such as email or word processing); the workflow being started by external applications.

Which approach is best depends on the circumstances of a given situation, and the resources and timescales that prevail.

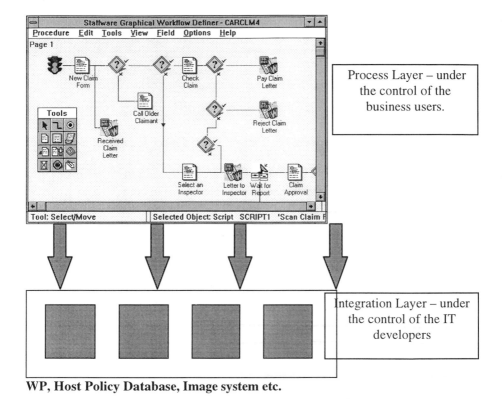

WP, Host Policy Database, Image system etc.

Figure 3   Separating Process and Integration Layers

Virtually all insurance companies already have well-established policy administration systems. The workflow system obviously has to be integrated with these; however, this need not necessarily mean a major software development project. The approach can be *incremental*.

The scenarios are outlined below. The first two options do not involve modifications to the existing application at all; the integration is achieved through the use of a programmable terminal emulation package (e.g. **Dynacomm** or **Attachmate**). Which package is used is determined by the terminal type that is being emulated.

In some situations the requirement is for the workflow system to be invoked by the application package. Most products provide APIs to allow this to be done, and again standards are available in the form of the Workflow Management Coalition's WAPI specification.

Integration Scenario One – Workflow to Guide You

The workflow acts to guide the user through the process, referring to and perhaps calling up an existing application. A workflow window provides instructions for the

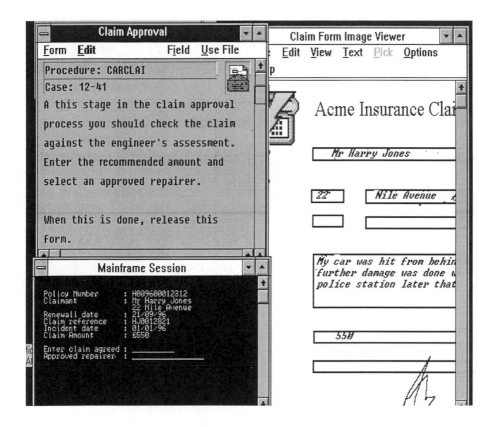

Figure 4   Sample Insurance Claim Screen

user and invokes the appropriate application screen via a terminal emulation package. In addition other relevant documents or information may be displayed such as related images. In this situation the user keys the main business-related data directly into the existing application. Figure 4 shows a sample claim screen.

Integration Scenario Two – Workflow Front-End

The technology used is the same as in Scenario One; however, the existing application is not visible. The workflow form invokes the terminal emulator which forces key strokes and reads the response from the host session, passing the key data to the workflow system. What the user sees is purely the workflow and its data entry forms; he or she keys in, say, a policy number and then sees the client's name and address displayed, together with the policy's expiry date.

This approach is often described as "Screen Scraping" and is commonly used as it provides a graphical environment without having to modify the application system. However, since a program is "reading" the screen it is vulnerable to layout and other functional changes in the application system.

Integration Scenario Three – Workflow Integrated

In this scenario the workflow accesses the application system data through either SQL or specially developed routines. The benefit of this approach is that it is more robust and possibly better performing, but generally takes more development effort than Scenario Two. From the user's perspective there is no change from Scenario Two.

Integration Scenario Four – Application Invokes Workflow Engine

In this situation the application system is the user interface that the user sees. Calls are made to the workflow system when, for example, a new case is started in a process, or the application needs to change the state of the process. Increasingly workflow products allow themselves to be used purely as "workflow engines", not visible to the user, but in the background orchestrating the processes.

Conclusion

For a number of years workflow technology has had the potential to have a substantial impact on the way that insurance companies operate. The newness of the technology, the lack of a sound networking infrastructure and the lack of implementation skills have all played a part in slowing uptake. These issues are being overcome; industry standards, robust proven products and most importantly maturing knowledge of how to apply workflow mean that workflow is no longer a "bleeding edge" technology.

Add to this the growing acceptance of electronic commerce (for example, the Polaris initiative) and new opportunities for workflow to be delivered by Internet World Wide Web pages (for the technophiles – using Java-based applets) to third parties, home workers and customers, and the consequences are mind-boggling. Perhaps the heralding of a new industrial revolution might not be so crazy after all ....

Complex User Modifiable Workflow

Jesse T. Quatse
IA Corporation

This article outlines the history of and challenges associated with Remittance Processing. It gives an overview of a new workflow technology developed for this area.

Remittance Processing

Late in the 1970s the banking service known as the "lockbox" enjoyed increasing popularity as bank customers began to appreciate its potential to improve their cash management processes. Customers of a bank could direct their retail customers to send their payment checks to a post-office box which was, physically, a lockbox in the bank's mailroom. The bank opened the payer's envelope, recorded the amount shown on the coupon which accompanied the check, verified the amount and other MICR line (magnetic ink character recognition) information, and conveyed the checks to the payer's bank. Figure 1 illustrates the most obvious benefit of the service: the elimination of one leg from the transit time of the check and therefore the elimination of a day or more of interest lost by the payee. A "wholesale" lockbox service extended the benefits to commercial customers who pay on invoices rather than coupons.

As the experience and technology advanced, more and more services were offered by lockbox banks until, now, most lockbox services offer change of address registration, allocation of funds, more comprehensive exception processing, higher quality assurance, and in some cases even survey data collection and order processing such as subscription renewals.

The results of the lockbox services end up as printed reports and bookkeeping entries in mainframes. All of the lockbox services are receptive to automation, image data entry, intelligent recognition, data communication technologies, and workflow. The technology for processing the contents of the lockbox is called a "Remittance Processing" system.

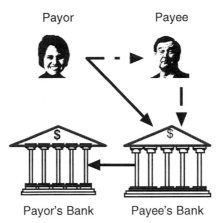

Payor   Payee

Payor's Bank   Payee's Bank

Figure 1   Check Transit

Current Limitations

Many installed Remittance Processing systems are unable to keep pace with the increasing workflow complexity required by the major banks and lockbox outsourcing service vendors. Retail and wholesale services are provided by separate systems, each with custom environments. Older systems are paper-based, and offer only check image printing, rather than image-based data entry. Each customer-specific workflow step must be hard coded, at the cost of professional programmer rates and sometimes weeks of delay. The workflow is single-threaded in the sense that only one process can be enacted on the system at one time. In short, the workflows are simple, hard coded, paper based, and single-threaded.

Single-threaded workflow is severely limiting because each of the bank's customers may require a different workflow process. The payment of a home mortgage is an example. The dollar value of a payment check might exceed the amount specified on the enclosed coupon. One mortgage service company might allocate the overpayment to interest, another to the next month's payment, and another to the principal. Cable companies might allocate differently from mortgage service companies. A single-threaded workflow executes one process for all work items.

Workflow complexity is not the only problem. Many installed systems are unable to meet the related demands for high productivity, high performance, wide area networking, and automation of quality assurance. Banks are enjoying a sustained, nationwide growth, internally and by acquisitions. For example, Mellon Bank provides the world's largest bank lockbox service. Mellon processes over 400 million payments per year and has experienced double-digit annual growth rates, without acquisitions, since the early 1980s. Remittance Processing must be managed on a nationwide seven-site network.

Yet new bank customers, each with his or her own specific requirements, must be added quickly and uniformly to all sites. Performance also depends upon quality assurance and productivity of the system. Quality assurance is labor-intensive and currently weak in automated support. The productivity tools are meager and inconsistent. The number of transactions per worker has reached a plateau. To add new customer services, or to increase the volume of transactions, the answer is always to add more people to the workforce.

A New Technology

A new workflow technology overcomes the current limitations by supporting geographic distribution and increased workflow complexity, user modifiability, and scaleability. All services are provided by one integrated system, including those of both retail and wholesale lockboxes. The workflow services extend beyond those of traditional Remittance Processing, for example to order entry and automatic step-by-step quality assurance consistency checks. Traditional services are improved. For example, a "knowledge worker" concept in wholesale lockbox enables a highly skilled participant to encircle important parameters on scanned images that are keyed in later by a less skilled participant. Close deadline management allows the banks to notify their customers of deposit amounts any time of the day. The priorities of work items are adjusted automatically as their individual deadlines approach. High priority work items can be split so that several workflow participants can work on the same work item concurrently. The flexibility to decompose the process into independent concurrent sequence segments exploits a difference between sequential workflow systems and Transaction Monitors, which manage transactions as single atomic activities rather than decomposable sequential processes.

User modifiability appears in several forms. The setup of a new customer account is parameterized so that the business rules of each work item are no longer hard coded but selectable by fields in a process definition form. The contents of the form can be downloaded to all sites in order to synchronize the account profile databases. Business rules which are not anticipated by the account profile can be introduced by the user in Visual Basic.

Although the Platform Product and the Remittance Processing Framework are both written in C++, new workflow activities and services can be written in Visual Basic by the user. The activity network, referred to as the "Map", allows process modifications and the routing to new workflow activities by the user. The system is productized, not customized, so that the components are understandable, robust, and designed for user modifiability. The scaleability is increased in two dimensions. Each site can be scaled to very high performance by the addition of servers and the replication of engines. New sites can be rapidly updated so that volume peaks can be balanced between sites.

Custom Application	Workflow Activities Admin. Activities Database Activities
Remittance Processing **O-O Framework Product**	Workflow Classes Database Classes I/O Classes
Workflow Management **Platform Product**	Work Manager FolderStore Event Manager Recognition Server Archive Server Operability Server I/O Servers
Open System **General Purpose Products**	Databases Operating Systems Utilities Drivers

Figure 2   Product Layers

The Product Structure

The Remittance Processing System is constructed from the four-level product model of Figure 2. Each layer tailors the software services of the layer beneath to be more specifically suited to the requirements of the application. At the topmost layer, the system is customized to the exact needs of the individual customer.

The general purpose products appear at the bottom level. They include the network managers, the RDB Managers (**Oracle, Sybase, and Informix**), and the operating systems (**Windows NT, OS/2, and UNIX**). The utilities include viewers, image processors, recognition engines, word processors, and others. The Drivers control the system equipment.

The Platform Product represents all of the services provided at the general product layer as compatible clients and servers having consistent API classes. The Platform Product makes a subtle but much more significant contribution. It provides a lucid paradigm for designing the sequential enactment of processing steps. The workflow engine is based upon physical and logical queues which simplify the visualization of the workflow process. The Event Manager notifies all workflow activities of events in which they have expressed interest. The FolderStore manages highly structured folders which contain images and other application data. Without a clear and effective design paradigm, the designers of a complex workflow systems can produce "spaghetti logic" which leads to project development overruns, tenacious bugs, and system fragility. The added complexity of user modifiability can be out of reach.

The Remittance Processing layer is an object-oriented framework product which contains the business classes for Remittance Processing and the declarations which specialize the Platform Product for all Remittance Processing applications. The workflow classes define the data structure of the FolderStore and the work item, as well as the methods used by their clients. The database classes define the customer account and bank site profiles which are retrieved by all clients and servers to enact a different workflow for each work item. They also define the results which update the database at the end of the workflow process.

At the top layer, the Custom Application adapts the Remittance Processing Framework to the needs of each specific bank. Equipment configuration and workflow alternatives are defined by configuration files and server deployment. Recognition forms are defined by using a form definition tool. Workflow deviations for specific bank customers are defined by entries in the set of database forms. Tools are provided for the bank to associate data communication protocols with each bank customer, and to define print and fax formats.

The Remittance Processing Architecture

The product structure is not visible in the final Remittance Processing architecture. At the diagram level, as well as the GUI level, the user cannot distinguish which features and functions are provided by each layer. For example, the Monitor and Control environment is provided by the Platform Product and specialized by the Object-Oriented Framework.

A significant principle of the architecture is that the relational database (RDB) is not the centerpiece of the workflow management system. It is at the side, available to every workflow activity that needs it. At the center is a very high speed, generalized, queue manager which is part of the workflow engine of the Platform Product. A work item is represented on a queue by a token called the "Transmittal Sheet". To move through the workflow process, a transmittal sheet 'for each work item moves from queue to queue. The Map determines which queue is next in the process for each individual work item. The primary API functions are "get_next" and "put_transmittal". Each physical queue can be organized, during workflow enactment, as a set of logical queues which are defined by their selection criteria. For example, a work item might be selected from a physical queue by the criterion "dollar value exceeds $10,000". All items in the physical queue which match the criterion form a logical queue of which the "get_next" acts as if it were a LIFO.

The lucidity of the "queue centric" architecture comes from the fact that the workflow designers, be they professional programmers or users, are able to think clearly about individual workflow activities, each of which is cleanly interfaced to the overall process by moving work to and from the queues. Scaleability comes from the fact that the workflow engine can be replicated and deployed to as many servers as needed.

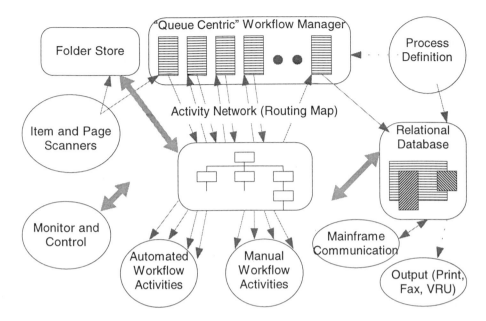

Figure 3   Architecture of Remittance Processing System

The application data for all workflow activities is accessible from one of three generalized servers. The database server provides the profile of the customer to which the work item belongs, and the profile of the site itself. A different workflow process for each work item is easy to visualize because each item has an associated profile which defines its individual process. The FolderStore server manages all bulk data such as the check image, the coupon image, ICR (intelligent character recognition) and data entry values, and MICR fields on checks or OCR fields on coupons. The folder can have an arbitrarily complex structure of documents and nested folders. The remaining server is the workflow engine itself. The transmittal sheet contains parameter values and references to folder items or any other file anywhere in the system. It acts as a global file system that is unique for each work item.

From the point of view of the queues, there is no distinction between manual workflow activities and those that are automatic. They are all just clients. A work item begins life at the scanners. The item scanners access the customer account profile to control the passage of each individual check and coupon down the transport track, millisecond by millisecond. Scanned checks and coupons are batched into a folder and passed to FolderStore. At the same time, a transmittal is created for the entire batch and passed to the first queue. The automatic workflow activities include stop check files through data communication, credit card checking through data communication, and ICR of dollar values, change of address, and survey or subscription marks. Quality is assured by an automatic activity in which each activity of the process is checked for consistency, step by step. In the end, automatic activities make one final end-to-end quality check, store the complete folder in a tape archive, and enter the results of the workflow process in the database. The manual workflow activities are enacted between scanning and database updating. They include dollar entry and verification, looping on errors, MICR repair, funds allocation, and resolution of inconsistencies. They all make use of the transmittal from the engine, the folder from FolderStore, and the customer account profile from the database.

The Results

A new high performance client/server workflow architecture supports geographic distribution and complex workflow processes which can be specialized for each work item and independently modified by each bank. The architecture simplifies the design of complex workflows by a lucid "queue centric" design paradigm in which all work activities get and put work on logical queues. All application data is passed as folders, database records, or work item transmittal sheets, all of which are standardized for the application. The simplification of the workflow management and the application data passing supports high complexity in the workflow process. The banks benefit from improved system services, new products, greater quality assurance, greater productivity, and user modifiability.

User modifiability is obtained by shielding the user from the intricacies of C++ and the details of the system. The user can select process alternatives by completing forms which update an account profile database. The routing of work can be modified through the routing Map. Workflow activities which are written in C++ can be modified by the user in Visual Basic.

In the near future, geographically distributed processing will be expanded to include automatic load balancing between sites and remote capture and exception processing of large centralized Remittance Processing systems.

Workflow Enabled Applications for Dresdner Bank

Jürgen Edelmann
Dresdner Bank AG
Frankfurt am Main, Germany

Michele A. Rochefort
IAB GmbH
Ottobrunn, Germany

Since December 1994, workflow management has been running on all workstations in all of Dresdner Bank's German branches - approximately 1200. This article draws on this experience to shed light on the practical aspects of implementing a large workflow system, including user acceptance, system integration and administration.

Introduction

Today, bank products can be characterized by a shorter lifetime and an increased flexibility when compared to their traditional counterparts; this influences the software that provides for the technical support which is demanded. The development of Dresdner Bank's software therefore aims to build modular, reusable and object-oriented components leading to solutions with less development time and reduced costs. To form support for an entire product, such components need to be glued together. Dresdner Bank employs workflow management for this purpose.

The employment of workflow management for the coordination of software components offers many benefits due to the inherent features of the technology. Among them the following are of special interest for the user:

- Handling of interruptions occurring for whatever reason – work on a business process can be suspended and resumed later
- The user can deviate from the predefined business process by delegating, adding or removing tasks provided he holds the required rights to do so
- All open tasks become manageable via a single point of access regardless of their type or source, thereby assisting the user in organizing his own work
- If tasks are ignored for whatever reason, escalation mechanisms are applied to ensure timely handling

These benefits led to the decision to install the **ProMInanD** workflow management system, developed by the German company **IABG**, in Dresdner Bank's production environment in December 1994. It is currently available in all 1,200 German branches on approximately 8,000 workstations. During the first phase of the project, some comparatively simple business processes were released and are currently running in parallel with traditional programs. The experiences gained throughout the project have served to establish a sound foundation for further and more complex business processes. By Q3 1996 the system will be running about 250,000 business processes per month.

Yet, despite the large number of business processes which can be handled effectively by workflow management, it is important to be aware that not all tasks are to be handled in this fashion. *Ad hoc* tasks which are supported by groupware applications or traditional programs will always exist. Consequently, software running under the control of a workflow management system must be able to coexist with applications running independently. The design of such coexisting software formed one of the main milestones in the introduction of workflow management. In fact, the utilization of this technology had to bear in mind that a single application should handle business processes and *ad hoc* tasks in parallel. Such applications are hence called workflow enabled.

In this article the major issues concerning workflow enabled applications will be addressed through an example description. In addition it will be seen how the Workflow Management Coalition's (WfMC) Interfaces 2 and 3 are used to meet requirements from users as well as software developers. Throughout this text, we refer to WfMC's work whenever possible, therefore it is assumed that the reader is familiar with WfMC's Glossary, Reference Model and the emerging standards for the particular interfaces (see *Section 2 – Standards –* in this Handbook).

Example

An illustrated example concerning the checking of data will show how workflow management is approached at Dresdner Bank. The rule applied within this example is that whenever a clerk has entered data – as in the case of a new customer – another clerk has to check the consistency of this data. If he approves, the data is released, otherwise it is sent back to the first clerk for correction. The whole business process has to be finished within five days, otherwise another clerk is to be informed.

Hence the following scenario:

1. One clerk enters data about a new customer in an application, called "Customer", followed by data about a new checking account for this customer in another application, called Checking Account.
2. A second clerk decides to perform all checking tasks currently available to him. The workflow management system invokes an application called "Checking" appearing in a separate window on his screen.
3. For each previously selected task, the data entered by the first clerk is displayed. He might approve the customer data which will then be released and the business process will be finished. If he disapproves the checking account, he may annotate the data and return the business process to the first clerk. Once the first clerk has updated the data, the checking might lead to the approval and release of data, thus the business process is finished.

This example requires two business processes which are depicted in Figure 1.

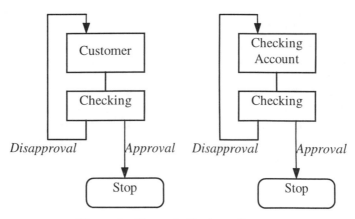

Figure 1   Example Business Processes

This simple example already indicates several requirements addressed by workflow management:

- The business processes follow predefined rules which, in this case, must not be circumvented
- More than one person is involved which requires transfer of information between persons and information about the arrival of transferred information
- Open tasks are to be managed such that a user can easily gain an overview of tasks available to him at a particular moment

- If the checking is not handled in a timely manner, an escalation procedure (not included in Figure 1) must be applied
- The "Checking" application is used in more than one business process, and thereby represents a reusable software module

User's Needs

To elaborate on the main features of workflow-enabled software, it is worth looking at the user's requirements when handling a particular business process.

The example indicates that a user does not necessarily think in terms of business processes. Instead he has a list of open tasks to be processed. Therefore a tool is introduced for the management of all open tasks for a user regardless of their type or source. To draw the user's attention, this tool has to actively inform if a new task arrives. The tool also supports non-standard task operations such as resubmitting, delegating to a colleague, cancellation of a business process and so on. Furthermore, it supports a task's processing by invoking the required application and supplying it with the appropriate application data. The actual tool is determined by the workflow engine through an inspection of the business process to which the task belongs. Thus, from a technical point of view, this tool mainly performs operations as defined in sections of WfMC's Interface 2.

Furthermore, the interactions between user and the applications on his desk must be minimized. This means that information which has already been entered by the user is automatically available in further situations. The checking of data is a typical example: once the user has approved the data, this application data has to be released and the business process should be forwarded accordingly by finishing the task and thus the entire business process. This means that the handling of the business process is based on the approval of application data without further interactions. Similarly, when new customer data is entered, a new business process instance is to be created without user interaction by applying the bank's guidelines within the application.

Though this seems to be an obvious requirement, it is typically not met by most current workflow management products. Instead it is assumed that a user handles application data in its application and afterwards decides separately on the business process in a workflow management front-end. To overcome this situation, it is necessary to couple parts of WfMC's Interface 2 with invoked applications.

The example also shows a further situation typically not addressed in current workflow management systems: not all business processes are handled individually, as often shown, for example, with loan applications. Instead, bulk handling of all business processes of the same type occurs as in the case of checking data. In such a situation, it is necessary to invoke the required application only once for all selected business processes which are subsequently handled within this application. Invocation and completion of an application for each task would not be accepted by the user. The individual handling of a business process is viewed by him as the special case of "bulk" handling with only one business process involved. Again, this important requirement is often neglected by current products which invoke an application for one task of a single business process only.

Software Requirements

Beside the user's needs, technical requirements influence the architecture of workflow enabled software. As already mentioned, such software must coexist with traditional programs. To ease handling and reduce training costs, it is essential that both types of software have a homogeneous user interface. This implies that workflow management cannot appear to the user as a desk controlling all his applications. Instead, applications may be invoked by a user through the rather traditional manner or via the tool managing open tasks.

This coexistence also implies that application data is processed in parallel by workflow enabled software as well as by traditional programs, which might cross-check databases, for instance. Therefore a workflow engine does not handle the application data itself but rather references it, as in the case of database keys, and the invoked application has to retrieve the actual data.

Additionally, it is not sufficient to allow for the coexistence of these two kinds of software in different applications. The design of a new application may lead to the decision that it has to handle a business process as well as an *ad hoc* task. For instance, if new data is entered into the "Customer" application, a new business process has to be created. If, instead, existing customer data is retrieved by the same application, workflow management is not needed. Both cases can occur even within one session.

It can be seen that running an application is not correlated with the handling of a business process task. Rather, an application will load and store tasks from the workflow engine at run-time or handle further *ad hoc* tasks in an arbitrary manner. This behaviour is well understood from current office software, e.g. text processing tools like MS-Word; once invoked, such tools are able to load and store several documents or even handle them in parallel in separate windows. Business process tasks will be handled in an equivalent way if workflow management is sufficiently integrated.

Workflow management products often choose to check the handling of a task by invocation and completion of the associated application. Since this approach cannot be applied, it is necessary to let the application actively signal the status of a particular task to the workflow engine by issuing WAPI-calls (WfMC Interface 2) [see Section 2].

Furthermore, the workflow engine cannot invoke an application and forward associated application data as parameters. Instead, the application has to retrieve its application data on demand from the workflow engine to allow for the handling of more than one business process.

Resulting Software Architecture

The listed requirements have shown that invoked applications have to be enriched by several WAPI calls. The integration of such calls causes the applications to become, in one sense, active: they signal to the workflow engine their need for data, finishing of a task, creation of a new business process and so on.

On the other hand, it is not necessary to include individual WAPI calls in an application. Instead, Dresdner Bank decided to bundle several WAPI calls into meaningful units made available to all applications as standardized components for arbitrary usage. Since these components do not own a user interface they can be deliberately integrated depending on the application logic. Typical examples of such components are:

- Load a task together with its application data
- Signal the beginning of a task
- Signal the finishing of a task with extra information like OK, try again, resubmit, and similar
- Create a new business process

The encapsulation into standardized components of calls to a particular service without user interface is commonly applied in Dresdner Bank's software design. With respect to WAPI it allows the programmer to view workflow management like any other service, e.g. data management, thus reducing training needs for programmers. It also ensures that the above mentioned requirements are fulfilled and the benefits of workflow management are gained with minimal efforts. If new versions of the WAPI standard emerge, it is sufficient to update these standardized components without affecting the applications themselves.

The resulting architecture of a workflow-enabled application is depicted in Figure 2.

Figure 3 gives an overview of the program structure for the "Checking" application introduced in the example. Rectangular boxes represent normal program elements, whereas ovals indicate components containing WAPI calls.

It can easily be seen how the workflow enabling of software is achieved by adding components to a program. It should be kept in mind that this mechanism is applied only to the handling of business process instances. The definition of a business process is entirely separated and not left to the application programmer. Rather, it is undertaken within the framework of an entire project where a new bank product is developed.

Conclusion

This article has sketched how workflow-enabled applications are designed for Dresdner Bank's production environment. The approach can easily be adopted to

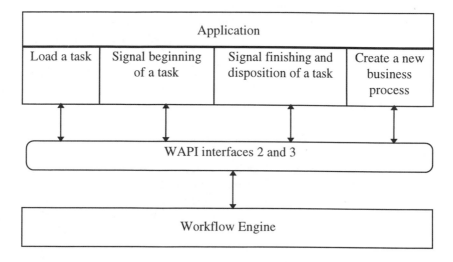

Figure 2   Architecture of a Workflow-Enabled Application

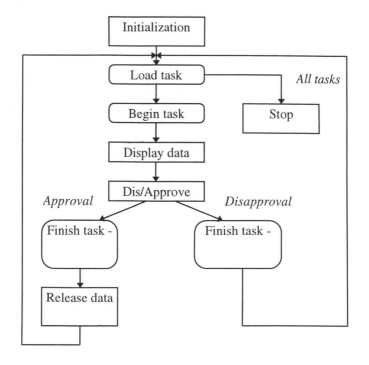

Figure 3   Structure of the "Checking" Application

the integration of standard applications into business processes like text processing. Such applications can be enriched by the standard components described, such as the loading and storage of tasks, which are to be made accessible to the user, for example via further menu entries.

The implementation shows that workflow technology is recognized by Dresdner Bank as a flexible and important way to handle daily tasks, thereby reducing costs and improving quality in the production environment. It also allows for the integration of many different aspects of software technology into a well conceptualized and efficient system. User requirements are to be considered first and foremost.

The investment in this new technology is justified only if standards exist which provide for stable availability of interoperable products. This can be applied in a heterogeneous environment and forms a guideline for their implementation. Thus, the approach described is in full conformance with WfMC's work, i.e. Reference Model and emerging standards. It gives positive proof that concepts and standards developed by the WfMC allow for successful implementations of workflow management. The actual implementation also points out some enhancements of WfMC standards which are necessary to run a workflow management system on a large scale. Therefore, Dresdner Bank is interested in the refinement and improvement of existing WfMC standards as well as the development of further standards on topics not yet addressed by WfMC.

Acknowledgments

The design and implementation of the approach described would not have been possible without a highly motivated and competent team which formed the solution for the implementation of workflow management within Dresdner Bank. Furthermore, the authors are indebted to Dr N. Ramsperger for fruitful comments on earlier versions of this article.

A Workflow Recipe for Healthy Customer Service

Dave Ruiz

ViewStar Corporation

Dave Ruiz documents the successful outcome of England's PPP healthcare service which employed workflow as a key component. Implementation increased staff productivity and showed visible service improvements.

Introduction

To unravel the mystery of business process automation, take 101 different document types, distribute around 3 LANs, 1 WAN and 640 desks; throw in a jumble of hardware and software, super-fast state-of-the-art scanners, jukeboxes and the latest in workflow technology; whiz together with a legacy mainframe system and it is possible to begin!

It is true that not every business process automation program will take this mix of new and used IT as its infrastructure. However, these are the raw ingredients exploited to great effect by England's Private Patients Plan (PPP) healthcare. PPP healthcare has just implemented a workflow strategy, which is already delivering dividends by cutting out "red tape" and increasing staff productivity. PPP healthcare's mission is to supply its 2.2 million customers with the ultimate in service. In fact, so successful has its implementation been, that it now claims to have an infrastructure that is increasing customer loyalty with visible improvements in service.

Customer Satisfaction is Key

PPP healthcare's brand awareness is very important to the company and its future growth. It has steadfastly developed and activated high-profile marketing programs to promote its caring and personal approach, which it claims to provide every step of the way. To this end PPP healthcare has introduced a range of products and services to satisfy a myriad of healthcare needs. But products alone do not build a consistent market image. Mike Tinsley, business project manager, planning and development division at PPP healthcare explained: "We can all design and sell new products – but the reality is that people buy, and buy again, based on service, quality and satisfaction. It is the service in our business that will make or break customer loyalty." This in some way explains why PPP healthcare has invested heavily in an IT infrastructure, which it expects to deliver on its brand promises. "The technology we have in place today enables us to provide the best customer service in the business, in that we can respond to a customer inquiry instantly" he continued.

To reach the point whereby PPP healthcare can guarantee the best available service, it looked very closely at its customer support and response processes. At this time it recognized that workflow technology was key to overall improvements. PPP healthcare's process involves a large variety of inbound and outbound documents from various sources, such as general correspondence, claims, hospital and consultant/specialist provider accounts, being merged into a single case file.

Previously, this resulted in a lot of paper work, handling and filing. Following information collation and gathering, the file was passed to the responsible personal adviser for action. Once a file was closed, and a customer claim dealt with, it was archived on microfiche. The whole process was paper, people and time intensive, with many opportunities for human error. Moreover, it required a large number of staff for the microfiche handling alone.

An Integrated Process

Having examined the process, PPP healthcare established that the new system needed to remove all opportunity for error and allow for future developments and growth. Consequently, the decision was taken to totally integrate the process from start to finish.

The new system scans, indexes, merges legacy and current data on the fly, and delivers information automatically to the desktop of the designated personal adviser. It goes a stage further than this: all staff have instant access to all information and any member of the team can provide a customer with exact, up-to-the-minute details on the status of his or her claim. All documents are electronically available, managed, merged and produced out of the **ViewStar** workflow system.

Technology Requirements

PPP healthcare selected **ViewStar**, as its chosen workflow/business process environment, in late 1993. The whole system is designed to serve the needs of PPP healthcare's three main offices in and around Tunbridge Wells, Kent, and Eastbourne, Sussex. It comprises two **Novell** Local Area Networks connecting 16 NT **Compaq** servers and **AST** Windows clients. There are two **Kodak** scanners on the third LAN taking care of incoming post and two Hewlett-Packard juke boxes for optical disk storage and archiving. A Wide Area Network connects the LANs and users to the mainframe, which holds valuable customer legacy data.

Currently, scanning takes care of 10,000 documents per day, although when the system is running to full capacity, Tinsley expects to fully consume 30,000 documents into the workflow system daily. "There are literally too many document types to mention; they could be anything from a birth certificate through to handwritten bills sent in by specialist providers – but whatever the content or type of document they will need to be assigned and managed", added Tinsley.

The system integrates all components onto the desktop, merging, tracking and delivering information no matter what its origin, for example scanned documents or those generated internally by accounting or word processing applications. The workflow system also interacts with the mainframe, retrieving legacy data that resides on the **Amdahl/MVS** and here integrates with the terminal emulation software, **Attachmate**.

Implementation

In the early stages of its implementation, in addition to network issues, PPP healthcare encountered many unforeseen difficulties. For example, every time there was a technical problem, it had to be isolated so that the right supplier could be contacted for support. In addition to orchestrating the installation and system integration, PPP healthcare found that it had to overcome a massive learning curve.

It is hard to imagine the frustration of PPP healthcare when it discovered that it had successfully set up and invested in a system that the customer perceived to be slow – even though it was actually delivering a much improved service. PPP healthcare understood that it had a weak link in its system. The culprit was the highly visible personal computer. PPP healthcare's staff were equipped with 486-based PCs. "By switching the 486s to Pentium-based technology we immediately improved the retrieval times - the result is the customer perceives instant response times", Tinsley explained. Indeed, PPP healthcare's personal advisers wait no more than nine seconds to retrieve every relevant item of information. Besides upgrading its PCs, PPP healthcare found that it could improve system performance by migrating its database to NT **SQL Server**.

The System's Impact

Today, the workflow system is available to 300 PPP healthcare staff, with plans to further expand the system, making it the working environment for all of PPP healthcare's 640 staff who deal with customers, by the middle of 1996. However, the company is already benefiting from 10% gains in total productivity and is using the system as a marketing tool.

PPP healthcare has unraveled the mystery of business process automation to benefit its customers and its staff and ultimately to contribute to its future growth.

IT-Supported Process Management in a Public Agency

Nicole Koerber

The environment in which workflow is implemented is a vital factor in determining the success or failure of the system. This includes both the technical infrastructure and wider political issues, inside and outside the organisation concerned. This article provides a study of the factors which made the workflow implementation in the Government of Brandenburg work.

There was never a more opportune time for the Government of Brandenburg, a federal state in Germany, to establish and use an IT-supported process management system for its public agencies. Following the reunification of Germany, reorganization was necessary, but had to be made with minimum effect on organization and existing processes while reducing the costs and simplifying workflows. A further prerequisite was that the existing number of workstations equipped with PCs was quite high.

In fact, about 70% of workstations within the organization had a PC – higher than the average when compared to other federal or state government agencies. The Brandenburg government employees were open to technical innovations and ready to use their technical knowhow on this project. As the budget and personnel available were limited, technical remedies to reduce the everyday workload had to be found quickly. Thus, the idea of using an IT-supported process management system in the public agencies was born.

Integrated Process Management

Through a process management system the traditional, almost Prussian, process management system, which included a wide division of labor within a business case, was to be replaced with an integrated processing system. At the same time, it was ascertained to what extent existing isolated software tools could be integrated into a unified users' environment. All of the participants knew in advance that they would face considerable hurdles of various kinds during this unique project. Therefore, one had to concentrate especially on the conceptualization in order to bring the entire project to a successful conclusion.

The use of a process management system is extremely complicated. It is not just a word processor or a spreadsheet but also a solution that includes almost all areas of activity. Skeptical looks from co-workers are to be expected and restructuring previous work habits is partly unavoidable. Indeed, it is even more demanding to put a process management system into use in a public agency.

Already, at the beginning of this century, the sociologist Max Weber had summarized the following principles upon which actions in public administrations are based:

- Administrative actions are regulated by numerous business rules and provisions and their flexibility is severely limited. Therefore, the process management system to be used must be highly flexible in order to be suitable for this rigid organization
- Continuous division of labor: each task is assigned to an accountable employee ("That's (not) my responsibility!")
- The privileges and responsibilities of each individual involved are based upon the hierarchy of the agency. Thus, the process management system has to be able to allow business processes to be worked on independently of unforeseeable events which are caused by higher levels within the hierarchy
- Documentation of all processes. All steps and activities performed upon a process must be recorded and be able to be traced back to the responsible employee. One has to take into account the processing stations, acknowledgments, signatures, the creation of different versions of the same document, etc. ("The case is being processed, but where?")

To work upon such processes with the help of an IT supported solution, special challenges will be placed on the system and its users. Therefore, the public sector demands specific software requirements.

Special Requirements for a Process Management System

Flexibility

The software must be able to be integrated into an organization which is regulated by numerous business rules and provisions. During the selection of the product, the government of Brandenburg paid particular attention to the flexibility of the product in the area of process definition, process routes, and the subsequent influence on the routing of processes already in motion.

Established individual privileges allow the process route to be changed in the case of unforeseeable events. These privileges are:

- Invocation privilege: the right to bring or call up a process
- Annulment privilege: the right to reverse a decision
- Privilege to control and supervise based upon specialization and hierarchy
- Instruction privileges
- Official channels principle

Due to the privileges listed above, administrative processes are often unstructured. The necessary software solution must be able to react to these unforeseeable events.

In addition, it must be flexible and the organization's administrative language must be used in the solution.

Recording of Processes

All steps and activities performed upon a process must be recorded and be able to be traced back, step-by-step. Thus, it is important that this information is generated automatically by the system and need not be entered by the users.

General Requirements for a Process Management System

- Integration of existing software products

One of the most important requirements for the Government of Brandenburg was the integration of existing software. WordPerfect, WordPerfect Office and MS Excel were already in use. These applications should continue to be available to the employees as they had already been trained on these applications. They also wanted the freedom in the future to be able to purchase or acquire more cost-efficient solutions than the applications already in use.

- Intuitive use of the product. The use of the product should be logical. User-friendliness and easy to learn working steps were the premise, and the constant use of handbooks should not be necessary
- The stability and maturity of the system – looking for extensive experience from the manufacturer in this area
- Sufficient performance based upon the PC's capabilities

- High security of data
- Flawless data protection devices

Segmentation of the Market through a Call for Public Bids

In 1993, a call for public bids was carried out in this field. None of the solutions available on the market was able to fulfill all of the requirements. It was decided to introduce two products as a result of this. A leading office software package was chosen to meet the "general needs", e.g. electronic mail, calendar, telephone and address book. A workflow product was selected to fulfill the categories of "process management" and "applications integration". It was discovered later that this product could not fulfill the promises of the manufacturer and meet the expectations of Brandenburg's Interior Ministry regarding the integration of existing solutions for office communications. In addition, the solution proved to be unsatisfactory in dealing with processes which were partly paper and partly electronic. The project was therefore discontinued and the product was returned.

The project was continued later on with a different workflow software solution, CSE/WorkFlow from CSE Systems. During a new project assessment, this workflow product was convincing in its flexibility, performance capabilities, the integration capabilities with existing software, and its user-friendliness. It was also appraised based upon the experiences of the previous project. Additionally, INFORA GmbH, an external consulting firm, was entrusted with the task of conceptualizing and organizing the project. The goal was to install the software solution over approximately 1,500 work stations. The realization called for long-term planning, which is why the Brandenburg government insisted, if possible, that a step-by-step procedure be used in installation of the process management system.

Introduction of the Workflow Solution

At first, 60 workstations located in different agencies of the Brandenburg government were equipped with workflow software for six months. These agencies included the Ministries for the Interior, for the Environment, Nature Conservation and Regional Planning, and for the Development of Cities, Housing, and Transportation.

The client–server solution was installed on the hardware/software environment shown in Table 1.

The different working areas in which the process management system were to be used, were divided into three:

- IT-supported registration of incoming mail
- IT-supported documentation of processes
- IT-supported management of processes

Table 1 Hardware/Software Environment

Server	HP 9000
Database	INFORMIX 5 Online
Network	LAN-Manager/X -MS TCP/IP
PC	DOS/Windows 3.1
Applications	WordPerfect 5.1 for DOS Excel 4.0 WordPerfect 6.0 for Windows dBase WordPerfect Office 4.0
Workflow	CSE/WorkFlow
Document Administration	SINAD

Data security was realized through a security program which saves all documents and descriptive data on tape and is located on the server. An excellent security concept is integrated in the workflow product and provides for data protection.

IT-Supported Registration of Incoming Mail

The proper registration of incoming mail provides the basis for the processing of business process instances. After all, the receipt of a letter is often the reason why a process is created. For their internal solutions, the State of Brandenburg decided in favour of a document administration system. The product is called SINAD (**Sch**riftgut**in**formations- und **Ad**ministrationssystem – Written Information and Administration System) which it was possible to integrate with the workflow software without any problems. Additionally, a form was established to contain further information about each incoming letter.

Through the use of this software solution for incoming registration, analysis using different criteria can now be carried out. Conventional incoming mail logbooks and other means of registration belong in the past. Another important advantage is the decentralized availability of all registration data which minimizes search time and the work involved in giving out information.

IT-Supported Documentation of Processes

In order to document and trace a process, it must be first created. Thus, the appointment of codes or description to a file takes on a special meaning. CSE/WorkFlow's online access to the file plan, the hierarchy of organizational units as well as the plausibility control during the creation of a business code is necessary for the correct entry of file codes. In this manner, redundancies can be avoided.

IT-Supported Management of Processes

In order to achieve an efficient level of process management, the results (text, tables, database searches) must be immediately obtainable from the process. The workflow solution organizes the access to programs and data. Because unforeseeable events can change the planned route of a process, the user has the ability to change routes in the system. In order to prevent misuse in these situations, a step-like system of access mechanisms has been integrated in CSE/WorkFlow.

Problems and Solutions

Duality of Paper and Electronic Data

Due to legal and organizational considerations, it is not possible to access and electronically process all documents belonging to a business process. As long as administrative laws do not allow electronic signatures, as a minimum, the final document must be in paper form. For this reason, there will be no purely electronic processes in the near future. The goal is, therefore, not a paperless, but rather a paper saving administration. Also, the documentation of paper and electronic cases must be synchronized. The workflow solution used here has the capability to handle these mixed media types seamlessly. So-called meta data are integrated into the electronic process and contain information referencing the paper documents. At the same time, a reference will be made in the paper process to show the existence of an electronic process. The unique business code allows the electronic and paper processes to be related.

Acceptance by Employees

A process management system strongly affects the employees' usual work habits. Acceptance problems could be the result. Employees fear the constant supervision of their activities or they think that their work will be determined by this system. Furthermore, co-workers will be forced to bend the work style as defined in the business order. Often, this has been rejected as "bureaucratic" and "impractical", and thus the use of a process management system is seen as a Trojan horse.

In order to minimize these acceptance problems, the project group focused much time and energy on this matter. Throughout the project, participants were given the opportunity to take part in presentations and/or product workshops. Additionally, a users' information hour was established. The IT-solution providers established a hotline to handle urgent inquiries from the Federal Government of Brandenburg. Courses for users and system administrators were conducted where all project participants were trained. The complete support of the co-workers was given in an "on-the-job" environment. After a period of time, the intensity of the support was reduced, step-by-step.

Unstructured Processes

Due to technical circumstances in the administration, the workflow solution used had to work with partially structured processes. Partially structured means that because of unforeseeable events:

- The process time cannot be precisely calculated
- Users may change in the course of a process
- No process classes can be assigned
- Spawned processes with their own process history can be modeled
- Responsibility can be transferred from one employee to another

The deciding factor in choosing the workflow solution was its flexibility.

Benefits and Advantages

Based upon the ruling management style of division of labor which was still present in the public administration, there existed a number of shortcomings which were improved through the use of workflow.

At the conclusion of the first project phase, the following benefits were summarized as resulting from the utilization of a workflow solution:

- Easy and retraceable assignment of documents and processes
- Decentralized availability of data which minimizes search time and the work involved in giving out information
- Reduction in paper. Through the ability to find processes quickly, it is no longer necessary to have individual files of copies
- Optimizing the coordination process. An employee is always in a position to duplicate or reproduce the contents of a case. This factor proves to be extremely positive in dealing with cases involving multiple responsibility. Earlier, one had to telephone one's respective colleague for confirmation; now one only has to look in the workflow system
- Reduction in multiple data storage. The use of workflow allows employees to quickly relocate documents and processes, therefore multiple storage of common data is unnecessary

- Efficient supervision of deadlines and suspend/resume operations. Earlier, important deadlines had to be registered by the employees; now the workflow-based solution handles this task automatically and reliably
- Cutbacks in personnel. Through the removal of costly search and investigation activities, especially in the assistants' area, long-term employment positions can be cut
- Cutbacks in office supplies, especially in paper and copying costs
- Improved employee motivation caused by more direct responsibility (because the process history is retraceable) as well as concentration on the critical activities through the reduction of routine work
- Increased productivity through the reduction of transport and idle time and the minimization of errors

CSE/WorkFlow is used not only as a process management system for the automation of business case processing, but also as an integration platform for various office tools and data under a uniform surface. Further to the qualities identified above, CSE/WorkFlow has been in use for a number of years in numerous administrations/agencies and Brandenburg did not need to be used as a guinea pig for product testing.

Future Work

Since the realization of the technical requirements of the software products were the focus in the first phase of the project, further experience in practical use will be gathered in the second phase. To do this, the heads of the various departments will now be included. Furthermore, a clear, functional separation of the workflow solution and the office software package will be carried out.

Using Workflow and BPR for 45-fold Improvement

Fred van Leeuwen
Managing Consultant
DCE Netherlands b.v.

Olav Gribnau
Innovation and Quality Management Group
DCC

The incentive for addressing business processes and considering their automation with workflow often comes from external changes imposed on an organization. Such was the case with the Dutch Defence Computer Centre. Productivity gains, return on investment, and response times are all documented here to show how major improvements have been made using workflow.

On 1 January 1994, the Dutch Defence Computer Centre (Duyverman Computer Centre or DCC) formally changed from being a government staff department into a semi-autonomous service, known as an "Agency". For the first time in DCC's history, there was now a direct relation between satisfying its clients' needs and securing cash flow. This imposed the need for significant changes, affecting all aspects of DCC's business. Using workflow and groupware technologies, major improvements have been made.

One of the worst-performing business processes, the so-called On-line Services Installation Process, was selected for drastic improvement. The scope of this process was configuring and installing decentralized online facilities. Its performance was 225 days' in response 90% of instances and a first time right score which was oscillating between 40% and 70%.

Assisted by DCE Nederland b.v., a consultancy company with hands-on experience in business process reengineering and workflow, DCC designed and implemented a new process. The major results so far are the capability to install within three days if desired, a five-day response in well over 50% of the instances (on its way to 90%), a first time right score of nearly 95% and an expected 50% return on the project investment. Furthermore, it is now possible to plan and confirm an installation while the client is still on the phone, and deliver according to promise! The project's objectives are summarized in Figure 1.

These significant improvements were realized by decimating the number of departments and roles involved in the process, by empowering the employees, by registering all information electronically once only – as soon as it comes into existence – and by improving logistics.

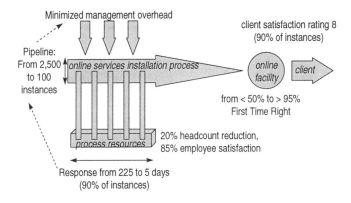

Figure 1   Project Objectives

The main technologies used were workflow combined with database applications for real-time planning & reservation (manpower and materials), groupware to maintain the so-called product recipes (defining the requirements, norms and instructions for each type of network installation) and a loosely-coupled portable computer for instructions to and registration by the installation engineer.

DCC – From Central Financing to Providing Competitive Services

In large parts of the world, politicians and governments are reconsidering the role and position of the public service. Like the business community, public administrations have become much more aware of what constitutes the main reason for their existence. The term "core business" is becoming more commonly used these days, even in government circles. As a result, all tasks which do not have a direct relevance to the core activities are potentially subject to change. Such change can take many forms, including outsourcing, undertaking public–private partnerships and the creation of (semi-)autonomous units.

Seen in this perspective, the transition which has taken place in the past few years in the Dutch Defence Computer Centre (Duyverman Computer Centre or DCC) may not seem to be a very amazing event, but for DCC management and the 550 employees the changes had significant impact. In January 1994, DCC became a so-called "Agentschap" (Agency) a specific construction for semi-autonomous units within the Dutch government. The major implication is that DCC, although still reporting to the Ministry of Defence, no longer gets financed by its "mother". Instead the budget is distributed to its clients, who can use it to purchase the services of DCC (Figure 2). One can imagine the effects this has on an organization. A coherent program of change is needed, covering a multitude of financial, legal, commercial, personnel, cultural, technical and organizational aspects. This article will illustrate the changes made by highlighting one specific project: the reengineering of the On-line Services Installation Process. First it will address the question: what is DCC?

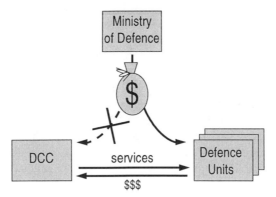

Figure 2   Transition to an Agency

DCC's Reason for Existence

DCC exists to provide highly secure and reliable IT services for the Dutch Defence Ministry, enabling defence units to concentrate on their core business.

Within the Dutch Ministry of Defence, the Duyverman Computer Centre traditionally is the focal point for all computing activities in logistical and administrative applications. The Centre is based in Maasland, near Hook of Holland. Large computers and application systems are being operated, allowing the Defence Ministry to take advantage of economies of scale (DCC owns computer equipment with a current book value of $30 million). Equipment installed includes mainframes and midrange computers from DEC, HP, IBM, Siemens and Unisys. DCC is not only running these systems and the applications; it also has a significant role in application development and maintenance. These combined activities generate annual revenues of about $90 million.

DCC's core competence lies in the highly secure and reliable IT services that military applications demand. The Centre operates an extremely fail-safe infrastructure, including a full-blown backup facility. The ambition is to provide turnkey solutions, which allow DCC's clients to concentrate on their own core activities, executing these in the most effective and efficient manner.

Organic Growth

Over the years, the accelerating use of terminals, personal computers, minicomputers and PC networks has added a new dimension to DCC's existing central computing facility: that of a distributed computer network. One of the effects this has had is the growth of a new set of services: handling clients' requests to install, move, reconfigure or replace "networked facilities". For instance, a new maintenance system for the Air Force is likely to require the installation of workstations (terminals or PCs) and network infrastructure. Reorganization of a Navy unit may trigger the reallocation of authorizations for the online usage of network facilities and applications. A political decision to allow the Dutch Army to provide support in Bosnia will trigger local installation of computer equipment and its connection to the Defence Network. Such requests are handled using the On-line Services Installation Process. An average of 55 requests come in every week

As usual with business processes, it was hard to recognize any specific design in the old process. It was the result of organic growth over a period of some 25 years, on the back of a distributed computer network evolving out of a central computing facility, and it represented a myriad of process steps which had accumulated over time. Moreover, the process embodied the rigidity of the computer networks that were once the norm in the IT industry. A total of 110 staff were involved in the process, of which 40 were on a full-time basis, divided over 15 organizational entities, and a rich variety of information systems was used in the various steps, most of them poorly connected and difficult to use (see Figure 3).

The result was that the probability of any installation being successfully completed during the first visit to the client oscillated between 40% and 70%. The average time from client request to installation and normal operation was 225 days in 90% of cases. In the pre-Agency situation each case had been accepted as a fact of life by the individuals involved, including the client, and as such the problem had been a hidden one; the poor overall process performance had hardly been noticed at the time.

Now that circumstances had changed, it became clear that improvement was needed. The problem was that the old process made it impossible for the employees involved to influence the final output in any significant way as individuals. As a result the majority of the staff were demotivated and customers were increasingly dissatisfied. In 1994, the first year of operating as an Agency, it became apparent that this situation was a real threat to the continuity of the On-line Services Product Group, generating about 20% of DCC's revenues.

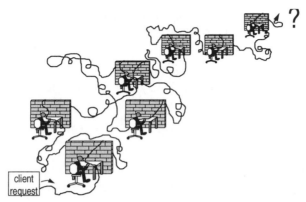

Figure 3   The Old On-line Services Installation Process

"No Guts, No Glory" the Initial Step

After analyzing the situation, it was decided to attack the problem in two stages. It was clear that there was little time left and therefore the first step had to be based on simple, straightforward action. This step found its roots in a Total Quality Management (TQM) program that DCC had by now adopted. An ambitious goal was set: to improve the first time right score from 40–70% to a constant minimum of 90% within four months. The title of this action communicated the new attitude that was required: "No guts, no glory". The emphasis was on raising the commitment of all staff involved by sheer enthusiasm and improvisation, and making departmental boundaries irrelevant by creating a strong feeling of team responsibility. That way it would be possible to achieve a drastic improvement, without changing anything structurally. The opportunities to increase efficiency would have to wait; boosting effectiveness was much more urgent.

After a successful team session at the end of November 1994, committing each and every one of the 110 people, the Product Group managed to improve its performance rapidly. The last week of January 1995 (only nine weeks after starting) saw a first time right score of 90%; the result had already been achieved and has since been maintained with only a few exceptions.

Challenging the Organization Further: Back to 72-Hour Delivery!

Now the platform was there to think about more structural solutions. The need was also there: it was clear that people could not be asked to improvise indefinitely. It had also become obvious how much more room for improvement there was, if one could only crack the old process.

A 15-person Process Management Team, consisting of the most involved line managers, shop floor workers, product managers and several staff specialists, was formed and another challenging goal was set. The major elements were as follows:

- To be able to deliver within three working days, from client request to installation
- To deliver within five working days in 90% of cases (a 45-fold improvement!)
- To sustain the first time right score and even improve it to 95% or more

Targets were also defined for client satisfaction and for employee satisfaction.

The Areas of Change

DCC engaged DCE Nederland b.v., a 95-staff consultancy company based in Badhoevedorp, The Netherlands, with hands-on experience in business process re-engineering and workflow, to assist in the project. The redesign resulted in five areas of change:

1. Process design
2. Organization and people
3. Electronic registration facilities
4. Logistics
5. Process management and integration
6. Each of these areas will be explained in the following text.

Process Design

The new process reduces incomprehensible complexity to six simple steps: acceptance, configuring, planning, material acquisition, installation, and aftercare. During the acceptance, the request forms – coming in through mail and fax – are being registered and validated. Configuring starts with contacting the client to discuss his or her needs and local infrastructure. During the telephone conversation the availability of materials and engineering capacity is checked, reservations for these resources are made and the installation date is agreed. Where necessary, a parallel step is triggered to acquire materials and data communications lines.

Planning is a very straightforward step. By now, each assignment has an amount of reserved engineering capacity linked to it. Planning allocates this capacity reservation to an individual installation engineer, while securing an optimal planning route. The installation consists of visiting DCC's central warehouse to pick up the order and the associated materials, traveling to the client and installing and testing the network facility. Aftercare entails completing the registration of all information related to the new facility and its installation, contacting the client to see if he is happy and confirming the new subscription fee (or the installation fee) that will be billed to the client.

Organization and People

The goal in this area was to balance employee empowerment and management control. In the new situation, for a standard installation, most of the work is done by only two organizational entities: the Estimators Group (14 people) and the Installation Group (18 people). Three more entities are involved on a part-time basis in specific parts of the process: Sales, Warehouse, and Installation Planning. This gives a total of five organizational entities involved (Figure 4), a vast improvement over the 15 groups that were needed in the old process! The employees who participate in the new process have improved their skills (particularly their commercial skills) and have adopted a team player's attitude. The workflow management system (which will be described later) created the opportunity to introduce state-of-the-art management concepts, including output-oriented planning and control and staff empowerment. To elaborate on this, the advanced line management for the new situation includes:

- Concentrating on coaching and facilitating (rather than day-to-day supervision)
- Maintaining case and process management responsibility at the bottom of the organization
- Making people development an explicit performance measure for managers
- Making continuous improvement an explicit performance measure for everyone

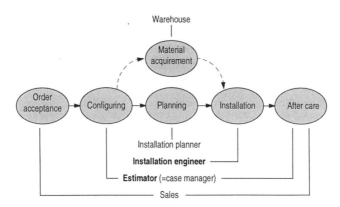

Figure 4   The New Process

Each group operates as a team of people exercising a specific role, related to one or more steps in the process. Accessibility of real-time information on the status of individual cases and on the overall process performance facilitates task integration and creates the possibility of agreeing on concrete targets for each group. The groups are being managed on the basis of group performance. Should performance drop below target, then the manager will get the group to resolve the problem amongst themselves. In other words, an explicit decision has been taken that the electronic information on an individual's performance will not be used by the manager. Instead, figures on individual performance are consolidated for each role and only used in that form.

The estimator carries responsibility for the handling of a case, during its entire lifetime. As a result, the team leader of the estimators is responsible for the overall process performance (within the constraints of the existing implementation, including performance norms). The installation engineer is responsible for achieving his or her output (installation accepted by the client) within quality and productivity norms. The team leaders of both estimators and installation engineers are responsible for the availability of appropriate staff and instrumentation, achieving cost-coverage according to budget and, as pointed out earlier, for staff development. All these responsibilities have been implemented in the management controls, supported by management information systems.

Electronic Registration Facilities

Accurate administration is vital, but how to get it out of engineering hands? The solution is electronic registration facilities.

A very significant improvement is that *all information is registered at the time it is generated*. As with all technical staff, the engineers involved do not see administrative tasks as their biggest challenge in life! Therefore to achieve the objective of immediate registration, the capturing of information must be enforced and highly automated. This also helps to boost efficiency, because it avoids delays in registration while helping everyone to concentrate on the activities that really add customer value. One example of this approach is that during the "configuring" step, once it is clear what the new configuration of the client will be, the workflow enforces a tentative registration in both the configuration database and in the change management database.

A second example is the new, streamlined, but nevertheless highly secure, authorization procedure. This is facilitated by a single uniform input mechanism, referred to as "The (Authorization) Peel" because of its encapsulating and protective effect. While the workflow system enforces definition of the authorizations at an early stage during the process, "The Peel" accepts this as an input, determines the types of authorization involved, generates the correct authorization formats for each type and passes them on to the appropriate systems. This is another major improvement, since authorization used to be unnecessarily complicated, resulting in omissions which delayed usability of the network facility. This is a good example of how things changed when DCC started looking from the client perspective. Previously, security enforcement was the dominating performance criterion which could push away all other considerations. The installation engineer would be relieved once he had successfully installed and tested the equipment and was convinced that the client would now be in the same state of happiness. Today, everybody involved in the process realizes that only at the moment when the facility becomes practically usable (including application accessibility) does customer value jump from 0% to 100%.

A third essential new component is the so-called "Remote Registration Facility". This allows the installation engineer to connect his portable computer to DCC in the evening, while at home (this is one of the situations in which DCC's special competence to provide secure, location-independent access is paying off). The installation engineer then automatically receives all information which is relevant to the installation tasks that are scheduled for his next working day. During his work at the client, the portable computer continuously provides him with information, which is perfectly tuned to each step in the installation process. When he has to deviate from the plan (a very common situation, which used to cause great inaccuracies in the registration of configurations, materials and engineering hours), this now triggers immediate registration of the changes. Also, the portable computer is fitted with a scanning pencil to fix the relation between logical configuration components and the hardware serial numbers, immediately after the final test has proved that the installed facility is working. During the installation engineer's once-a-day online session in the evening, all information is transmitted back to DCC, after which definite registration follows within half a working day. This compares very favorably to the old process, where it was not uncommon for registration activity to behave like a "comet's tail" following the actual installation at great distance (Figure 5). Finishing this tail of registration activities could last many months, causing significant inaccuracies and inefficiencies. Correct registration is vital; without it the services would not be billed or would be wrongly billed, it would be impossible to monitor material stocks, and the help-desk would not be able to assist a client who is calling for service.

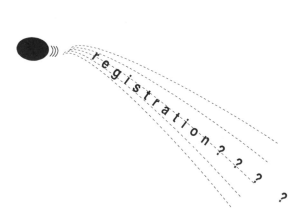

Figure 5   Registration Followed Behind

Logistics

The aims in this area were standardization, proactive procedures and an attempt to influence the external telecoms provider.

Installation services, materials and supplies are much more standardized than in the past, thus it is possible to undertake more than 90% of the installations rapidly, using stocked material. This reduces inventory costs and logistic delays. In a similar way, groups of network addresses are predefined in the network software (creating a "warehouse of addresses") and updating of the Network Control Program is done dynamically, avoiding weekly down hours and delays. Bandwidth is planned proactively, to minimize situations in which ordering a data communications line becomes the critical path for a network installation. Since this cannot always be avoided, the DCC Process Management Team appealed to the ambition of PTT (the Dutch telecom operator) to be a partner in business; it started to challenge PTT to improve their timeliness and accuracy as well.

Process Management and Integration

Real-time process management, practical empowerment and systems integration presented an unprecedented challenge.

Being able to install within three working days and to agree the installation date while the client is on the phone places heavy demands on the process management. During configuring, the estimator must be able to answer the following questions:

- What type of installation will this be and which steps must be taken?
- Which resources will be required during each step, and how much of each resource? This relates to staff capacity as well as materials
- Are all these resources available within the timeframe desired by the client?

Also, to run the process with minimum delay and to inform the client adequately in all cases, each individual involved must be able to check on the status of instances in the pipeline. The motto which triggered the first improvement action, "No guts, no glory", remains valid. Much emphasis is put on staff responsibility for maximum motivation and quality in client service. This is reflected in the approach for allocating work to staff: where possible it is left up to the individual employee which case he selects as his next task and when he does so. Of course a mechanism is required to monitor the time period during which cases remain in the "electronic in-tray", queuing for the subsequent role in the process. In case of time-out, the group manager must be triggered to take action. Staff performance is kept at the required levels by the team performance monitoring mechanism which was explained earlier.

For process integration, the historical archipelago of information islands had to be bridged. Sixteen separate information systems and data tables are used in the process. At the same time, as a result of the overall change program of DCC, six of these systems were in the process of being replaced by new systems. This situation created an extraordinary challenge to the management of the project. It was met by marrying workflow to groupware, with sophisticated process management and integration, as well as dispersed, yet up-to-date engineering instructions.

The workflow system that was implemented to provide the described process management and integration has become the information backbone of the new process. It was built using Staffware as a workflow tool and Lotus Notes for maintaining replicated documents and to build a multi-user database, registering human resource capacity. As described earlier, different types of network installation can be distinguished: e.g., adding a 3270-terminal to an existing cluster controller is one thing, but installing a complete local network of PCs, connected to the Defence Network through a gateway, is something quite different. Fifteen different types of installation have each been described in a so-called product recipe. The recipe defines the process route and the associated norm times for each installation type. It also defines a checklist that the estimator will use during his conversation with the client, as well as a framework for the instruction of the installation engineer. This instruction is tailored to the specific case during configuring. Finally, the recipe refers to materials and supplies needed for this installation type. Most of the recipe information system is built as a document-oriented groupware application, fully integrated with the workflow. Complementary to and integrated with the workflow there is a database, maintaining engineering capacity and reservations thereof. This database can be accessed and updated by each estimator.

The workflow system keeps control of all installation requests in the pipeline, it allows anyone involved to give an adequate reaction to a client who is calling for information, it manages the work queues in such a way that employee empowerment and management control go hand in hand, and finally it registers all performance information in such a way that process improvement is becoming a continuous effort. In its current implementation, the workflow integrates ten different vertical systems and tools (Figure 6). By integrating the old vertical systems, the workflow resolved redundancies, inconsistencies, inefficiencies and ergonomic problems.

The combined workflow/recipe system was designed and built in a sub-project led by the external BPR/workflow consultant (DCE) and supported by Cadenz Informatisering – a systems integrator based in Capelle a/d IJssel, Holland. By organizing it this way, DCC secured intense interaction between workflow and process redesign. The resulting integration of managerial, technological and organizational aspects enabled DCC to grasp the full benefit of state-of-the-art technology combined with advanced management concepts.

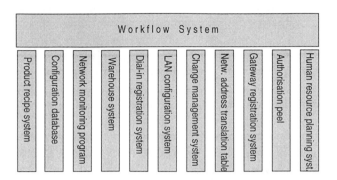

Figure 6   Integrating Vertical Systems

Project Management

The only way to meet a real challenge was through state-of-the-art project management! The management of the project was convinced that revolutionary results could only be achieved by following a non-standard approach. Important factors leading to success were:

- A *prominent goal*, which is easy to understand and can be expressed in a few words: **72 hour delivery!** Combined with continuous and intensive communication on goals, requirements and status of the project
- A *holistic attitude*, recognizing that it would be pound-foolish to look at the change measures as isolated entities which one could pick and choose at will or implement in a segregated manner
- A *substantial role for DCC management and staff*, not only in the project's management but also in its day-to-day activities. External parties were involved to bring in experience with reengineering and with workflow integration, hence securing timeliness and quality of implementation
- Much *emphasis by management on the required improvements in commercial skills and attitude*, supported by an action-oriented program for learning and team building, called "Discovery"
- An implementation strategy, focused on *rapid visibility of improved business results*. Initially, the "No guts, no glory" action took care of this. During the subsequent BPR, once the redesign had been carried out, the smallest possible step was defined which would lead to further visible improvement. Instead of creating a critical path of building new information systems and structures, a small team of six people (representing the various roles) was selected to start the processing of installation requests based on the new process. Since they fitted in one office, referred to as the Base Camp, for the time being they could exercise "workflow on

the whiteboard". In other words, long before the new systems were introduced, they were able to demonstrate that the project goals were achievable. As a result, the first three-day delivery took place within only six weeks after management had approved the implementation plan; client reactions were very encouraging!

- The same team of people played a major role in the *incremental system development* that followed. Within a week of the development environment being installed, the first workflow process implementation could be demonstrated to the inhabitants of the Base Camp
- *Two stages of systems integration* were defined: one which would lead to quick results, using screen scraping techniques, and one which would deliver a more advanced API-based integration at a later stage, for ease of system management and maintenance. Only seven weeks after availability of the systems development environment, the first release of integrated workflow could be installed in the Base Camp

Summarizing, the ambitious project goals and the state-of-the-art technology they required would not have been attainable using a traditional project approach. "State-of-the-art project management", as described above, was the solution in meeting the challenge!

Objectives and Achievements

Was BPR drastic, hence risky? Not to apply it would have been riskier and, anyway, the result is astonishing!

With most of the implementation done, the main objective, 72 hour delivery, has been achieved. *It is now possible to satisfy clients who want their installation within three days* of DCC receiving the request, provided the installation is standard and material is in stock, and that existing data communications lines can be used. Also, in practice, *the majority of the installations are already being delivered within five working days.* There is only one thing left that separates DCC from the desired "90% within five days" score: the problem of non-standard components (which cannot be kept in stock and complicates the estimates). Measures have been taken to further standardize facilities and components to swiftly resolve this remaining problem.

Nearly 95% of the installations are successful at the first attempt and the staff involved find it a lot easier now to maintain this score. Their experience is that the workflow system has relieved them from the tedious task of dealing with a multitude of vertical systems. Moreover, their task is much better organized and they can concentrate on the client's problem, instead of having to deal with internal problems. Also it has become more rewarding to put forward new ideas for further improvement, now that in the new situation the implementation of those ideas has become a lot easier.

The clients react very positively to the improved service, especially in situations where speed of delivery is important to the client's own performance. *Clients are pleasantly surprised by the new service standards.*

The $1.2 million project investment (including external cost, as well as all internal hours) is going to generate a *yearly return of $0.6 million*, mainly as a result of productivity gains, more accurate and timely billing, reduced capital allocation and market share security.

Lessons Learnt

Integration has its own risks; the same applies to user involvement and to workflow flexibility; speed of action is a dominating success factor.

Every project creates learning opportunities and an ambitious project such as this creates a lot of them. Important lessons were:

- The ability of a workflow tool to integrate the underlying information systems can contribute significantly to success, but this does demand a lot from the PC and network infrastructure in terms of memory and processor requirements, uniformity and connectivity. The first place where this will hit a project is the development environment. The big potential for integration also implies another risk: the system will affect large parts of the organization, thereby generating a fair amount of resistance.

- Incremental, user-driven development is very helpful in implementing a workable process and in securing user acceptance. The two risks to be managed are avoiding innovation being constrained by the difficulty for staff to think beyond their current working situation, and being aware of the human tendency to defer real serious thinking until the implementation is close at hand (in other words, even if the user has already given a lot of feedback, always expect a lot of last-minute change requests).

- Once people realize how easy it is to build a workflow system, the chances are that they will come forward with many old wishes and new ideas. Resist the temptation to build lots of non-workflow functionality in the workflow system; maintain a design in which non-workflow functions are implemented only as an invoked application.

- Rapid implementation of results is extremely important for success. The first reason for this is that workflow systems tend to be introduced by organizations that are changing. With a traditional project, lasting multiple years, the chances are that it will take less time for the circumstances to change than it will for the project to finish. The second reason is that the best way to overcome resistance to change is to demonstrate very quickly that the ambitions for business improvement can be met in practice.

Further Improvements

Most of the implementation has been carried out; remaining improvements are imaged request forms, remote registration and standardization of products. The workflow's flexibility will be further challenged by the planned renewal of underlying systems.

As explained earlier, so far the majority of the implementation has been carried out. A few missing elements will be put in place before or during the second half of 1996:

- Integration of an imaging facility in the workflow, so that client request forms can be scanned as soon as they enter DCC. This will further increase the efficiency and speed of operation. No longer will there be the need to physically transfer the request forms a couple of times a day. To achieve this, DCC will implement its own XREGIS product, in particular the imaging, fax-input, document management system and workflow integration modules.
- The remote registration facility, which will take away the need for an installation engineer to go physically to DCC for information exchange. In January 1996, IBM Netherlands delivered a client–server based prototype, which demonstrated the feasibility of the idea. That convinced management, who then took the decision to write out a tender for a production version; this will be operational by the end of 1996. This facility, connected into the workflow, will be the final step in reaching the ideal of immediate and automatic registration.

More work will be done on standardizing the online facilities of DCC and of its clients and the components that are needed to build these. It is fair to say that making this happen has prove to be the most tedious task of all; it will take more time than originally expected.

Finally, as a result of other projects, part of the old vertical systems will be replaced by new systems during the second half of 1996. This will provide a further degree of integrated information processing throughout the process.

Conclusions

Without workflow and without state-of-the-art management, this result could not have been achieved.

An unusually ambitious goal was set and achieved in this project. The improved service contributes strongly to one of DCC's main objectives: providing a total service and increasing customer satisfaction. Also the 50% return-on-investment helps to maintain DCC's financial health and the appreciation of DCC's mother: the Ministry of Defence. It is hard to imagine how this improvement could have been implemented without using workflow. Workflow technology provided the essential ingredients of real-time process management, the tracking and tracing of client requests, the process enforcement (including the immediate registration of information) and the accessibility of process information to each individual, facilitating a new combination of staff empowerment and management control. Also essential for success were the abilities to integrate the vertical information systems throughout the process and to build the workflow rapidly and in a flexible manner. This flexibility will be a lasting advantage, since it facilitates the ongoing and rapid implementation of new ideas for improvement. That capability, combined with the process performance information and the new management concepts which were implemented, will further accelerate the learning organization that DCC has become in the past few years.

The final conclusion has to be that all the technology in the world would not have brought about this success, if a traditional project approach had been followed. The combination of modern information technology, state-of-the-art project management and advanced line management has been the recipe for success. The rapidly visible improvements, both during the "No guts, no glory" TQM phase and during the start of the BPR's Base Camp, created enthusiasm which has fuelled all further successes.

Implementing Workflow

Workflow Success Starts with Application Understanding

Peter Lawrence
Concordium

Implementing workflow automation successfully means more than just picking a product and installing it; there are wider implications on the organization. The first thing to do is to understand your own requirements, and that means knowing the right questions to ask.

Workflow and Changing Organizations

The wide takeup of workflow automation as a concept has resulted in an ever-increasing range of potential product solutions to any application problem, all of which could be, and are, given the label of "workflow". Buzzword status has its drawbacks.

Implementing a workflow project is not the same as any other. At the very least it will change the way the work is passed to staff in the organization. But it is even more likely to change the actual work which people do – the greatest successes for workflow come where there is an accompanying change in who does what, such as skilling-up customer service representatives to handle more of the tasks for each customer. Suppliers of technology do not always see that it is within their scope to advise on organizational change. Add this to the inevitable fact that knowledge about workflow is not yet widespread among users who need it, and the potential for dissatisfaction becomes apparent.

The need for a way of characterizing a potential workflow application more methodically became apparent. This resulted from the belief that the best approach must be for the *users* of technology to understand their requirements more thoroughly, since only they can understand the organization's imperatives.

A Framework for Understanding

The *Workflow Application Classification Scheme* – WACS – was the result. It consists of twelve characteristics of workflow applications, each of which can take a range of values. To use a familiar analogy, a person buying a car has a set of characteristics to look for: the configuration – such as Saloon, Hatchback, Estate; the engine size – with possible values of 1000 cc upwards; and so on. For workflow applications, those characteristics are not so well known, but they exist nevertheless; hence the need for WACS.

WACS is not only applicable to prospective workflow applications, however. It can also be applied to workflow products themselves to help tease out the range of application types which the product is suited to. In theory, then, it should be possible to look for a "best fit" between application requirements and potential products. In practice this would tend to obscure some other vital aspects, such as the relationship with the supplier. But it might at least help avoid the worst mismatches.

The method is for each of the twelve characteristics to be reviewed, and values for each one to be assigned. Although the end result can be a graphical representation of the requirement, the biggest benefit comes from the increased understanding which comes from a detailed consideration of the application.

The WACS Characteristics

The Reason for Implementing Workflow

Although this characteristic may not provide much guidance as to which products to put on a shortlist, it is nevertheless a good place to start. It is essential to capture and, where appropriate, to make known the benefits to the organization which are being sought. Possible values for this characteristic include *Better customer service, Being more responsive, Using less staff, Doing more work with the same staff, Losing less paperwork,* etc.

Who Implements the Workflow Application

Possible values are *the Supplier, the IT department, Business Process Analysts, Users.* Here we begin to see some real differentiation between products, and a matching difference in expectations between users. The expectations here will start to turn a long list of potential products into a shortlist. The characteristic will probably need to be refined further to ask who implements <u>which aspects</u> of the application: process design, workflow implementation, administration, etc.

What Flows

Not an obvious question to ask, but experience shows that users typically have an unstated expectation here; most commonly they assume that the equivalent of a paper form is being passed around by the workflow system. Some will expect this to be an image of a real paper form, others expect an "electronic form", or perhaps whatever the user chooses to put into the "case folder". Any of those could be the most appropriate, and any could be supplied; but the question needs to be addressed.

How Often New Work is Started

Whether new work is started once a second or once a year is a key part of the system design. If a product's architecture is unsuited to the requirements, the application will have problems – either the system will not cope in a high volume situation, or a high-powered product will have administration requirements (database tuning, etc.) which are too onerous for a smaller application.

How Well-Defined the Process is

If users need to be able to define *ad hoc* workflows, then the choice of product needs to support that. More commonly today, although this will change, the flow is fairly well prescribed, the objective very often being to ensure that people do what the organization requires of them. A product will not handle both well defined and *ad hoc* types of workflow well. There is, of course, a middle ground, too: the flow may be well-defined in terms of *what* is done, but the ability to choose *who* does it, and by *when,* may need to be delegated to users while the flow is proceeding. There is nothing more likely to make a workflow project fail than trying to be too prescriptive, and removing choices from users who are quite able to make them.

Who Chooses the Work to be Done

Another aspect of choice is how much opportunity users have to choose their own work. As an alternative, the work may be automatically assigned based, for instance, on a predefined priority for each piece of work. So possible values for who chooses are *Each user, A supervisor, An automated scheduler.* The purpose of a particular workflow application may point in a particular direction, here. For a full "production" workflow application, users are typically given little choice, their work being determined automatically by the priorities of the outstanding work.

Where the Work is Done

Another aspect of workflow which will change over time is the location of those involved in a workflow. Increasingly we will see the need to automate business processes which are distributed between offices, buildings, or countries. In addition, mobile or teleworking workers will need to be incorporated into the flow. An application's requirements need to be brought to the surface and matched against product capabilities.

Lifetime of Work Items

A help-desk system may have short duration work items – just enough time to pass a problem to a help-desk analyst and have the issue resolved. But there are many workflow applications which take several months to complete the process. For long-duration work, products need to have strong support for backup/restore facilities, and to be able to introduce new versions of the workflow software and the other applications which they use with live work on the system.

Complexity of Flow

A simple flow will have a straightforward sequence of one step following another. More complex flows are typically required, however, including parallel sub-flows, conditional routing, looping, etc. Although it is not realistic or desirable to design the details of the flow before selecting a product, it is nevertheless essential to have a general idea of the shape of the flow so that product capabilities can be assessed against the required complexity.

Level of Integration Needed

Workflow is "glueware". It will almost always be used to tie together other applications, whether "legacy" systems, or systems implemented in parallel such as document image processing, and links to telephony systems. Questions like *"Where is the integration to be done: client or server?"* and *"What integration facilities are required: API, DDE, ...?"* need to be addressed.

Computing Platforms

Just as with any IT acquisition, constraints on the platform to be applied to the workflow application need considering: operating systems, hardware, network, etc.

Monitoring and Control Requirements

For many users, a key perceived advantage of implementing a workflow system is a greater ability to know the status of work, and to control it more effectively. This breaks down into two aspects: the need to know the status of individual pieces of work so that a customer can be told what's happening, and the need to know overall workloads, so that current bottlenecks can be identified and dealt with. Depending on the objective in a particular application, either or both of these aspects may be relevant.

Merging the Characteristics

For a graphical representation of the result, numeric values can be assigned to the twelve WACS characteristics, and the resulting profile of a particular application can be plotted on a "radar chart" – see Figure 1. By itself, this is simply another way of representing what is already known. However, the profile can then be mapped onto the profile for similar workflow application types which will provide a better feel for how typical a particular application is within its "type".

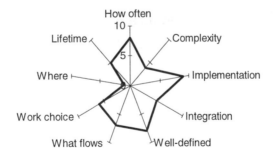

Figure 1   An Example WACS Profile for a Workflow Application

A common way of classifying workflow applications at a high level is to split them into four broad types: Production, Administrative, Collaborative, and Ad hoc. Inevitably, applications within each of these four types exhibit common traits. For example, in production workflow applications, the business process will be "fairly" to "very" well defined (WACS 5), whereas in an *ad hoc* workflow application the process will not be predefined at all, the application providing no more than a framework for individuals to flow their own work.

In this way, each type of workflow application can be given typical values for each WACS characteristic, and then plotted resulting in a band on the radar chart. Figure 2 shows the results for production and *ad hoc* workflow types.

Mapping the WACS profile of a specific workflow application onto these generic profiles will then show up where an application might differ from the norm – perhaps pointing to an aspect which needs particular attention when reviewing requirements with potential suppliers.

There are many common aspects between workflow applications and types of IT system. But there are aspects which are unique as well. It is these which WACS addresses, with a view to reducing risk in implementation and extending the success of workflow systems yet further.

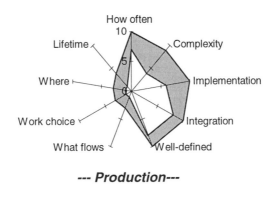

--- *Production*---

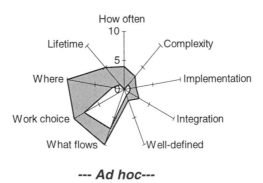

--- *Ad hoc*---

Figure 2　WACS Profiles for Production and Ad hoc Workflow Applications

What is Workflow Enabling?

Jon Pyke
Staffware plc

The primary objective of Workflow Enabling is to provide routing capabilities to new and existing applications thereby fully integrating them into a single environment. This means that an application can be used as part of a larger business process. So how does Workflow Enabling work?

Methods of Workflow Enabling

Current technology provides three methods of workflow enabling an existing application.

The first method would be utilized in a database-based architecture. The existing system will access and update the database as it does now, the workflow engine will concurrently access the same database and once a predefined change is detected (record added, updated, etc.) the workflow will be initiated. For example, supposing the workflow enabled system provides a link between the Sales Order Processing system and the Stock Control/Purchasing system. When the workflow element detects a stock level falling below a predefined reorder level, a Stock Reordering procedure can be automatically initiated, rather than a report being produced which results in a user having to scan the report, detect the need to reorder and manually start the process. This approach could enable organizations to run lower stock levels, reduce potential errors with reordering and reduce costs. Using Interorganizational workflow could even automatically initiate the supplier's workflow system to begin the necessary procedures to deliver within the required timescales.

A less obvious method of integrating existing applications into the workflow environment can be via messaging services, such as electronic mail. The workflow engine will monitor the mail system and react once a certain type of message is received. Messages can be simple forms for routing through an organization depending on content, deadlines, etc., or even specific request messages, i.e. those which are designed to initiate a specific instance of the workflow. This method provides significant benefits and advantages when trying to tie many disparate systems together. Message based workflow integration will become increasingly important in conjunction with the Internet.

The final method of integrating existing systems into the workflow environment applies, in the main, to the client/server environment. By having a workflow engine capable of responding to interprocess communications, it will be possible to instigate workflow procedures using such methods as Object Request Brokers, Named Pipes, Remote Procedure Calls and other client/server architectures.

The above suggestions will enable organizations to implement workflow processing without having to rewrite or discard existing systems. It will also assist in integrating existing systems into a single environment. If the workflow engine is able to provide the user interface, or communicate directly with the user interface of choice, it will be possible to have a consistent look and feel to applications right across the enterprise – with all the benefits and advantages that brings to staff flexibility and reduced training investment.

Workflow as an Enabling Technology

In order for us to understand how these systems will be implemented and how they will differ from what appears to be the current understanding of workflow, a new approach to workflow thinking is required.

The notion that workflow in some way only relates to document imaging and forms processing, needs to change. The term "document" needs to be interpreted in its widest sense, to encompass all aspects of a company's information. Once this is understood, workflow can be viewed and used as a tool to bind and deliver applications to the end users in a proactive and rules-driven environment. What this means in practical terms is that the user interface to the workflow system will become less and less important. Workflow automation will become an enabling technology, part of the organization's infrastructure, rather than a self contained, distinct technology. User interaction will still have its uses, especially in those instances where the workflow is an *ad hoc* application such as a simple purchase requisition and authorization system rather than critical line-of-business applications.

Only when the thinking changes, and potential adopters of workflow see it as a mechanism for bringing together what they already have, will the promise of the technology be fulfilled. It is changing; the author's own experience shows that few of the recent successes have been developed in isolation. System integrators are also seeing that the technology can be used as a way of quickly reengineering the way in which companies derive benefit from their existing investments.

It is vital for those critical line-of-business high volume applications that the integration capabilities of the selected workflow solution, coupled with the way in which the workflow is initiated, must be at the top of the selection criteria.

The Benefits of Workflow Enabling

What are the benefits of Workflow Enabling, and why is it so vital? The answer may be obvious, but it is worth examining these reasons in more detail.

One of the essential elements of workflow automation is the ability to integrate with existing, or "legacy", systems. Indeed, workflow without extensive integration capabilities makes little or no sense. Workflow automation can be considered as a set of software tools whose primary aim is to collect documents and information from one environment and move them on to the next person or system in the process. Integrating the workflow application with line-of-business applications is one of the most critical aspects to consider when evaluating a particular system. Workflow is the glue that binds the systems and environments together.

These integration capabilities need to cover all aspects of the business process. It is almost inevitable that systems currently utilized to meet the business requirements will be integrated into the automated procedures at some stage. For example, the Stationery Requisition procedure may appear to be completely isolated from other, mainstream, business applications such as Purchasing Ordering or Stock Control. However, consider the scenario where the procedure for purchasing new office equipment is automated by a workflow system. The procedure could ensure that correct level of authorization is obtained (by accessing the Human Resource system), update the Assets Register records with the new serial number and depreciation costs (in the case of Capital Expenditure) and service contract details, etc., whilst at the same time updating the accounting systems, for cheque processing and the purchase ledger. The organization could be sure that every aspect of Capital Expenditure is handled in a consistent and timely way by one single system.

When workflow automation is considered alongside a Business Process Reengineering (BPR) project many take the view, which some pundits encourage, that legacy systems should be discarded in favor of brand new ones. This line of thinking results in organizations feeling forced to obliterate and replace what they currently use. Clearly this approach can be costly, very risky, unnecessary and difficult to implement, and could possibly be one of the main reasons why the high level of interest in workflow is not resulting in high levels of implementation.

The apparent confusion concerning investment in legacy systems, and how they can be used in conjunction with workflow automation and BPR, is causing concern. To remove this fear, and increase the level of payback achieved from workflow automation and BPR, ways need to be found to protect investment in existing IT systems. There is no suggestion that retaining existing systems should override the potential for change, but retention must be considered along with every other aspect of the business processes under review.

Suppliers of workflow automation need to change this way of thinking, and look at the retention of existing systems to be an essential element in the BPR exercise. Those considering workflow need take a much wider perspective, and look at the technology as a mechanism for binding the existing environment together into a single, virtual, system – one which retains all the benefits of the old, whilst profiting from the efficiency and ease of use of the new. Workflow is the glue, the tool to deliver full systems integration.

What we need to do is to workflow-enable existing, relevant, systems. In this way workflow automation can be seen as an enabling technology. However, it is not just about the technology, it is much more than that – it is a notion, an environment which enables technology and an organization's procedures to merge together, to integrate into a consistent and seamless range of business processes and to understand how those procedures and processes help an organization to meet its business objectives.

Workflow enabling the enterprise ensures that organizations will benefit from:

- Consistent handling of work
- Consistent decision making
- Maximized return on investments from legacy systems
- Improved management control
- Reduced vulnerability
- Minimized risk

Integrating Workflow Systems and the World Wide Web

Herbert Groiss, Johann Eder
Institut für Informatik, Universität Klagenfurt, Austria

This article presents a prototype workflow management system which integrates workflow management with the World Wide Web. Incentives for addressing this area include the need to support distributed companies, and links between different organizations.

Introduction

Workflow systems are a key technology for supporting the management of processes as requested by modern organizational approaches. Several workflow management products are already on the market with a different set of features and different degrees of support (see [GHS 1995] for an overview). Although there is an increasing number of success stories, there are still several technical problems to solve. One of the urgent issues is to increase the openness and interoperability of workflow systems in several directions:

- Companies spread over many distributed locations need to be integrated. Some applications link together more than 4,000 sites, geographically distributed, using heterogeneous platforms [MAGK 1995]
- Interfaces to users outside the organizations must be available – a business process typically starts *outside* an organization, for example by submitting requests or orders
- Workflow systems of different companies should be able to cooperate in business processes

We present the prototype workflow management system Panta Rhei which takes care of the demands outlined above by using the World Wide Web (WWW) as the medium for interaction with the system. The Internet and the WWW are widely available and used and many users are familiar with these media. Employing these systems as a front end to a workflow management system and as communication vehicle for the exchange of forms (documents), we can easily meet the demands outlined above.

The Panta Rhei[1] System

We demonstrate the integration of the WWW with workflow systems on our prototype Panta Rhei. In this system the definition of workflows relies on the form flow metaphor [HEA 1990]. Within a single organization, the coordination between the tasks is achieved by forwarding forms which contain the data necessary for performing a task.

The communication between two (or more) enterprises is typically handled through exchange of documents (orders, bills, etc.). The reception of a document initiates or continues a business process on the receiver's side. Sending a document to another enterprise is a (partial) result of a business process. Therefore, we can also use the form flow metaphor for the cooperation of workflows in different organizations.

The Panta Rhei workflow system is completely integrated with the Web; it can send and receive forms, and every user interaction is done via a WWW browser. The workflow management system consists of three parts. The *HTTP server* is the interface between the user and the workflow engine. Requests from the user, which are interpreted as workflow procedures, result in calls to the corresponding procedure of the workflow engine. The *workflow engine* is a collection of procedures which are invoked from the HTTP server. They usually connect the database and retrieve or update some data stored there. The *database management system* holds all information relevant for the execution of processes. This includes the static information about document structures and process definitions as well as the dynamic information of processes, like contents of forms, state of processes, etc.

The various types of interaction with a workflow system over the Internet are described in the next section.

The Modes of Interaction

Communication between business partners has many aspects. A customer can view information about an organization, start a business process, make further interaction by exchanging documents, monitor the progress of the process, or interact directly with the workflow system as a registered user. Each of these modes of communication can be performed using the Web.

---

[1]Heraklit: "Everything flows".

The simplest mode of communication with an organization on the Web is browsing information about the company (products, services, address, etc.). A workflow system is not needed for this kind of interaction, but providing online information is a precondition for interacting electronically and giving the customer the information and motivation (advertising!) to contact the organization.

Initialization of a Process

The initialization of a business process is usually triggered from outside the organization. Examples are orders, applications, registrations, reservations and many others. Enabling the initializer of a process to start the process directly over the Internet saves a lot of time and costs. Moreover, when the customer starts the process by interacting with the workflow system and its helper applications – for example an online catalog, store systems, or price calculations – he can be provided with all necessary available information. The customer can be supported to provide all data needed from him to make the handling of the case more efficient and reduce communication costs. In the workflow system the documents can be routed to the person or department responsible for handling them.

In Panta Rhei processes can be initialized by sending HTML forms to the workflow server. These forms can be generated by the workflow system or any other applications.

Cooperation

Once initialized, most processes need further communication between the partners. Three different modes are possible: (a) the person dealing with the process sends a message to the initializer of the process, (b) the customer sends additional information to the workflow system, (c) the customer wants to monitor the progress of the initialized case.

Conventional interaction via electronic data interchange (EDI) requires that the business partners agree on the protocols used to exchange documents. The Web allows an open architecture in using the HTTP protocol for exchanging documents and HTML for formatting these documents. With the same mechanism as above, the sending of forms, we organize the interaction between two workflow systems.

Every participating workflow system provides a description of the forms it can receive, which process will be started on receiving, and whether it answers with a form and of which type this answer form is. Additionally, the interface description should have an entry for receiving a form of the type *message* and start an email-like process on receiving. This ensures that a workflow system can receive all kinds of messages and allows for the full correspondence between two organizations to be done using the workflow systems without specifying any process. This contrasts with other approaches where the processes have to be well defined before interaction is possible [CCPP 1996; BLWW 1995]. Using standardized documents, for example the UN/EDIFACT standard [Rap 1995], a high degree of initial interoperability can be achieved.

Sending documents to a partner who has no workflow system installed, is done by email. Using a mail reader that can interpret HTML documents, like the **Netscape browser** [Net 1995], the partner can read the mail, fill in the attached forms and submit them in one window. No proprietary software is needed on the client side.

Distributed Execution

In distributed or multinational organizations it is necessary to handle business processes which can be executed distributed over several locations. Although it would be possible to have a single workflow server and connect to it over the Internet, it is not feasible for performance and security reasons. The exchanging of forms is used for implementing distributed execution, too.

Monitoring

The user who initialized a process or performed a task of a process should be able to see what happened with "his" process. For this purpose a monitoring component allowing users to inspect the processes depending on their roles and privileges is necessary.

On the other hand, a system operator needs to monitor the state of all processes, the individual work lists, etc. Using databases for storing the process information and WWW browsers as interface allows a simple implementation of such an add-on.

Moreover, the possibilities of hypertext representation allow new kinds of presentation: for example, the user can browse through process descriptions with hyper-links to the tasks and the involved users and roles. The size of work lists may be represented by bar charts, generated on the fly from the process data.

User Interface

Complete integration of a workflow system into the Web is possible when WWW browsers are used as the standard user interface. Figure 1 shows this component of the Panta Rhei system. After identification, the registered user receives a "tasklist"; this page contains all tasks which are currently assigned to this user or a role in which the user is in. In the second case the task has been broadcast to all users belonging to the role with the intention that one of them takes the task for processing it. This can be done by clicking on the "take it" link. Tasks already assigned to the user can be processed and are finished by pressing the "submit" link. The icons in the document column are links to the corresponding documents. Process name and task name in the second and third columns are links to the process and task description.

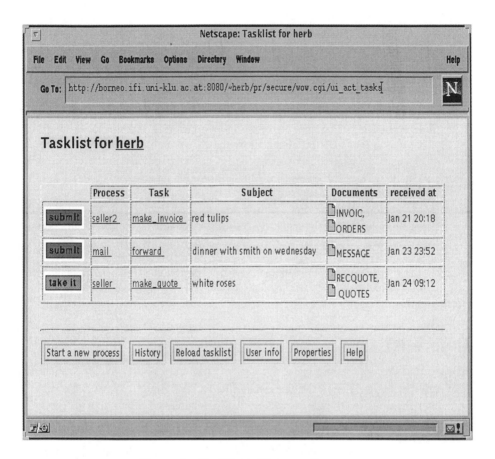

Figure 1 Tasklist in Netscape Browser

Conclusions

We have presented a methodology for integrating workflow systems into the Web. Our approach is evolutionary and allows various degrees of interoperability. Everybody who has access to the WWW and an email address can communicate with the workflow system. If he or she has a workflow system too, they can use it for interaction with other systems without specifying any process. The advantages of this approach are:

1. Support for different platforms. It would need a lot of manpower to write and maintain clients for different platforms and it is impossible to rival the developers of WWW browsers in porting clients to other machines or operating systems. Moreover, on different platforms users can work with their favourite browser.

2. Users are familiar with the technology. Web browsers are widely used for getting information from the Internet, therefore most potential workflow users know them; the browsers are widely available, some of them even public domain (e.g. **Mosaic**) or part of the operating system (e.g. in **OS/2 Warp**). Online help and documentation is available. Switching from performing a workflow task to other work is easy with the interface.

3. Mobile computing. The support of different platforms and the loose coupling between the server and the client allow the distributed execution of a task. A user can start the execution of a task on his or her computer in the office, save the forms to a floppy disk, work offline at home or on a journey and reload the results from another computer.

4. Simple implementation. In addition to the advantage of no client-side implementation, the implementation on the server side is easy, because many commercial database management systems already offer WWW gateways.

A prototype of the system is implemented using the Oracle database management system, the **WOW Oracle-Web gateway** [ORA 1995] and the **NCSA http server** [NCSA 1995].

References

[BLWW 1995]
> Bons, R. W. H., Lee, R. M., Wagenaar, R. W., Wrigley, C. D. Modelling inter-organizational trade procedures using documentary Petri nets. In: *Proc. 28th Hawaii Int. Conf. on System Sciences*, Volume III, 1995, pp. 189–198.

[CCPP 1996]
> Casati, F., Ceri, S., Pernici, B., Pozzi, G. Semantic WorkFlow interoperability. In: *Conf. on Extending Database Technology*, 1996.

[EGN 1994]
> Eder, J., Groiss, H., Nekvasil, H. A workflow system based on active Databases. in: Chroust, G., Benczur, A. (Eds), *CON 94: Workflow Management: Challenges, Paradigms and Products*, Oldenburg, Linz, Austria, 1994.

[GHS 1995]
> Georgakopoulos, D., Hornick, M., Sheth, A. An overview of workflow management: from process modeling to workflow automation infrastructure, *Distributed and Parallel Databases*, 3(2), 1995.

[HEA 1990]
> Hämmäinen, H., Eloranta, E., Alasuvanto, J. Distributed form management, *ACM Transactions on Information Systems*, 8(1), January 1990.

[MAGK 1995]
> Mohan, C. Alonso, G. Günthör, R., Kamath, M. Exotica: a research perspective on workflow management systems, *Bulletin of the Technical Committee on Data Engineering*, 18(1), March 1995.

[NCSA 1995]
NCSA, NCSA httpd. http://hoohoo.ncsa.uiuc.edu/, 1995.
[Net 1995]
Netscape, *Netscape Browser 2.0*. http://home.netscape.com, 1995.
[ORA 1995]
ORACLE, *The Oracle World Wide Web Interface Kit*,
http://dozer.us.oracle.com:8080/, 1995.
[Rap 1995]
UN/EDIFACT Rapporteurs, *United Nations Directories for Electronic Data Interchange for Administration, Commerce and Transport*, United Nations, 1995, http://www.unicc.org/unece/trade/untid/Welcome.html.

Organization and Role Models for Workflow Processes

Walter Rupietta
Siemens Nixdorf Informationssysteme AG

This article proposes a framework for organization modeling and a concept of process-related roles allowing workflow processes to be connected to organizational entities. In the first section, a framework for organization modeling is presented. Organizational structures are modeled using concepts for employees, positions, organizational units, organizational roles and authorities. The second section describes a concept for process-related roles in conjunction with an organizational model.

Organization Modeling

The organizational structure of an enterprise or public authority sets the framework for its business processes – both manual processes and workflow processes. Organization determines when and how tasks are processed and by whom. It includes static structure as well as the dynamics of business processes taking place in the framework of the static structure. Organization determines division of labor, official channels and cooperation. The support of regulated communication and cooperation between members of an enterprise in workflow management systems requires that organizational rules be closely followed. Workflow processes automate portions of business processes. Consequently, they need information on the enterprise organization in order to fulfill their tasks according to the underlying organizational structure.

Workflow management systems enable the implementation of workflow processes, i.e. the dynamic aspects of organization. Organizational models are used for the analysis and simulation of business processes and for related purposes. They can also be employed in workflow processes and other applications to follow organizational rules. An organizational model which extends traditional concepts of business organization theory by the addition of the generic concept of authority is introduced in this section as a basis for assigning workflow process activities to persons that perform them.

Required Features of Organizational Models

Traditional concepts of business organization theory require that the hierarchy of organizational units reflect the decomposition of an enterprise's business goal into tasks and sub-tasks and their grouping into operational units. Structuring is guided by Tayloristic principles and basically consists of grouping similar sub-tasks into operational units, resulting in business process execution distributed across the organization. Hierarchy is introduced to maintain the overall connection between individual sub-tasks and to manage complexity. Consequently, the hierarchy of organizational units and positions contains information on responsibilities and authorizations of the employees with respect to the task decomposition.

Business process reengineering aspires to radically optimize business processes by redesigning and reallocating them from scratch. As the focus shifts from functional structure to processes, organizational structures tend to flatten with respect to the hierarchy of organizational units and positions. The tasks of individual employees in turn are enriched. Employees perform more holistic tasks in the context of business processes in contrast to former Tayloristic structures.

When hierarchies are flattened, the information they represented is lost. At the same time, the authorities of individual positions or employees within the organization become more differentiated. Therefore an organizational model must represent not only the traditional hierarchy of positions and organizational units but also the *network of authorities* which can replace the information lost in a flattened hierarchy. The assignment of work and authorizations is no longer based on the hierarchy but depends on the individual authorities.

A Modeling Framework

An organizational model represents the organizational structure of an enterprise or public authority in terms of persons (employees), positions, organizational units, organizational roles and authorities. It incorporates the hierarchy of organizational units and positions as well as the assignment of organizational roles and authorities.

In this article we will present a basic model of related object classes representing the corresponding concepts without detail. Examples of commercially available organizational models can be found in [Rup 1994] and [WFB+ 1995]. Basic entities of an organizational model are described in Table 1.

Table 1 Basic Entities of an Organizational Model

Employees	The people working in the enterprise. Employees are integrated into the organization by assignment to positions. They may act as *workflow participants* in (workflow) processes.
Organizational units	Organizational units are sets of positions with common or related tasks grouped together to form a larger operational unit. Organizational units can be subordinate to other organizational units and can themselves have subordinate organizational units, i.e. they can form *hierarchies*.
Positions	A position represents the workplace of an employee and thus is a kind of *"abstract employee"*. Positions are the basic elements that constitute an organization.
Organizational roles	Organizational functions such as department manager, accounting clerk or secretary are assigned to positions. An organizational role refers to all individuals who have a certain set of characteristic tasks or authorities in common.
Authorities	Authority is a generic term subsuming *authorizations* for tasks like signatures, *rights* to access or use resources, *responsibilities* for specific tasks, areas or topics of work and any combination of these elements.

Organizational structures are formed by instantiating these entities and connecting them according to the diagram shown in Figure 1. Organizational units can be subordinate to other organizational units, forming hierarchies (hierarchical subordination). Every position belongs to an organizational unit (position assignment). A position can be occupied by an employee (employee assignment) and can play an organizational role (role assignment). Employees, positions, organizational units and roles can have authorities (authority assignment). An authority can be assigned to an arbitrary number of employees, positions, organizational units and roles.

The entities and their relationships provide the *vocabulary* for describing organizational structures. The model possesses sufficient expressive power to describe real enterprise organizational structures. At the same time it is flexible enough to model small workgroup organizations and their network of authorities as well as large hierarchically structured organizations.

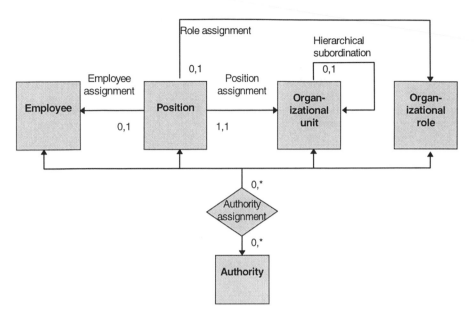

Figure 1   Entity/Relationship Diagram of a Basic Organizational Model
(cardinalities of relations given in min,max notation)

As an example, the model makes it possible to express statements like "Jones is the manager of the accounting department. He is authorized to sign payment orders up to 5000 EURO. The accounting department is part of the internal administration section." This statement can be modeled by defining an employee object named "Jones", which is assigned to a position object in the organizational unit object "Accounting". The latter is subordinate to the organizational unit object "Internal Administration". An organizational role named "Manager" can be assigned to Jone's position. An authority object representing the authorization for signing payment orders can be defined and assigned to the "Manager" role.

Process-Related Roles

A connection between such an organizational model and a workflow process can be established via the concept of a *process-related role*. Basically, a process-related role is a simple placeholder whose purpose is to provide an abstraction for the actor (person or application) assigned to a workflow process activity or any other task related to a workflow process. However, combined with an organizational model, it can be associated with organizational entities and relationships and thus become a very powerful mechanism for defining generic workflow processes that automatically adapt to specific organizational structures.

Roles at Definition Time

In a workflow process definition, a process-related role is a placeholder (or a name) for the performer of a process-related task, especially a workflow process activity. "Workflow participant" is such a process-related role. At definition time, the process-related roles for all activities of the process are defined. Such a definition is a *profile* that specifies a set of candidates as potential performers who are responsible and authorized to perform the corresponding activity during process execution.

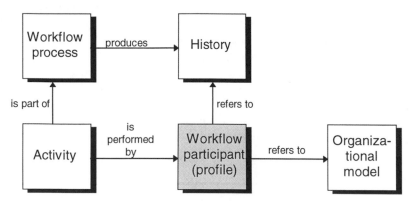

Figure 2   Connecting Workflow Processes and Organizational Models

The profile (see Figure 2) defining the process-related role of a workflow participant can be an expression referring to:

- The process history (e.g. performer of any preceding activity)
- Elements and relationships from an organizational model (e.g. an employee with the organizational role "Manager" and the authority "Signature for Payment Orders")
- Non-human actors (applications), that can either be referenced as external instances or be integrated in the organizational model, expanding it to an organizational and resources model
- An application-specific function that returns an identification of a user and is called when the profile is evaluated

Such a profile selects the set of potential performers of the activity. In this way, workflow processes can be tied to entities of the enterprise organizational structure and do not depend on specific users. Workflow participants can be specified with reference to positions, organizational roles or authorities, for example, and not to specific employees. If the assignments of employees to positions or assignments of authorities change, the workflow process definition remains unaffected because it relies on abstract concepts rather than on concrete users.

Roles at Execution Time

At execution time, each executable workflow activity instance must be assigned to (potential) workflow participants. This is done by instantiating the corresponding process-related role, i.e. the profile is evaluated to find the set of potential performers of the activity. Given this set, the workflow enactment service can employ an active or passive strategy for the actual assignment of work (see Table 2). Depending on the complexity of the profile, the evaluation of a process-related role can be a rather complicated procedure.

The role concept enables dynamic assignment of actors to workflow process activities, since the evaluation of a process-related role at execution time may result in a different set of candidates than the evaluation at process definition time. Thus, while changes in the organizational structure do not necessarily require modification of process definitions, process execution nonetheless follows organizational regulations valid at execution time.

Table 2   Strategies for Instantiating Process-Related Roles

Active strategy	The workflow enactment service actively selects one of the candidates and puts the corresponding work item on his or her work list. Selection may occur according to strategies for work balancing. The selected candidate can be automatically notified of the arrival of a new work item.
Passive strategy	The corresponding work item is added to the work lists of all candidates. One of them eventually chooses to perform the activity. This means that each process-related role is like a hat which may be picked up by certain users if it fits them. What happens at the time of process execution is that one of these candidates really picks up the hat, plays the role and performs the activity.

The process-related role concept presented so far is not limited to workflow activities, but can be extended to comprise other roles related to a workflow process. For every process a supervisor role can be defined in the same way as the workflow participants of the individual activities of the process.

Conclusion

In its current version, the WfMC Reference Model makes no assumptions on how workflow participants are assigned to activities. This topic is covered by the organizational and role model presented in this article as a possible extension of the WfMC model. The concept is useful, for example, in banks: authorities can be defined for different levels to automatically assign activities within a loan application workflow process to the appropriate persons depending on the amount of money involved. This ensures that an employee who is assigned a task is also given the necessary authorizations and rights to perform it. Signing and stand-in arrangements can be implemented based on the organizational structure. The major elements of the concepts in this article have been implemented in the WorkParty system described in [Rup 1995]. Experience shows that describing existing organizational structures or designing new structures in terms of the organizational and role model is an important first step in introducing a workflow management process.

The use of an organizational model is not limited to workflow processes. Arbitrary applications, including, of course, client workflow applications as well as invoked workflow applications, can refer to the organizational model to adapt themselves to specific regulations of an enterprise or to implement an organization-dependent access control scheme. This can be achieved using a comparable role model.

References

[IK1988]
> Ishii, H., Kubota, K. Office procedure knowledge base for organization office work support. in: *Office Information Systems*, The Design Process. Working Conference, IFIP WG 8.4, August 15-17, 1988, Linz, Austria, pp. 40–57.

[Rup 1994]
> Rupietta, W. Organization models for cooperative office applications, in: Karagiannis, D. (Ed.), *Database and Expert Systems Applications. 5th International Conference, DEXA '94*, Athens, Greece, 7–9 September, 1994, *Proceedings*, Springer-Verlag, Berlin, Heidelberg, New York, 1994, pp. 114–124.

[Rup 1995]
> Rupietta, W. Flexible Geschäftsprozesse mit Workflow-Anwendungen, in:

Proc. of Conf. *"Geschäftsprozesse und Workflow-Systeme in der evolutionären Unternehmung"*, Bamberg, October 1995.
[WFB+ 1995]
      Wächter, H., Fritz, F. J., Berthold, A. Drittler, B., Eckert, H., Gerstner, R., Götzinger, R., Krause, R., Schaeff, A., Schlögel, C., Weber, R., Modellierung und Ausführung flexibler Geschäftsprozesse mit SAP Business Workflow 3.0, in: *Proc. GI/SI-Jahrestagung 1995*, Zurich, September 1995.
[WfMC1994]
      Glossary, WfMC, Brussels, November 1994.

Reusing Tasks Between Workflow Applications

Thomas S. Magg
Lucent Technologies

The ability to realistically reuse software has long been an objective among developers. In workflow systems, where different applications use common tasks, those process steps can become reusable components which can be linked with others via the workflow manager to create new applications more quickly and cheaply. This article describes methods of cataloguing common process steps to facilitate their reuse.

Introduction

Workflow Management is becoming a hot item in corporations looking for more efficient ways to automate their business processes [Sta 1995]. A workflow manager allows a process model to be defined and then acts as the engine that executes the process model. A workflow manager abstracts the control and the monitoring aspects of an application. The process model can be changed without having to change the workflow manager. The workflow manager is a reusable software component.

The process model consists of process steps and their dependencies. A process step can invoke a transaction in an application, called a task. Common tasks become reusable components of an application that can be linked together via the workflow manager and the process model to create an application cheaply and quickly. In a workflow manager framework, an end-user can define both the process model and the linking of process steps to the appropriate tasks.

To aid the end-user in linking the process steps to tasks, a catalog or library of tasks must be available. This paper describes methods of cataloging common tasks to facilitate their reuse across process models.

Workflow Management

The term "workflow manager" lacks a clear definition [Lin 1995]. There are several groups working to provide workflow standards [OSI 1995] [Ubo 1995]. This section sets the context for the rest of this paper by describing a typical workflow management system, and how through a process model it will interact with an application.

A workflow manager is a software component that:

- Guides work items though a process model consisting of process steps
- Updates tracking data as the process steps complete

A work item is a data store that is maintained and managed by an application. The work item is what is processed through a process model, and which follows a process model through to completion. Examples of a work item are a trouble ticket, service request, or a sales contract. Examples of an application are a trouble management, order management, or sales negotiation system. The workflow manager will invoke transactions or tasks against a work item via the application.

A process model is a definition of a business process. It is a series of process steps and the dependencies between the steps. Typically, a process model is defined using a graphical tool. Process steps can be either tasks, logical steps, or procedural steps. A task can be either automatic or manual. Logical steps are either OR or AND steps and are used for parallelism and synchronization. Procedural steps are a reference to another process model and facilitate reuse of common process models.

A task can have one or more outcomes that will guide the work item through the process. For instance, a task may have SUCCESS and FAILURE outcomes defined. The process model will have branches to other tasks defined based on the possible outcomes. A task that succeeds will take the SUCCESS branch, and a task that fails will take the FAILURE branch.

In addition to guiding a work item through a process model, a workflow manager can perform project management function such as assigning manual tasks to workers, tracking the progress of the work item against its milestones, providing appropriate notification when the progress of a work item is in jeopardy, and providing process metrics.

A key tenet of a work managed solution is that a process model can easily be changed with little or no additional development. This facilitates a cycle of continuous process improvement [Sch].

A workflow manager can be considered a middleware component [Eck 1995]. Figure 1 shows a typical architecture of a system employing a workflow manager.

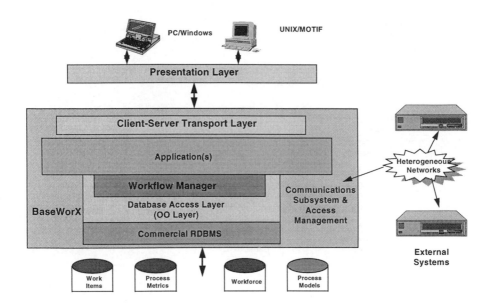

Figure 1   Typical Workflow Managed System Architecture

When the workflow manager encounters a step in a process model that is a task, it will make a call to the application, asking it to perform the appropriate transaction on a work item. This is illustrated in Figure 2. The workflow manager will provide the transaction name, the ID of the work item, the process step number, and transaction options. The transaction name and the ID of the work item are needed so that the application knows what to do, and what to do it on. The transaction options provide specialization for the transaction as described below.

On return, the application must provide the ID of the work item, and process step number for reference purposes. The outcome returned is used to determine which process steps to take next in the process model. The interface between the workflow manager and the application is the same for all application tasks that are invoked.

The set of tasks that are able to be performed by an application can be defined in a task catalog.

Figure 3 illustrates the relationships within the framework so far discussed.

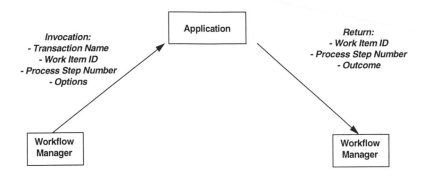

Figure 2   Task Invocation

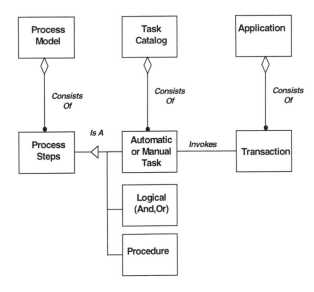

Figure 3   Workflow Manager Framework

Task Catalog

For each task in a process model, the process modeler must either:

- Reuse an existing task
- Make it a generic manual task
- Develop a new application transaction to associate with the task

To facilitate the reuse of existing tasks, the process modeler must be aware of what tasks are available to reuse. When the process modeler associates a process step with a task, they should be presented with a list of available tasks and the descriptions of the tasks. This can be called a task catalog. The task catalog provides documentation about each task. This documentation promotes reuse because it provides the process modeler with an understanding on what each task does and how to use it in a task model [AT&T 1994] [Ant 1994].

A task catalog format was used to provide a consistent means of defining tasks in the task catalog. Each task entry in the catalog consists of the following fields:

- Name – the name of the task and a brief one-line description
- Synopsis – the name of the task followed by all of its options
- Description – a description of what the task does
- Options – a description of each option that can be provided to the task, and what values are valid for each of the options
- Outcomes – a listing of the outcomes that the task can return
- Work Item Types – a listing of the types of work item that the task can be invoked against
- Availability – what release the task is at
- References – references to the detailed requirements for the task

An example task catalogue entry is shown in Figure 4. The task catalog should be available online with appropriate browsing capability. In order to find a task to reuse, the process modeler will locate a task that matches the description of what needs to be done. Next the process modeler needs to verify that the work item type(s) that the process model will support are supported by the task, and that it is available in the application(s) that the workflow manager will interact with.

Examples of tasks that might be found in a generic catalog are shown in Figure 5.

If a process engineer determines that a needed task is not present in the task catalog, they can make a request to Development to add it. If the missing task is general enough that it is expected to be used in more than one flow, it should be added to the general task catalog for future reuse. If the task is customer specific, or proprietary, it can be added to a customer-specific task catalog that can be used in conjunction with a general task catalog.

The task should be developed to support as many different work item types as relevant and practical to widen the scope of its potential reuse. Figure 6 shows the overall process for reusing and creating new tasks.

When creating a new task in the task catalog, two concepts must be taken into consideration: Task Granularity and Task Generalization.

FaxWI   **Last Update: Aug 12, 1995**

Name
FaxWI - Faxes a copy of a Work Item

Synopsis
FaxWI dest type [retry]

Description
This task sends a fax, whose contents are specified by type, to a destination specified by dest. Based on type of fax, the appropriate Work Item Attributes are sent.
If the send of the fax fails, this task will retry, a retry number of times. If after the last retry, the send fails, a failure outcome is returned; otherwise, a successful outcome is returned.

Options
dest - The destination to send the fax to which is either a telephone number, the name of an attribute in the Work Item that contains a fax telephone number.
type - The type of fax. Valid Values: Complete or Non-Proprietary Subset
retry - The number of times to retry sending the fax before failing

Outcomes
1 - Fax Succesfully Sent
98 - Fax Number Not Present in Work Item
99 - Fax Send Failed

Example
FaxWI 908-555-1212 Complete 7 - fax the Complete Work Item to 908-555-1212 retry up to 7 times

Work Item Types
Trouble Ticket, Insurance Contract

Availability
Application A Release 5.5, Application B Release 2.4

References
See requirements XYZ

Figure 4   Task Catalog Example

Task Granularity

The amount of functionality provided by a task is an important consideration when defining the task. At one extreme, a process model could consist of just one task that does everything. At the other extreme, a process model could consist of thousands of tasks performing atomic operations of disk reads and writes. The trade-off here is between process model size and control. For example, Figure 7 shows three functions A, B, C that need to be performed. They can be performed as either one task, or three separate tasks.

There are several reasons to "granularize" and have three separate tasks: 1) flexibility, (2) tracking, and (3) error handling. Figure 8 illustrates how the three separate tasks may be rearranged to allow B and C to be performed in parallel when A completes. For tracking purposes it may be important to know how long each of the functions is taking. For error handling, if task B was to fail, the process model may want to retry or skip B. If the three functions are combined into one task, this would not be possible.

- **ActivateChildrenWIs**
- **Alarms**
- **Assign**
- **BlockCancel**
- **Close**
- **CreateJob**
- **CreateWI**
- **Delay**
- **DisplayWI**
- **GetAttribute**
- **ManualCmp**
- **MilestoneComp**
- **MilestoneRem**
- **Notify**

- **ReactivateMilestone**
- **Recalc**
- **Reconcile**
- **Refer**
- **RetrieveWI**
- **Serial**
- **Service**
- **SetStatus**
- **StatusJob**
- **SupressJeopardy**
- **Suspend**
- **SuspendRelatedWIs**
- **UpdateDB**
- **UpdateSvcId**

Figure 5 Example Tasks

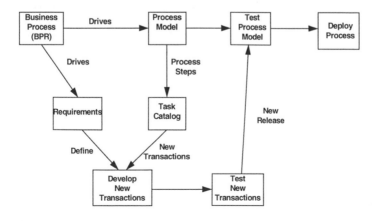

Figure 6 Process Model Creation

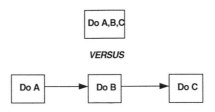

Figure 7   Task Granularity

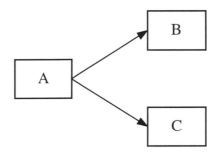

Figure 8   Granular Task Flexibility

There are also reasons not to "granularize": (1) if A, B, C must always occur in the same sequence, granularizing would only provide the process modeler the opportunity to model the flow incorrectly; and (2) to minimize the number of task entries in the task catalog.

Task Generalization

The generality of a task is another factor to consider in facilitating the reuse of a task. The workflow manager to application interface described above allows options to be passed into a task. The options passed in enable the grouping of functionally similar tasks into one task, with the options determining what specific functionality is needed for a specific instance of the task in a process model. For instance, we could have three specialized tasks as follows:

- Send Work Item to System X
- Send Work Item to System Y
- Send Work Item to System Z

Or we could have one generalized task "Send Work Item to System" with an option of "Destination" where destination can be either X, Y or Z.

Generalizing similar groups of tasks aids task catalog usability and task development. By generalizing similar groups of tasks, the number of tasks in a task catalog can be kept to a more manageable size. Similar tasks are also likely to have a large overlap of common code. For instance, in the send example above, the only differences among the three specialized sends may be the destination of the system and the protocol to use in communicating with that system. The retrieval of the work item, the formatting and sending of the work item data may all be the same.

There is an important balance in generalizing tasks as there was with task granularity. You could have one generalized task that does everything based on the options passed in, or you could have so many specialized tasks that it could be overwhelming. An appropriate medium needs to be found.

Task Generation

As middleware, a workflow manager provides for the control aspects of an application across many possible application domains. The tasks perform the functions provided by the applications. In many cases a task can be common across many domains. For instance, a task to fax a work item to a destination can be found in a telecommunications system domain as well as a financial system domain. The primary difference between the tasks in the two domains revolves around the last component of an application -- its data.

A task to fax a work item must know what attributes are needed to be sent and the format of the fax. For example, the task "FaxWI" was described above as having a type option of either "Complete" or "Non-Proprietary". The mechanics of retrieving the work item data, formatting the data, and sending it to the fax interface are the same across domains. What is different is the work item data that needs to be sent. Not only can this be different across a domain, but within a domain, a customer may want to customize or subclass the work items they plan to use.

Tasks in the task catalog should be designed as multi-use components with the requirement of being able to operate on different work items taken into consideration. Two possible ways of doing this would be (1) to have the task dynamically bind to the work item based on the combination of the type of work item and a user-managed parameter table describing what data to send and the format for each type of fax, or (2) to use a code generator to generate tasks specific to each different type of work item within a domain and across domains [HKGS]

Dynamically binding the task to a new work item type allows more flexibility, but it also requires more development effort to take into account the range of possible user flexibility that may be required.

A parameter file in conjunction with a code generator to generate tasks specific to work item types is less flexible; however, unlike introducing a new process model into a workflow managed environment, introducing a new work item or modifying an existing work item generally requires regeneration of the database and other parts of the application anyway.

Conclusion

A sampling of a set of process models defined by a typical customer using the above framework revealed the following for the 20 process models in the sample:

- Some tasks were being reused over 30 times
- Each task was being reused an average of five times

The process models represented three different domains of work items. The task catalog being used had 40 tasks defined. Although a few new tasks had to be added to the task catalog, most of the tasks needed in the 20 process models were reused from the task catalog.

Ideally, if all tasks needed by a given process model existed in the task catalog, the process could be provided immediately without any systems development.

References

[Ant 1994]
> Anthes, G. Users look for standards on reuse libraries, *Computerworld, 23* May 1994, p. 97(1).

[AT&T 1994]
> *A Guide to Designing Multiuse Components,* AT&T 365-101-600, Issue 1, April 1994.

[Eck 1995]
> Eckerson, W. Middleware vendors embrace workflow and GUIs, *Open Information Systems,* January 1995, p. 27(5).

[HKGS]
> Huston, W., Kaminski, J., Graven, J., Streger, R. *The Application of Code Generators within the ACTIVIEW Platform,* Unpublished presentation.

[Lin 1995]
> Linnet, E. Going with the flow, *Computer Weekly,* 22 June, 1995, p. 42(2).

[OSI 1995]
> Workflow Management Coalition releases first standards documents, *The OSINetter Newsletter,* April 1995, p. 34(1).

[Sch]
> Schreiber, R. Workflow imposes order on transaction processing, *Datamation,* 41(13), p. 57(3).

[Sta 1995]
> Stahl, S. Turning on the workflow: new partnerships and products rolled out, *Information Week,* 1 May 1995, p. 102(2).

[TB 1995]
  Tibbetts, J., Bernstein, B. Make reuse a reality, *Information Week,* Issue 514, 13 February, 1995, p. 76(1).
[Ubo 1995]
  Ubois, J. Meet the champions of open standards, *Midrange Systems,* 16 June, 1995, p. 35(1).

Learning from Experience in Workflow Projects

Fred van Leeuwen
Management Consultant
DCE Nederland b.v.

It seems that workflow projects need more than just automation experience and good intentions. Far too many of them are already stagnating at implementation time. If we are ever to confound the sceptics, isn't it time that we paid some serious attention to the success and failure factors? This article addresses workflow projects and their pitfalls.

The Advance of Workflow

When the conversation turns to market development, people who have spent time in workflow-land all say the same thing. Whereas 1993 was marked by information (articles and conferences) and 1994 by try-outs (non-obligatory pilots), 1995 began with the forecast that serious applications would now break through. I said as much myself on various occasions. But have the predictions proved true?

The answer to this is "Yes" and "No". There has been a clear increase in projects with objectives that went beyond the "let's see if it's technically viable" stage. On the other hand, very few implementations were actually successful. Here, in the Netherlands, we can count them literally on the fingers of one hand!

Could the IT industry have foiled us yet again? Has the wool been pulled over our eyes? Are the products still too immature? If this were so, the user organizations would have a ready-made excuse. Too bad: as we shall see, this time the malady and the cure lie mainly with themselves.

Let's try to uncover the pitfalls by looking at a few practical situations.

Council Lets Chance Slip By to Improve Production Time

Our first case comes from a county council and concerns the licensing process. Main problem was the fact that obtaining a licence took longer than it legally should. As a result, businesses felt that their interests were being jeopardized, the council ran the risk of lawsuits, and great political pressure was applied to improve the situation. The proposed workflow project would solve the problem of getting to grips with the process control. It would also provide a broad basis for the organizational changes that were needed to realize the objective. But the organizational changes fell under a separate category – in other words, it had no part in the workflow project.

The lead time of the workflow project amounted to several years. It was successfully developed by the automation department with some support from outside. But when the time came for it to be implemented, the internal circumstances had changed. The original improvements no longer had priority and the basis for implementation seemed to have vanished into thin air. For the time being, all that the multi-million investment can deliver is a sense of frustration mingled with indifference. We can learn two important lessons from this. Firstly, the longer a project lasts, the greater the chance that its objective will be outdated when the time comes for implementation. And secondly, it is dangerous to look upon a workflow project as an automation project. The only way to achieve the aim of a workflow project is by implementing a workflow management system and by adapting the organization to suit process-oriented operations. The whole affair can so easily go wrong if it is turned into two separate projects.

Paper Implementation in Indemnity Insurance

The second scenario is played out in the indemnity division of a commercial insurer. This company believed that market orientation also meant making business operations as easy as possible for the middleman. The middleman likes to deal with only one person in a company. But the company's problem was that this person had to be able to cope with a whole range of different insurance products. Workflow was seen as the solution. Tight uniformity would be brought into the production processes and each product would be so securely handled in the workflow that there would be far less dependence on the product knowledge of the contact person. Thus another aim would be realized: improved efficiency.

Before the workflow project was started, a Business Process Reengineering (BPR) study was carried out by an external agency. Blueprints for the new processes were available – but there was no follow-up plan and the implementation elements were only roughly defined. The automation department (which took no part in the BPR study) drew up its own plan which introduced not only workflow but a new administrative system as well. This was to entail the very latest technology: with reusable building blocks. As it turned out, they had bitten off more than they could chew of the apple of innovation ... nine months after the BPR study there was still no sign of development, let alone implementation.

The transition to the creative stage – actually getting down to things – never happened. Instead of steering the project along general management lines, the various disciplines started going their own way. It got back on track eventually. But, in the meantime, a lot of time and money had been invested and all that had been gained was a new formal structure for the organization.

What lesson can be learned from this? Firstly, it is not prudent to set up a BPR project with an objective that goes no farther than redesigning processes and organization. If the project manager doesn't have his sights set on realization, the project will run a high risk of stagnation. There will be little continuity in objective and approach and other people will follow their own agendas when processing the follow-up project. Secondly, this situation demonstrates that workflow must not be an automation project. The automation component is important since it plays a key role in the overall success, but it should be subordinate to the company aims. If it is not, the "neatest automation solution" may well gain the upper hand. Enter the umpteenth time-consuming project which has no practical or expedient contribution to make to the actual improvements that the company wants!

Mortgage Handling in 24 Hours – but in Fits and Starts

Our third case is a workflow classic when it comes to company processes. It concerns mortgages. The objective was to improve the control process so that a mortgage request could be dealt with in 24 hours. As in the case of the county council, experts were called in from outside and design and construction went smoothly. However, the acceptance test exposed a huge gap between the completed workflow and the way operations were run in the branch offices. The cause? The workflow was based on a concept that was developed at head-office. This led to a sizeable increase in effort and production time for a multi-million project. At the end of the day, it took two years to realize the first implementation. The reaction of the other branch offices when their turn comes still remains to be seen.

The moral of the tale? The automation expert must resist the temptation of focusing attention only on solutions to technical problems. Timely consultation with the real users is vital to ensure acceptance and suitability of the workflow.

Workflow Project Pitfalls

If we step outside the area of case history and look at other projects being carried out in our own market, we can get an overall idea of what can go wrong. The most common pitfalls are listed below under specific labels (Figure 1). We shall be

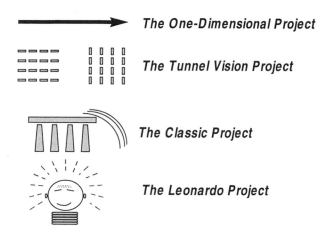

Figure 1   Some Workflow Project Labels

concentrating on the idiosyncrasies of the One-Dimensional Project, the Tunnel Vision Project, the Classic Project, the Leonardo Project, the Narcissus Project, the Unshored Bridge and the Optimistic Project. In real situations, projects are usually characterized by a combination of these.

The One-Dimensional Project

This project is dominated by one of the key specializations. Usually it's the automation expert, but other specialists can show similar preferences for getting their own way (if the management gives them the chance). Any results are more likely to be enhancements to a CV than the solution to a company problem. (Here we often see the upshot of a typical "staff" approach which creates a combination of Classic Project, Leonardo Project and Narcissus Project which will all be described later.)

The Tunnel Vision Project

The Tunnel Vision Project can be vertical or horizontal. In vertical tunnel vision we see consecutive stages being magnified to separate projects (e.g. the BPR project which was ready when there was still only a design). Horizontal tunnel vision is particularly popular in input-controlled organizations where the technology is stuffed into one project, the processes into another and the organization into a third. Everything looks as if it is under control but when it comes to the crunch only fragmentary results emerge and these do not reflect the company aims.

The Classic Project

This variation (regrettably) still applies in 95% of the cases. Although workflow gives us an instrument that delivers quick results, most of the market still works according to the philosophy of the waterfall approach (a relic from automation prehistory when functionality had to be cast in concrete). This means that the project takes too long. It is impossible to hold the attention of management and users, and often the circumstances have changed when Implementation Day finally dawns – or else the project dies an early but gentle death.

The Leonardo Project

Euphemistically known as "pilot projects", over 90% of Leonardo Projects suffer from the one-dimensional approach. It is the worst nightmare of the workflow-tool supplier who invests a small fortune in pilots in the vain hope of stockpiling user licenses. In the meantime the value-added reseller or the external consultant gets richer and even exploits the pilot to gain some experience of workflow for himself. But a pilot project Leonardo-style doesn't even get the interest of the line, let alone the commitment. In the best of cases it becomes a toy and that's where it stays.

The Narcissus Project

More workflow project labels are shown in Figure 2. In the Narcissus Project, the team members concentrate on the design and construction of a project that they themselves find thrilling, but they tend to forget that, at the end of the day, it is one person – the user – who determines whether everything works as it should. What he gets is a "theoretically correct" workflow, or at best, something which works but fails to capture his heart. The consequence is to go back to the drawing table with all the extra costs and delay, or to make do with a system that is only 50% functional.

The Unshored Bridge

In this case the project manager does not realize the implications of linking up islands (with workflow). The management and information islands have grown considerably in recent years; they are surrounded with hidden dangers which disrupt the linking of data, systems and stages. They are often difficult to detect because no one has an overall picture. The question is: can the project manager unearth them in time? If he can, he will make space in his planning for further analysis and solutions. If he can't, he is working on incorrect assumptions and the workflow will simply "hang in the air" or (as happens more often) he will spot the problem too late and then overrun the project time and budget.

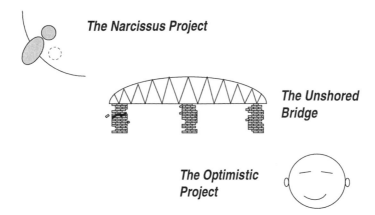

Figure 2   More Workflow Project Labels

The Optimistic Project

Here, lack of experience means that important technological and organizational
risks go unnoticed. Many projects begin stagnating even when the workflow tool is
being installed. Worries develop around component integration: the computer
platform, the database management system and the communication system – which
is so crucial to workflow. Sometimes this happens because the project is the first in
the world to combine certain software and/or versions. Or because the client–server
infrastructure is still unfamiliar. But by far the most common situation is that the
integration is perfectly possible but the project manager has failed to find the
necessary local expertise. Moreover, many projects do not realize that the challenge
of workflow is 50% organizational. Here the main dangers are the "big brother"
effect" (lack of anticipation means that, sooner or later, users discover the risks for
themselves and become more and more uncompromising) and implementing process
control which no one uses because responsibility for the process is non-existent.

Why are We Suffering Like This?

Why do we make so many mistakes on such a large scale? Have we lost the knack
of organizing projects with a reasonable chance of success? Or are we being asked
to do something which is fundamentally different from what we are accustomed to?

The second answer is correct. The explanation is entirely logical and lies in the
nature of the concept. Workflow has two specific characteristics: integration and
change. This is compounded by the fact that workflow is a new and relatively
unknown phenomenon. These characteristics and their ramifications are summarized
in Table 1.

Table 1. Workflow characteristics and their ramifications.

Workflow characteristics	Ramifications
Integration	Required: across organizational units across roles/disciplines across information systems across technical infrastructure
Change	Awareness is created by information on process performance Awareness is created by thinking about the flow Inducement to real-time (self) control Greater flexibility (for the flow as well as the project)
New and unknown	Success and failure factors are underestimated Skepticism or underestimation regarding applicability

It looks as if we need not be ashamed of our flops after all. We needed this run-up to make us face the facts: workflow is not a continuation of what we have been used to. It is a new phenomenon that gives us the chance to extend our horizons but, at the same time, makes fundamental new demands.

Lost Investment or the Price of Learning?

What can we do to ensure that the missed opportunities of the past do not end up as lost investments but as dividends for the future? From now on we want to stop our project from earning any of the above labels. The main steps for doing so are set out for each project type in Table 2.

Explicitness and Nerve

One familiar problem which we haven't yet discussed is mixing two contradictory aims in one project. We could label this the Ambivalent Project. It's easily identified. The project manager has (consciously or otherwise) created management expectations that workflow will improve the company performance within a reasonable period of time. At the same time he finds himself with a second aim: that workflow will serve as a learning process for everyone who is involved. This is shown in Figure 3.

There is a simple way of avoiding this misery: take the bull by the horns and force a clear purpose-based choice between the two.

Table 2   Steps in Preventing Lost Investments

Project label	Main means of prevention
The One-Dimensional Project The Tunnel Vision Project	Fix the project limits so that everything that is needed to realize the desired performance improvement is contained in the project. Make sure that the project is set up and managed from the perspective of general management.
The Classic Project The Leonardo Project The Narcissus Project	Make sure that the project management comes from the management line. Use the project to make the team members customer-oriented, effective and efficient. See that it is run with this in mind.
The Unshored Bridge The Optimistic Project	Start by looking at other projects and analyze their successes and failures. Take responsibility in advance for the availability of broad and specialist workflow experience.

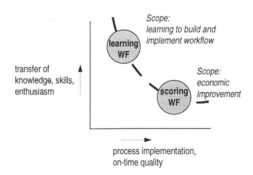

Figure 3   Two Types of Workflow Project

Learning Comes First

The aim is to maximize the learning effect over the long term. The economic results are not crucial; on-time delivery and the quality of the implementation do not have priority. There is plenty of scope for trial and error. Identify beforehand the areas where you could run into something new, be sensible about phasing (so that you don't bump into all sorts of obstacles at the same time), formulate the learning aims as concretely as possible and gear the project towards them.

Scoring Comes First

Quality and on-time delivery are vital. In this case you must be assured of manageability, insight and practical experience. Don't forget that both specialist and general workflow experience is needed. If you call in external support, organize it so that the result is guaranteed and that there is still something to be learned.

A less successful project is exasperating but at least something can be learned from it. Things are really in a bad way when no one dares to grasp the nettle and start a project up. This brings us to the ninth and last label: The Coward's Project.

Table 3   Preventing the Ambivalent and Coward's Projects

Project label	Main means of prevention
The Ambivalent Project	Force a clear choice: learning or scoring
The Coward's Project	Overcome the scepticism and rise to the challenge

Let us round off with a comment from Machiavelli: "the indifference which greets change originates in the skepticism of Man who does not believe in anything new until he has experienced it for himself." It's clear where the challenge lies: don't be frightened off by what could go wrong. Take on the new, but be serious about the recommended preventative steps. Only then can risks be kept within limits.

Workflow Transactions[1]

Johann Eder, Walter Liebhart
Institut für Informatik, Universität of Klagenfurt, Austria

The concept of Workflow Transactions is introduced in this article. The need for a new concept arises since classical software ("ACID") transactions are too constraining for long-lived computations. Nevertheless, process-oriented workflow systems do require transaction support in order to guarantee consistent and reliable execution of business processes in a multi-user and failure-free environment.

Introduction

Workflow management systems (WFMSs) may be roughly divided into document-oriented and process-oriented systems [EL 1996a]. *Document-oriented* systems mainly support the flexible and often *ad hoc* coordination and cooperation of humans who are responsible for consistent execution results. *Process-oriented* systems control and coordinate the execution of (complex) business processes consisting of heterogeneous, distributed and/or autonomous tasks which are executed with little or no human intervention. Process-oriented systems especially require transactional support in order to ensure correct and reliable process execution in a multi-user and non-failure-free environment. Unfortunately, classical (ACID) transactions are in many aspects too constraining for workflow applications. Therefore numerous advanced transaction models have been developed, which allow a more complex transaction structure and/or relax (at least some of) the ACID properties. However, while most of these newer transaction models offer valuable concepts for workflow applications, they are too database-centered and therefore not directly applicable in the workflow context. *Workflow transactions* can be seen as an approach to fill the gap between advanced transaction models and process-oriented workflow models. How to realize workflows with workflow transactions is illustrated by the workflow activity model WAMO [EL 1995].

[1] This research was supported, in part, by CSE-Systems, Computer & Software Engineering GmbH, Klagenfurt, Austria.

Basic Transaction Concepts

The basic idea of transaction processing is to guarantee a consistent and reliable execution of applications in the presence of concurrency and failures. A database transaction is a sequence of operations which transfers a database from one consistent state into another (not necessarily different) consistent state. Transaction processing technology ensures that each transaction executed either to completion or not at all, and that concurrently executed transactions behave as though each transaction executes in isolation. Additionally, these guarantees are upheld despite various types of failures (e.g. computer components). In general, these requirements are realized by a concurrency control unit and a recovery unit.

Transaction processing systems pioneered many concepts in distributed and fault-tolerant computing. Most important, they introduced the transaction ACID properties – atomicity, consistency, isolation, and durability – that have emerged as the unifying concepts for distributed computing [GR 1993]:

- *Atomicity*: A state transition is atomic if it appears to jump from the initial state to the result state without any observable intermediate states – or if it appears as though it had never left the initial state (all-or-nothing principle).
- *Consistency*: A transaction produces consistent results only; otherwise it aborts. A result is consistent if the new state of the database fulfills all the consistency constraints of the application. Since it is impossible to check all constraints each time a transaction is started, it is assumed that the data is consistent in the initial database state or if it has been produced by a committed transaction.
- *Isolation*: Isolation means that a program running under transaction protection in a multi-user environment must behave exactly as it would in single-user mode. This topic is variously called consistency (the static property), concurrency control (the problem), serializability (the underlying theory), or locking (the technique).
- *Durability*: Durability requires that results of transactions that have completed successfully must not be forgotten by the system; from its perspective, they have become part of reality.

From Traditional Transactions to Advanced Transactions

In the database area *flat transactions* represent the most common (and simplest) type of transactions, and for almost all existing systems is the only type that is supported at the application programming level. Nevertheless, they are too restrictive and inflexible for non-traditional applications, such as for example workflows. These applications have the following characteristics.

Long Duration

Traditional transactions were invented for very short transactions whereas workflow activities have a much longer duration, touch many objects and have a complex control flow. Executing a long-running activity as a single ACID transaction can significantly delay the execution of other high-priority short transactions, increase the probability of deadlocks (because of locking) and hence cause high transaction abort rates. In most cases it is necessary to externalize uncommitted results or make them visible to other activities in order to achieve acceptable performance.

Of course, since the results are uncommitted they may become invalid later in the process. This fact in general can be tolerated from an application point of view but it requires adequate consistency preserving mechanisms (for example partial backward recovery with compensation). Additionally, it is not tolerable to rollback the whole workflow, and maybe the work of a day, if somewhere a failure (or exception) occurs.

Cooperation and Concurrency

In contrast to traditional applications, workflow activities are more in cooperative nature where different sub-activities are allowed to concurrently access shared, persistent data (e.g. working on a common document). Of course, there is some kind of synchronization is necessary to control the concurrent access but workflows have weaker synchronization requirements than traditional applications – for example, they tolerate inconsistent results to some extent. Serializability as a global correctness criterion is not applicable in the workflow domain because business processes themselves are not serial.

Another important aspect is the cooperation issues. There are not only intra-workflow dependencies (dependencies between activities within one workflow) but also *inter-workflow dependencies* (dependencies between different workflows) which must be supported adequately. Classical (ACID) transactions are seen as concurrent and completely unrelated units of work. This means that there are no *application independent* system services for specifying (inter- and intra-) dependencies except for putting all these control features into the application code.

Complex Structure

Flat transactions have only one layer of control which can be used by the application. Everything between "begin work" and "commit work" is at the same level which means that there is no way of committing or aborting parts of transactions, or committing results in several steps, and so forth. But especially transaction based workflow applications require more dimensions of control in order to manage the control flow over distributed and autonomous applications within a workflow.

The shortcomings of flat transactions motivated the development of more sophisticated – extended and relaxed – transaction models, as for example are summarized in [Elm 1992]. *Extended transactions* permit grouping of their operations into hierarchical structures (e.g. nested transactions) and *relaxed transactions* indicate that (some of) the ACID requirements are relaxed (e.g. open nested transactions relax the isolation requirement) [RS 1994]. However, in defining new transaction models it must be kept in mind that the success of flat transactions was its *simplicity* in isolating the application from faults. Extending transactions for non-traditional applications is not a case of "the more the better"; rather, a delicate balance between expressive power and usability (simplicity) [GR 1993].

From Advanced Transactions to Workflow Transactions

As stated in [AKA+ 1995a, RS 1994], most of the advanced transaction models for non-traditional applications are developed from a database point of view, where preserving the consistency of the shared database by using transactions is the main objective. A basic fact behind these models is the attempt to use traditional transactions as building blocks which restricts the applicability in the workflow domain. Workflow activities are in general not database transactions which are, for example, started automatically and therefore the concepts of advanced transaction models cannot be applied directly.

Major work in expanding advanced transaction models for workflow requirements was done in the area of transactional workflows, e.g. [RS 1993, Hsu 1993, BDS+ 1993], and long-running activities, e.g. [DHL 1991, WR 1992]. Nevertheless, this work is still strongly influenced by a database point of view and therefore is not directly applicable to workflow systems.

Modern WFMSs have to support complex, long-running business processes in a heterogeneous and/or distributed environment. It has been pointed out in [GHS 1995] that most of these systems lack the ability to ensure correctness and reliability of workflow execution in the presence of failures. Therefore a strong motivation of merging advanced transaction models with workflow models becomes evident. *Workflow Transactions* [EL 1996b] incorporate the basic ideas of traditional transactions extended by several features of advanced transaction models required for workflow execution. Currently there are several approaches reflecting this idea, e.g., [KS 1995, MAA+ 1995, AKA+ 1995b, Ley 1995, EL 1995]. The main characteristics of workflow transactions may be summarized as follows.

Analogies

A flat transaction is a sequence of operations which transfers a database from one consistent state into another consistent state. A transaction is executed in isolation from concurrent transactions and if one operation within a transaction fails, the whole transaction is rolled back. In analogy to this, a workflow transaction is a *sequence of workflow activities* which transfers a business process from one consistent state into the next consistent state. Activities themselves are again workflow transactions. From this point of view, we talk about workflow transaction on a more abstract level than we are used to talking about traditional transactions.

Transaction Structure

Workflow transactions must allow a hierarchical structure in order to be applicable to complex applications. A workflow typically consists of several activities which themselves again may be composed of (sub-)activities. Each activity is a workflow transaction. The nesting must be supported over as many levels as there are abstraction layers in the application. The most elementary activities finally represent an application program, a flat transaction or, for example, a human task (e.g. making a phone call).

Atomicity

Since workflow activities are in general of long duration, application dependent (user-defined) failure atomicity is required. The goal is not to undo everything in case of a failure but instead to *selectively roll back* parts of the work until the most recent consistent state (within the transaction) is reached. In order to find such a consistent state the workflow transaction manager needs support from a human expert (e.g. in WAMO [EL 1995] such states can be identified during run-time, based on specific information given by the workflow designer). Additionally, it would not be a realistic option in online systems to go back to the past (which corresponds to a rollback operation). Instead, more advanced recovery concepts [EL 1996b, Ley 1995] have to be provided. Having reached the latest consistent point, forward execution of the process – perhaps on an alternative path – must be supported. Summing up, workflow transactions relax the "nothing" property of the all-or-nothing concept of traditional transactions.

Consistency

As for traditional transactions, the scope of consistent executions does not focus on the work which is done within an activity (a transaction) but only on the correct execution order of activities. The "commit" of an activity is taken as a guarantee that the activity has produced a consistent result. If an activity aborts or fails (it is necessary to distinguish between abnormal termination and unsuccessful termination of an activity [EL 1996b]) then an inconsistent state may be the consequence. As for flat transactions, inconsistent states cannot be tolerated and must therefore be removed – ideally automatically. If compensating activities are involved in a recovery process then these activities have to terminate successfully in order to preserve consistency. At this point it must also be emphasized that a compensation of activities is not always possible (e.g. drilling a hole) or that a compensation can become very complex (e.g. starting a new workflow).

Isolation

Because of the nature of workflow applications (long duration, cooperation, concurrency) it is not possible to execute workflow transactions fully isolated from concurrent transactions. As mentioned earlier, serializability as the correctness criterion for concurrent processing is too restrictive. There exist several theoretical approaches to overcome this problem without compromising consistency, e.g. [BDS+ 1993, Sch 1994], as for example semantic serializability. The goal is to exploit the semantics of the activities (by a human expert) by defining compatibility specifications between the activities. Compatibility between two activities means that the ordering of the two activities in the schedule is insignificant from an application point of view. Additionally, isolation is relaxed in the sense that sub-activities externalize their results as soon as they commit in order to increase concurrency and hence performance. Of course, since precommitted results may later become invalid the application must be able to handle such situations.

Durability

As soon as a (sub-)activity (workflow transaction) commits, its effects are persistent. Of course, these effects may later be undone semantically if the parent activity aborts or is compensated.

The workflow activity model WAMO [EL 1995] realizes most of the concepts presented above. WAMO supports the hierarchical structuring of workflows by using complex activities which are workflow transactions. Control flow operators allow the specification of control flow dependencies between activities and hence transactions. Failure atomicity can be controlled by *vital* activities. Elementary activities – tasks – may be associated with compensation tasks which are necessary for recovery. *Critical* tasks are not compensatable (at least without human intervention). WAMO's concepts currently are integrated into the prototype WFMS Panta Rhei [EGN 1994].

Conclusions

In order to ensure a consistent and reliable execution of process-oriented workflows, we have investigated workflow specific requirements for a transaction-based execution of workflow applications. We started by discussing classical (ACID) transactions which are very successful in traditional applications (because of their simplicity) but too constraining for long-lived computations, such as for example workflow applications. Then we focused on advanced transaction models, developed for non-traditional applications. Unfortunately, these models are very database-centered and therefore not directly applicable in the workflow domain. Considering this fact, we developed the concept of workflow transactions which allows a transaction-based definition of workflows.

References

[AKA+ 1995a]
  Alonso, G., Kamath, M., Agrawal, D., El Abbadi, A., Günthör, R., and Mohan, C. *Advanced transaction models in workflow contexts*, Technical report, IBM Almaden Research Center, 1995.
[AKA+ 1995b]
  Alonso, G., Kamath, M., Agrawal, D., El Abbadi, A., Günthör, R., Mohan, C. *Failure handling in large scale workflow management systems*, Technical report, IBM Almaden Research Center, 1995.
[BDS+ 1993]
  Breitbart, Y., Deacon, A., Schek, H.-J., Shet, A., Weikum, G. Merging application-centric and data-centric approaches to support transaction-oriented multi-system workflows, *SIG-MOD Record*, 22(3), Sep. 1993, pp. 23–30.
[DHL 1991]
  Dayal, U., Hsu, H., Ladin, R. A transactional model for long-running activities, In: *Proc. 17th Int. Conf. on VLDBs*, Barcelona, September 1991.
[EGN 1994]
  Eder, J., Groiss, H., Nekvasil, H. A workflow system based on active databases, In: Chroust, G., Benczur, A. (Eds), *CON 94: Workflow Management: Challenges, Paradigms and Products*, Oldenburg, Linz, Austria, 1994, pp. 249–265.
[EL 1995]
  Eder, J., Liebhart, W. The workflow activity model wamo, in: *Proc. 3rd Int. Conf. on Cooperative Information Systems*, Vienna, Austria, May 1995.
[EL 1996a]
  Eder, J., Liebhart, W. *A workflow classification framework*, Technical report, University of Klagenfurt, Department of Informatics, January 1996.

[EL 1996b]
   Eder, J., Liebhart, W. *Workflow recovery*, submitted elsewhere, January 1996.
[Elm 1992]
   Elmagarmid, A. K. *Database Transaction Models for Advanced Applications*,
   Morgan Kaufmann, 1992.
[GHS 1995]
   Georgakopoulos, D., Hornick, M., Shet, A. An overview of workflow
   management: From process modeling to workflow automation, in
   Elmagarmid, A. (Ed.), *Distributed and Parallel Databases*, Vol. 3, Kluwer
   Academic Publ., Boston, 1995.
[GR 1993]
   Gray, J., Reuter, A. *Transaction Processing: Concepts and Techniques*,
   Morgan Kaufmann, 1993.
[Hsu 1993]
   Hsu, M. Special issue on workflow and extended transaction systems, *Bulletin
   of the Technical Committee on Data Engineering*, 16(2), June 1993.
[KS 1995]
   Krishnakumar, N., Shet, A. Managing heterogeneous multi-system tasks to
   support enterprise-wide operations, in Elmagarmid, A. (Ed.), *Distributed and
   Parallel Databases*, Vol. 3, Kluwer Academic Publ., Boston, 1995.
[Ley 1995]
   Leymann, F. Supporting business transactions via partial backward recovery in
   workflow management systems, in Lausen, G. (Ed.), *GI-Fachtagung:
   Datenbanksysteme in Büro, Technik und Wissenschaft*, Dresden, Springer-
   Verlag, March 1995.
[MAA+ 1995]
   Mohan, C., Agrawal, D., Alonso, G., El Abbadi, A., Günthör, R., Kamath, M.
   Exotica: A project on advanced transaction management and workflow
   systems, *ACM SIGOIS Bulletin*, 16(1), 1995.
[RS 1993]
   Rusinkiewicz, M., Shet, A. On transactional workflows, *Bulletin of the
   Technical Committee on Data Engineering*, 16(2), 1993.
[RS 1994]
   Rusinkiewicz, M., Shet, A. Specification and execution of transactional
   workflows, in Kim, W. (Ed.), *Modern Database Systems: The Object Model,
   Interoperability, and Beyond*, ACM Press, June 1994.
[Sch 1994]
   Schwenkreis, F. A formal approach to synchronize long-lived computations,
   in: *Proc. 5th Australasian Conference on Information Systems*, Melbourne,
   1994.
[WR 1992]
   Waechter, H., Reuter, A. The contract model, in: Elmagarmid, A.K. (Ed.),
   Database Transaction Models for Advanced Applications, chapter 7, Morgan
   Kaufmann, 1992.

The Future of Workflow

Planning for the Clustered Corporation
John Williams

Workflow Interoperability Between Businesses
Dr. Thomas Adams, Steve Dworkin

Growth and Challenges in Enterprise Workflow
Dave Ruiz

Workflow Engines as Transaction Monitors
Martin Ader

Planning for the Clustered Corporation

John Williams
Integrated Work

As standards appear that will make it possible for companies to let their workflow systems work together, how should they plan to take advantage of them? John Williams puts forward his view of what workflow interoperability might mean for businesses and how they should prepare for the possibilities.

Evolving Technologies and Organizations

If you are reading this then you probably already have a good idea of what workflow is. You may already have experienced its benefits for teams or departments in your own organization. Those same benefits can be multiplied when processes are allowed to break out of the boundaries between single departments or, even more so, single companies. Today few vendors offer true multi-departmental or multi-site workflow systems but in the future your company may need to handle processes that cross departments and go beyond the company's boundary. As companies rethink their business processes they will discover new roles for other companies to play in the chain of actions that runs from the perception of market need to its successful exploitation in the form of goods or services, paid for by customers. Using technology to support these new networks of companies will become a core competency for tomorrow's organizations.

It is certainly possible that, in a few years from now, clusters of companies, each bringing their own skills to a discrete part of the business, will build joint enterprises. The growth of the Internet as a carrier and the explosion of technologies around the infrastructure of the World Wide Web promises ease of connection, if not of communication. The emergence of these corporate clusters will break the paradigm of the supplier–vendor relationship with its sterile contracts and service level agreements. Instead a new paradigm will emerge of cooperating networks of corporations in which shared interest and experience becomes a greater bond than contractual ties. Building such networks can be expected to yield great opportunities in flexibility and responsiveness to addressing markets but success will depend on technology to link the clustered corporation. The key competencies of many organizations will move from being able to execute all parts of a business process to achieving excellence in orchestrating the cluster of enterprises and in understanding how the interconnection opportunities presented by the Internet can be translated into new business operating models. Workflow will be a key technology in achieving this, integrating systems, people and information and orchestrating the progress of work across the Internet-connected clustered corporation in the same way as it does today within departments.

Wide Area Workflow and the WfMC Standards

Whatever the future holds for organizations, we can be certain of one thing. Different companies (and sometimes different departments) will have selected differing workflow products as their way of implementing automated business processes. The problem for companies trying to create a single, seamless business process across and beyond the corporation will be a challenge of interfacing different workflow systems.

Even for corporations working with today's business approaches, this will be a problem area as they confront the challenges of systems that need to be brought together as a result of mergers and take-overs. Here the work of the Workflow Management Coalition is expected to make an important contribution. One of the standards being developed by the Coalition will provide a standard way for workflow systems from different vendors to connect to one another. Once the WfMC standards have been defined and taken up by the industry, users will be able to implement processes that depend on interconnected workflow systems.

The introduction of these standards will also be a driving force in developing the possibility for companies to do business with one another electronically – electronic commerce.

Electronic commerce, also known as e-commerce, is being hailed as the next major opportunity for companies to re-shape the way they do business. It will become the backbone upon which the clustered corporations are built. Companies have exchanged data electronically for some years. Electronic data interchange (EDI) is a pre-requisite for e-commerce but exchanging data is not its only aspect. E-commerce adds the concepts of electronic products (goods or services that only exist in electronic forms) and the idea of virtual corporations and marketplaces that exist as the result of companies' ability to interact with their suppliers, their partners and their customers electronically. To date most business process reengineering projects have focused on the processes inside a company. Using technologies such as workflow and document image processing, companies have made substantial improvements in staff productivity and in the cycle times associated with new product development or customer service. E-commerce offers companies the opportunity to take this same thinking beyond the boundaries of the corporation.

This will allow groups of companies to build new models of business operation using the activities of individual member companies in the best way to achieve an overall result. Doing this requires standards for interoperation, however. It is in this area that the WfMC will make the biggest contribution to the future of e-commerce.

Planning for the Clustered Corporation

How should a company plan for the technologies needed for a clustered corporation? In the first instance it is essential to build a clear model of the boundaries of the corporation today. What comes into the corporation and what goes out? Who manages the relationships with companies that allow your organization to achieve its goals? How do those relationships contribute to your company's goals? Only when questions like these have been answered can the planning for intercompany workflow begin. The problem is in many respects like that of assessing the role of any performer in a workflow. The key things are to build a picture of the attributes of the corporation, its role, its responsibility and authority.

It may help to examine the paper exchanged between corporations but, just as in workflow within the organization, beware of simply automating existing practices. Many documents exchanged between organizations exist because of the nature of the contractual relationship between the companies involved. But imagine if the supplier of components for a product was paid on the basis of sales of the final product. What use would there be for orders and invoices along the way? The role of workflow would be to ensure that the component supplier and the product manufacturer coordinated their activities so well that sales of the product were maximized with minimum use of components to both sides' benefit in reduced paperwork and operational administration. Of course most intercompany workflows will not be as radical in their effect as this. But the challenge of such an end goal can be a powerful catalyst for radical thought about the current and future relationships (and thus roles in the overall work processes) of corporations.

In essence the key questions are "What do we want to achieve?", "What are the boundaries of my company and my partners today? What should they be?" and "What comes in and goes out? Does it (and will it) need to?".

Looking at the Boundaries

Planning for multi-enterprise workflow will need to assess the style of cooperation that the two companies plan in the process. Is the intention to deliver a seamless process or is there to be a clear dividing line between the two companies? If the former, it becomes possible to envisage a process flow in which "work" passes backwards and forwards freely across the intercompany divide. If the latter, there will be clear and controlled points at which information passes. While the former becomes achievable with the advent of interconnected workflow systems it can be expected that for many organizations, at least, a model where process segments with clear boundaries are "owned" by each entity is the most likely. A useful model is that shown in Figure 1. In the cooperating corporations each organization establishes workflows that extend across their respective boundaries. The task is to define the roles of each, the activities they will carry out and the characteristics of the boundaries. In the clustered corporation the challenge is to build a process that functions within the shared space occupied by both organizations.

Inter-company workflow
Cooperating Corporations

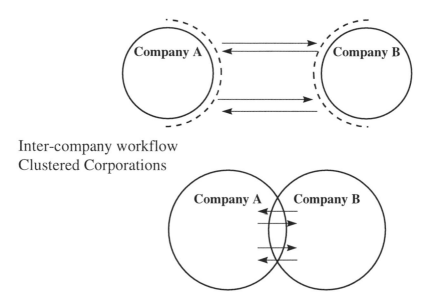

Inter-company workflow
Clustered Corporations

Figure 1   Cooperating and Clustered Corporations

Implementation Issues

Whatever organizational model is chosen the practical problems of implementing inter-company workflow are likely to be the same. Some of these will relate to the geographical distribution of the organizations, their location, the availability of high bandwidth communications links between them and security/reliability/privacy issues related to transferring information on the Internet. Some will relate to different IT infrastructures existing within the companies and the need to engineer interfaces between heterogeneous systems. In all these areas standards for interconnection are vital but when it comes to workflow it is essential that the systems are able to understand the data they exchange. Telephones provide interconnection between people in different countries thanks to CCITT standards. Communication is only possible, however, if the people at either end share a common language as well. WfMC standards will help this for wide area workflow. For planning purposes it is sufficient to concentrate on what a "work packet" would look like if you had to encapsulate all the information required in one package. WfMC standards will ensure that systems at both ends are able to understand it. Organizations can concentrate on the interfaces between each other, considering why work packages carry the information they do. Above all they should review the extent to which effort in the shared process is focused on achieving the ends of the process rather than that being done as a means to that end.

Table 1   Guidelines for Intercompany Process Design

- Look at the companies involved as "performers" in the process, each with their own roles, attributes, responsibilities and authorities
- Start with a process, break it down into flows
- Look for measures at the process level
- Control access to the process but trust the process to work
- Eliminate measures that look inside the process (what is needed to run the business = what is needed to run the process)
- Consider who needs what visibility of work within the process

If you believe that intercompany workflow may be needed by your company in the future you should look carefully at the interconnection capabilities of vendors' products as well as at their basic workflow functionality. Look for systems which interface to the most common data network types and offer the performance and scaleability that will be needed. Examine their support of common mail protocols such as MAPI, SMTP/MIME and X.400 so that messaging approaches can be used for information delivery where relevant. Seek systems with interfaces sufficiently flexible and open so that the user can produce applications to work with data related to work items and the materials that the workflow is concerned with. But, for the best bet in planning for interoperation between systems in the future, ensure that the vendor supports the WfMC standards. Today, that is the best guarantee that users can give themselves for investments that will be protected in the future, whatever the shape of their company and its business processes.

Workflow Interoperability Between Businesses

Dr Thomas Adams, Steve Dworkin
Computron Software, Inc.

Different workflow engines will soon start to talk to each other in practical applications. This will bring benefits but also technical problems where workflows cross boundaries between companies, processes and workflow systems. The interoperability standards address the mechanics but not yet the content of the conversations. The AI community has proposed several standards and methods for communication between independent computerised agents. This article surveys the work in this area.

The Promise of Workflow Interoperability

We can anticipate major benefits from interoperable workflows in the following areas:

- Processes which involve the individual consumers of a company's product
- Processes which govern the exchanges between strategic business partners
- Interactions between major processes within a company
- Interactions between online and casual participants in a process

Many existing workflows interact with the individual consumers of a company's product, such as the purchasers of a distributor's goods, the contractors for a company's services, or the claimants on an insurer's policies. However, these consumers are usually given only small windows into the provider's processing, through a claim or order form, form letters, or phone conversations. If they were given the ability to freely query the status of their order or claim wherever it was in the process, or even add information as it was needed in the process, wouldn't they get better service? The provider would also spend less on special forms, letters, and phone clerks. Companies are beginning to provide this kind of consumer involvement through the Internet, faxes, and free home-PC software.

While an individual consumer would not have a workflow engine to handle their side of the process, when two large companies deal with each other, they might each implement a separate workflow for their side of the exchange. For example, one company is running a procurement process while the other is running a sales order process, both dealing with the same order. They exchange paper or EDI documents at various points, such as order forms, invoices, and bank check, but each interprets them their own way in their own workflow. In fact, the order is really going through a single process, and really has a single status at any point. The two companies are passing back and forth the responsibility for the order as it progresses from initial commitment to final payment (Figure 1). If we could implement this as a single workflow process, we would have a single shared view of the status of the order at any point.

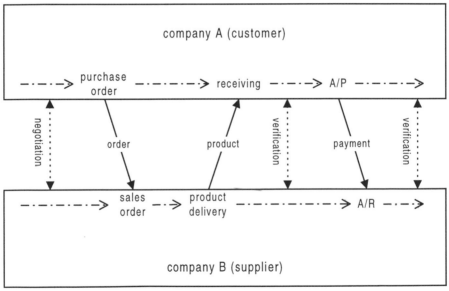

Figure 1   Process Involving Two Companies

Likewise, a single company can operate several different workflows that interact, but lack a common, higher-level viewpoint (Figure 2). The sales order process, for example, affects the manufacturing process by creating commitments for certain goods to be in inventory during a certain time-period in order to fulfill the sales order. However, the sales organization typically uses a different computer system than the manufacturing floor, so it is hard for their workflows to interoperate. A single, enterprise-wide process view would allow us to control the interactions between sales and manufacturing, for example.

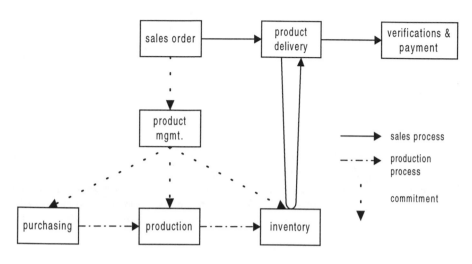

Figure 2   Two Interacting Processes Within the Same Company

A single process within a company can also benefit from workflow interoperability, by integrating different types of work-processing software. Some workers, such as order checkers, use a centralized, online workflow system for daily processing. Others, such as project planners or information service providers, use collaborative software for most of their work, but also need to tie into production processes. Others use email to interact with workflows less formally, for occasional use, from remote locations, or because they prefer the email environment. An interoperability standard allows these different work-processing systems to participate in a single "process".

The Problem of Workflow Interoperability

As soon as we start to implement some of the scenarios above, we run into some real-world problems. These concern the need to share information and to share responsibility in order to share a common process.

Workflow systems have always shared and distributed work, and therefore information and responsibility, among different workers. These systems have restricted themselves, however, to a single organization with a single set of interests (which all the workers are pledged to serve), and even to a single computer system. Now two or more organizations or individuals, each with their own interests, legal rights, vocabulary, protocols, and computer systems, have to cooperate and share a single process.

Organizations have, in fact, always cooperated and "shared a process" by following elaborate protocols. For example, to exchange goods or services between organizations, the protocol involves invoices, terms-of-agreement, and so on. Our job is to take these protocols out of the manual realm and let computers handle the drudge-work of verifying each step in the process.

If one computer system is going to talk to another in a meaningful way about whether it has fulfilled an agreed-upon commitment, they need at least to understand the full content of these "verifications" such as orders and invoices. It is a rare case when one system can say simply "my invoice #ABC is in response to your order #123" and be done with it. More often, one invoice may cover several orders, or part of one, or a production lot may cover parts of several different orders. Different systems must therefore exchange messages concerning the detailed content of the process, and this detailed content will be different for each domain from car parts to college courses. Therefore, they have to share common vocabularies in each specific domain.

We see this problem in EDI (Electronic Data Interchange), where committees have worked out elaborate standards covering the meaning of each piece of each exchange document. Even so, these standards just govern the content of the documents; each pair of organizations must work out another elaborate, ad hoc agreement to cover the *processing* of the document ("Company A will cancel the order if it does not get a response to document 123 from Company B within 10 business days"). A shared workflow would automate this processing, rather than rely on written agreements. But a shared workflow requires a shared domain-specific vocabulary to describe the process details.

It is easy to share a vocabulary if you share a common physical database. Each field name represents a specific type of information, and different applications can easily translate these field names into intelligible labels. All the scenarios above run into problems because they do not share that physical database. A computer will not even necessarily associate a field named CUST_NAME in one database with a field named CUST_NAM in another. We need a different common vocabulary.

As companies share more responsibilities via workflow, such as a car manufacturer delegating part of its manufacturing process to an electric-parts company, the need for electronic verifications, shared rules, and common vocabularies will grow. Now that we have outlined the problem in a workflow context, let us see what solutions we can borrow from the more general work on interagent collaboration.

An Agent-Based Approach to Workflow Interoperability

The previous discussion illustrates that in order to achieve workflow interoperability, two requirements must be met. First, the individual agents must share a consistent semantic understanding of the information exchanged. For example, the purchase order agent of customer company A and the sales order agent of supplier company B in Figure 1 must share a common understanding of the order concept. Second, there must be a mutual understanding of the means for coordinating the various activities of the workflow. For example, customer company A in Figure 1 may negotiate with supplier company B about product specifications and prices prior to preparing a purchase order.

In agent-based software engineering [TOVE], programmers write their programs as individual software agents. This is done without considering the details or even the existence of other programs, and without knowledge of the hardware configuration on which those programs will be run. The operating system takes the responsibility for assuring that those individual programs interoperate correctly. This approach imposes three requirements on the environment:

1. There must be a shared understanding of the basic concepts· in the domain; all communication between agents must be based on this common conceptualization.
2. The system must support a basic repertoire of interagent communication.
3. The interaction of the agents must be coordinated, whenever they must mutually accomplish some joint activity.

The requirement for obtaining mutual understanding of shared information has been addressed by developing task-independent domain ontologies that represent the domain objects and domain-independent task ontologies that describe problem-solving methods in a general way. The requirement for a shared understanding of interagent communication is addressed by defining an agent communication language that declaratively describes a core set of communication acts. Agent coordination is implemented by a federation architecture in which the problem-solving agents interact with each other through the services of specialized agents known as facilitators. We discuss each of these issues very briefly below and then indicate their relevance to workflow interoperability.

Ontologies

In order to interoperate, the individual agents must share a set of concepts (e.g., entities, attributes, processes), their definitions and their interrelationships. Ontologies are agreements about such shared conceptualizations. In much existing software the ontologies are implicit. For example, an accounting application makes use of concepts describing invoices and products. These conceptualizations may differ in syntax and semantics from similar concepts used by an inventory management software application or by existing standards for intercommunication between enterprises, such as EDI [ANSI 1994].

A first attempt to address these problems would be to simply agree on terminology. If this vocabulary is expressed loosely in natural language, then it is possible for programmers to anticipate any inconsistencies and unwanted interactions, but there is no way to automatically translate between representations or to guarantee correctness of the interactions between the independently programmed agents. Furthermore, the informal nature of the specification may result in ambiguous interpretations by various users of the ontology. A significant improvement can be obtained by expressing the vocabulary in a restricted and structured form of natural language, where care is taken to define terms unambiguously. An example of this level of specification is the Workflow Management Coalition Glossary [WfMC 1994]. This Glossary gives definitions, descriptions of typical usage, and synonyms for the various terms in a workflow management system.

The next layer of sophistication would be to express the concept descriptions in a formally defined language. One of the most significant accomplishments in this direction is the Knowledge Interchange Format (KIF) [GF+ 1992], a language developed by the Interlingua Working Group, under the DARPA Knowledge Sharing Initiative to facilitate knowledge sharing. The important features of KIF are its declarative semantics, its expressive power, its provision for the representation of knowledge about knowledge (meta-knowledge), and the ability to represent non-monotonic reasoning rules. KIF has been used as the basis of several useful knowledge representation languages:

1. **Ontolingua** [Gru] extends KIF with standard primitives for defining classes and for organizing knowledge in object-centered hierarchies with inheritance. It is the basis of an Ontology Editor developed by the Stanford University Knowledge Systems Laboratory. The KSL Ontology editor is a set of tools for building, importing, analyzing and translating ontologies into a variety of representation languages.
2. The **Process Interchange Format** (PIF) [LY+ 1994] supports the exchange of business process descriptions among different process representations. Tools interoperate by translating between their native format and PIF. A PIF process description consists of a file of objects, such as activity, actor, and resource objects. Each object has a particular set of attributes defined for it; each attribute describes some aspect of the object. For example, an actor object has a skills attribute listing the actor's skills. The syntax of PIF adopts that of KIF. PIF can thus be described as a domain-specific specialization of KIF that supports reasoning about business processes.

There are two large scale projects that are developing a collection of terms and definitions related to business enterprises. The Toronto Virtual Enterprise (TOVE) Project [FCF+ 1993], coordinated by the University of Toronto Enterprise Integration Laboratory, is developing an enterprise ontology with formal semantics, including proofs of such properties as soundness and completeness, and applying it to a wide range of business applications, such as integrated supply chain management and enterprise engineering.

The Enterprise Ontology [UKMZ 1995] is a collection of terms and definitions relevant to business enterprises developed as part of the Enterprise Project, a collaborative effort led by the Artificial Intelligence Applications Institute (AIAI) at the University of Edinburgh. The overall objective of the Enterprise Project is to develop a framework for integrating methods and tools which are appropriate to enterprise modeling and the management of change.

There is a considerable overlap in the core ontologies used by the Enterprise Ontology and the TOVE Ontology. Both ontologies includes terms related to activities, authority, resource allocation and time, and terms related to how organizations are structured. The Enterprise Ontology also includes terms describing the task of planning. The plan concept elaborates the activity concept by associating a purpose with activities. A strategy ontology is also defined that introduces terms related to high level planning for an enterprise such as critical success factor, decisions, and mission. The planning aspects of the ontology were motivated by the AIAI Open Planning Architecture, which provides a uniform framework for strategic planning, tactical planning and plan execution [TDK 1994]. The Enterprise Ontology also includes terms related to marketing and selling goods and services.

An important contribution of the TOVE Project to second generation knowledge engineering is the concept of competency questions. The competency of an ontology is, intuitively speaking, a specification of the problems it is capable of solving. The competency is formally expressed as a set of questions that the ontology must be able to answer. Competency provides an important mechanism for comparing ontologies and for evaluating the expressiveness of an ontology. The TOVE Project also developed ontologies for activity-based costing and quality.

Interagent Communication

The difficulty of running applications in dynamic, distributed environments has driven the development of standards and protocols (CORBA, OpenDoc, OLE, etc.) that ensure that applications can exchange their data structures and methods across different platforms. Although these efforts have been promulgated as solutions to the agent communication problem, they are best viewed as substrates on which agent languages can be built. Languages that facilitate high-level communication are an essential part of an intelligent software agent architecture. Such a language should have the following characteristics [MLF]:

1. Declarative, syntactically simple, and readable by people
2. Supports a core set of primitives that captures most of our intuitions about what constitutes a communicative act irrespective of application
3. Grounded in theory and unambiguous
4. Efficient, in terms of both speed and bandwidth utilization

5. Supports all of the basic networking connection types (point-to-point, multicast, and broadcast) and both asynchronous and synchronous communications
6. Supports interoperability with other languages and protocols, knowledge discovery in large networks, and is easily attachable to legacy systems
7. Supports reliable and secure communication among agents

Knowledge Query Manipulation Language (KQML) [FMF 1992] is a language that is designed to support interaction among intelligent software agents. It addresses many (although not all) of the needs described above. The KQML language can be viewed as being divided into three layers: the content layer, the message layer, and the communication layer. KQML messages are oblivious to the content they carry. The message layer consists of a small set of basic communication primitives (e.g., assert, query, command, subscribe) with explicitly defined semantics. The communication layer encodes in the message a set of features that describe lower-level communication parameters (such as the identity of the sender and recipient, and a unique identifier associated with the communication). There are currently a number of KQML software suites that have been implemented and are in use (e.g., COOL, KAPI, KATS, LogicWare, Magenta).

Interagent Coordination

The current specification for the workflow interoperability interface deals with the implementation of manually specified coordination mechanisms, but does not address how to evaluate the effectiveness of a given coordination mechanism nor how a group of autonomous agents would dynamically interact to create a coordination protocol.

Intelligent agents should be able to:

1. Work together to accomplish complex goals
2. Act on their own initiative
3. Use local information and knowledge to manage local resources
4. Handle requests from peer agents

The client–server architecture [SJKB] is too restrictive to allow this. Some agents need to interact as both clients and servers depending upon with whom they are interacting. On the other hand, peer-to-peer interaction between every agent in the system introduces complex coordination problems. A reasonable compromise is to introduce a special class of agent called facilitators, whose role is to facilitate inter-operation between a set of process agents. Facilitators assist the process agents in collaborating by providing several interaction services [SG 1995]. Examples of the services that a facilitator must provide are:

1. Brokering for the services of the agents in its community (e.g., determination of the appropriate recipient for undirected messages, content-based routing)
2. Translation of messages from one form to another
3. Problem decomposition (e.g., determining that a query consists of two parts that can be addressed by different agents and assembling the response to be returned to the requesting agent)

Agents and facilitators are linked in what is often called a federation architecture (Figure 3). Agents communicate with their facilitators; facilitators communicate with each other and their associated agents. The agents form a federation in which they surrender their communication autonomy to the facilitator.

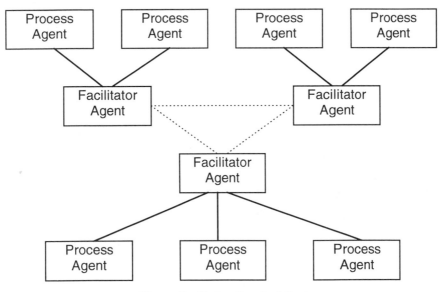

Figure 3   Federation Architecture

Summary

The federated agent-based approach to knowledge sharing provides a way to integrate various workflow application modules that were developed by different vendors. It is not necessary to impose a uniform approach on any of the individual modules. A unifying framework consisting of the underlying concepts, their definitions, and interrelations serves as the basis for achieving system integration. Each workflow module remains unchanged; agents act as brokers between the individual modules. Each agent translates the encoding used by the independent module into the representation used by the unifying framework and vice versa. The number of translations that need to be defined is equal to the number of modules, n. Without the unifying framework, n^2 translators would be required.

Enterprise ontologies constitute an integrated enterprise model, providing support for more powerful reasoning in problems that require multiple ontologies. This integrated view explicitly models the interactions between objects shared by independently defined workflows, such as the products which must both be delivered by the sales workflow and produced by the production management workflow in Figure 2. The product ontology is shared by both sales order and inventory ontologies, and any instances manipulated by the sales workflow are also seen by the product management workflow.

References

[TOVE]
> TOVE Manual.

[ANSI 1994]
> ANSI, *X12 Standard*, ANSI, Alexandria, VA, February 1994.

[WfMC1994]
> Workflow Management Coalition, *Glossary*, A Workflow Management Coalition Specification, November 1994.

[GF+ 1992]
> Genesereth, M. R., Fikes, R. E., *et al.*, *Knowledge Interchange Format, Version 3.0, Reference Manual*, Report Logic-92-1, Computer Science Department, Stanford University, June 1992.

[Gruber]
> Gruber, T., *Ontolingua: A Mechanism to Support Portable Ontologies*.

[LY+ 1994]
> Lee, J., Yost, G., PIF Working Group. *The PIF Process Interchange Format and Framework*, Version 1.0, 16 November, 1994.

[Fox 1993]
> Fox, M. S., Chionglo, J., Fadel, F. G., A common sense model of the enterprise, *Proc. 2nd Industrial Engineering Research Conf. (IERC)*, Los Angeles, CA, 20–27 May 1993.

[UKMZ 1995]
> Uschold, M., King, M., Moralee, S., Zorgios, Y., *The Enterprise Ontology*, 1995.

[Tate 1994]
> Tate, A., Drabble, B., Kirby, R., O-Plan2: an open architecture for command, planning, and control, in: Fox, M. S., Zweken, M. S. (Eds), *Intelligent Scheduling*, Morgan Kaufmann, 1994.

[Mayfield]
> Mayfield, J., Labrou, Y., Finin, T., *Evaluation of KQML as an Agent Communication Language*.

[Finin 1992]
Finin, T., McKay, D., Fritzson, R. (Eds.). The KQML Advisory Group. *An Overview of KQML: A Knowledge Query and Manipulation Language,* 2 March, 1992.

[Schuster]
Schuster, H., Jablonski, S., Kirsche, T., Bussler, C., *A Client/Server Architecture for Distributed Workflow Management Systems.*

[Singh 1995]
Singh, N. P., Gisi, M. A., *Coordinating Distributed Objects With Declarative Interfaces*, 24 March, 1995.

Growth and Challenges in Enterprise Workflow

Dave Ruiz
ViewStar Corporation

As large companies have decentralized, disparate and distributed collections of people, processes and systems that have lost touch with each other have resulted. As the business cycle comes full circle, decentralized companies find compelling needs for large scale workflow platforms - true enterprise workflow solutions that recognize and address their distributed business processes. This article reviews the growth and looks at the challenges in this area.

Definitions

Because it can mean such different things to different people, it is prudent to begin any discussion of "enterprise workflow" with a definition of the three major types of applications that characterize workflow of an enterprise scale.

- **Pervasive applications that enable workgroup and interpersonal productivity.** These are mega-applications involving many thousands of users across an enterprise. Usually based on a messaging paradigm, these systems enable both administrative and team-oriented workflows over local and wide area networks. Example products used in this category include **Microsoft Exchange** and **Lotus Notes**.
- **Multiple business processing applications that are implemented throughout an organization.** These discrete workflow applications involve tens or hundreds of users focused on automation of strategic and functional business processes. An example might be workflow systems implemented in different departments to automate accounts payable, loan processing, customer service and correspondence management. These *logically distributed* processes can occur in multiple business units or operating departments.
- **Automated business processes that cross organizational boundaries.** Also focused on automation of strategic and functional business processes, these

applications typically involve hundreds or even thousands of users participating as part of a single, distributed workflow. An example might occur in an insurance company with offices in several states or countries that shares a common set of procedures for claims processing. In this case, a single application is *physically distributed* among multiple geographic locations and time zones.

Characteristics of True Enterprise Workflow Applications

It is important to establish the essential application and platform characteristics of enterprise workflow systems.

Application Characteristics

The key application characteristics common to all enterprise workflow systems and solutions are described below. These characteristics include the ability to address distributed processes, scaleability, ability to address multiple applications, large capacity, high transaction rates, ability to integrate with desktop and personal productivity products, a high level of complexity and a high level of service availability.

Physical and Logical Distribution

Perhaps the primary characteristic of enterprise workflow systems is their ability to address distributed workflow processes. This includes *physically* distributed processes that span multiple geographic locations and time zones as well as *logically* distributed processes that span multiple business units or operating departments.

An example of physical distribution might be a purchasing operation that exists at several locations, but shares a common set of procedures for accounts payable processing. In this example, invoices received at distributed sites are automatically routed to a central site for payment. That same purchasing operation might need to share documents or coordinate activities with the manufacturing department to satisfy a common set of business objectives. The flow of purchasing documents or information into manufacturing for inventory-control purposes is an example of a logically distributed process – even if the manufacturing department is located at the same physical site.

Concurrency and Scaleability

A key indicator of the performance of enterprise systems is *concurrency*. Concurrency quantifies the maximum number of users a system is capable of supporting at the same time. While the industry average for a production workflow application is well under 50 concurrent users, enterprise solutions typically involve several hundred, perhaps thousands of concurrent users for a single system. A system's ability to scale up to meet increasing expectations for concurrency is one measure of its *scaleability*.

Multiple Applications

Enterprise solutions often address multiple applications – involving single or multiple business units – that could be separated by space and time. Even if not adopted as the "corporate standard", workflow software that has applicability across the physical and organizational boundaries of a company is generally considered enterprise calibre.

Large Capacity

Often, systems of enterprise scale must manage immense volumes of documents. These documents include work-in-progress data and archived document information that has completed the workflow. Typical volumes of documents, folders and cases managed in an enterprise system can range from 10 to well over 100 million records.

High Transaction Rates

Enterprise systems must be capable of processing high volumes of workflow data, where transactions are measured in the hundreds of thousands per business day. Typical volumes for incoming cases range from 100,000 to 250,000 per day, and overall transaction volume – the product of the total caseload times the number of discrete steps in the workflow – can run from 250,000 to 500,000 per day and above.

Flexible Integration

Even at a departmental level, production workflow applications often require integration with both desktop or personal productivity products and existing information systems. This need continues to grow as the workflow system expands to address the needs of the enterprise. Integration with legacy applications, such as the 3270 and 5250 terminal interfaces, and with the new generation of client/server transaction systems, such as those offered by **SAP**, **PeopleSoft** and **Oracle Financials**, is increasingly required.

Workflow Complexity

Given the previously defined needs for distributed processing, multiple application support and system integration, it should be clear that enterprise workflow solutions typically involve automation of the most complex business processes. These applications represent significant data-management, decision-modeling and document-routing challenges.

High Service Availability

Enterprise workflow systems are used to automate those strategic and functional business processes that are most critical to an organization's operational success. Because these systems process essential business transactions and manage vital assets, they must be based on platforms that provide the highest possible degree of service availability.

Platform Characteristics

There are also a number of platform-related characteristics that are typical of true enterprise workflow systems. These characteristics include an open architecture, compliance with *de facto* industry standards and the ability to use standard system management tools with the selected hardware and software.

Open Architecture

The primary platform characteristic of enterprise workflow systems is their ability to operate using the major client/server platforms, networks, databases and communication protocols installed throughout the enterprise.

Standards Compliance

True enterprise workflow solutions must support the industry and *de facto* standards necessary to maintain regulatory compliance and support corporate interoperability objectives.

Systems Management

To acceptably span the enterprise, workflow systems must enable the use of standard network and systems management tools. This standardization establishes a consistent framework for system operations and maintenance across the organization.

Enterprise workflow systems should offer maximum leverage of the supporting infrastructure, not as it is defined by the workflow vendor, but as it is defined by the corporation itself. This leverage includes:

- Direct utilization of standard hardware, software and network components
- Use of the tools already in place to support the above system components
- Leveraging of the knowledge, training and experience of existing IT resources
- Workflow solutions that fail to address any of the above characteristics will fall short in satisfying the enterprise needs of large organizations.

The Challenge of Enterprise Computing

For every solution there is a problem or challenge that precedes it, and this is certainly the case for enterprise workflow automation. Corporations would be well advised to understand the challenges of implementing such systems before determining what solutions are right for their organizations. Without this understanding, customers with enterprise objectives can fall short in terms of both project deliverables and management expectations. Given the dynamic, competitive nature of the corporate marketplace, falling short is a political risk that can and should be avoided.

Client/Server Challenges

Many of the challenges associated with developing and deploying enterprise workflow systems are directly traceable to the client/server platform on which the systems execute. Although client/server systems continue to enjoy widespread adoption, there are a number of configuration-related complexities associated with implementing and maintaining them. These challenges become particularly thorny when implementation is done on an enterprise scale. Some of these challenges are attributable to the relative immaturity of client/server architectures; just as many are due to the lack of training and the discipline required to manage these systems in production.

Before making a final selection of an enterprise workflow vendor, corporate customers should carefully consider the following realities of enterprise client/server computing: the diversity of the environment, the cost of maintenance and support, the lack of trained personnel and the lack of a unified network infrastructure.

Diversity of the Environment

Client/server systems provide the ultimate in flexibility, presenting customers with a complex array of choices between vendors, components and configuration alternatives. The challenge lies in selecting those components that will best serve the system and application needs of the enterprise. Because the components comprising today's client/server platforms are in a constant state of evolution, informed decision-making is particularly difficult. Despite vendor hype to the contrary, the market has not yet witnessed the arrival of "plug-and-play" client/server computing.

Cost of Maintenance and Support

Corporate customers continually underestimate the true cost of supporting client/server systems. Costs include those for routine maintenance, monitoring, change management, application delivery and production support. In the era of mainframe-centered systems, customers could always rely on the platform vendor to act as a one-stop source for maintenance and support. The client/server computing model does not allow a single vendor to provide a complete solution. The solution is, in essence, the sum of the parts.

Lack of Trained Personnel

Most IT personnel lack training and experience with client/server technology. While some of the discipline associated with legacy-system management remains relevant, the complexity of distributed client/server applications demands a much more proactive approach to system management, maintenance and administration. Many corporate IT organizations are ill-equipped to handle this responsibility.

Lack of a Unified Network Infrastructure

In spite of clear and compelling needs for enterprise workflow processing, customers often lack the network infrastructure required to create a seamless operating environment that can bridge multiple business units and physical sites. Even if persistent network connections between sites do exist, incompatibilities between network components that were installed at different times and to different specifications are likely to occur. These incompatibilities must be resolved before any serious enterprise project can proceed.

Additionally, enterprise client/server systems suffer from the lack of an overall system management framework for monitoring and maintaining distributed workflow applications. Although this situation is rapidly changing with the advent of **Microsoft Windows NT** and the visual administration tools it provides, customers today must compile their own system management toolkits – including network managers, DBA consoles and backup utilities – to provide the infrastructure support mandated by enterprise workflow systems.

Process Automation Challenges

There are other application-related challenges that customers must address before proceeding with enterprise workflow initiatives. Careful consideration of these challenges, which are both technical and political in nature, could expose new process automation opportunities that might otherwise be overlooked. These challenges include the lack of an enterprise workflow perspective, the need for effective distribution of information, the variety of available usage models and delivery environments, and the demand for local autonomy, all of which are described below.

Lack of Enterprise Workflow Perspective

Although corporate reengineering initiatives are on the increase, it is rare for such initiatives to span the enterprise. While business processes are reengineered and automated at a local level, conflicting business objectives as well as the physical, political and cultural boundaries that exist in any large corporation have naturally inhibited attempts at enterprise process automation. Customers must challenge themselves to adopt a broader, enterprise perspective to avoid creation of locally optimized workflows that cannot inter-operate with other applications in the enterprise. Workflow solutions must allow users to analyze and redesign their business processes to best support the enterprise as a whole.

Need for Effective Distribution of Process Information

With organizations becoming more and more decentralized, there is a growing need to replicate and synchronize workflow definitions and data across multiple departments and physical sites. The challenge is in determining whether to use standard messaging and transport infrastructure or a proprietary application service provided by a workflow vendor.

Variety of Usage Models and Delivery Environments

Enterprise workflow solutions traditionally involve a variety of users with differing skill sets and responsibilities. Some users may have direct involvement and responsibility for driving key aspects of the workflow. Others may only be occasional participants or may simply require workflow status information. In designing and developing workflow solutions for the enterprise, organizations should consider the full range of usage models and specify the application delivery environment that is best suited for each type of user.

Demand for Local Autonomy

As corporations drive to create workflow applications that span the enterprise, they must maintain awareness of the physical and political boundaries being crossed. Previously independent business units may be resistant to change or, as a minimum, demand operational autonomy for their applications and data. Enterprise workflow strategists should carefully examine the system and application impact of supporting locally autonomous computing infrastructures.

Facing the Enterprise Challenge

The architectural demands placed on enterprise workflow systems are directly proportional to the complexity of the applications being built and the service levels those applications require. As applications grow in complexity and scale, so too does the client/server infrastructure required to support successful sustained operations. Although there are significant challenges to be faced in these implementations, solutions are available today that can satisfy the growing market demand for enterprise workflow applications. The key is selecting a vendor with the product and technology components, the implementation skills and the advisory service capabilities to engage as a partner in joint pursuit of enterprise workflow objectives.

Workflow Engines as Transaction Monitors

Martin Ader
Wang Europe

For 25 years transaction monitors have provided secure, low cost, instant distant access to shared databases via private and public networks. Workflow engines linked to document management systems will offer these and new benefits opening up totally new areas to automation. In turn, this will impose new requirements on workflow engines.

Transaction monitors have enabled a major breakthrough in information processing productivity by providing remote capabilities to update central databases as soon as the relevant event occurs, where it occurs, and with the needed response time and security. Their usage has spread widely inside enterprises, worldwide, in all economic sectors, with a special mention for banking, insurance and industry where rapid developments would have been impossible without them. Transaction processing applications account for the steady extension of the demand for more power and memory for installed host computer systems in the past 20 years.

It is contended that workflow engines will play similar roles when used together with document management systems. They will provide new opportunities to deploy workflow applications bringing astonishing productivity gains, drastically reduced time to service customers, and full control of costs and quality of information processing inside corporations and organizations. They will thus be a major new source of hardware revenues for manufacturers.[1] This contention comes from two findings. First, in the same way as transaction monitors enable an update to a database from the place where the event occurred, workflow engines enable an update to the documentbase by the right people at the right time. These similarities suggest the same effects: enhanced productivity and customer service. Second,

---

[1] Major hardware vendors have to date introduced a workflow offering in their catalogue, and are preparing to support sales aggressively.

workflow engines provide totally new features that allow them to address new areas of applications. These areas will prove much larger than those already addressed by transaction monitors.

In order to support this prediction, this article provides an overview of transaction monitors, document management systems, and workflow engines. In addition, it presents a comparison of the features of transaction monitors and workflow engines and shows where they compare and how they differ. This is followed by a comparison of users' views and users' benefits. These elements lead to the conclusion summarized above. They imply, however, that a list of new requirements will be satisfied in the coming years.

Transaction Monitors Bring Productivity and Service Improvements

Transaction monitors first appeared on the market around 1970, five years after the first database management systems, and at the same time as the availability of telecommunications technologies and terminals at reasonable prices. Transaction processing boosted the growth of DBMSs, made mandatory by the concept of real time update, the *raison d'être* of transaction monitors. At that time, the association of database management systems and transaction monitors brought a true revolution in the work organization of computer-assisted tasks. This in turn implied a complete re-organization of many units in the enterprise. In most cases, this reorganization was nothing other than a return to the old situation, before the development of centralized batch-based information processing centres, surrounded by their huge data entry factories where all documents converged before processing. Freedom of work organization was passed back – thanks to powerful means of information processing – to where and when it appeared.

Transaction monitors enabled enterprises to get rid of those giant data entry factories, and to give back to lines of business the full responsibility for their data entry and processing. Even more important, they generated major enhancements of services provided to corporation customers by processing data in seconds where it took previously from one to several days. Productivity gains and enhanced services are the fundamental benefits that enterprises have derived from transaction processing developments since 1970.

Document Management for the Whole Enterprise

Just as with database management systems and an enterprise's data, the goal of document management systems is to integrate all of an enterprise's documents in a coherent and easily accessible way. Their use – up to now limited by hardware costs – is beginning to take off with the incentive of low cost and ever increasing performance. It brings drastic reductions in floor space, quasi-immediate document access through flexible requests mechanisms, and instant transfer through more and more efficient networks. Document management is beginning to be as important now as the database was in the past. However, as databases needed transaction processing capabilities, document management will find its true forte only in association with workflow.

Workflow Engines Address Business Processes

Documents are not electronically stored only with the perspective of later retrieving them. The need to store and retrieve them is only justified by their participation in the processing of administrative cases corresponding to the mission of the enterprise. Workflow deals essentially with those business cases. It enables organizations to:

- Represent the procedure that must be followed by various business cases
- Precisely define case processing at each step
- Specify rules for task dispatching to enterprise participants in accordance with the principles of the organization and with load leveling strategies

As transaction monitors handle the dynamics of how elementary processing pieces can lead to consistent database updates, workflow defines the dynamic of processing business cases for periods that can last from days – for a simple loan – up to several months for compulsory purchases by government. Document-bases thus reflect at any time the current state of processing of the work.

Workflow and document management jointly bring a new dynamic to ever increasing automation by taking into account administrative processes. They reduce the duration of processing by factors that can reach 10, doing in days what was achieved before in weeks. Workflow applications can generate double-figure productivity gains (up to 50%) by ensuring task scheduling and dispatching to participants, retrieval of data and documents needed by each task, and automatic calling and chaining of the tools which are needed. As a result of precise and comprehensive statistics collected by workflow engines, it becomes possible to measure efficiency and quality of information work. With workflow and document management, the proximity of participants becomes of little importance. Decisions related to organization and localization can be made with a new degree of freedom.

Transaction and Workflow Features Compared

As processed by transaction monitors, a transaction is a piece of processing invoked by a recognized user from a terminal and involving a series of interactions between the application and the terminal. The main assumptions are that interactions with the user are form-based on a terminal, data transfer at each interaction is light (hundreds of characters) and the whole transaction duration is a few minutes with response time in the range of seconds. The possible updates on the database made by the transaction are either all done and done only once, or not done at all (atomicity), this being ensured by the monitor. Recording the receipt of a payment of a policy premium is a typical example with information transfer of less than 100 characters, and transaction time of around 15 seconds in normal cases.

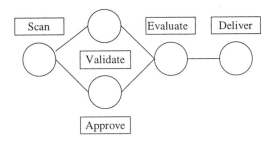

Figure 1   A Procedure Consists of Activities

In contrast, a procedure as seen by a workflow engine is made up of a series of activities (Figure 1). Each activity is executed by a user of the workflow system (a participant) in isolation from the others. Activities are created as soon as they can potentially be executed. Their execution order is managed by the workflow engine. For this, the engine refers to an explicit procedure description. Examples of procedures are claim processing in insurance, loan processing in banks, order processing in retailing, and material control in manufacturing.

An activity is created by the workflow system. It is picked up by the user from a list of activities he or she is allowed to execute, which is maintained by the engine. When the activity executes, it activates several possible actions (Figure 2). Each action is either a piece of code implementing the action (for example in **Visual Basic**) or a call to another pre-existing tool like a transaction in a transaction monitor, a text editor, a form manager, or any tool either on a server on the network or on the workstation. Typical activities can be to enter an order, approve a travel request, or compute a health claim amount.

Whereas a transaction involves only one user, the one that requested it, a procedure can involve several users, simultaneously in some circumstances (and potentially as many as there are activities in the network defining the procedure, and can be executed for the case). This is illustrated in Figure 3 where the respective role of the transaction monitor and workflow engines are depicted, together with office tools used for the implementation of activities. It indicates the essential roles of a workflow engine which is to take into account all the actions needed to process a case, regardless of the number of participants that will be involved and the number of tools, including the transactions that must be activated to complete them.

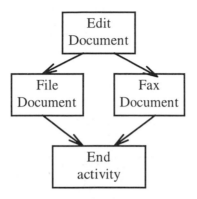

Figure 2   An Activity Consists of Actions

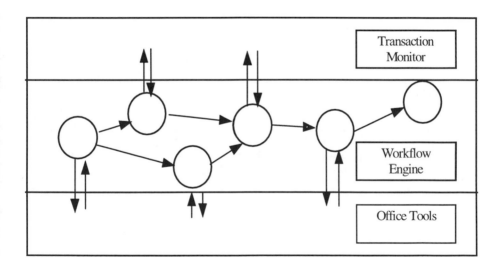

Figure 3   Workflow Engine and Transaction Monitor Roles

Transactions, activities, and procedures share some essential parameters and characteristics and a more detailed comparison is worth making. Table 1 shows the essential elements of this comparison.

From this table the most significant differences that must be highlighted are:

- Differences in duration from seconds for a transaction to days or even months[2] for a procedure

---

[2]Duration is domain specific: a simple loan can be processed in one day, a lawsuit may last years.

Table 1   Main Transaction, Activity and Procedure Features Compared

Characteristics	Transaction	Activity	Procedure
Duration	Seconds to minutes	Seconds to hours	Hours to months
Input/output	Hundreds of characters	Thousands to millions of characters	Thousands to millions of characters
Participants involved	One	One	One to 100
Execution mode	By host computer	Cooperation between workstation, servers and hosts systems	Cooperation and distribution
Cooperation	None (but batch spawn)	Cooperation is the basis of activity execution	Yes
Statistics	Started, Ended, User	Created, Started, Ended, User, Location, Cost	Created, Started, Ended, Cost, Location, Responsible
Time control	None	Deadlines, trigger points, reminders	Deadlines monitoring, periodic activation
Participant selection	No, it's the user that invokes a transaction	Yes, by the engine, based on rules	Yes, by the engine, based on rules
Administration	Yes	Yes	Yes
Response time	Seconds	Seconds to minutes	Seconds to minutes

- A transaction handles hundreds of characters, an activity can handle millions[3] of characters
- Multiple participants for a single procedure[4], only one for a transaction
- Handling of time constraints by workflow engines
- Workflow engines take into account the organization structure for dispatching
- Workflow processing is essentially distributed and cooperative

---

[3]Volume is also domain specific. One scanned page is 50 000 characters, 20 pages makes 1 MC document.

[4]One is obviously an exceptional situation; average case will involve 5 to 10 participants. Complex cases with many experts might involve 100 participants.

User Interface Differences

Table 2 attempts to highlight differences between workflow engines and transaction monitors in the view which they offer to end-users on their terminal or workstation.

Table 2 Transaction and Workflow External Visibility

Visibility	Transaction monitor	Workflow engine
Offered interface	Hundreds of atomic transactions	Tens of complex procedures, each made of tens of activities, each made of several actions
Organization support	List of users with transactions access control list	Full organization model, users, groups, roles, privileges, and rules for task allocation
User view	A menu of transactions to select	Worklist and procedure diagram

A transaction monitor offers a long list of possible transactions, each of them corresponding to a small action like updating a client address, entry of an account movement, or registering an order. By contrast, a workflow engine proposes to the user a list of activities that have to be performed by him and which he can select for execution, and a list of procedures that he can start. Activities can be complex, such as producing a letter with a text editor from a model proposed by the engine followed by sending the letter by fax and filing it in a folder. Procedures can involve multiple activities handled by several actors over a period of several days, weeks, or months.

A transaction monitor knows the list of users that have the appropriate access rights to reach him. For each user the transaction monitor maintains the list of transactions the user can activate. A workflow engine will maintain a much more detailed representation of the organization including participants, groups, and roles of participants inside groups. The workflow engine uses this organization description to interpret dispatching rules to be applied to each activity in order to allocate it to the proper participant according to the specific activity context.

Workflow Users Have Additional Benefits

Like transaction monitors, workflow engines provide essential benefits to users including enhanced productivity, better response time, and enforced security controls to the information system (Table 3).

Table 3   Transaction and Workflow compared benefits

Benefits	Transaction monitor	Workflow engine
Productivity	Yes	Yes
Response time	Yes	Yes
Security	Yes	Yes
State of affairs	No	Yes
Quality & costs measurements	No	Yes
Tools integration	No	Yes
Organisation handling	No	Yes

However, workflow engines provide additional user benefits of a totally new nature. They can precisely and instantly inform anyone on the present status of a case: what has been done so far, by whom; what are the pending activities and those responsible; and present all the data and documents related to the case. Workflow engines register all parameters related to case execution, and are able to produce from this data extensive quality and cost measurements. They enable integration of tools at the activity level including transactions, personal office tools, and collective services provided by servers. And finally they take into account the organization description in automatically dispatching activities to the proper participant.

Workflow Promises Additional Benefits

The similarity between workflow engines and transaction monitors is clear if we replace database by document-base. Workflow engines handle events like input documents where they appear to instantly update a document-base reflecting the state of current business processes. They will certainly provide similar effects: mainly greater productivity and better service by improving response time.

In addition, they provide different features and views to users. This is a result of the scope that they address: administrative cases governed by procedures, and organizational representation. This scope is much wider than that of transaction monitors; they much more directly concern the enterprise's operational goals themselves, and enter deeply into the direct support of the organization. Furthermore, together with document management systems, workflow engines address documents in addition to data, with volumes perhaps hundreds of times larger.

Transaction monitors took more than 25 years to deploy, and they have not yet saturated all potential targets, even if all possible applications have already been experimented with. Workflow engines cover a much wider area of the enterprise, in a way that is aligned more closely with the operational goals of the enterprise and its organization. They provide more intensive effects than transaction monitors did. At the beginning of the next century workflow effects on the economy will really show up. At that time, thanks to an efficient flow of work, enterprises which are business-case driven and organisation minded will become more productive and more time responsive. With the availability of measurements, cost management and quality control will be improved, too.

Workflow Engines will Have to Support New Requirements

With that perspective, workflow engines will have to evolve in the coming 10 years to provide better support for essential features like time management, organization support, extended statistics, scaleability, distribution, enhanced atomicity support, and remote operation of servers.

- *Time management* - Time calculations based upon an agenda registering working hours and holidays will have to be supported in order to compute duration within working time. Internal time representation and computations will be done in absolute time to accommodate procedure execution covering several time zones.
- *Organization support* - will have to be extended to give better and more realistic support to real organization representations including objects like line units, and functional units such as projects and committees.
- *Extended statistics* - will be needed to reflect more precisely and accurately the activity of users and the performance of procedures. Tools for analysis of the collected figures will need to be extended accordingly.
- *Scaleability* is needed due to the very large scope of systems that will need to be operated: up to 100,000 participants in the largest corporations. In addition, support of a large range of activities per unit of time and per user, going from 5 to 10 a day up to 400 an hour, will be required.
- *Distribution* is a mandatory requirement since it is impossible to rely upon only one server for large applications. The requirement is to enable distribution of execution on several servers of different activities or parts of the same procedure.
- *Enhanced atomicity support* is required for the ever increasing requirements for integration between transaction processing and other tools. The atomic property of a transaction should, in certain situations, be supported at the activity level so that operations done by an activity using a transaction are bounded to the transaction itself.
- *Remote operation of servers* is related to distribution and scaleability. It will be needed to reduce the need for multiple administrators by centralizing the operations of several distant servers in one location.

Section 2

Workflow Standards

The Workflow Reference Model

This section is based on version 1.1 of the Workflow Reference Model. Document reference: WFMC-TC00-1003.

1. Workflow Systems Overview

1.1 What is Workflow?

Workflow is concerned with the automation of procedures where documents, information or tasks are passed between participants according to a defined set of rules to achieve, or contribute to, an overall business goal. Whilst workflow may be manually organised, in practice most workflow is normally organised within the context of an IT system to provide computerised support for the procedural automation and it is to this area that the work of the Coalition is directed.

> **DEFINITION - WORKFLOW**
>
> The computerised facilitation or automation of a business process, in whole or part.

Workflow is often associated with Business Process Reengineering, which is concerned with the assessment, analysis, modelling, definition and subsequent operational implementation of the core business processes of an organisation (or other business entity). Although not all BPR activities result in workflow implementations, workflow technology is often an appropriate solution as it provides separation of the business procedure logic and its IT operational support, enabling subsequent changes to be incorporated into the procedural rules defining the business process. Conversely, not all workflow implementations necessarily form part of a BPR exercise, for example implementations to automate an existing business procedure.

A Workflow Management System is one which provides procedural automation of a business process by management of the sequence of work activities and the invocation of appropriate human and/or IT resources associated with the various activity steps.

DEFINITION - WORKFLOW MANAGEMENT SYSTEM
A system that completely defines, manages and executes "workflows" through the execution of software whose order of execution is driven by a computer representation of the workflow logic.

An individual business process may have a life cycle ranging from minutes to days (or even months), depending upon its complexity and the duration of the various constituent activities. Such systems may be implemented in a variety of ways, use a wide variety of IT and communications infrastructure and operate in an environment ranging from small local workgroup to inter-enterprise. The Workflow Reference Model thus takes a broad view of workflow management, which is intended to accommodate the variety of implementation techniques and operational environments which characterise this technology.

Despite this variety, all WFM systems exhibit certain common characteristics, which provide a basis for developing integration and interoperability capability between different products. The Reference Model describes a common model for the construction of workflow systems and identifies how it may be related to various alternative implementation approaches.

At the highest level, all WFM systems may be characterised as providing support in three functional areas:

• Build-time functions, concerned with defining, and possibly modelling, the workflow process and its constituent activities
• Run-time control functions concerned with managing the workflow processes in an operational environment and sequencing the various activities to be handled as part of each process
• Run-time interactions with human users and IT application tools for processing the various activity steps

Figure 1 illustrates the basic characteristics of WFM systems and the relationships between these main functions.

1.1.1 Build-time Functions

The Build-time functions are those which result in a computerised definition of a business process. During this phase, a business process is translated from the real world into a formal, computer processable definition by the use of one or more analysis, modelling and system definition techniques. The resulting definition is sometimes called a process model, a process template, process metadata, or a process definition. For purposes of this document, the term 'process definition' will be used.

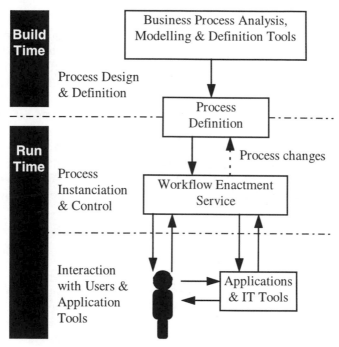

Figure 1   Workflow System Characteristics

DEFINITION - PROCESS DEFINITION

The computerised representation of a process that includes the manual definition and workflow definition.

A process definition normally comprises a number of discrete activity steps, with associated computer and/or human operations and rules governing the progression of the process through the various activity steps. The process definition may be expressed in textual or graphical form or in a formal language notation. Some workflow systems may allow dynamic alterations to process definitions from the run-time operational environment, as indicated by the feed-back arrow in the above diagram.

Coalition members do not consider the initial creation of process definitions to be an area of standardisation. Rather, this is considered to be a major distinguishing area between products in the marketplace. However, the result of the Build-time operation, the process definition, is identified as one of the potential areas of standardisation to enable the interchange of process definition data between different build-time tools and run-time products.

1.1.2 Run-time Process Control Functions

At run-time the process definition is interpreted by software which is responsible for creating and controlling operational instances of the process, scheduling the various activities steps within the process and invoking the appropriate human and IT application resources, etc. These run-time process control functions act as the linkage between the process as modelled within the process definition and the process as it is seen in the real world, reflected in the runtime interactions of users and IT application tools. The core component is the basic workflow management control software (or "engine"), responsible for process creation & deletion, control of the activity scheduling within an operational process and interaction with application tools or human resources. This software is often distributed across a number of computer platforms to cope with processes which operate over a wide geographic basis.

1.1.3 Run-time Activity Interactions

Individual activities within a workflow process are typically concerned with human operations, often realised in conjunction with the use of a particular IT tool (for example, form filling), or with information processing operations requiring a particular application program to operate on some defined information (for example, updating an orders database with a new record). Interaction with the process control software is necessary to transfer control between activities, to ascertain the operational status of processes, to invoke application tools and pass the appropriate data, etc. There are several benefits in having a standardised framework for supporting this type of interaction, including the use of a consistent interface to multiple workflow systems and the ability to develop common application tools to work with different workflow products.

1.1.4 Distribution & System Interfaces

The ability to distribute tasks and information between participants is a major distinguishing feature of workflow runtime infrastructure. The distribution function may operate at a variety of levels (workgroup to inter-organisation) depending upon the scope of the workflows; it may use a variety of underlying communications mechanisms (electronic mail, messaging passing, distributed object technology, etc.). An alternative top-level view of workflow architecture which emphasises this distribution aspect is shown in Figure 2 below.

The workflow enactment service is shown as the core infrastructure function with interfaces to users and applications distributed across the workflow domain. Each of these interfaces is a potential point of integration between the workflow enactment service and other infrastructure or application components.

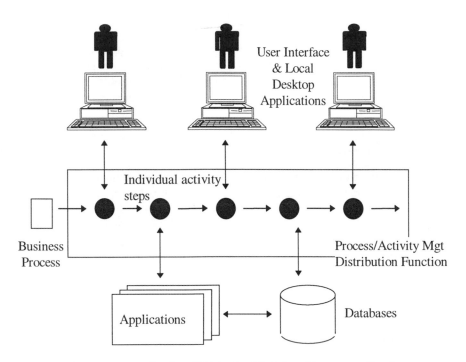

Figure 2 Distribution Within the Workflow Enactment Service

The flow of work may involve the transfer of tasks between different vendors workflow products to enable different parts of the business process to be enacted on different platforms or sub-networks using particular products suited to that stage of the process. In this scenario the flow within the central box passes between two or more workflow products - for example activities 1,2 and 5 may be executed by one workflow system and activities 3 and 4 by a different system, with control passed between them at appropriate points within the overall workflow. Standards to support this transfer of workflow control enable the development of composite workflow applications using several different workflow products operating together as a single logical entity.

The full range of interfaces being defined by the WFM Coalition therefore covers:

- Specifications for process definition data and its interchange
- Interfaces to support interoperability between different workflow systems
- Interfaces to support interaction with a variety of IT application types
- Interfaces to support interaction with user interface desktop functions
- Interfaces to provide system monitoring and metric functions to facilitate the management of composite workflow application environments

These are further developed in Section 2.

1.2 The Evolution of Workflow

Many types of product in the IT market have supported aspects of workflow functionality for a number of years, yet it is only comparatively recently that its importance has been recognised in its own right. The evolution of workflow as a technology has thus encompassed a number of different product areas.

1.2.1 Image Processing

Workflow has been closely associated with image systems and many image systems have workflow capability either built-in or supplied in conjunction with a specific workflow product. Many business procedures involve interaction with paper-based information, which may need to be captured as image data as part of an automation process. Once paper based information has been captured electronically as image data, it is often required to be passed between a number of different participants for different purposes within the process, possibly involving interaction with other IT applications, thereby creating a requirement for workflow functionality.

1.2.2 Document Management

Document management technology is concerned with managing the lifecycle of electronic documents. Increasingly, this is including facilities for managing document repositories distributed within an organisation as a shared resource with facilities for routing documents (or even separate parts of documents) to individuals for information access or updating according to their specific roles relating to a specific document. The document may form part of a particular business procedure which requires access to the document by individual staff undertaking separate activities according to a particular sequence according to some procedural rules - i.e. a document-centric form of workflow.

1.2.3 Electronic Mail & Directories

Electronic mail provides powerful facilities for distributing information between individuals within an organisation or between organisations; the use of directory mechanisms not only provides a way of identifying individual participants within an email domain but also potentially recording information about individual user attributes, such as organisation roles or other attributes relating to business procedures. Thus electronic mail systems have themselves been progressing towards workflow functionality through the addition of routing commands to define a sequence of recipients for particular types of mail items in response to some form of identified business procedure.

1.2.4 Groupware Applications

The groupware industry has introduced a wide range of software applications designed to support and improve the interactions between groups of individuals. Initially many of these applications supported improvements in group working via informal processes, accessing group bulletin boards or diary/scheduling applications on an ad-hoc basis. As the scope of such applications has spread towards more formal business focused group interactions there has been an increasing requirement to provide a more formal and controllable procedural framework to support the use of groupware applications. Workflow technology provides a solution to this type of requirement.

1.2.5 Transaction-based Applications

For many years applications to support certain classes of business procedures ("transactions") have been developed using transaction management facilities within TP monitors and/or Database Management software. From the initial centralised style of working, such application software has increasingly enabled the distribution of transaction based applications across a number of computer platforms. Transaction based applications typically exhibit important characteristics of robustness and support for "atomic" properties of the transaction; however, they do not typically exhibit a separation between the business procedure logic and the invocation of the various application tools which may be required to support individual activities within the business process. Over time, this is leading to a requirement to consolidate workflow capabilities to control the business procedures with the ability to invoke traditional transaction application programs for appropriate parts of the business process, as well as other types of application (document or office based, etc..) for other parts of the business process.

1.2.6 Project Support Software

Software to handle complex IT application project development (e.g. IPSEs - "Integrated Project Support Environments") has often provided a form of workflow functionality within the project environment, for "transferring" development tasks between individuals and routing information between individuals to support these tasks. In some cases this type of software has been generalised to support a wider, business-oriented view of process and a wider range of application tools - offering a more general workflow capability.

1.2.7 BPR and Structured System Design Tools

Business Process Reengineering tools have provided IT based support for the activities of analysing, modelling and (re-)defining the core business processes of an organisation and the potential effects of change in such processes or organisational roles and responsibilities associated with such processes. This may include analysis of the process structure and information flows supporting it, the roles of individuals or organisational units within the process and actions taken in response to different events, etc. A natural extension of such tools is to facilitate the implementation of the process with IT support infrastructure to control the flows of work and associated activities within the business process.

1.2.8 Separation of Workflow Functionality

The market for workflow has evolved from requirements across a spectrum of the IT industry and is likely to continue to do so, with a wide range of products focused on one or more particular aspects of the overall workflow requirement. Some may be provided in conjunction with other areas of technology, such as image processing or document management, others may be more general purpose. This multiplicity of products will allow wide choice for individual implementation circumstances and is recognised as something to be encouraged. However, it also increases the need for standards within the industry to enable different products to work together and integrate within a consistent overall architecture.

The reference architecture described in this document provides a framework which separates the various functions within a workflow environment and identifies various interface points at which product integration and interworking may be accomplished. It forms the template within which the individual interfaces and interchange specifications are being developed by the Coalition..

1.3 Product Implementation Model

1.3.1 Overview

Despite the variety in workflow products in the market, it has proved feasible to construct a general implementation model of a workflow system which can be matched to most products in the marketplace thereby providing a common basis for developing interoperability scenarios.

This approach identifies the main functional components within a workflow system and the interfaces between them as an abstract model. It is recognised that many different concrete implementation variants of this abstract model will exist and therefore the interfaces specified may be realised across a number of different platform and underlying distribution technologies. Furthermore not all vendors may choose to expose every interface between the functional components within the model; this will be dealt with by the specification of a variety of conformance levels which will identify the particular interworking functions where open interfaces are supported for multivendor integration.

The main functional components of a generic workflow system are illustrated in Figure 3.

The generic model has three types of component:

- Software components which provide support for various functions within the workflow system (shown in dark fill)
- Various types of system definition and control data (shown unfilled) which are used by one or more software components
- Applications and application databases (shown in light fill) which are not part of the workflow product, but which may be invoked by it as part of the total workflow system

The roles of the major functional components within this system are described below.

Process Definition Tool

The process definition tool is used to create the process description in a computer processable form. This may be based on a formal process definition language, an object relationship model, or in simpler systems, a script or a set of routing commands to transfer information between participating users. The definition tool may be supplied as part of a specific workflow product or may be part of a business process analysis product, which has other components to handle analysis or modelling of business operations. In this latter case there must be a compatible interchange format to transfer the process definitions to/from the run-time workflow software.

1.3.2 Process Definition

The process definition contains all necessary information about the process to enable it to be executed by the workflow enactment software. This includes information about its starting and completion conditions, constituent activities and rules for navigating between them, user tasks to be undertaken, references to applications which may to be invoked, definition of any workflow relevant data which may need to be referenced, etc..

The process definition may refer to an Organisation / Role model which contains information concerning organisational structure and roles within the organisation (e.g. an organisational directory). This enables the process definition to be specified in terms of organisational entities and role functions associated with particular activities or information objects, rather than specific participants. The workflow enactment service then has the responsibility of linking organisational entities or roles with the specific participants within the workflow runtime environment.

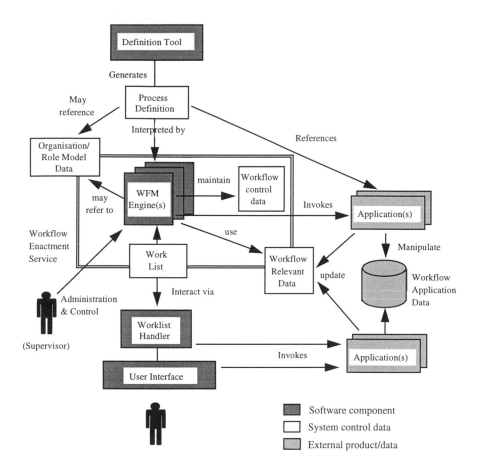

Figure 3   Generic Workflow Product Structure

1.3.3 Workflow Enactment Service

The workflow enactment software interprets the process description and controls the instantiation of processes and sequencing of activities, adding work items to the user work lists and invoking application tools as necessary. This is done through one or more co-operating workflow management engines, which manage(s) the execution of individual instances of the various processes. The workflow enactment service maintains internal control data either centralised or distributed across a set of workflow engines; this workflow control data includes the internal state information associated with the various process and activity instances under execution and may also include checkpointing and recovery/restart information used by the workflow engines to co-ordinate and recover from failure conditions.

The process definition, in conjunction with any (run-time) workflow relevant data is used to control the navigation through the various activity steps within the process, providing information about the entry and exit criteria for individual activity steps, parallel or sequential execution options for different activities, user tasks or IT applications associated with each activity, etc.. This may require access to organisation / role model data, if the process definition includes constructs relating to these entity types.

The workflow engines also include some form of application tool invocation capability to activate applications necessary to execute particular activities. The generality of such mechanisms may vary greatly, with some simple systems only offering support of a single fixed tool such as a form or document editor, whereas others may provide methods for the invocation of a wider range of tools, both local and remote to the Workflow engine.

1.3.4 Workflow Relevant Data and Application Data

Where process navigation decisions, or other control operations within the workflow engine, are based on data generated or updated by workflow application programs, such data is accessible to the workflow engine and termed workflow relevant data (also known as "case data"); this is the only type of application data accessible to the workflow engine. Workflow application data is manipulated directly (and only) by the invoked applications, although the workflow engines may be responsible for transferring such data between applications (if necessary), as different applications are invoked at different activity points within the workflow process.

1.3.5 Worklists

Where user interactions are necessary within the process execution, the workflow engine(s) place items on to worklists for attention by the worklist handler, which manages the interactions with the workflow participants. This process may be invisible to the workflow participants with the worklist maintained within the workflow software and the user being presented sequentially with the next task to be performed. On other systems the worklist may be visible to the user, who has the responsibility of selecting individual items of work from the list and progressing them independently, with the worklist being used to indicate task completions.

WORKLIST HANDLER & USER INTERFACE

The worklist handler is a software component which manages the interaction between workflow participants and the workflow enactment service. It is responsible for progressing work requiring user attention and interacts with the workflow enactment software via the worklist. In some systems, this may be little more than a desktop application providing a simple in-tray of work items awaiting user attention. In other systems this may be far more sophisticated, controlling the allocation of work amongst a set of users to provide facilities such as load balancing and work reassignment. In addition to these worklist handling functions, workflow engines typically support a wider range of interactions with client applications, including sign-on and -off of workflow participants, requesting the commencement of an instance of particular process types, requesting workitems queued for particular participants, etc.. Within the Reference Model the term *workflow client application* is used in preference to "worklist handler" to reflect this wider range of potential usage, which includes process control functions as well as worklist manipulation.

In the diagram the User Interface is shown as a separate software component, responsible for the look and feel of the user dialogue and control of the local interface with the user. In certain systems this may be combined with the Worklist Handler into a single functional entity. It also expected that some client applications will interact with several different workflow services, enabling workitems from such services to be consolidated into a unified task list for presentation to participants via a common user interface.

Invocation of local applications may be necessary to support the user in the particular tasks to be undertaken. This may be done by the Worklist Handler, for example at the time of presenting workitems to the user, or may be the responsibility of the user, using general facilities available at the User Interface software to load appropriate supporting applications. There is a distinction between application invocation at the Worklist Handler/User Interface (which is not directly controlled from the workflow engine and may not be visible to it) and direct application invocation by the workflow enactment software.

SUPERVISORY OPERATIONS

Within a workflow system there are a number of supervisory functions which are normally provided; these are typically supported on the basis of supervisory privilege to a particular workstation or user(s). These functions may enable supervisors to alter work allocation rules, to identify participants for specific organisational roles within a process, to track alerts for missed deadlines or other forms of event, to trace the history of a particular process instance, to enquire about work throughput or other statistics, etc.. Where distributed workflow engines are used there may need to be specific commands to transfer such control operations or (partial) responses between different workflow engines to provide a single administrative interface.

EXPOSED AND EMBEDDED INTERFACES

Whilst the majority of workflow products can be related to the above structure, not all products offer exposed interfaces between the various individual system functional components; some products may implement several functional components together as a single logical entity with the interfaces embedded within the software component and not available for third party product use. The WFM specifications will identify, for each interface, the role of that interface in achieving interoperability, so that individual products can identify conformance against particular interoperability criteria. (For example, a particular product might offer an exposed interface for worklist manipulation but not for process definition interchange.)

1.4 Alternative Implementation Scenarios

The structural model of a generic workflow product identifies a series of software components and interfaces. In a concrete product implementation this structure may be realised in a variety of different ways; this is an important area of product differentiation. Major distinguishing factors between products include choice of platform and network infrastructure, as well as the inherent functionality of the workflow software itself. This section illustrates how the generic model copes with this variety of implementation approach, whilst retaining visible interfaces to facilitate multi-vendor product interworking.

A full discussion of all potential implementation design issues lies outside the scope of this document. Amongst the main alternatives considered are:

- Centralised or distributed workflow enactment service
- Worklist handler location(s) and distribution mechanism

1.4.1 Workflow Enactment Software - Alternative Approaches

The workflow enactment software consists of one or more workflow engines, which are responsible for managing all, or part, of the execution of individual process instances. This may be set up as a centralised system with a single workflow engine responsible for managing all process execution or as a distributed system in which several engines cooperate, each managing part of the overall execution.

In the above scenario the two workflow services exhibit common properties at the boundary but follow different internal implementation architectures, whose characteristics may be product dependent.

Where several workflow engines cooperate in the execution of a process instance, the control data associated with the process instance must be accessible to the different engines. This workflow control data may be distributed across the engines, located at a master engine or held as a shared filestore resource, or some combination of these. The particular implementation approaches by which this data is made available to the engines is considered to be outside the current scope for standardisation. Similarly, the process definition data may be distributed across all engines or parts transferred to individual engines from some master source during process execution. Interfaces to handle supervisory operations or application invocation may be supported as distributed features or localised to particular engines. The implementation approaches to manage distribution of workflow across multiple engines are thus complex and numerous.

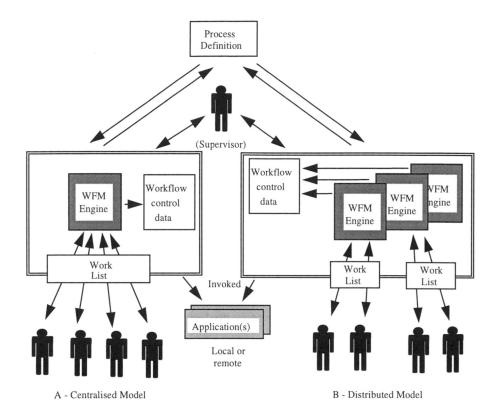

Figure 4   Standard Workflow Enactment Service Boundary

The approach taken by the Coalition is to define a boundary around the workflow enactment service, which exhibits various standard functional attributes accessible via a set of common APIs. The internal mechanisms by which the enactment service delivers this capability are not defined and may include one or more homogenous workflow engines, communicating in a variety of ways.

To support interworking between different products, interfaces are defined for specific co-operative functions between different enactment services so that a composite multi-vendor workflow application may execute parts of a particular process on different enactment services (each comprising one or more specific vendors workflow engines). This is considered a more realistic approach (except perhaps in the long term) than attempting to standardise the internal interfaces and state data of a distributed workflow service.

1.4.2 Workflow Client Applications - Alternative Approaches

In the workflow model interaction occurs between the worklist handler and a particular workflow engine through a well defined interface embracing the concept of a worklist - the queue of work items assigned to a particular user (or, possibly, group of common users) by the workflow enactment service. At the simplest level the worklist is accessible to the workflow engine for the purposes of assigning work items and to the worklist handler (i.e. the workflow client application) for the purpose of retrieving work items for presentation to the user for processing.

There are various possible product implementations of this worklist interaction model depending upon the nature of the product implementation and, in particular, on the type of infrastructure used to support the distribution of worklist handling.

Four possible approaches are illustrated in the following diagram, one supporting centralised worklist handling and three using a distributed worklist handler function.

The four example scenarios are as follows:

- Host based Model - the client worklist handler application is host based and communications with the worklist via a local interface at the workflow engine. In this case the user interface function may be driven via a terminal or a remote workstation MMI.
- Shared filestore model - the worklist handler application is implemented as a client function and communication is via a shared filestore, which lies on the boundary between host and client platform environments and is accessible to both.

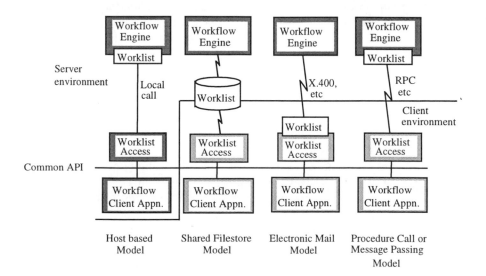

Figure 5   Alternative Client Worklist Handler Implementations

- Electronic mail model - communication is via electronic mail, which supports the distribution of work items to individual participants for local processing. In this scenario the worklist would normally lie at the client.
- Procedure Call or Message Passing model - communication is via procedure call, or other message passing mechanism. In this scenario the worklist may be physically located on the workflow engine or at the worklist handler according to the particular implementation characteristics.

In each case it is feasible to construct a common API, which supports worklist handler access to the worklist and workflow engine functions, but which is located behind a specific worklist access function appropriate to the product implementation style.

1.5 The Need for Standardisation

The basic rationale to achieve standardisation of important workflow functional interfaces is driven by two major considerations:

- Ongoing support for business re-engineering & operational flexibility
- Integration requirements resulting from product specialisation and market variety

1.5.1 Business Reengineering & Operational Flexibility

The strategic importance of business process re-engineering and associated workflow implementations will lead to the requirement for sufficient flexibility of product to cope with ongoing business change, indeed this is one of the key motivations behind the use of the technology. This will include cases where several separate business processes have been implemented using different workflow products, and require to be re-engineered into a single composite process involving interaction between existing workflows. These requirements may arise due to reorganisation, legislative changes, changing business objectives, etc.. As the use of electronic data interchange develops, these workflows are likely to embrace inter-organisation communications as well as those internal to a single organisation.

In these situations it is extremely likely that different products will be in use within different organisations or departments and the inability of such products to interoperate will cause a significant potential problem in coping with business change. The market projections for the penetration of workflow technology suggest very widespread adoption during the next 5–10 years, leading to the potential incompatibility problems seen in previous generations of information technology unless appropriate interworking standards are developed.

The early availability of such standards with subsequent product implementations will provide a degree of confidence to the market critical to the effective take up of workflow technology.

1.5.2 Specialisation and Market Variety

There are currently estimated to be in excess of a hundred different workflow (and related) products in the market, focused on different aspects of functionality and data/application integration. The development of interworking standards will allow application choice of "best of breed" products for individual aspects of a workflow implementation. This may embrace process analysis and definition products from one vendor, coupled with workflow engine software from a different vendor, integrated with a client worklist handling application from a third.

An individual workflow may conveniently be broken down into several sub-processes each enacted on a specialist product suited to the specific data type, platform or network environment related to that particular sub-process. The availability of interworking standards will provide the opportunity to implement composite solutions to business process requirements, linking several such specialist products to meet the precise needs of the process.

Furthermore, many workflow applications require to integrate with other, existing or emerging applications, ranging from desktop office functions to corporate transaction processing / database. The provision of a standard interface to support this will reduce product complexity and the amount of specialist integration skills necessary during implementation.

Members of the Coalition, both vendors and users, recognise the potential importance of standards in all these areas and are cooperating in their definition.

2. Workflow Reference Model

2.1 Overview

The Workflow Reference Model has been developed from the generic workflow application structure by identifying the interfaces within this structure which enable products to interoperate at a variety of levels. All workflow systems contain a number of generic components which interact in a defined set of ways; different products will typically exhibit different levels of capability within each of these generic components. To achieve interoperability between workflow products a standardised set of interfaces and data interchange formats between such components is necessary. A number of distinct interoperability scenarios can then be constructed by reference to such interfaces, identifying different levels of functional conformance as appropriate to the range of products in the market.

2.2 The Workflow Model

Figure 6 illustrates the major components and interfaces within the workflow architecture.

The architecture identifies the major components and interfaces. These are considered in turn in the following sections. As far as possible, the detail of the individual interfaces (APIs and interchange formats) will be developed as a common core set using additional parameters as necessary to cope with individual requirements of particular interfaces.

The interface around the workflow enactment service is designated WAPI - Workflow APIs and Interchange formats, which may be considered as a set of constructs by which the services of the workflow system may be accessed and which regulate the interactions between the workflow control software and other system components. Many of the functions within the five interface areas are common to two or more interface services hence it is more appropriate to consider WAPI as a unified service interface which is used to support workflow management functions across the five functional areas, rather than five individual interfaces.

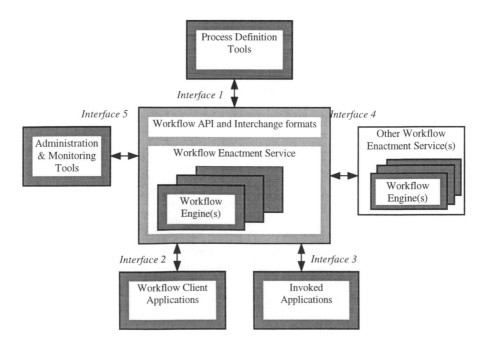

Figure 6   Workflow Reference Model - Components & Interfaces

2.3 Workflow Enactment Services

2.3.1 What is a Workflow Enactment Service?

The workflow enactment service provides the run-time environment in which process instantiation and activation occurs, utilising one or more workflow management engines, responsible for interpreting and activating part, or all, of the process definition and interacting with the external resources necessary to process the various activities.

DEFINITION - WORKFLOW ENACTMENT SERVICE

A software service that may consist of one or more workflow engines in order to create, manage and execute workflow instances. Applications may interface to this service via the workflow application programming interface (WAPI).

In the model adopted, there is a logical separation between this process and activity control logic, which constitutes the workflow enactment service, and the application tools and end user tasks which constitute the processing associated with each activity. This separation provides the opportunity for a wide range of industry standard or user specific application tools to be integrated within a particular workflow application.

Interaction with external resources accessible to the particular enactment service occurs via one of two interfaces:

- The client application interface, through which a workflow engine interacts with a worklist handler, responsible for organising work on behalf of a user resource. It is the responsibility of the worklist handler to select and progress individual work items from the work list. Activation of application tools may be under the control of the worklist handler or the end-user.
- The invoked application interface, which enables the workflow engine to directly activate a specific tool to undertake a particular activity. This would typically be a server-based application with no user interface; where a particular activity uses a tool which requires end-user interaction it would normally be invoked via the worklist interface to provide more flexibility for user task scheduling. By using a standard interface for tool invocation, future application tools may be workflow enabled in a standardised manner.

These interfaces are described in sections 2.5 and 2.6 respectively.

Within this section, the workflow enactment service has been discussed as a single logical entity, although physically it may be either centralised or functionally distributed.

In a distributed workflow enactment service, several workflow engines each control a part of the process enactment and interact with that subset of users and application tools related to the activities within the process for which they are responsible. Such an enactment service is considered to have common naming and administrative scope, so that process definitions (or subsets) and user/application names may be handled on a consistent basis. Distributed workflow systems make use of specific protocols and interchange formats between Workflow engines to synchronise their operations and exchange process and activity control information. Workflow relevant data may also be transferred between workflow engines. Within a single homogeneous workflow enactment service, such operations are vendor specific.

Where heterogeneous products are involved, a standardised interchange is necessary between workflow engines. Using interface 4, the enactment service may transfer activities or sub-processes to another (heterogeneous) enactment service for execution. Within the Workflow Reference Model this is termed Workflow Engine Interchange and is considered under section 2.7.

Common administration and monitoring functions may also be required in such a heterogeneous environment; these are considered in section 2.8.

2.3.2 The Workflow Engine

A workflow engine is responsible for part (or all) of the runtime control environment within an enactment service.

DEFINITION - WORKFLOW ENGINE

A software service or "engine" that provides the run time execution environment for a workflow instance.

Typically such software provides facilities to handle:

- interpretation of the process definition
- control of process instances - creation, activation, suspension, termination, etc.
- navigation between process activities, which may involve sequential or parallel operations, deadline scheduling, interpretation of workflow relevant data, etc.
- sign-on and sign-off of specific participants
- identification of work items for user attention and an interface to support user interactions
- maintenance of workflow control data and workflow relevant data, passing workflow relevant data to/from applications or users
- an interface to invoke external applications and link any workflow relevant data
- supervisory actions for control, administration and audit purposes

A workflow engine can control the execution of a set of process, or sub-process, instances with a defined scope - determined by the range of object types, and their attributes, which it can interpret within the process definition(s).

In an enactment service consisting of multiple workflow engines, there is a partitioning of process execution across the constituent engines. This may be by process type, with a particular engine controlling a particular process type in its entirety, by functional distribution, with a particular engine controlling those parts of a process requiring user or resource allocation within its own control domain, or some other partitioning mechanism.

2.3.3 Homogeneous & Heterogeneous Workflow Enactment Services

An homogeneous workflow enactment service comprises one or more compatible workflow engines which provide the runtime execution environment for workflow processes with a defined set of (product specific) process definition attributes. The mechanisms by which process execution is organised across the various workflow engines and protocols and interchange formats used to support this are product specific and not standardised.

A heterogeneous workflow enactment service comprises two or more homogeneous services, which follow common standards for interoperability at a defined conformance level. It is envisaged that a number of conformance levels will be defined to support increasing levels of common functionality.

These are expected to include (amongst other things):

- A common naming scheme across the heterogeneous domain
- Support for common process definition objects and attributes across the domain
- Support for workflow relevant data transfer across the domain
- Support for process, sub-process or activity transfer between heterogeneous workflow engines
- Support for common administration and monitoring functions within the domain

Support for common workflow control data and its interchange (e.g. shared process and activity state data) would be necessary to support totally open interworking between heterogeneous products; whilst an interesting standardisation challenge it is considered unattainable in the foreseeable future, hence the emphasis on levels of interoperability governed by defined conformance criteria.

PROCESS AND ACTIVITY STATE TRANSITIONS

The workflow enactment service may be considered as a state transition machine, where individual process or activity instances change states in response to external events (e.g. completion of an activity) or to specific control decisions taken by a workflow engine (e.g. navigation to the next activity step within a process).

An illustrative basic state transition scheme for process instances is shown below.

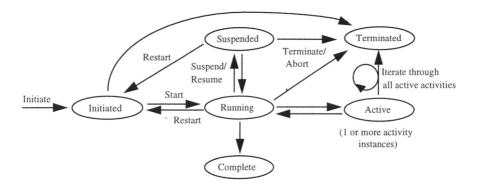

Figure 7   Example State Transitions for a Process Instance

Within the above diagram, transition between states (represented by the arrows) take place in response to the particular WAPI commands identified; transition between certain states will also take place as a result of transition conditions within the process definition being met (e.g. as the result of an external event, or time or data dependent condition, etc.) The basic states are:

- *Initiated* - a process instance has been created, including any associated process state date and workflow relevant data, but the process has not (yet) fulfilled the conditions to cause it to start execution
- *Running* - the process instance has started execution and any of its activities may be started (once any appropriate activity start conditions have been met)
- *Active* - one or more of its activities has been started (ie a workitem has been created and assigned to an appropriate activity instance)
- *Suspended* - the process instance is quiescent and no activities are started until the process has returned to the running state (via a resume command)
- *Completed* - the process instance has fulfilled the conditions for completion; any internal post-completion operations such as logging audit data or statistics will be performed and the process instance destroyed
- *Terminated* - execution of the process instance has been stopped before its normal completion; any internal operations such as error logging or logging recovery data may be performed and the process instance destroyed

Activities may be non-interruptable; ie once a workflow service has started a particular activity within a process instance, it may not be possible to suspend or terminate that activity. This means that suspension / restart / terminate functions cannot be completed until all active activities have completed and the process instance returned to a running state. In addition, it may be required to mark a set of activities as an atomic unit, which are either executed in entirety or the process instance "rolled-back" to a restart point. The potential treatment of interruptable activities and atomic activity units with restart capability will require further consideration and is beyond the initial work of the Coalition.

Ignoring these additional complexities, a simple illustration of the basic states and transitions for an activity instance is thus:

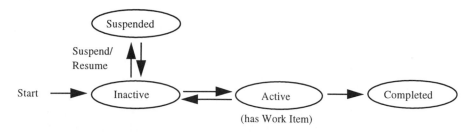

Figure 8   Example State Transitions for Activity Instances

The basic states of an activity instance are:

- *Inactive* - the activity within the process instance has been created but has not yet been activated (e.g. because activity entry conditions have not been met) and has no workitem for processing
- *Active* - a workitem has been created and assigned to the activity instance for processing
- *Suspended* - the activity instance is quiescent (e.g. as a result of a change_state_of_activity_instance command) and will not be allocated a workitem until returned to the running (inactive) state
- *Completed* - execution of the activity instance has completed (and any post-activity transition conditions will be evaluated)

A particular product implementation may, of course, support additional state types or use a different representation of the basic states and transitions shown above. The reference model does not attempt to prescribe standardised internal behaviour of workflow systems but the state transitions illustrate the basic underlying concepts which are necessary to scope the effects of the API command set which the Coalition is developing.

2.3.4 Workflow Application Programming Interface & Interchange

The WAPI may be regarded as a set of API calls and interchange functions supported by a workflow enactment service at its boundary for interaction with other resources and applications. Although this architecture refers to five "interfaces" within WAPI, a number of the functions within each of these interfaces are common (for example process status calls may be issued from the client application interface or the administration interface). The WAPI is thus being defined as a common core of API calls /interchange formats with specific extensions where necessary to cater individually for each of the five functional areas.

The majority of WAPI functions comprises of APIs calls with defined parameter sets / results codes. Where appropriate it also defines interchange data formats, for example for the exchange of process definitions. The use of WAPI within each of the five functional areas is described within the following sections (2.4 - 2.8).

2.3.5 Workflow Control, Workflow Relevant and Workflow Application Data

The workflow enactment service maintains internal control data to identify the state of individual process or activity instances and may support other internal status information. This data is not accessible or interchangeable, as such, via the WAPI commands, but some of the information content may be provided in response to specific commands (e.g. query process status, give performance metrics, etc.). Homogeneous workflow enactment services may exchange such information between workflow engines by specific private dialogue.

> **DEFINITION - WORKFLOW CONTROL DATA**
> Internal data that is managed by the workflow management system and/or workflow engine.

Workflow Relevant Data is used by a workflow management system to determine particular transition conditions and may affect the choice of the next activity to be executed. Such data is potentially accessible to workflow applications for operations on the data and thus may need to be transferred between activities by the workflow enactment software. When operating in a heterogeneous environment, such data may need to be transferred between workflow engines, where the process execution sequence spans two or more workflow engines; this process may (potentially) require name mapping or data conversion.

> **DEFINITION - WORKFLOW RELEVANT DATA**
> Data that is used by a workflow management system to determine the state transition of a workflow process instance.

Manipulation of application data may be required within each activity of a process definition, for example by a particular tool or application, either under the direct control of the application or in conjunction with some form of user interaction. The workflow model must, therefore, cope with any necessary interchange of case data between the various activities. In some circumstances this may also require some form of case data transformation between different tool data formats, for example conversion of a document or spreadsheet from one application format to another. (In some systems this may be a function of the workflow enactment service, in others data conversion may be defined as an activity in its own right within the process definition.)

DEFINITION - WORKFLOW APPLICATION DATA

Data that is application specific and not accessible by the workflow management system.

Workflow application data is not used by the workflow enactment software and is relevant only to the applications or user tasks executed during the workflow. As with workflow relevant data, it may need to be transferred (and/or transformed) between workflow engines in a heterogeneous enactment service, so as to be made available to the appropriate activities executed on the individual engines.

The relationship between an application and any workflow relevant or application data it needs to manipulate will normally be defined within the process definition. In some cases this may be an implicit relationship (for example in those systems where case data is physically transferred to the next activity as part of the activity navigation within the process), whereas in others (for example access to a shared object store) it may be an explicit relationship defining a specific object name and application access path. Within the reference model the former scenario will be called direct data interchange and the latter indirect data interchange.

2.3.6 Data Interchange

Interchange of workflow relevant and application data is (potentially) required across the WAPI to support interworking within three runtime functions

- Worklist handler (interface 2)
- Invoked application (interface 3)
- Workflow engine interchange (interface 4)

This section covers the general principles of data interchange; this area will require further specification work. The proposed API command set may include specific calls to accept/return workflow relevant data from/to the enactment service across the WAPI; variants of these could be defined for both direct and indirect case data interchange.

The direct interchange of application data is typified by email driven workflow systems in which the data is physically transferred between activities, either application or user-driven. In this situation there is no need to define an explicit relationship between activities and application data; the data is transferred as part of the standard workflow activity navigation and locally linked to the application on invocation. Where there is a requirement to provide data format conversion between activities, the model recognises that a particular application may define, as an attribute, the data type (or types) with which it is associated (this attribute information may be held local to a particular software environment or global to the entire workflow service - for example in a directory). This enables systems which are constructed to use heterogeneous workflow applications to provide data conversion (where necessary) on the basis of attribute types defined for the respective applications. Conventions will need to be adopted (or developed) for transferring and retaining the data type information, for example by the use of X.400 body part object identifiers or the Internet mail MIME mechanism (RFC-1341).

Some types of workflow system (for example, those implemented via a shared document store) do not physically transfer application data between activities. In these systems, data is accessed in situ by the application using an appropriate access path (which may be networked). In this case, the access path naming scheme must be global to all applications which may be invoked within the workflow service and appropriate access permissions must be available and controlled for each active process instance. Data format conversion in this scenario, if necessary, may be modelled as an activity in its own right, using an appropriate application tool (for example a document converter).

Homogenous systems may use private conventions for object names and access permissions, but heterogeneous systems require a common scheme. In this case, either the (common) process definition must include access path references to the application data object storage, or the navigation between activities must include transfer of the necessary access path references for any data objects to be transferred between activities.

Where interworking between heterogeneous workflow products is planned they must either follow the same approach to application data interchange or interwork through a gateway mechanism (section 2.7), which can map between the two approaches and/or handle any differences in object naming and data type conventions by appropriate conversion. Further work is required on the detail in this area, but it is possible that alternative interchange conformance criteria could be identified to cover the two cases.

The way in which application or workflow relevant data interchange is to be handled across the three interfaces is for more detailed study; the following notes identify some initial options.

Client applications - workflow relevant data may be embedded in the workitem and extracted from the worklist for presentation to the user or for linkage to a particular application tool (for example by the worklist handler locating it in a particular local directory). Alternatively, the data may be indirectly passed to a specific application via some form of shared object store (for example by the use of a common file for data in transit between applications, or by passing a specific file reference embedded as part of the workitem.)

Invoked applications - the data interchange will depend upon the nature of the application invocation interface (section 2.6) and may require the invocation service to embed the data within a specific application protocol. APIs for reading /writing workflow relevant data are feasible for specific workflow-enabled applications or to construct generalised application agents.

Workflow engine interoperability - considerations are similar to the Client Application interface, although where the different systems support different application data interchange approaches, the use of a gateway function will be necessary to map between the two schemes and, possibly, handle name resolution.

2.4 Process Definition

2.4.1 Process Definition Tools

A variety of different tools may be used to analyse, model, describe and document a business process; such tools may vary from the informal ("pencil and paper") to sophisticated and highly formalised. The workflow model is not concerned with the particular nature of such tools nor how they interact during the build-time process. As noted earlier, such tools may be supplied as part of a workflow product or as a separate, for example, BPR product toolset.

Where a workflow product provides its own process definition tool, the resultant process definitions will normally be held within the workflow product domain and may, or may not, be accessible via a programming interface for reading and writing information. Where separate products are used for defining and executing the process, the process definitions may be transferred between the products as and when required or may be stored in a separate repository, accessible to both products (and possibly other development tools).

The final output from this process modelling and design activity is a process definition which can be interpreted at runtime by the workflow engine(s) within the enactment service. For today's workflow products each individual process definition is typically in a form specialised to the particular workflow management software for which it was designed. The workflow definition interchange interface will enable more flexibility in this area.

The process analysis, modelling and definition tools may include the ability to model processes in the context of an organisation structure (although this is not a mandatory aspect of the workflow reference model). Where an organisation model is incorporated into such tools the process definition will include organisation related objects such as roles. These are related (typically) to system control data such as role: actor relationships (e.g. within an organisational directory) which may be referenced during process execution.

2.4.2 Workflow Definition Interchange (Interface 1)

The interface between the modelling and definition tools and the runtime workflow management software is termed the process definition import/export interface. The nature of the interface is an interchange format and API calls, which can support the exchange of process definition information over a variety of physical or electronic interchange media. The interface may support the exchange of a complete process definition or a subset - for example a set of process definition changes or the attributes of a particular activity within the process definition.

There are clear benefits in using a standardised form for this definition.

Firstly, it defines a point of separation between the build-time and runtime environments, enabling a process definition generated by one modelling tool to be used as input to a number of different workflow runtime products. This enables user choice of modelling tools and workflow runtime products to be independent.

Secondly, it offers the potential to export a process definition to several different workflow products which could co-operate to provide a distributed runtime enactment service. (The ability to exchange process definition data is only one aspect of such a distributed service; there are other requirements in terms of runtime interactions between WFM-Engine, which are considered in section 2.8.)

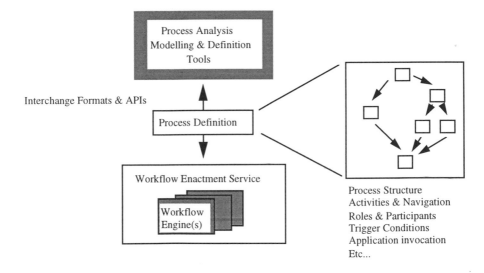

Figure 9   Process Definition Interchange

There are two aspects to the Coalition's work in this area:

1. Derivation of a meta-model which can be used to express the objects, their relationships and attributes within a process definition and which can form the basis for a set of interchange formats to exchange this information between products

2. API calls (within the WAPI) between workflow systems or between a workflow system and process definition product, providing a common way to access workflow process definitions. Access may be read, read/write or write only and may manipulate the set of standard objects defined within the meta-model or a product-specific set (for example defined in a product type register).

A BASIC META-MODEL

The Coalition is developing a meta-model for the process definition, which identifies a basic set of object types appropriate to an initial level for the interchange of relatively simple process definitions. Further object types may be added, either by vendor specific extensions and/or by defining additional conformance levels with added functionality.

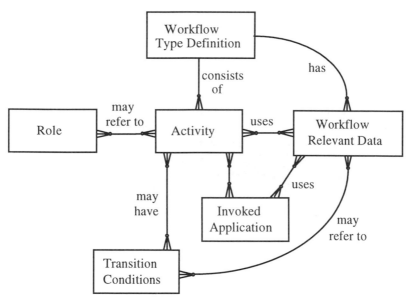

Figure 10   Basic Process Definition Meta-model

It is envisaged that particular attributes of the following types will be defined:

WORKFLOW TYPE DEFINITION

- Workflow process name
- Version number
- Process start and termination conditions
- Security, audit or other control data

ACTIVITY

- Activity name
- Activity type (subflow, atomic flow, etc.)
- Pre- and post- activity conditions
- Other scheduling constraints

TRANSITION CONDITIONS

- Flow or Execution conditions

WORKFLOW RELEVANT DATA

- Data name and path
- Data types

ROLE

- Name and organisational entity

INVOKED APPLICATION

- Generic type or name
- Execution parameters
- Location or access path

In the case of distributed services, an allocation of activities to individual workflow engines may also need to be made within the process definition, as an additional activity attribute. Process definition aspects affecting security and administration, for example controls over privileged or supervisory activities within the process, also require consideration in the longer term.

In defining interchange formats, it is assumed that a symbolic naming scheme would be supported which could be unambiguously mapped to real names and addresses in the runtime enactment service. This may be handled by dynamic address resolution mechanisms (for example by the use of a directory service) or by other mechanism external to the process definition. There are other industry groups working in related areas such as process modelling and CASE interchange tools; the proposed Coalition approach in this area is to work with other groups to advance the definition of suitable interchange formats.

APIS TO ACCESS PROCESS DEFINITIONS

A set of API commands within WAPI is under development to support access to process definition data. It is expected that such specifications will cover a number of functions of the following general types. Commands are expected to be provided which operate on a list, or on individual objects or attributes.

Session Establishment
- Connection / disconnection of sessions between participating systems

Workflow Definition Operations
- Retrieval of lists of workflow process definition names from a repository or other source list
- Selection / de-selection of a workflow process definition to provide a session handle for further object level operations
- Read/write top level workflow process definition object

Workflow Definition Object Operations
- Creation, retrieval & deletion of objects within a workflow definition
- Retrieval, setting and deletion of object attributes

2.5 Workflow Client Functions

2.5.1 Workflow Client Applications

The worklist handler is the software entity which interacts with the end-user in those activities which require involve human resources. The worklist handler may be supplied as part of a workflow management product or may be written by a user, for example to provide a particular common house style for use with a number of different workflow applications utilising different vendor's products. In other cases, workflow may be integrated into a common desktop environment alongside other office services such as mail and work-in-progress folders to provide a unified task management system for the end-user. There is thus a need for a flexible mechanism of communication between a workflow enactment service and workflow client applications to support the construction of the many different operational systems which are expected to be encountered.

In the workflow model interaction occurs between the client application and the workflow engine through a well defined interface embracing the concept of a worklist - the queue of work items assigned to a particular user (or, possibly, group of common users) by the workflow engine. At the simplest level the worklist is accessible to the workflow engine for the purposes of assigning work items and to the worklist handler for the purpose of retrieving work items for presentation to the user for processing. There are various possible product implementations of this worklist interaction (see section 1.4).

Activation of individual work items from the worklist (for example launching application and linking workflow relevant data) may be under the control of the workflow client application or the end-user. A range of procedures is defined between the workflow client application and the workflow enactment service to enable new items to be added to the worklist, completed activities to be removed from the worklist, activities to be temporarily suspended, etc.. These are described in section 2.5.2

Application invocation may also be handled from the worklist handler, either directly or under the control of the end-user. In general it is expected that the range of applications invoked from the worklist handler would be predominantly local to that environment, although it may place an unnecessary constraint on the generality of the model to assume that this will always be the case.

Part of the activity related data associated with the worklist is the necessary information to enable the worklist handler to invoke the appropriate applications(s). Where the application data is strongly typed, an association may be stored at the worklist handler and used for this purpose. In other cases an interchange of the full application name and address information may be necessary between the worklist handler and Workflow engine, in which case the workflow Client Application may also implements some functions from the invoked application interface (Interface 3) to obtain the necessary information.

A worklist may contain items relating to several different active instances of a single process and/or individual items from activations of several different processes. A worklist handler might potentially be interacting with several different Workflow engines and several different enactment services. (According to individual product implementation, separate physical worklists may be maintained for each process type, or the worklist handler may consolidate the various worklists items into a single representation to the end-user.) .

The interface between the client workflow application and Workflow engine must therefore be sufficiently flexible in terms of its use of:

- process and activity identifiers
- resource names and addresses
- data references and data structures
- alternative communications mechanisms

to contain these variations of implementation approach.

2.5.2 *Workflow Client Application Interface (Interface 2)*

The approach to meet the above requirement is to contain the variety behind a standard set of APIs (the WAPI), which may be used in a consistent manner for access from a workflow application to the Workflow engine and worklist, irrespective of the nature of actual product implementation.

The APIs and its parameters will be mapped onto several alternative communications mechanisms to fit the variety of workflow implementation models. (In the case of email based communications it is also possible, of course, for a worklist handler to directly access the incoming mailbox for incoming work items using any local mailbox access interface, rather than via specific WAPI calls. In this case the worklist handler application will take responsibility for filtering any non-workflow email items and handling them in an appropriate manner. Similarly commands or responses directed at the workflow engine by the workflow application may be submitted directly to an outgoing mailbox handler. In this scenario a simple level of interoperability is achieved through the use of standardised mail interchange formats, rather than the full WAPI.)

The overall approach to the client application API is shown in figure 11, following.

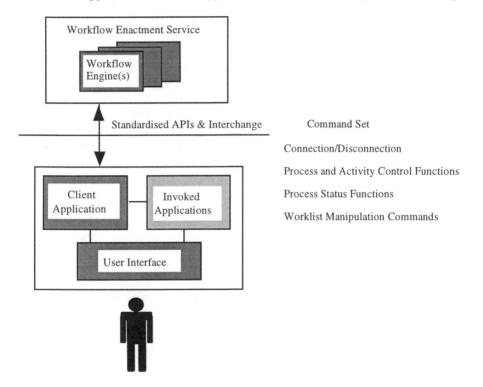

Figure 11   Client Application Interface

The API specifications are published in a separate Coalition document; the following provides an overview of the intended APIs for client application use, grouped into various functional areas. Commands are provided for operations on individual or collective process or activity instances as well as worklist manipulation.

Session Establishment
• Connection / disconnection of sessions between participating systems

Workflow Definition Operations
• Retrieval / query functions (with optional selection criteria) on workflow process definition names or attributes

Process Control Functions
• Creation / starting / termination of an individual process instance

- Suspension / resumption of an individual process instance
- Forcing a state change within an individual process instance or activity instance
- Assignment or query of an attribute (e.g. priority) of a process or activity instance

Process Status Functions
- Opening / closing a process or activity instances query, setting optional filter criteria
- Fetching details of process instances or activity instances, filtered as specified
- Fetching details of a specific (individual) process or activity instance

Worklist/Workitem Handling Functions
- Opening / closing a worklist query, setting optional filter criteria
- Fetching worklist items, filtered as specified
- Notification of selection / reassignment / completion of a (specific) workitem
- Assignment or query of a workitem attribute

Process Supervisory Functions
(The following functions operate on all process or activity instances and are deemed to operate in the context of a supervisory privilege level, which may, or may not, be granted to a specific client application or user logged onto such application.)

- Changing the operational status of a workflow process definition and/or its extant process instances
- Changing the state of all process or activity instances of a specified type
- Assigning attribute(s) to all process or activity instances of a specified type
- Termination of all process instances

Data Handling Functions
- Retrieval / return of workflow relevant or application data

Administration Functions
Support for additional administration functions across the WAPI may be appropriate for certain client applications. A subset of the operations discussed in 2.8.2 may be included in a future conformance level.

Application Invocation
The functions outlined above provide a base level of functionality to support application invocation by the worklist handler function (e.g. by providing access to process/activity/workitem attributes and workflow relevant data). Some of the proposed commands for the application invocation function (section 2.6.2) may also be relevant to the client application environment.

It is possible that some product implementations may wish to support a subset of the full WAPI; further consideration will be given to identifying conformance levels to cater for the different interoperability requirements arising from the range of workflow products available in the market.

2.6 Invoked Application Functions

2.6.1 Invoked Applications

It may be assumed that any particular WFM implementation will not have sufficient logic to understand how to invoke all potential applications which might exist in an heterogeneous product environment. This would require the logic to cope with invocation across (potentially) all platform and network environments, together with a means of transferring application or workflow relevant data in a common format and encoding (or transforming it to the individual application environments).

However there are many workflow systems which deal with a more restrictive range of applications, particularly those where the data is strongly typed and may be directly associated (for example via a directory) with a particular application tool such as a word processor or spreadsheet. In other cases invocation of an operation by a particular application may be accomplished through a standard interchange mechanism such as the OSI TP protocol or X.400. Some implementations use the concept of a "Application Agent" to contain this variety of method invocation behind a standard interface into the workflow enactment service. There is also the possibility of developing "workflow enabled" application tools which use a standard set of APIs to communicate with the workflow enactment service - to accept application data, signal and respond to activity events, etc.. Such APIs may be used directly by an application tool or by a application agent process acting as a front end for interaction with heritage or other applications written without a specific knowledge of workflow.

Some of the possible types of interface for application invocation are identified in the following table.

Table 1 Application Invocation Interfaces

Interface Type	Workflow Relevant Data Access	Standardisation Candidate
Local Process Call	Local File	No
Shell Script	Local File	POSIX environments?
ORB Call (e.g. object linking and launch service)	Via reference (call parameters)	Yes
Remote Execution Call	Via reference (call parameters)	Yes
Message Passing (e.g. X.400)	Embedded or via reference	Yes
Transaction (e.g. OSI-TP)	Embedded or via reference	Yes

Further discussion will be required on the full range of possible options for application invocation. The initial work of the Coalition is likely to focus on developing a catalogue of interface types, together with a set of APIs for use in future workflow specific applications.

2.6.2 Invoked Applications Interface (Interface 3)

The diagram following shows the scope of this interface, which is intended to be applicable to application agents and (longer term) applications which have been designed to be "workflow enabled" (ie to interact directly with a workflow engine).

In the simple case, application invocation is handled locally to a workflow engine, using information within the process definition to identify the nature of the activity, the type of application to be invoked and any data requirements. The invoked application may be local to the workflow engine, co-resident on the same platform or located on a separate, network accessible platform; the process definition contains sufficient application type and addressing information (specific to the needs of the workflow engine) to invoke the application. In this case the conventions for application naming and addressing are local between the process definition and the workflow engine.

The detailed semantics and syntax of an API set for application invocation are for further study and will be documented as part of the Coalition specification set. Operation is envisaged over a variety of underlying interfaces, including a selection from the above table, some of which may operate synchronously and others asynchronously. The operation of the API is assumed at this stage to be potentially either single- or multi-threaded (in the latter case using an activity id handle for thread discrimination). The following provides an outline of a possible command set applicable to application invocation functions.

SESSION ESTABLISHMENT
- Connection / disconnection of application (or application agent) session

ACTIVITY MANAGEMENT FUNCTIONS
(workflow engine to application)
- Start activity (workflow engine to application)
- Suspend/Resume/Abort activity (where an asynchronous application interface is available)
(application to workflow engine)
- Activity complete notification
- Signal event (e.g. synchronisation)
- Query activity attributes

DATA HANDLING FUNCTIONS
- Give workflow relevant data (pre-activity to application, post activity from application)
- Give application data or data address

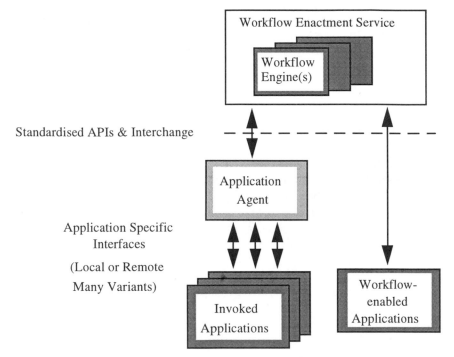

Figure 12   Invoked Application Interface

More complex scenarios, involving interworking between heterogeneous Workflow engines, may require application invocation information to be transferred between Workflow engines, either as part of the run-time interchange or by importing (parts) of the process definition after the process development phase. This is considered under section 2.7 (Workflow Interoperability).

2.7 Workflow Interoperability

2.7.1 Heterogeneous Workflow Enactment Services

A key objective of the Coalition is to define standards that will allow workflow systems produced by different vendors to pass work items seamlessly between one another.

Workflow products are diverse in nature ranging from those used for more ad-hoc routing of tasks or data to those aimed at highly regularised production processes. In its drive for interoperability standards the Coalition is determined not to force workflow product vendors to choose between providing a strong product focused on the needs of its customers and giving up those strengths just to provide interoperability.

The work of the Coalition has therefore focused on developing a variety of interoperability scenarios which can operate at a number of levels from simple task passing through to full workflow application interoperability with complete interchange of process definition, workflow relevant data and a common look and feel. In this area it is expected that relatively simple interoperability scenarios will be supported initially, with the more complex situations requiring further work on interoperability definitions.

Although it is possible to consider the development of very complex interoperability scenarios in which a number of different vendor engines cooperate to deliver a single enactment service, this scenario is unlikely to be realised in the near future as it requires that all engines can interpret a common process definition and share a common set of workflow control data, in effect maintaining a shared view of process states across the heterogeneous workflow control engines. A more realistic target in the near term is the ability to transfer parts of a process for runtime support on a different enactment service.

Four possible interoperability models has been identified, covering various (increasing) levels of capability. The following sections describes these potential interoperability models; the illustrations use squares to indicate tasks or activities, with different shading to denote tasks co-ordinated by individual workflow enactment services.

SCENARIO 1 - CONNECTED DISCRETE (CHAINED)

This model allows a connection point within process A to connect to another point within process B. Although the illustration shows these connection points at the terminus and starting points of the processes, this is done for illustration purposes only. It is presumed that the connection points can be anywhere within the processes that makes sense for the meat-process created by the connection of the two.

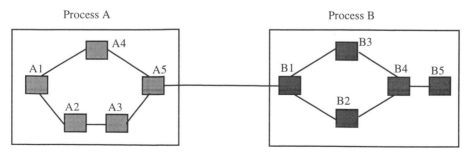

Figure 13   Chained Services Model

This model supports the transfer of a single item of work (a process instance or activity) between the two workflow environments, which then operates independently in the second environment with no further synchronisation. In implementation terms it may be realised via a gateway application function, handling data format conversion, process and activity name mapping, etc., or may be subsumed into one of the workflow services, for example when a standard API call is used between the two services.

2.7.2 Scenario 2 - Hierarchical (Nested Subprocesses)

This allows a process executed in a particular workflow domain to be completely encapsulated as a single task within a (superior) process executed in a different workflow domain. A hierarchic relationship exists between the superior process and the encapsulated process, which in effect forms a sub-process of the superior. The hierarchic relationship may be continued across several levels, forming a set of nested sub-processes. Recursion within this scenario may, or may not, be permitted by individual product implementations.

In the diagram, Workflow Service A has an activity defined (A3) which is enacted as a complete process (B) on Workflow Service B with control returned to Service A on completion. As in scenario 1 earlier, transfer of activity control may be via an applications gateway function or by direct API calls between the two workflow services. The diagram illustrates the simple case with a single entry and exit point in Process B, although activity navigation rules within B may permit other activity flow scenarios, for example process completion conditions enabling the process to be completed prior to activity B5 and control returned to workflow domain A.

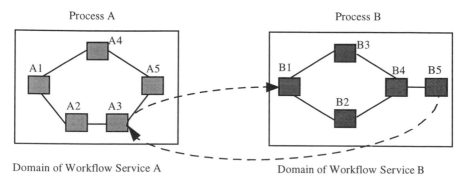

Figure 14   Nested Subprocesses Model

2.7.3 Scenario 3 - Connected Indiscrete (Peer-to-Peer)

This model allows a fully mixed environment; the diagram indicates a composite process C, which includes activities which may be executed across multiple workflow services, forming a shared domain. Activities C1, C2 and C5 could be co-ordinated by server A (or even several homogenous servers within a common domain) and activities C3, C4 and C6 co-ordinated by server B.

In this scenario, the process would progress transparently from task to task, without any specific actions by users or administrators, with interactions between the individual workflow engines taking place as necessary.

This scenario requires that both workflow services support common API sets for communication and that both can interpret a common process definition, either imported to both environments from a common build process or exported between services during the runtime phase. Workflow relevant and application data may also need to be passed between the various heterogeneous engines.

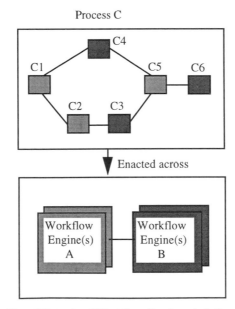

Shared Domain of Workflow Services A & B

Figure 15   Peer-Peer Model

Whilst simply illustrated as an interworking scenario, there are various complexities within the peer-peer model which will require further study. As shown each particular activity is associated with a specific workflow domain, for example predefined within the process definition. Further complexities arise where a specific activity may be executed on either of two independent workflow services or where a particular process instance can be created or terminated independently by either service. Systems administration, security and recovery across co-operating workflow services will also need to be addressed. In the extreme, the two different workflow enactment services may require to share much of the process state data normally maintained internally to each, in effect forming a single heterogeneous service. The Coalition intends to define a number of conformance levels, allowing earlier specifications to cope with simpler scenarios and additional functions to cope with more complex scenarios to be added in the future.

2.7.4 Scenario 4 - Parallel Synchronised

This model allows two processes to operate essentially independently, possibly across separate enactment services, but requires that synchronisation points exist between the two processes. Synchronisation requires that once the processes each reach a predefined point within their respective execution sequences, a common event is generated. This type of mechanism may be used to facilitate functions such as process scheduling across parallel execution threads, checkpointing of recovery data or the transfer of workflow relevant data between different process instances.

In the diagram following synchronisation is shown between activity A3 within process A and activity B4 within process B.

Matching pairs of work can thus be synchronised at specific points in each process. This requires an event co-ordination and tracking mechanism, in addition to both services being able to recognise tasks from the two process definitions. It is included for completeness but is recognised as lying beyond the scope of the Coalition's current specification activity.

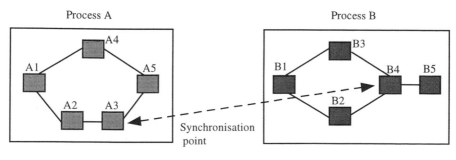

Figure 16   Parallel Synchronised Model

2.7.5 WAPI Interoperability Functions (Interface 4)

The general nature of the information and control flows between heterogeneous workflow systems is shown in Figure 17.

There are two major aspects to the necessary interoperability:

- The extent to which common interpretation of the process definition (or a subset) is necessary and can be achieved
- Runtime support for the interchange of various types of control information and to transfer workflow relevant and/or application data between the different enactment services

Interface 4

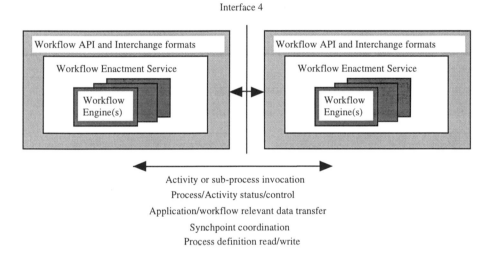

Activity or sub-process invocation
Process/Activity status/control
Application/workflow relevant data transfer
Synchpoint coordination
Process definition read/write

Figure 17   Workflow Interoperability Interface

USE OF PROCESS DEFINITIONS ACROSS MULTIPLE DOMAINS

Where both enactment services can interpret a common process definition, for example generated from a common build tool, this enables both environments to share a single view of the process definition objects and their attributes. This would include activity, application, organisation and role names, navigation conditions, etc.. This potentially enables individual workflow engines to transfer execution of activities or sub-processes to heterogeneous workflow engines within the context of a common naming and object model. This approach is particularly applicable to interoperability scenario 3, where several systems are co-operating at peer level, although can also be employed in simpler scenarios.

Where this shared view of a process definition is not feasible, the alternative approach of "exporting" details of a process definition subset as part of the runtime interchange may be possible. The process definition interchange APIs provide a means of requesting object and attribute data from a particular workflow service, thus enabling a workflow engine to obtain process definition data relevant to the execution of an individual activity or sub-process assigned to it in a co-operative enactment environment.

Where process definition interchange by either of the above approaches is infeasible, interoperability is constrained to a gateway approach, in which (typically a subset of) object names and attributes are mapped between the two environments via an application interworking gateway. In this simplest case, the two separate enactment services use their own process definition formats with any mapping between the two handled within the gateway. This approach effectively constrains interworking to the simpler scenarios 1 and 2 or relatively trivial examples of scenario 4.

RUNTIME CONTROL INTERACTIONS

At runtime, the WAPI calls are used to transfer control between workflow services to enact subprocesses or individual activities on a specific service. Where both services support a common level of WAPI calls and a common view of the process definition objects (including naming conventions and any workflow relevant or applications data) this will be done directly between Workflow engines - although this will require agreement on common protocol support for WAPI primitives.

Where this is not the case the WAPI calls can be used to construct a gateway function providing interworking between the two workflow services by mapping the different object and data views between the two environments and (where necessary) supporting different protocol environments into each workflow service. This is illustrated in the following diagram.

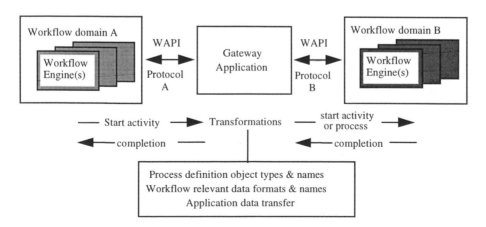

Figure 18   Gateway Operation Using WAPI

The diagram illustrates the main principles of gateway operation; depending upon the particular interworking scenario an individual activity from one domain (A) may be mapped to a single activity or a new process / subprocess in the second domain (B).

A large number of WAPI commands are (ultimately) likely to be exploited to support interoperability either by direct call between the two workflow services or via a gateway function. Many of the WAPI commands discussed earlier (sections 2.4.2, 2.5.2 & 2.6.2) are also potentially applicable in workflow interoperability interactions:

- Session establishment
- Operations on workflow definitions and their objects
- Process control and status functions
- Activity management functions
- Data handling operations

A degree of common administration between multiple workflow domains will also be necessary using functions developed for interface 5 (section 2.8.2).

Once activities are being enacted on a separate (subordinate) service, interactions from workflow client applications with the original service (for example query status of activity/process instance, or suspend/resume/terminate process instance) may need "referral" to the subordinate service. Some operations may thus need to be chained across several workflow engines (for example, where different activities within an active process instance are distributed across several machines). Some form of event notification service is also likely to be required to inform the initiating service of activity status changes and completion of activities and/or subprocesses. It is envisaged that a number of additional WAPI operations will be developed, over time, to support these and other functions arising from more complex interworking scenarios.

The range of possible interactions is relatively extensive and complex in terms of state transitions (including, for example aspects such as failure containment and recovery); further study will be required to develop the necessary conformance levels which could form a practical basis for interoperability between different products.

2.8 Systems Administration

2.8.1 Administration & Monitoring Tools

The final area of proposed specification is a common interface standard for administration and monitoring functions which will allow one vendor's management application to work with another's engine(s). This will provide a common interface which enables several workflow services to share a range of common administration and system monitoring functions.

Although process status commands are defined within the interfaces already described, there is a recognised requirement in some industries for a function to apply overall status monitoring and extract metrics information. The proposed interface is intended to allow a complete view of the status of work flowing through the organisation, regardless of which system it is in; it is also intended to present a comprehensive function set for administration purposes, including specific considerations of security, control and authorisation.

The interface will include specific commands within the WAPI set to manipulate designated administration and monitoring functions. In addition, further review is intended to ascertain to what extent this interface can exploit existing protocol mechanisms such as CMIP and SNMP to set and retrieve management status and statistical information defined in an open MIB (Management Information Base).

2.8.2 Administration & Monitoring Interface (Interface 5)

The interface as illustrated shows an independent management application interacting with different workflow domains, although alternative implementation scenarios are also feasible; for example the management application may be an integral part of one enactment service, although capable of managing various functions across additional (heterogeneous) workflow domains.

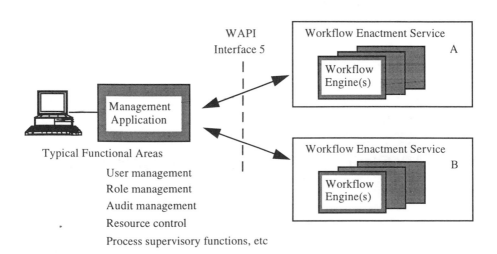

Figure 19   Systems Administration & Monitoring Interface

It is also feasible for the management application to take on other management functions, beyond those shown. For example, it may also manage workflow process definitions, acting as a repository and distributing process definitions to the various workflow domains via operations within interface 1.

The detail of this interface is for further study, but it is envisaged to include the following types of operation (some of which are common to other interface areas):

USER MANAGEMENT OPERATIONS

- Establishment / deletion / suspension / amendment of privileges of users or workgroups

ROLE MANAGEMENT OPERATIONS

- Define / delete / amend role:participant relationships
- Set or unset role attributes

AUDIT MANAGEMENT OPERATIONS

- Query / print / start new / delete audit trail or event log, etc.

RESOURCE CONTROL OPERATIONS

- Set / unset / modify process or activity concurrency levels
- Interrogate resource control data (counts, thresholds, usage parameters, etc.)

PROCESS SUPERVISORY FUNCTIONS

- Changing the operational status of a workflow process definition and/or its extant process instances
- Enabling or disabling particular versions of a process definition
- Changing the state of all process or activity instances of a specified type
- Assigning attribute(s) to all process or activity instances of a specified type
- Termination of all process instances

PROCESS STATUS FUNCTIONS

- Opening / closing a process or activity instances query, setting optional filter criteria
- Fetching details of process instances or activity instances, filtered as specified
- Fetching details of a specific (individual) process or activity instance

3.   WAPI Structure, Protocols and Conformance

3.1 WAPI - Functional Overview of APIs

The WAPI is envisaged as a common set of API calls and related interchange formats which may be grouped together as required to support each of the five functional interface areas. Operations already identified across these five interface areas (and discussed in section 2) include those in the following groups:

3.1.1 API Calls

- Session establishment
- Operations on workflow definitions and their objects
- Process control functions
- Process control supervisory functions
- Process status functions
- Activity management functions
- Data handling operations
- Worklist/Workitem Handling Functions
- User Management operations
- Role Management operations
- Audit Management operations
- Resource Control operations

3.1.2 Data Interchange Functions

Interchange formats are expected to be defined to cover:

- Process definition transfer
- Workflow relevant data transfer

3.1.3 API Call Structure and Naming

API calls will be defined initially in terms of their logical operations, the data types on which they may operate (i.e. as call parameters) and the supporting data structures referenced from such parameters. Language bindings are expected to be developed, initially for the C language and subsequently for other important development environments (both C++ and IDL are candidates for further study). Naming conventions are being specified for the call functions themselves, plus the supporting data type definitions, parameter types and data structures (see *WAPI Naming Conventions*).

3.2 WAPI Protocol Support

The WAPI calls will be able to function in two types of interconnection scenario:

1. Where an exposed WAPI interface is provided as a boundary function to a workflow enactment service (e.g. as vendor stub routines embedded in a client

application or application agent), vendor specific mappings may be used to encode the call and associated parameters to the particular vendor protocol environment used to communicate with the workflow engines.

2. Where direct interworking between different products is provided (e.g. interoperability between different workflow engines), open (common) protocol support will be necessary. This will require a standardised mapping from WAPI calls onto one or, more likely, several interworking protocols.

The expected areas of standardisation relating to these two scenarios are as illustrated in the following diagram.

The details of protocol usage within WAPI are for further study, but it is expected that WAPI mappings will be developed onto important communications environments, i.e. those widely used by workflow products available in the market. Initial support for client application integration and workflow interoperability via an application gateway can be achieved using approach 1 (with vendor specific protocols); however, this approach has some inherent limitations and the development of appropriate protocol usage specifications is a clear requirement in the medium term.

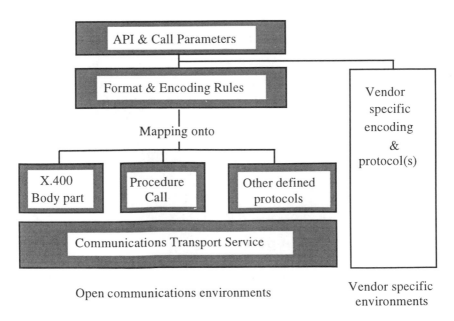

Figure 20 WAPI Protocol Support

Implementations would be expected to identify the particular communications environment(s) which are supported, along with the specific API command set options being implemented for the particular interchange function. This subject will be further considered as conformance rules are developed (see following section).

3.3 Conformance Principles

3.3.1 What does Conformance Mean?

Conformance will be defined against each particular functional area corresponding to one of the five interfaces, so that product vendors can offer an exposed interface for conformant interworking in one or more areas but do not have to implement all five functions to achieve interoperability.

For each interface it is expected that conformance will be classified at several levels, providing a minimum level of interoperability at level 1, with the option for more complex products to achieve conformance against a higher level of functionality for richer interworking, where appropriate. In the case of interface 4 functions, this will be particularly essential due to the potential complexities of workflow service interoperability. Products which achieve conformance at a particular level are expected to interwork with products at any conformance level below or equal to their own.

Conformance will need to be separately considered in terms of API support and protocol usage. It is likely that some form of matrix will need to be constructed indicating the particular API functions supported at a specific level and the protocol environments supported for interworking with other products.

It is possible that some form of interoperability testing or certification may be feasible, but this is an area requiring further investigation by the Coalition.

3.4 Interoperability Classifications & Conformance Levels

Conformance levels will be developed to assist in the classification of interoperable products.

The potential scope of workflow interoperability and application integration is very wide and to develop a full range of APIs and interchange formats to cater for all potential interoperability scenarios is a major task. For these reasons it is considered essential that a set of interoperability scenarios is developed, ranging from the simple to the complex, so that interfaces for the simpler scenarios can be developed earlier. This will enable some of the benefits of interoperable systems to be realised in the nearer term, whilst further development work is done to develop the more complex interfaces. Various conformance levels can be defined to group the particular APIs, interchange formats and protocol support necessary to meet specific interoperability scenarios. The remainder of this section documents a simple classification as a basis for further discussion in this area.

3.4.1 Definition Tool - Workflow Enactment Software

Purpose: to allow separate choice of products for development tools (modelling, definition, etc.) and runtime workflow service delivery or to enable storage and retrieval of process definitions from a repository.

Interoperability - based on support for the Process Definition Import/Export Interface. The process definition is exported by the definition tool and imported by the workflow enactment software.

Conformance levels - based on a basic (minimum) set of process definition objects with optional extensions to cater for more sophisticated process definitions. File interchange formats and API call details to be discussed.

3.4.2 Client Application Interoperating with Workflow Enactment Service(s)

Purpose:

1. To allow for the construction of a common worklist handler to provide worklist management for one or more workflow systems, for example to provide a common house style for task management dialogue with the user, independently of the workflow management software in use. This enables the delivery of several different workflow services to be combined at the desktop, giving the appearance to the end user of a single service.
2. To support simple interaction between the two workflow services controlled from the desktop environment (for example, workflow relevant data interchange between two process instantiated on different workflow services or an activity within one process enactment causing the start of a new process on the second service - the activity gateway approach)

Interoperability - based on support for the WAPI calls and interchange formats from interface 2.

Conformance levels - to support varying degrees of sophistication at the client application; details to be discussed. Protocol usage options - to be specified.

3.4.3 Application & Tool Integration

Purpose:

1. To allow applications or tools to be workflow-enabled in a standardised manner (for example, to interact with a workflow engine via activity control functions or to accept/return case data, etc.)

2. To allow the development of standardised application agents to interface non workflow-enabled applications in a similar manner

Interoperability - based on support for the subset of WAPI calls to handle application invocation and access to workflow relevant data.

Conformance levels - to be discussed, possibly classified by application type.

3.4.4 Workflow Service Interoperability

Purpose:

1. To support the development of process automation applications utilising different workflow enactment software products.
2. To enable existing (heterogeneous) workflow applications to exchange application or workflow relevant data, which is common to both processes, at an appropriate point within the processes.

Interoperability - based on support for the WAPI calls and interchange formats using either the activity gateway or direct interfaces. The gateway model is of more immediate applicability; direct interoperability requires agreement on common process definition interchange and compatible protocol support.

Conformance levels and protocol support - to be discussed, reflecting the various interoperability scenarios described in section 2.7.

3.4.5 Common Workflow Administration and Management

Purpose - to support common management, administration and audit function across several workflow management products

Interoperability - based on support for WAPI calls from interface 5 to enable administration and monitoring functions to be supported by a common management application.

Conformance levels and protocol usage - to be defined.

WAPI Specification – The Workflow Client Application Programming Interface

This section is based on Version 1.1 of the WAPI Specification, dated 15th May 1996. WfMC document reference: WFMC-TC-1009.

1. Overview

The support of these interfaces in workflow management (WFM) products allow the implementation of front-end applications which need to access WFM Engine functions (workflow services). Such implementations might be written by WFM exploiters or independent software vendors. Implementation of these API calls are also intended to allow the workflow applications to be adjusted to operate with different WFM Engines using this common API interface.

These API calls should allow a WFM exploiter to have a single end user interface and functions set regardless of the number of WFM products existing in an installation. WAPI calls may be implemented in a number of languages. The first Coalition specification will be for the 'C' language. The API operates as CALLS. No assumption is may regarding the underlying implementation of the CALLS in a particular WFM product implementation. The WAPI calls are for use at run-time. That is, when processes are executing or are to be executed. They would normally be used by workflow applications (e.g. worklist handlers, cooperating applications) but may also be used by a WFM Engine when it wishes to interact with another WFM product within the context of the API functions.

Through its set of functions, the WAPI provides a set of workflow services that a Workflow Enactment Service provides. The WAPI does not assume any specific user interface, but rather it specifically assumes that the user interface of the workflow enabled application, that uses these services, provides its own user interface, that depends solely on the application development environment facilities where it is implemented.

The WFM Engine functions can broadly be classified in the following areas:

- **WAPI Connection Functions**
- **WAPI Process Control Functions**
- **WAPI Activity Control Functions**
- **WAPI Process Status Functions**
- **WAPI Activity Status Functions**
- **WAPI Worklist Functions**
- **WAPI Administration Functions**

1.1 Design Assumptions

Incremental Set of Functions. It is assumed that as the WFM technology evolves, likewise the specifications defined in this document will evolve and will have additions in subsequent versions of this document.

- Strings are defined with buffer sizes allocated in bytes. Strings are assumed to be zero terminated.
- The workflow engine may have security restrictions that may cause an error to be returned to a user for some of the API calls.
- The specific calls to change state have to be supported by all vendors. The generic state changes are reserved for vendor specific states. In the future, it is expected that a common set of states will evolve.
- Each process definition must have a unique ID within an administrative scope.
- Each process instance must have a unique ID within an administrative scope.
- Each activity instance must have a unique ID within a process instance.
- Each work item must have a unique ID within a process instance.
- Process Instance ID is unique to the workflow engines from which it is available. It is the responsibility of the workflow engine to ensure a unique identifier within this scope.

1.2 Design Objectives

Ease of Implementation. The API specification must be easy to implement by a wide range of vendors. This also implies that the specification will be able to be implemented by multiple vendors in a reasonably short period of time.

1.3 Reference Documents

The following documents are associated with this document and should be used as a reference.

- The Workflow Reference Model
- The WfMC Glossary
- WAPI Naming Conventions

The terms used in this document are defined in The WfMC Glossary.
All of these documents are reproduced in this Handbook.

1.4 Conformance

A vendor cannot claim conformance to this or any other WfMC specification unless specifically authorized to make that claim by the WfMC. The WfMC grants this permission only upon the verification of the particular vendor's implementation of the published specification, according to the conformance requirements and applicable test procedures defined by the WfMC.

1.5 WAPI Naming Conventions

The Working Group has proposed a set of standards for handling the naming conventions of the different implementation of the Workflow API. These naming conventions standards are described in *WAPI Naming Conventions* reproduced in this Handbook.

2. WAPI Data Types

This section describes the WAPI data types. These data types are used in the WAPI calls as input and output parameters.

2.1 Basic WAPI Data Types

This subsection contains definitions of the basic Workflow Management types that are operating system or platform dependent.

```
typedef char              WMTInt8;
typedef short             WMTInt16;
typedef long              WMTInt32;
typedef unsigned char     WMTUInt8;
typedef unsigned short    WMTUInt16;
typedef unsigned long     WMTUInt32;

typedef        WMTInt8    WMTText;
```

```
typedef              WMTText     *WMTPText;
typedef              WMTInt8     *WMTPInt8;
typedef              WMTInt16    *WMTPInt16;
typedef              WMTInt32    *WMTPInt32;

typedef              WMTInt8     WMTBoolean;
typedef              WMTUInt8    *WMTPointer;
typedef              WMTText     *WMTPPrivate;

#define              WMNULL      ((WMTPointer)0)
#define              WMFalse0
#define              WMTrue      (!WMFalse)
```

2.2 Other WAPI Data Types

This subsection contains definitions of the Workflow Management types that are specific to the structures and objects defined in this specification.

Strings in this specification, are assumed to be zero terminated. The maximum string length for names, keywords and identifiers in this specification is 63 characters hosted in a 64 byte text array. The following macro definition specifies this typical size:

```
#define NAME_STRING_SIZE       64
```

All strings in this specification are defined as text arrays, such as:

```
WMTText                        user_identification[NAME_STRING_SIZE];
```

Given this, in the example above the string can include up to a maximum of 63 real characters.

In some other cases, the fixed size structures for data reference and unique ids are also defined through the following macro definitions:

```
#define UNIQUE_ID_SIZE         64
```

All WAPI function calls have a uniform error return datatype:

```
typedef struct
{
    WMTInt16       main_code;
    WMTInt16       sub_code;
} WMTErrRetType;
```

This data type is shared among all API calls. All other data types are shown along with the WAPI description for each individual call.

This error return datatype is a Int32 word that has two Int16 elements for error returns. The main_code element contains the main error return code, while the sub_code element contains a code that further specifies the nature of the error. For

example, the main_code error code WM_INVALID_PROCESS_INSTANCE (see Error
Return Codes below), would include in its sub_code set of codes a further, more
detailed reason why the process instance is invalid.

This specification assumes that the Coalition will specify a subset of the main_code
codes, leaving for vendor specific implementation the remaining main_code codes
and the set of sub_code codes to provide extensibility and specialization of error
codes.

```
typedef struct
{
   WMTText user_identification[NAME_STRING_SIZE];
                    // The identification of the workflow participant on  whose
                    behalf the Workflow Application will be operating.  The
                    value specified may represent a human, a device, etc.  This
                    identification is normally used for security checking,
                    accounting, etc.
   WMTText password[NAME_STRING_SIZE];
   WMTText engine_name[NAME_STRING_SIZE];
                    // The identification of the WFM Engine to whom the
                    subsequent API calls are to be directed.  This information
                    would not be required for some WFM products in the normal
                    case.  However, it is required for those Workflow
                    Applications which interact with multiple WFM Engines.
                    This would be a symbolic  name which is resolved through a
                    lookup facility.
   WMTText scope[NAME_STRING_SIZE];
                    // Identification of scope for the application.  If scope
                    is not relevant, then this field would be empty and
                    ignored.
}WMTConnectInfo;

typedef   WMTConnectInfo *WMTPConnectInfo;

typedef struct
{
     WMTUInt32      session_id; // locally unique ID for the session
     WMTPPrivate    pprivate;   // pointer to a private structure
                                // containing vendor specific information.
}WMTSessionHandle;

typedef   WMTSessionHandle *WMTPSessionHandle;

typedef struct
{
     WMTInt32       filter_type;// Includes basic types and SQL String
     WMTInt32       filter_length;      // Length (in bytes) of value
     WMTText                    attribute_name [NAME_STRING_SIZE]
     WMTUInt32      comparison; // one of: <, >, =, !=, <=, <=
     WMTPText       filter_string;
}WMTFilter;

typedef   WMTFilter *WMTPFilter;
```

// The first 255 filter types will be reserved. These will be used for
filtering on attributes of process control data and process relevant data.
The specific code values for these codes are included in the *WFM Coalition
Interface 2 WAPI Naming Conventions* specification document.

// In this specification there are two types of filters. One type is useful
for comparisons with and between attribute values. In this case, the
filter_string includes the attribute value that the attribute is compared
against. The second type is a more general mechanism in which the
filter_string represents the whole argument (typically a full SQL argument).
If filter_type is a SQL string, the filter_string will point to a SQL
clause with the syntax of a WHERE clause in the SQL 92 standard language
specification.

```
typedef struct
{
        WMTUInt32     query_handle;
}WMTQueryHandle;


typedef WMTQueryHandle *WMTPQueryHandle;


typedef struct
{
        WMTText       wf_participant[NAME_STRING_SIZE];
}WMTWflParticipant;


typedef WMTWflParticipant *WMTPWflParticipant;


typedef struct
{
        WMTText       proc_def_id[UNIQUE_ID_SIZE];
}WMTProcDefID;


typedef WMTProcDefID *WMTPProcDefID;


typedef struct
{
        WMTText       activity_id[NAME_STRING_SIZE];
}WMTActivityID;


typedef WMTActivityID *WMTPActivityID;


typedef struct
{
        WMTText       proc_def_state[NAME_STRING_SIZE];
}WMTProcDefState;


typedef WMTProcDefState *WMTPProcDefState;     // pointer to a 63-byte string

typedef struct
{
```

```
    //  This is the minimum list of elements at this time. Future versions to
        provide extensibility for this structure.
        WMTText              process_name[NAME_STRING_SIZE];
        WMTProcDefID         proc_def_id;
        WMTProcDefStat       estate;
}WMTProcDef;


typedef   WMTProcDef *WMTPProcDef;


typedef   struct
{
        WMTText     proc_inst_id[UNIQUE_ID_SIZE];
}WMTProcInstID;


typedef   WMTProcInstID *WMTPProcInstID;


typedef struct
{
        WMTText     proc_inst_state[NAME_STRING_SIZE];
}WMTProcInstState;


typedef   WMTProcInstState *WMTPProcInstState;
                                    // pointer to a 63-byte string
typedef struct
{
    //  This is the minimum list of elements at this time. Future versions to
    provide extensibility for this structure.
        WMTText              process_name[NAME_STRING_SIZE];
        WMTProcInstID        proc_inst_id;
        WMTProcDefID         proc_def_id;
        WMTProcInstState     state;
        WMTInt32                    priority;
        WMTWflParticipant           proc_participants[20];
//up to 20 63 character long participant identifiers
}WMTProcInst;


typedef   WMTProcInst *WMTPProcInst;


typedef struct
{
        WMTText     activity_inst_id[UNIQUE_ID_SIZE];
}WMTActivityInstID;


typedef   WMTActivityInstID *WMTPActivityInstID;


typedef struct
{
        WMTText     activity_inst_state[NAME_STRING_SIZE];
```

```
}WMTActivityInstState;

typedef   WMTActivityInstState *WMTPActivityInstState;

typedef struct
{
  // This is the minimum list of elements at this time. Future  versions to
  provide extensibility for this structure.
          WMTText                    activity_name[NAME_STRING_SIZE];
          WMTActivityInstID          activity_inst_id;
          WMTProcInstID              proc_inst_id;
          WMTActivityInstState       state;
          WMTInt32                   priority;
          WMTWflParticipant          activity_participants[10];
  //up to 10 63 character long participant identifiers
}WMTActivityInst;

typedef   WMTActivityInst *WMTPActivityInst;

typedef struct
{
          WMTText                    work_item_id[UNIQUE_ID_SIZE];
}WMTWorkItemID;

typedef   WMTWorkItemID *WMTPWorkItemID;

typedef struct
{
  // This is the minimum list of elements at this time. Future  versions to
  provide extensibility for this structure.
          WMTText                    workitem_name[NAME_STRING_SIZE];
          WMTWorkItemID              workitem_id;
          WMTActivityInstID          activity_inst_id;
          WMTProcInstID              proc_inst_id;
          WMTInt32                   priority;
          WMTWflParticipant          participant;
}WMTWorkItem;

typedef   WMTWorkItem *WMTPWorkItem;
```

2.3 Attributes

This specification does not make any assumption about the binding that workflow
applications will make of retrieved attributes and their values. It is up to the specific
application to manage this binding. The API manages attributes as a set of four elements:

```
        WMTText        attribute_name[NAME_STRING_SIZE];
```

```
WMTInt32        attribute_type;      // type of the attribute
WMTInt32        attribute_length;    // length of the attribute value
WMTPText        pattribute_value;    // pointer to the attribute value
```

All API calls in this specification that deal with attributes, take each individual element as separate parameter for the call.
The following type definitions are used for attribute name:

```
typedef         WMTText      WMTAttrName[NAME_STRING_SIZE];
typedef         WMTAttrName  *WMTPAttrName;
```

These attributes are of the kind called *Process Control* and *Process Relevant Data*. Some attributes of process instances, activity instances and work items could be: priority, state, start_time, description, instance_name, workflow_participant.

3. WAPI Error Return Codes

This section describes the minimal set of WAPI error return codes. These error codes correspond to the main_code element of the WMTErrRetType datatype defined above. The specific code values for these codes are included in the *WFM Coalition WAPI Naming Conventions* specification document.
The minimal set of main_code error return codes are:

WM_SUCCESS	Indicates that the API call completed successfully.
WM_CONNECT_FAILED	Indicates that the **WMConnect** call failed.
WM_INVALID_PROCESS_DEFINITION	Indicates that the process definition ID that was passed as parameter to an API call was not valid, or it was not recognized by the servicing workflow engine.
WM_INVALID_ACTIVITY_NAME	Indicates that the activity name that was passed as parameter to an API call was not valid, or was not recognized by the servicing workflow engine.
WM_INVALID_PROCESS_INSTANCE	Indicates that the process instance ID that was passed as parameter to an API call was not valid, or was not recognized by the servicing workflow engine.
WM_INVALID_ACTIVITY_INSTANCE	Indicates that the process instance ID that was passed as parameter to an API call was not valid, or was not recognized by the servicing workflow engine.
WM_INVALID_WORKITEM	Indicates that the work item ID that was passed as parameter to an API call was not valid, or was not recognized by the servicing workflow engine.

`WM_INVALID_ATTRIBUTE`	Indicates that the attribute that was passed as parameter to an API call was not valid, or was not recognized by the servicing workflow engine.
`WM_ATTRIBUTE_ASSIGNMENT_FAILED`	Indicates that the workflow engine was not able to complete the attribute assignment requested.
`WM_INVALID_STATE`	Indicates that a state was not valid, or was not recognized by the servicing workflow engine.
`WM_TRANSITION_NOT_ALLOWED`	Indicates that the state transition requested was not valid, or was not recognized by the servicing workflow engine.
`WM_INVALID_SESSION_HANDLE`	Indicates that the session ID that was passed as parameter to an API call was not valid, or was not recognized by the servicing workflow engine.
`WM_INVALID_QUERY_HANDLE`	Indicates that the query handle ID that was passed as parameter to an API call was not valid, or was not recognized by the servicing workflow engine.
`WM_INVALID_SOURCE_USER`	Indicates that the participant "source user" that was passed as parameter to an API call was not valid, or was not recognized by the servicing workflow engine.
`WM_INVALID_TARGET_USER`	Indicates that the participant "target user" that was passed as parameter to an API call was not valid, or was not recognized by the servicing workflow engine.
`WM_INVALID_FILTER`	Indicates that the filter structure or values that were passed as parameter to an API call was not valid, or was not recognized by the servicing workflow engine.
`WM_LOCKED`	Reserved for situations in which the servicing workflow engine implements "locking" of workflow entities (process definitions, process instances, activities, work items, etc.) to indicate that the entity is locked at the moment in which its access is requested.
`WM_NOT_LOCKED`	Reserved for situations in which the servicing workflow engine implements "locking" of workflow entities (process definitions, process instances, activities, work items, etc.) to indicate that the entity is **not** locked at the moment in which its access is requested.
`WM_NO_MORE_DATA`	Indicates that a **fetch** query call has reached the end of the list of valid entities to be returned. This error return code is used to implement queries of lists of workflow entities, it indicates that all the entities of the list that matched the selection criterion have already been returned.
`WM_INSUFFICIENT_BUFFER_SIZE`	Indicates that the buffer size that was passed to an API call is insufficient to hold the data that it is supposed to receive.

4. WAPI Descriptions

This section describes the WAPI calls. They are grouped as follows:

- **WAPI Connection Functions**
- **WAPI Process Control Functions**
- **WAPI Activity Control Functions**
- **WAPI Process Status Functions**
- **WAPI Activity Status Functions**
- **WAPI Worklist Functions**
- **WAPI Administration Functions**

The specification of the WAPI calls that follows includes a specification of parameters with indications of the direction of data passing:

in   for parameters with data being passed to the API from the calling application

out   for parameters with data being passed from the API to the calling application.

It should be noted, that in the "C" language interface, parameters that are specified as *out* require a pointer to be passed from the calling application to the API. The API in turn will return the appropriate data in the space pointed to by the pointer. The specification of these *in* and *out* parameters is provided to clarify the specific purpose of these parameters in the calls.

4.1 WAPI Connection Functions

CONNECTED/CONNECTEDLESS OVERVIEW

The Coalition **WMConnect /WMDisconnect** API commands are intended to bound a set of related work by the application using them. When issued, the **WMConnect** returns a handle whose value is used on all other Coalition API calls. The handle value is unique and relates API calls which are issued between a **WMConnect /WMDisconnect** pair instance. The **WMConnect** command allows information to be supplied once and to remain valid until a **WMDisconnect** occurs.

Information supplied during the **WMConnect** (see the ConnectInfo structure in the **WMConnect** call) includes identification information relating to who/what is requesting services from the WFM Engine for use by an authentication service. The structure of the session handle that is returned by the **WMConnect** call is a pointer to a structure that contains a session ID and another structure pointer containing vendor specific information. (See the Session Handle structure in the **WMConnect** call.)

For those workflow servers that establish a connection, the session ID and the pointer to the vendor specific information would be returned by the workflow engine. For those workflow servers that do not establish a connection, the session ID would be set to 0, and a pointer to the connection information that was passed in by the user will be stored in the private structure contained in the session handle structure.

OPERATION BETWEEN THE API AND THE ENGINE

The construction of the Coalition API calls are intended to have little impact on the operational structure of how a WFM product supports them. The API calls are considered to be protocol neutral in that once the API boundary is crossed, different types of mechanisms may be employed to deliver the request to the WFM engine. A particular WFM product's method of interacting between the API calls and the WFM Engine functions may be RPC, conversational, messaging (connectedless) or others.

If a messaging mechanism is used by a WFM product, the receipt of a **WMConnect** may result in the determination of what messaging queue is to be used for interaction between its API support and the WFM engine functions, plus establishing control information to link that queue to subsequent API calls which use a particular handle. If the WFM engine is remote, it may also send a setup type of message to the engine.

If a conversational mechanism is used by a WFM product, and the WFM engine is remote, the receipt of a **WMConnect** may result in the establishment of a communications session between the code supporting the API calls and the WFM engine.

If a database is being used, one of the results of the **WMConnect** may be the establishment of a connection to the appropriate data store facility.

A particular WFM product may choose to accept the **WMConnect** command, return a handle, and ignore the fact that it occurred.

The above are examples of possible operations performed by different WFM products in support of a **WMConnect** command. Obviously, more are possible.

In some cases, a product will be required to connect a single workstation to multiple WFM engines. It is possible that multiple **WMConnect** commands are active concurrently and the subsequent API commands be directed to the correct WFM engine. The **WMConnect** command may be used to designate a particular engine. The handle returned from the **WMConnect** command may be used on subsequent API calls to link those which relate to a engine.

The results of a **WMDisconnect** command is may vary, again depending upon a particular WFM product implementation. Its purpose is to indicate that the application issuing the preceding API calls will no longer be accessing the WFM engine functions within the previous context. In some products, upon receipt of a **WMDisconnect** command, communications and other resource types may be released.

APPLICATION OPERATION WHEN USING THE API CALLS

The operational structure of an application as it relates to the use of the Coalition API calls is affected by the way the API calls are constructed. The current construction of the Coalition API calls result in the code segment of the application making the API call to run in blocked mode. That is, the application will issue an API command and 'wait' for a response from what it perceives as the WFM engine. When making the API call, the application code segment gives up control to the API and does not regain control until the API command is satisfied.

Much of the time, the API commands will be issued due to a workflow participant's direction via the application's End User Interface (EUI). Most of the current API commands are not such that a workflow participant would be interested in making the request, doing something else, and then sometime later (via a process/queue/whatever) viewing the real response to the request. With the request types supported by the API set, it would normally be the case that a workflow participant would want to see the response to the request as soon as possible.

The API calls could be constructed in such a way to allow the application code segment making the API call to run in unblocked mode. That is, to make the API call 'immediate return' rather than waiting for the actual response to the requested action. If this were done, the Coalition would need to define additional functions to support connectedless mode of operation (in some manner, get the asynchronous response when it did arrive and get it to the workflow participant).

The **WMConnect / WMDisconnect** API commands themselves have nothing to do with the ability of an application to run connected or connectedless as they are now defined.

SYNCHRONOUS VERSUS ASYNCHRONOUS CALLS

Most API calls in the WAPI call set are synchronous calls. In particular all the query related API calls are synchronous. Other calls may have some asynchronous behavior in that the call itself will return synchronously to the caller program, but the work specified by the call may be executed by the Workflow Engine at a later time, letting the application proceed. This set of API calls will not include any Call-Back mechanism to synchronize asynchronous calls.

4.1.1 WMConnect

NAME

WMConnect - Connect to the WFM Engine for this series of interactions

DESCRIPTION

The **WMConnect** command informs the WFM Engine that other commands will be originating from this source.

```
WMTErrRetType WMConnect (
        in  WMTPConnectInfo pconnect_info,
        out WMTPSessionHandle psession_handle)
```

Argument	Description
pconnect_info	Pointer to structure containing the information required to create a connection.
psession_handle	Pointer to a structure containing information which can be passed to the WFM Engine on all subsequent API calls which would identify interactions within the **WMConnect / WMDisconnect** bounds, that define a participant's session interaction with the Engine. These handles are opaque so that in connectedless environments the handles include participants identities and passwords rather than session identification. There will be a special value for a handle to indicate failure of the function.

ERROR RETURN VALUE

WM_SUCCESS
WM_CONNECT_FAILED

4.1.2 WMDisconnect

NAME

WMDisconnect - Disconnect from the WFM Engine for this series of interactions

DESCRIPTION

The **WMDisconnect** command tells the WFM Engine that no more API calls will be issued from this source using the named handle. The WFM Engine could discard state data being held or take other closure actions.

```
WMTErrRetType WMDisconnect (
      in WMTPSessionHandle psession_handle)
```

ERROR RETURN VALUE

WM_SUCCESS
WM_INVALID_SESSION_HANDLE

4.2 WAPI Process Control Functions

Process Control Functions can be defined as those which change the operational state of one or more process instances. These API calls are intended for use by the WFM end user application. However, some of the API calls, or parameters within some of the API calls, may affect multiple users and would normally be restricted to the use of a process administrator.

4.2.1 WMOpenProcessDefinitionsList

NAME

WMOpenProcessDefinitionsList - Specifies and opens the query to produce a list of all process definitions that meet the selection criterion of the filter.

DESCRIPTION

This command may also be used by a manager or process administrator to get a list of process definitions so they may view which processes are startable by particular persons. This command directs the WFM Engine to open the query to provide a list of process definitions which are available to a particular workflow participant, some of which may be startable by the participant. It is assumed that not all processes in an organization may be started by all workflow participants. One of the uses of this API is to allow a workflow participant to view which processes he/she can start with the expectation that the next action by the workflow participant would be to pick one to be started.

This command will return a query handle for a list of process definitions that match the specified value for the attribute. The command will also return, optionally, the total *count* of definitions available. If the count is requested and the implementation does not support it, the command will return a pcount value of -1. If pproc_def_filter is NULL, then the function, with the corresponding fetch calls will return the list of ALL process definitions.

(**Note**: This API does not change the state of process or activity instances per the definition above of Process Control Functions. It is included in this section because it might normally lead to the execution of other API calls which would cause operational state changes.)

```
WMTErrRetType WMOpenProcessDefinitionsList (
      in   WMTPSessionHandle psession_handle,
      in   WMTPFilter pproc_def_filter,
      in   WMTBoolean count_flag,
      out  WMTPQueryHandle pquery_handle,
      out  WMTPInt32 pcount)
```

Argument Name	Description
psession_handle	Pointer to a structure containing information about the context for this action.
pproc_def_filter	Filter associated with the process definition.

`count_flag`	Boolean flag that indicates if the total count of definitions should be returned.
`pquery_handle`	Pointer to a structure containing a unique query information.
`pcount`	Total number of process definitions that fulfill the filter condition.

ERROR RETURN VALUE

WM_SUCCESS
WM_INVALID_SESSION_HANDLE
WM_INVALID_FILTER

REQUIREMENTS

No requirements are assumed to exist with regard to the type of process model.
No requirements are assumed to exist with regard to how workflow participant's
are identified within the WFM Engine.

RATIONALE FOR API

This command and the corresponding fetch calls allows a workflow participant to
retrieve the process definition ids which a workflow participant is authorized to
start. They might be used in conjunction with the WMCreateProcessInstance and
WMStartProcess API calls to start a particular named process.

4.2.2 WMFetchProcessDefinition

NAME

WMFetchProcessDefinition - Returns the next process definition from the set of
process definitions that met the selection criterion stated in the
WMOpenProcessDefinitionsList call.

DESCRIPTION

This command directs the WFM Engine to provide one process definition from the
list of process definitions which are available to a particular workflow participant,
some of which may be startable by the participant. It is assumed that not all
processes in an organization may be started by all workflow participants. One of the
uses of this API is to allow a workflow participant to view which processes he/she
can start with the expectation that the next action by the workflow participant would
be to pick one to be started. This fetch function, as well as all other fetch functions
in this API, will return subsequent items after every call, one at a time. The fetch
process is complete when the function returns the error WM_NO_MORE_DATA. The sort
order in which the items are returned is specific of the workflow engine servicing
the call, no specific order should be assumed.

WMTErrRetType **WMFetchProcessDefinition** (
    in WMTPSessionHandle **psession_handle,**
    in WMTPQueryHandle **pquery_handle,**
    out WMTPProcDef **pproc_def_buf_ptr)**

Argument Name	Description
psession_handle	Pointer to a structure containing information about the context for this action.
pquery_handle	Identification of the specific query handle returned by the WMOpenProcessDefinitionsList query command.
pproc_def_buf_ ptr	Pointer to a buffer area provided by the client application where the process definition structure will be placed.

ERROR RETURN VALUE

WM_SUCCESS
WM_INVALID_SESSION_HANDLE
WM_INVALID_PROCESS_DEFINITION
WM_INVALID_QUERY_HANDLE
WM_NO_MORE_DATA

4.2.3 *WMCloseProcessDefinitionsList*

NAME

WMCloseProcessDefinitionsList - Closes the query of process definitions.

DESCRIPTION

WMTErrRetType **WMCloseProcessDefinitionsList(**
    in WMTPSessionHandle **psession_handle,**
    in WMTPQueryHandle **pquery_handle)**

Argument Name	Description
psession_handle	Pointer to a structure containing information about the context for this action.
pquery_handle	Identification of the specific query handle returned by the WMOpenProcessDefinitionsList query command.

ERROR RETURN VALUE

WM_SUCCESS
WM_INVALID_SESSION_HANDLE
WM_INVALID_QUERY_HANDLE

4.2.4 *WMOpenProcessDefinitionStatesList*

NAME

WMOpenProcessDefinitionStatesList - Specifies and opens the query to produce the list of states of the process definition that match the filter criterion.

DESCRIPTION

This command will return a query handle for a list of states for a process definition. The command will also return, optionally, the total *count* of definitions available. If the count is requested and the implementation does not support it, the command will return a pcount value of -1.

One of the uses of this API, together with the corresponding fetch and close calls is to allow a workflow application to query the Workflow Engine for the available states of the process definition that match the filter criterion, in order to offer this list to the application user. For example, process definitions can be in states such as *disabled* (thus disallowing temporarily the creation of new process definitions), or *enabled* (thus allowing again the creation of new process definitions based on the named definition). If pproc_def_state_filter is NULL, then the function, with the corresponding fetch calls will return the list of ALL states available for the definition.

```
WMTErrRetType WMOpenProcessDefinitionStatesList (
    in  WMTPSessionHandle psession_handle,
    in  WMTPProcDefID pproc_def_id,
    in  WMTPFilter pproc_def_state_filter,
    in  WMTBoolean count_flag,
    out WMTPQueryHandle pquery_handle,
    out WMTUInt32 pcount)
```

Argument Name	Description
psession_handle	Pointer to a structure containing information about the context for this action.
pproc_def_id	Pointer to a structure containing the unique process definition ID.
pproc_def_state_filter	Filter associated with the process definition state.
count_flag	Boolean flag that indicates if the total count of process definition states should be returned.
pquery_handle	Pointer to a structure containing a unique query information.
pcount	Total number of states for this process definition.

ERROR RETURN VALUE

WM_SUCCESS
WM_INVALID_SESSION_HANDLE
WM_INVALID_PROCESS_DEFINITION

4.2.5 *WMFetchProcessDefinitionState*

NAME

WMFetchProcessDefinitionState - Returns the next process definition state, from the list of states of the process definition that match the filter criterion.

DESCRIPTION

This command returns a process definition state. This fetch function will return subsequent process definition states after every call. The fetch process is complete when the function returns the error WM_NO_MORE_DATA.

WMTErrRetType **WMFetchProcessDefinitionState** (
    in WMTPSessionHandle psession_handle,
    in WMTPQueryHandle pquery_handle,
    out WMTPProcDefState pproc_def_state)

Argument Name	Description
psession_handle	Pointer to a structure containing information about the context for this action.
pquery_handle	Identification of the specific query handle returned by the **WMOpenProcessDefinitionStatesList** query command.
pproc_def_state	Pointer to a buffer area provided by the client application where the state name will be placed.

ERROR RETURN VALUE

WM_SUCCESS
WM_INVALID_SESSION_HANDLE
WM_INVALID_QUERY_HANDLE
WM_NO_MORE_DATA

4.2.6 *WMCloseProcessDefinitionStatesList*

NAME

WMCloseProcessDefinitionStatesList - Closes the query for process definition states.

DESCRIPTION

WMTErrRetType **WMCloseProcessDefinitionStatesList** (

    in   WMTPSessionHandle psession_handle,

    in   WMTPQueryHandle pquery_handle)

Argument Name	**Description**
psession_handle	Pointer to a structure containing information about the context for this action.
pquery_handle	Identification of the specific query handle returned by the **WMOpenProcessDefinitionStatesList** query command.

ERROR RETURN VALUE

WM_SUCCESS

WM_INVALID_SESSION_HANDLE

WM_INVALID_QUERY_HANDLE

4.2.7 WMChangeProcessDefinitionState

NAME

WMChangeProcessDefinitionState - Changes the state of the named process definition.

DESCRIPTION

This command is defined to allow a process definition to be changed temporarily to a specific state such as *disabled* (thus disallowing temporarily the creation of new process definitions), or *enabled* (thus allowing again the creation of new process definitions based on the named definition).

WMTErrRetType **WMChangeProcessDefinitionState** (

    in   WMTPSessionHandle psession_handle,

    in   WMTPProcDefID pproc_def_id,

    in   WMTPProcDefState pproc_def_state)

Argument Name	Description
psession_handle	Pointer to a structure containing information about the context for this action.
pproc_def_id	Pointer to a structure containing a unique process definition ID.
pproc_def_state	Pointer to a structure that contains the name of the state to change the process definition to.

ERROR RETURN VALUE

WM_SUCCESS

```
WM_INVALID_SESSION_HANDLE
WM_INVALID_PROCESS_DEFINITION
WM_INVALID_STATE
WM_TRANSITION_NOT_ALLOWED
```

REQUIREMENTS

Each process definition must have a unique ID within an administrative scope.

RATIONALE FOR API

This API allows the possible intervention of a process administrator in a running process.   This might be for the purpose of changing the process definition and having all subsequently created definitions reflect the new definition.

4.2.8 WMCreateProcessInstance

NAME

WMCreateProcessInstance - Create an instance of a previously defined process.

DESCRIPTION

An operational instance of the named process definition will be created by a WFM Engine as the result of this command. A call to WMStartProcess would then start the process.

To assign attributes to the process instance, you will make multiple calls to WMAssignProcessInstanceAttribute.

The process instance ID returned by this call is valid and reliable until WMStartProcess is called, at which time it may be reassigned to a new value.

```
WMTErrRetType WMCreateProcessInstance (
    in  WMTPSessionHandle psession_handle,
    in  WMTPProcDefID  pproc_def_id,
    in  WMTPText pproc_inst_name,
    out WMTPProcInstID pproc_inst_id)
```

Argument Name	Description
psession_handle	Pointer to a structure containing information about the context for this action.
pproc_def_id	Pointer to a structure containing a unique process definition ID.
pproc_inst_name	Pointer to the name for the process instance created by this call.
pproc_inst_id	Pointer to a structure containing the process instance ID created by this call.

ERROR RETURN VALUE

WM_SUCCESS
WM_INVALID_SESSION_HANDLE
WM_INVALID_PROCESS_DEFINITION

REQUIREMENTS

No requirements exist with regard to process model type.

RATIONALE FOR API

This API allows a workflow participant to create an instance of a process.   It is
anticipated that vendor's implementations will be of at least 2 types: one in which
the creation of a process instance and the starting of the same are a single
functionality and another in which this functionality is separate. The calls in this
API definition are thus separated to accommodate both types of implementation.
Vendors that provide the single functionality will implement the creation and start of
a process through the creation of a temporary (possibly local) proc_inst_id
through WMCreateProcessInstance, assign attributes to it and then call
WMStartProcess.

4.2.9 WMStartProcess

NAME

WMStartProcess - Start the named process.

DESCRIPTION

The **WMStartProcess** command directs the WFM Engine to begin executing a
process, for which an instance has been created. When a process is started through
this command, the first activity(s) of the process will be started. The process
instance ID returned by this call will be valid for the life of the process instance.
Note: The programmer needs to maintain the association between the new process
instance ID and the session in order to identify which session they need to connect
to for future calls.

```
WMTErrRetType WMStartProcess (
        in  WMTPSessionHandle psession_handle,
        in  WMTPProcInstID  pproc_inst_id,
        out WMTPProcInstID pnew_proc_inst_id)
```

Argument Name	**Description**
psession_handle	Pointer to a structure containing information about the context for this action.

| `pproc_inst_id` | Pointer to a structure containing the process instance ID returned by the WMCreateProcessInstance call. |
| `pnew_proc_inst_id` | Pointer to a structure containing the process instance ID created by this call. This ID will be valid for the life of the process instance. |

ERROR RETURN VALUE

WM_SUCCESS
WM_INVALID_SESSION_HANDLE
WM_INVALID_PROCESS_INSTANCE
WM_INVALID_ATTRIBUTE

REQUIREMENTS

The process instance to be started has a unique id within an administrative scope. No requirements exist with regard to process model type.

RATIONALE FOR API

This API allows a workflow participant to start a created process instance. It is anticipated that vendor's implementations will be of at least 2 types: one in which the creation of a process instance and the starting of the same are a single functionality and another in which this functionality is separate. The calls in this API definition are thus separated to accommodate both types of implementation. Vendors that provide the single functionality will implement the creation and start of a process through the creation of a temporary (possibly local) `proc_inst_id` through WMCreateProcessInstance, assign attributes to it and then call WMStartProcess.

4.2.10 *WMTerminateProcessInstance*

NAME

WMTerminateProcessInstance - Terminate a process instance.

DESCRIPTION

This command provides the capability of gracefully terminating a process without aborting the process instance. Return from this call does not imply that the process instance has terminated, for example, the process instance could be stopped when currently running activities are complete. The exact behavior of currently running activities is system dependent.

```
WMTErrRetType        WMTerminateProcessInstance (
     in  WMTPSessionHandle psession_handle,
     in  WMTPProcInstID pproc_inst_id)
```

Argument Name	Description
psession_handle	Pointer to a structure containing information about the context for this action.
pproc_inst_id	A pointer to a structure that indicates the process instance that you want to terminate.

ERROR RETURN VALUE

WM_SUCCESS
WM_INVALID_SESSION_HANDLE
WM_INVALID_PROCESS_INSTANCE

REQUIREMENTS

None

RATIONALE FOR API

To allow a process instances to be terminated.

4.2.11 *WMOpenProcessInstanceStatesList*

NAME

WMOpenProcessInstanceStatesList - Specifies and opens the query to produce the list of states of the process instance that match the filter criterion.

DESCRIPTION

This command will return a query handle for a list of states for a process instance. The command will also return, optionally, the total *count* of states available. If the count is requested and the implementation does not support it, the command will return a pcount value of -1. The meaning of states is dependent upon the particular WFM Engine implementation. For example, the process instance can have states such as *suspended* or *in-progress*.

One of the uses of this API, together with the corresponding fetch and close calls is to allow a workflow application to query the Workflow Engine for the available states of the process instance that match the filter criterion, in order to offer this list to the application user. If pproc_inst_state_filter is NULL, then the function, with the corresponding fetch calls will return the list of ALL states available for the process instance.

WMTErrRetType **WMOpenProcessInstanceStatesList** (
    in WMTPSessionHandle psession_handle,
    in WMTPProcInstID pproc_inst_id,
    in WMTPFilter pproc_inst_state_filter,
    in WMTBoolean count_flag,
    out WMTPQueryHandle pquery_handle,
    out WMTPInt32 pcount)

Argument Name	Description
psession_handle	Pointer to a structure containing information about the context for this action.
pproc_inst_id	Pointer to a structure containing the unique process instance ID.
pproc_inst_state_filter	Filter associated with the process instance state.
count_flag	Boolean flag that indicates if the total count of process instance states should be returned.
pquery_handle	Pointer to a structure containing a unique query information.
pcount	Total number of states for this process instance.

ERROR RETURN VALUE

WM_SUCCESS
WM_INVALID_SESSION_HANDLE
WM_INVALID_PROCESS_INSTANCE

4.2.12 *WMFetchProcessInstanceState*

NAME

WMFetchProcessInstanceState - Returns the next process instance state from the list of states of the process instance that match the filter criterion.

DESCRIPTION

This command returns a process instance state. This fetch function will return subsequent process instance states after every call. The fetch process is complete when the function returns the error WM_NO_MORE_DATA.

WMTErrRetType **WMFetchProcessInstanceState** (

```
in  WMTPSessionHandle psession_handle,
in  WMTPQueryHandle pquery_handle,
out WMTPProcInstState pproc_inst_state)
```

Argument Name	Description
psession_handle	Pointer to a structure containing information about the context for this action.
pquery_handle	Identification of the specific query handle returned by the **WMOpenProcessInstanceStatesList** query command.
pproc_inst_state	Pointer to a buffer area provided by the client application where the state name will be placed.

ERROR RETURN VALUE

```
WM_SUCCESS
WM_INVALID_SESSION_HANDLE
WM_INVALID_QUERY_HANDLE
WM_NO_MORE_DATA
```

4.2.13 *WMCloseProcessInstanceStatesList*

NAME

WMCloseProcessInstanceStatesList - Closes the query for process instance states.

DESCRIPTION

WMTErrRetType **WMCloseProcessInstanceStatesList** (
```
in  WMTPSessionHandle psession_handle,
in  WMTPQueryHandle pquery_handle)
```

Argument Name	Description
psession_handle	Pointer to a structure containing information about the context for this action.
pquery_handle	Identification of the specific query handle returned by the **WMOpenProcessInstanceStatesList** query command.

ERROR RETURN VALUE

```
WM_SUCCESS
WM_INVALID_SESSION_HANDLE
WM_INVALID_QUERY_HANDLE
```

4.2.14 *WMChangeProcessInstanceState*

NAME

WMChangeProcessInstanceState - Changes the state of the named process instance.

DESCRIPTION

This command is defined to allow a process instance to be changed temporarily to a specific state such as *suspended*.

Execution of this command will cause the single process instance that is named to be transitioned to a new state. In this case, the meaning of all states is dependent upon the particular WFM Engine implementation. This command will set the state attribute of the process instance to a state such as *suspended* or *in-progress*.

WMTErrRetType **WMChangeProcessInstanceState** (
    in   WMTPSessionHandle psession_handle,
    in   WMTPProcInstID pproc_inst_id,
    in   WMTPProcInstState pproc_inst_state)

Argument Name	Description
psession_handle	Pointer to a structure containing information about the context for this action.
pproc_inst_id	Pointer to a structure containing a unique process instance ID.
pproc_inst_state	Pointer to a structure that contains the name of the process state that you want to change the instance to.

ERROR RETURN VALUE

WM_SUCCESS
WM_INVALID_SESSION_HANDLE
WM_INVALID_PROCESS_INSTANCE
WM_INVALID_STATE
WM_TRANSITION_NOT_ALLOWED

REQUIREMENTS

Each process instance must have a unique ID within an administrative scope.

RATIONALE FOR API

This API allows the possible intervention of a workflow participant in a running process.

4.2.15 *WMOpenProcessInstanceAttributesList*

NAME

WMOpenProcessInstanceAttributesList - Specifies and opens the query to produce the list of attributes that match the filter criterion.

DESCRIPTION

This command will return a query handle for a list of attributes for a process instance. The command will also return, optionally, the total *count* of attributes available. If the count is requested and the implementation does not support it, the command will return a pcount value of -1.

One of the uses of this API, together with the corresponding fetch and close calls is to allow a workflow application to query the Workflow Engine for the available attributes that can be assigned to the process instance, in order to offer this list to the application user. Attribute values can be obtained as well provided that a buffer of enough size is passed in the fetch call. Individual attribute values can also be retrieved with the **WMGetProcessInstanceAttributeValue** call. If pproc_inst_attr_filter is NULL, then the function, with the corresponding fetch calls will return the list of ALL attributes available for the process instance.

WMTErrRetType **WMOpenProcessInstanceAttributesList** (
    in WMTPSessionHandle psession_handle,
    in WMTPProcInstID pproc_inst_id,
    in WMTPFilter pproc_inst_attr_filter,
    in WMTBoolean count_flag,
    out WMTPQueryHandle pquery_handle,
    out WMTPInt32 pcount)

Argument Name	Description
psession_handle	Pointer to a structure containing information about the context for this action.
pproc_inst_id	Pointer to a structure containing the unique process instance ID.
pproc_inst_attr_filter	Filter associated with the process instance attributes.
count_flag	Boolean flag that indicates if the total count of process instance attributes should be returned.
pquery_handle	Pointer to a structure containing a unique query information.
pcount	Total number of attributes for this process instance.

ERROR RETURN VALUE
WM_SUCCESS
WM_INVALID_SESSION_HANDLE
WM_INVALID_PROCESS_INSTANCE

4.2.16 *WMFetchProcessInstanceAttribute*

NAME

WMFetchProcessInstanceAttribute - Returns the next process instance attribute from the list of attributes that match the filter criterion.

DESCRIPTION

This command returns a process instance attribute. This fetch function will return subsequent process instance attributes after every call. The fetch process is complete when the function returns the error WM_NO_MORE_DATA. The fetch function will return the attribute value as well in a buffer specified in the call. If buffer_size is NULL then the attribute value will not be returned. If buffer_size is not large enough to hold the attribute value then the function will return as much of the attribute value as can be fit in the buffer. The proper length of the attribute value is available in the attribute_length field. The application can compare the attribute_length with the buffer_size to determine if the full value was returned.

WMTErrRetType **WMFetchProcessInstanceAttribute** (
     in WMTPSessionHandle psession_handle,
     in WMTPQueryHandle pquery_handle,
     out WMTPAttrName pattribute_name,
     out WMTPInt32 pattribute_type,
     out WMTPInt32 pattribute_length,
     out WMTPText pattribute_value,
     in WMTInt32 buffer_size)

Argument Name	Description
psession_handle	Pointer to a structure containing information about the context for this action.
pquery_handle	Identification of the specific query handle returned by the **WMOpenProcessInstanceAttributesList** query command.
pattribute_name	Pointer to the name of the attribute.
pattribute_type	Pointer to the type of the attribute.
pattribute_length	Pointer to the length of the attribute value.
pattribute_value	Pointer to a buffer area provided by the client application where the attribute value will be placed.
buffer_size	Size of the buffer.

ERROR RETURN VALUE

WM_SUCCESS
WM_INVALID_SESSION_HANDLE
WM_INVALID_QUERY_HANDLE
WM_NO_MORE_DATA

4.2.17 *WMCloseProcessInstanceAttributesList*

NAME

WMCloseProcessInstanceAttributesList - Closes the query for process instance attributes.

DESCRIPTION

WMTErrRetType **WMCloseProcessInstanceAttributesList** (
    in WMTPSessionHandle psession_handle,
    in WMTPQueryHandle pquery_handle)

Argument Name	Description
psession_handle	Pointer to a structure containing information about the context for this action.
pquery_handle	Identification of the specific query handle returned by the **WMOpenProcessInstanceAttributesList** query command.

ERROR RETURN VALUE

WM_SUCCESS
WM_INVALID_SESSION_HANDLE
WM_INVALID_QUERY_HANDLE

4.2.18 WMGetProcessInstanceAttributeValue

NAME

WMGetProcessInstanceAttributeValue - Returns the value, type and length of a process instance attribute specified by the proc_inst_id and attribute_name parameters.

DESCRIPTION

This command will return the value of a process instance attribute in the buffer specified in the call.

WMTErrRetType **WMGetProcessInstanceAttributeValue** (
    in WMTPSessionHandle psession_handle,
    in WMTPProcInstID pproc_inst_id,
    in WMTPAttrName pattribute_name,
    out WMTPInt32 pattribute_type,
    out WMTPInt32 pattribute_length,
    out WMTPText pattribute_value,
    in WMTInt32 buffer_size)

Argument Name	Description
psession_handle	Pointer to a structure containing information about the context for this action.

`pproc_inst_id`	Pointer to a structure containing the unique process instance ID.
`pattribute_name`	Pointer to the name of the attribute.
`pattribute_type`	Pointer to the type of the attribute.
`pattribute_length`	Pointer to the length of the attribute value.
`pattribute_value`	Pointer to a buffer area provided by the client application where the attribute value will be placed.
`buffer_size`	Size of the buffer to be filled.

ERROR RETURN VALUE

WM_SUCCESS
WM_INVALID_SESSION_HANDLE
WM_INVALID_ATTRIBUTE
WM_INSUFFICIENT_BUFFER_SIZE

4.2.19 *WMAssignProcessInstanceAttribute*

NAME

WMAssignProcessInstanceAttribute -   Assign the proper attribute to process instance(s)

DESCRIPTION

This command tells the WFM Engine to assign an attribute, change an attribute or to change the value of an attribute of a process instance.

This command changes the value of an attribute of a process instance. Attributes of process instances are of the kind called *Process Control   and Process Relevant Data*. These attributes are specified as quadruplets of *name, type, length* and *value*.

WMTErrRetType **WMAssignProcessInstanceAttribute (**
    in WMTPSessionHandle psession_handle,
    in WMTPProcInstID pproc_inst_id,
    in WMTPAttrName pattribute_name,
    in WMTInt32 attribute_type,
    in WMTInt32 attribute_length,
    in WMTPText pattribute_value)

Argument Name	Description
`psession_handle`	Pointer to a structure containing information about the context for this action.
`pproc_inst_id`	Pointer to a structure containing the process instance ID that indicates the process for which the attribute will be assigned.

`pattribute_name`	Pointer to the name of the attribute.
`attribute_type`	Type of the attribute.
`attribute_length`	Length of the attribute value.
`pattribute_value`	Pointer to a buffer area provided by the client application where the attribute value will be placed.

ERROR RETURN VALUE

WM_SUCCESS
WM_INVALID_SESSION_HANDLE
WM_INVALID_PROCESS_INSTANCE
WM_INVALID_ATTRIBUTE
WM_ATTRIBUTE_ASSIGNMENT_FAILED

REQUIREMENTS

None

RATIONALE FOR API

For various business reasons, certain pieces of work are required to be handled with particular attributes (e.g. priority) relative to other pieces of like work. This command allows attributes to be set on those pieces of work. In some cases, these attributes are determined by the WFM product based upon data values existing during process execution. The setting of these attributes through the use of this API is provided to cover the cases where applications set them upon requests from users.

4.3 WAPI Activity Control Functions

Activity Control Functions can be defined as those which change the operational state of one or more activity instances. These API calls are intended for use by the WFM end user. However, some of the API calls, or parameters within some of the API calls, may affect multiple users and would normally be restricted to the use of a process administrator.

4.3.1 *WMOpenActivityInstanceStatesList*

NAME

WMOpenActivityInstanceStatesList - Specifies and opens the query to produce the list of states of the activity instance that match the filter criterion.

DESCRIPTION

This command will return a query handle for a list of states for an activity instance. The command will also return, optionally, the total *count* of states available. If the count is requested and the implementation does not support it, the command will return a pcount value of -1.

One of the uses of this API, together with the corresponding fetch and close calls is to allow a workflow application to query the Workflow Engine for the available states of the activity instance that match the filter criterion, in order to offer this list to the application user. If pact_inst_state_filter is NULL, then the function, with the corresponding fetch calls will return the list of ALL states available for the activity instance.

WMTErrRetType **WMOpenActivityInstanceStatesList** (
    in   WMTPSessionHandle **psession_handle,**
    in   WMTPProcInstID **pproc_inst_id,**
    in   WMTPActivityInstID **pactivity_inst_id,**
    in   WMTPFilter **pact_inst_state_filter,**
    in   WMTBoolean **count_flag,**
    out   WMTPQueryHandle **pquery_handle,**
    out   WMTPInt32 **pcount)**

Argument Name	Description
psession_handle	Pointer to a structure containing information about the context for this action.
pproc_inst_id	Pointer to a structure containing a unique process instance ID.
pactivity_inst_id	Pointer to a structure containing the unique activity instance ID.
pact_inst_state_filter	Filter associated with the activity instance state.
count_flag	Boolean flag that indicates if the total count of activity instance states should be returned.
pquery_handle	Pointer to a structure containing a unique query information.
pcount	Total number of states for this activity instance.

ERROR RETURN VALUE

WM_SUCCESS
WM_INVALID_SESSION_HANDLE
WM_INVALID_PROCESS_INSTANCE
WM_INVALID_ACTIVITY_INSTANCE

4.3.2 *WMFetchActivityInstanceState*

NAME

WMFetchActivityInstanceState - Returns the next activity instance state, from the list of states of the activity instance that match the filter criterion.

DESCRIPTION

This command returns an activity state. This fetch function will return subsequent activity states after every call. The fetch process is complete when the function returns the error WM_NO_MORE_DATA.

WMTErrRetType **WMFetchActivityInstanceState** (
    in WMTPSessionHandle psession_handle,
    in WMTPQueryHandle pquery_handle,
    out WMTPActivityInstState pactivity_inst_state)

Argument Name	Description
psession_handle	Pointer to a structure containing information about the context for this action.
pquery_handle	Identification of the specific query handle returned by the **WMOpenActivityInstanceStatesList** query command.
pactivity_inst_state	Pointer to a buffer area provided by the client application where the state name will be placed.

ERROR RETURN VALUE

WM_SUCCESS
WM_INVALID_SESSION_HANDLE
WM_INVALID_QUERY_HANDLE
WM_NO_MORE_DATA

4.3.3 WMCloseActivityInstanceStatesList

NAME

WMCloseActivityInstanceStatesList - Closes the query for activity instance states.

DESCRIPTION

WMTErrRetType **WMCloseActivityInstanceStatesList** (
    in WMTPSessionHandle psession_handle,
    in WMTPQueryHandle pquery_handle)

Argument Name	Description
psession_handle	Pointer to a structure containing information about the context for this action.
pquery_handle	Identification of the specific query handle returned by the **WMOpenActivityInstanceStatesList** query command.

ERROR RETURN VALUE

WM_SUCCESS
WM_INVALID_SESSION_HANDLE
WM_INVALID_QUERY_HANDLE

4.3.4 *WMChangeActivityInstanceState*

NAME

WMChangeActivityInstanceState - Changes the state of the named activity instance.

DESCRIPTION

This command directs a WFM Engine to change the state of a single activity instance within a process instance. This allows the state of one activity instance to be changed, without impacting others in the process instance.

For example, this command will be used to change the state of an activity instance to *suspended*. This command can be used afterwards to change the state of the activity instance back to *in-progress*. The implementation documentation will provide the names and semantics of the supported activity states for a particular implementation.

WMTErrRetType **WMChangeActivityInstanceState (**
    in WMTPSessionHandle **psession_handle,**
    in WMTPProcInstID **pproc_inst_id,**
    in WMTPActivityInstID **pactivity_inst_id,**
    in WMTPActivityInstState **pactivity_inst_state)**

Argument Name	Description
psession_handle	Pointer to a structure containing information about the context for this action.
pproc_inst_id	Pointer to a structure containing a unique process instance ID.
pactivity_inst_id	Pointer to structure containing the activity instance ID of the activity whose state to change.
pactivity_inst_ state	Pointer to a structure that contains the name of the activity instance state that you want to change to.

ERROR RETURN VALUE

WM_SUCCESS
WM_INVALID_SESSION_HANDLE
WM_INVALID_PROCESS_INSTANCE
WM_INVALID_ACTIVITY_INSTANCE
WM_INVALID_STATE
WM_TRANSITION_NOT_ALLOWED

REQUIREMENTS

Each process instance must have a unique ID within an administrative scope.

Each activity instance must have a unique ID within a process instance.

RATIONALE FOR API

A workflow participant may wish to modify the state attributes associated with a particular activity instance.

4.3.5 *WMOpenActivityInstanceAttributesList*

NAME

WMOpenActivityInstanceAttributesList - Specifies and opens the query to produce the list of activity attributes that match the filter criterion.

DESCRIPTION

This command will return a query handle for a list of attributes for an activity instance. The command will also return, optionally, the total *count* of attributes available. If the count is requested and the implementation does not support it, the command will return a `pcount` value of -1.

One of the uses of this API, together with the corresponding fetch and close calls is to allow a workflow application to query the Workflow Engine for the available attributes that can be assigned to the activity instance, in order to offer this list to the application user. Attribute values can be obtained as well provided that a buffer of enough size is passed in the fetch call. Individual attribute values can also be retrieved with the **WMGetActivityInstanceAttributeValue** call. If `pact_inst_attr_filter` is NULL, then the function, with the corresponding fetch calls will return the list of ALL attributes available for the activity instance.

```
WMTErrRetType WMOpenActivityInstanceAttributesList (
        in   WMTPSessionHandle psession_handle,
        in   WMTPProcInstID pproc_inst_id,
        in   WMTPActivityInstID pactivity_inst_id,
        in   WMTPFilter pact_inst_attr_filter,
        in   WMTBoolean count_flag,
        out  WMTPQueryHandle pquery_handle,
        out  WMTPInt32 pcount)
```

Argument Name	Description
psession_handle	Pointer to a structure containing information about the context for this action.
pproc_inst_id	Pointer to a structure containing the unique process instance ID.
pactivity_inst_id	Pointer to a structure containing the unique activity instance ID.
pact_inst_attr_filter	Filter associated with the activity instance attributes.

`count_flag`	Boolean flag that indicates if the total count of activity instance attributes should be returned.
`pquery_handle`	Pointer to a structure containing a unique query information.
`pcount`	Total number of attributes for this activity instance.

ERROR RETURN VALUE

WM_SUCCESS
WM_INVALID_SESSION_HANDLE
WM_INVALID_PROCESS_INSTANCE
WM_INVALID_ACTIVITY_INSTANCE

4.3.6 WMFetchActivityInstanceAttribute

NAME

WMFetchActivityInstanceAttribute - Returns the next activity instance attribute from the list of activity attributes that match the filter criterion.

DESCRIPTION

This command returns a activity instance attribute. This fetch function will return subsequent activity instance attributes after every call. The fetch process is complete when the function returns the error WM_NO_MORE_DATA. The fetch function will return the attribute value as well in a buffer specified in the call. If `buffer_size` is NULL then the attribute value will not be returned. If `buffer_size` is not large enough to hold the attribute value then the function will return as much of the attribute value as can be fit in the buffer. The proper length of the attribute value is available in the `attribute_length` field. The application can compare the `attribute_length` with the `buffer_size` to determine if the full value was returned.

```
WMTErrRetType WMFetchActivityInstanceAttribute (
    in   WMTPSessionHandle psession_handle,
    in   WMTPQueryHandle pquery_handle,
    out  WMTPAttrName pattribute_name,
    out  WMTPInt32 pattribute_type,
    out  WMTPInt32 pattribute_length,
    out  WMTPText pattribute_value,
    in   WMTInt32 buffer_size)
```

Argument Name	Description
`psession_handle`	Pointer to a structure containing information about the context for this action.
`pquery_handle`	Identification of the specific query handle returned by the **WMOpenActivityInstanceAttributesList** query command.
`pattribute_name`	Pointer to the name of the attribute.

`pattribute_type`	Pointer to the type of the attribute.
`pattribute_length`	Pointer to the length of the attribute value.
`pattribute_value`	Pointer to a buffer area provided by the client application where the attribute value will be placed.
`buffer_size`	Size of the buffer.

ERROR RETURN VALUE

WM_SUCCESS
WM_INVALID_SESSION_HANDLE
WM_INVALID_QUERY_HANDLE
WM_NO_MORE_DATA

4.3.7 *WMCloseActivityInstanceAttributesList*

NAME

WMCloseActivityInstanceAttributesList - Closes the query for activity instance attributes.

DESCRIPTION

WMTErrRetType **WMCloseActivityInstanceAttributesList** (
    in WMTPSessionHandle psession_handle,
    in WMTPQueryHandle pquery_handle)

Argument Name	Description
`psession_handle`	Pointer to a structure containing information about the context for this action.
`pquery_handle`	Identification of the specific query handle returned by the **WMOpenActivityInstanceAttributesList** query command.

ERROR RETURN VALUE

WM_SUCCESS
WM_INVALID_SESSION_HANDLE
WM_INVALID_QUERY_HANDLE

4.3.8 *WMGetActivityInstanceAttributeValue*

NAME

WMGetActivityInstanceAttributeValue - Returns the value, type and length of an activity instance attribute specified by the `pproc_inst_id,` `pactivity_inst_id` and `attribute_name` parameters.

DESCRIPTION

This command will return the value of an activity instance attribute in the buffer specified in the call.

WMTErrRetType **WMGetActivityInstanceAttributeValue** (
    _in_ WMTPSessionHandle psession_handle,
    _in_ WMTPProcInstID pproc_inst_id,
    _in_ WMTPActivityInstID pactivity_inst_id,
    _in_ WMTPAttrName pattribute_name,
    out WMTPInt32 pattribute_type,
    out WMTPInt32 pattribute_length,
    out WMTPText pattribute_value,
    _in_ WMTInt32 buffer_size)

Argument Name	Description
`psession_handle`	Pointer to a structure containing information about the context for this action.
`pproc_inst_id`	Pointer to a structure containing the unique process instance ID.
`pactivity_inst_id`	Pointer to a structure containing the unique activity instance ID.
`pattribute_name`	Pointer to the name of the attribute.
`pattribute_type`	Pointer to the type of the attribute.
`pattribute_length`	Pointer to the length of the attribute value.
`pattribute_value`	Pointer to a buffer area provided by the client application where the attribute value will be placed.
`buffer_size`	Size of the buffer to be filled.

ERROR RETURN VALUE

WM_SUCCESS
WM_INVALID_SESSION_HANDLE
WM_INVALID_ATTRIBUTE
WM_INSUFFICIENT_BUFFER_SIZE

4.3.9 WMAssignActivityInstanceAttribute

NAME

WMAssignActivityInstanceAttribute - Assign an attribute to an activity instance.

DESCRIPTION

This command tells the WFM Engine to assign an attribute, to change an attribute or to change the value of an attribute of the activity instance within a named process definition.

This command changes the value of the attributes of a activity instance. These attributes of activity instances are of the kind called *Process Control and Process*

Relevant Data. These attributes are specified as quadruplets of *name, type, length* and *value.*

WMTErrRetType **WMAssignActivityInstanceAttribute** (
    in WMTPSessionHandle psession_handle,
    in WMTPProcDefID pproc_def_id,
    in WMTPActivityInstID pactivity_inst_id,
    in WMTPAttrName pattribute_name,
    in WMTInt32 attribute_type,
    in WMTInt32 attribute_length,
    in WMTPText pattribute_value)

Argument Name	**Description**
`psession_handle`	Pointer to a structure containing information about the context for this action.
`pproc_inst_id`	Pointer to a structure containing the unique process instance ID.
`pactivity_inst_id`	Pointer to a structure containing the activity instance identification for which the attribute will be assigned.
`pattribute_name`	Pointer to the name of the attribute.
`attribute_type`	Type of the attribute.
`attribute_length`	Length of the attribute value.
`pattribute_value`	Pointer to a buffer area provided by the client application where the attribute value will be placed.

ERROR RETURN VALUE

WM_SUCCESS
WM_INVALID_SESSION_HANDLE
WM_INVALID_PROCESS_INSTANCE
WM_INVALID_ACTIVITY_INSTANCE
WM_INVALID_ATTRIBUTE
WM_ATTRIBUTE_ASSIGNMENT_FAILED

REQUIREMENTS

None

4.4 WAPI Process Status Functions

The process status functions are intended to provide a view of the work done, work to be done, work associated with a workflow participant or group of workflow participants, etc. The status queries may be requested by a normal workflow participant or may be requested by a manager or process administrator who wishes to view the progress of work within his/her domain.

The status API calls are structured such that they provide views ranging from a view of global work to a view of work within a single process instance. These views are as follows:

1	All the process instances associated with a process definition.	**WM(Open+Fetch+Close)ProcessInstancesList**
2	A view of a single process instance.	**WMGetProcessInstance**

In addition, various filters (parameters) are provided with the calls such that the information returned may be tailored.

The API functions associated with these API calls are described in this section.

4.4.1 WMOpenProcessInstancesList

NAME

WMOpenProcessInstancesList - Specifies and opens the query to produce a list of process instances that match the filter criterion.

DESCRIPTION

This command will return a query handle for a list of process instances that match the specified value for the *attribute*. The command will also return, optionally, the total *count* of instances available. If the count is requested and the implementation does not support it, the command will return a pcount value of -1.

This command will be used to set up a wide variety of queries of process instances. For example, this command will be used to set up the query for a list of completed or suspended process instances. If pproc_inst_filter is NULL, then the function, with the corresponding fetch calls will return the list of ALL accessible process instances.

```
WMTErrRetType WMOpenProcessInstancesList (
    in  WMTPSessionHandle psession_handle,
    in  WMTPFilter pproc_inst_filter,
    in  WMTBoolean count_flag,
    out WMTPQueryHandle pquery_handle,
    out WMTPInt32 pcount)
```

Argument Name	Description
psession_handle	Pointer to a structure containing information about the context for this action.

pproc_inst_ filter	Pointer to a structure containing the information for this request.
count_flag	Boolean flag that indicates if the total count of process instances should be returned.
pquery_handle	Pointer to a structure containing a unique query information.
pcount	Total number of process instances that fulfill the filter condition.

ERROR RETURN VALUE

WM_SUCCESS
WM_INVALID_SESSION_HANDLE
WM_INVALID_FILTER

REQUIREMENTS

None

RATIONALE FOR API

The requester of the information needs to know what work of a particular type is in process or needs to know what work has completed.

4.4.2 WMFetchProcessInstance

NAME

WMFetchProcessInstance - Returns the next process instance from the list of process instances that met the selection criterion stated in the corresponding WMOpenProcessInstancesList call.

DESCRIPTION

This command returns a process instance. This fetch function will return subsequent process instances after every call. The fetch process is complete when the function returns the error WM_NO_MORE_DATA.

```
WMTErrRetType WMFetchProcessInstance (
    in   WMTPSessionHandle psession_handle,
    in   WMTPQueryHandle pquery_handle,
    out  WMTPProcInst pproc_inst_buf_ptr)
```

Argument Name	**Description**
psession_handle	Pointer to a structure containing information about the context for this action.

`pquery_handle`	Identification of the specific query handle returned by the **WMOpenProcessInstancesList** query command.
`pproc_inst_buf_ptr`	Pointer to a buffer area provided by the client application where the set of process instances will be placed.

ERROR RETURN VALUE

WM_SUCCESS
WM_INVALID_SESSION_HANDLE
WM_INVALID_QUERY_HANDLE
WM_NO_MORE_DATA

REQUIREMENTS

None

4.4.3 WMCloseProcessInstancesList

NAME

WMCloseProcessInstancesList - Closes the query of process instances.

DESCRIPTION

This command will close the query of process instances that match the specified query *attribute*, specified in the **WMOpenProcessInstancesList** command. The *query handle* can no longer be used.

```
WMTErrRetType WMCloseProcessInstancesList (
     in   WMTPSessionHandle psession_handle,
     in   WMTPQueryHandle pquery_handle)
```

Argument Name	Description
`psession_handle`	Pointer to a structure containing information about the context for this action.
`pquery_handle`	Identification of the specific query handle returned by the **WMOpenProcessInstancesList** query command.

ERROR RETURN VALUE

WM_SUCCESS
WM_INVALID_SESSION_HANDLE
WM_INVALID_QUERY_HANDLE

4.4.*4 WMGetProcessInstance*

NAME

WMGetProcessInstance - Return a specific process instance record.

DESCRIPTION

The **WMGetProcessInstance** provides information about what work has been done within a process instance and what is the current work being done within the process instance.

WMTErrRetType **WMGetProcessInstance (**
        in   WMTPSessionHandle psession_handle,
        in   WMTPProcInstID pproc_inst_id,
        out WMTPProcInst pproc_inst)

Argument Name	Description
psession_handle	Pointer to a structure containing information about the context for this action.
pproc_inst_id	Pointer to the process instance identification.
pproc_inst	Pointer to a structure containing the requested process instance information. Includes the state and other attributes of the process instance.

ERROR RETURN VALUE

WM_SUCCESS
WM_INVALID_SESSION_HANDLE
WM_INVALID_PROCESS_INSTANCE

REQUIREMENTS

None

4.5 WAPI Activity Status Functions

The process status functions are intended to provide a view of the work done, work to be done, work associated with a workflow participant or group of workflow participants, etc. The status queries may be requested by a normal workflow participant or may be requested by a manager or process administrator who wishes to view the progress of work within his/her domain.

The status API calls are structured such that they provide views ranging from a view of global work to a view of work within a single activity instance. These views are as follows:

1	All the activity instances associated to a process definition or instance	**WM(Open+Fetch+Close)Activity InstancesList**
2	A view of a single activity within a process instance.	**WMGetActivityInstance**

In addition, various filters (parameters) are provided with the calls such that the information returned may be tailored.

The API functions associated with these API calls are described in this section.

4.5.1 *WMOpenActivityInstancesList*

NAME

WMOpenActivityInstancesList - Specifies and opens the query to produce a list of activity instances that match the criterion of the filter.

DESCRIPTION

This command will return a query handle for a list of activity instances that match the criterion of the filter. The command will also return, optionally, the total *count* of activity instances available. If the count is requested and the implementation does not support it, the command will return a pcount value of -1.

This command will be used to set up a wide variety of queries of activity instances. For example, this command will be used to set up the query for a list of completed or suspended activity instances. If pactivity_inst_filter is NULL, then the function, with the corresponding fetch calls will return the list of ALL accessible activity instances.

```
WMTErrRetType WMOpenActivityInstancesList (
    in   WMTPSessionHandle psession_handle,
    in   WMTPFilter pactivity_inst_filter,
    in   WMTBoolean count_flag,
    out  WMTPQueryHandle pquery_handle,
    out  WMTPInt32 pcount)
```

Argument Name	Description
`psession_handle`	Pointer to a structure containing information about the context for this action.
`pactivity_inst_filter`	Pointer to a structure containing the information for this request.
`count_flag`	Boolean flag that indicates if the total count of activity instances should be returned.
`pquery_handle`	Pointer to a structure containing a unique query information returned by this function.
`pcount`	Total number of activity instances that fulfill the filter condition.

ERROR RETURN VALUE

WM_SUCCESS
WM_INVALID_SESSION_HANDLE
WM_INVALID_FILTER

REQUIREMENTS

None

RATIONALE FOR API

The requester of the information needs to know what work of a particular type is in process or needs to know what work has completed.

4.5.2 *WMFetchActivityInstance*

NAME

WMFetchActivityInstance - Returns the next activity instance from the list of activity instances that met the selection criterion in the corresponding WMOpenActivityInstancesList call.

DESCRIPTION

This command returns an activity instance.   This fetch function will return subsequent activity instances after every call. The fetch process is complete when the function returns the error WM_NO_MORE_DATA.

```
WMTErrRetType WMFetchActivityInstance (
        in  WMTPSessionHandle psession_handle,
        in  WMTPQueryHandle pquery_handle,
        out WMTPActivityInst pactivity_inst)
```

Argument Name	Description
psession_handle	Pointer to a structure containing information about the context for this action.
pquery_handle	Identification of the specific query handle returned by the **WMOpenActivityInstancesList** query command.
pactivity_inst	Pointer to a buffer area provided by the client application where the set of activity instances will be placed.

ERROR RETURN VALUE

WM_SUCCESS
WM_INVALID_SESSION_HANDLE
WM_INVALID_QUERY_HANDLE
WM_NO_MORE_DATA

REQUIREMENTS

None

4.5.3 *WMCloseActivityInstancesList*

NAME

WMCloseActivityInstancesList - Closes the query of activity instances.

DESCRIPTION

This command will close the query of activity instances that match the specified query *attribute*, specified in the **WMOpenActivityInstancesList** command. The *query handle* can no longer be used.

```
WMTErrRetType WMCloseActivityInstancesList (
        in WMTPSessionHandle psession_handle,
        in WMTPQueryHandle pquery_handle)
```

Argument Name	Description
psession_handle	Pointer to a structure containing information about the context for this action.
pquery_handle	Identification of the specific query handle returned by the **WMOpenActivityInstancesList** query command.

ERROR RETURN VALUE

WM_SUCCESS
WM_INVALID_SESSION_HANDLE
WM_INVALID_QUERY_HANDLE

REQUIREMENTS

None

4.5.4 *WMGetActivityInstance*

NAME

WMGetActivityInstance - Returns the record of a specific activity instance.

DESCRIPTION

The **WMGetActivityInstance** command provides status about an activity within a process instance.

WMTErrRetType **WMGetActivityInstance** (
    in WMTPSessionHandle psession_handle,
    in WMTPProcInstID pproc_inst_id,
    in WMTPActivityInstID pactivity_inst_id,
    out WMTPActivityInst pactivity_inst)

Argument Name	Description
psession_handle	Pointer to a structure containing information about the context for this action.
pproc_inst_id	Pointer to a structure containing the process instance identification.
pactivity_inst_id	Pointer to a structure containing the identification of the activity instance.
pactivity_inst	Pointer to a structure containing the activity instance information.

ERROR RETURN VALUE

WM_SUCCESS
WM_INVALID_SESSION_HANDLE
WM_INVALID_PROCESS_INSTANCE
WM_INVALID_ACTIVITY_INSTANCE

REQUIREMENTS

None

4.6 WAPI Worklist Functions

The WAPI worklist API calls provide workflow participants access to information about work to which they have been assigned. As described by the WfMC reference model, a process consists of a set of activities connected in such a way to control the sequencing of application invocation. An activity is associated with one or more applications to be invoked and also, during run time, is associated with the person(s) who has been assigned to do the work. Depending upon a WFM product's implementation, a workflow participant may be assigned one or more pieces of work at any one time. Each piece of work assigned to a workflow participant is called a 'work item' and the collection of all work items assigned to a workflow participant is called that workflow participant's 'worklist'.

(**Note**: To clarify the difference between an 'activity' and a 'work item' the following discussion is included. When a process is being defined (build time), an 'activity' is the construct used to define a piece of work to be done. It serves as a type of anchor point for further descriptions of that work to be done (i.e., the name of the application to be invoked, possibly a reference to skills needed to do the work, a symbolic name denoting the network address where the application is to be executed, etc.). During run time, when the activity is ready to be executed and one or more candidate persons are assigned to do the work, a work item is created and placed on that person(s) worklist. So, even though an activity and a work item both represent a piece of work, they come into existence at different points in time, there may be more than one work item for an activity and some operational characteristics may be different.)

A worklist then is defined as: the result of an implementation-defined query against the work item space. It is a list of work items and a work item is one element in a worklist.

The API calls in this section exist for the manipulation of work items and worklists.

4.6.1 WMOpenWorkList

NAME

WMOpenWorkList - Specifies and opens the query to produce the worklist that matches the criterion of the filter.

DESCRIPTION

This command provides the capability of returning a list of work items assigned to a specified workflow participant or a workgroup. The requester may be making the request on behalf of himself or may be a manager wanting to know what work has been assigned to a particular person or a workgroup.

A query handle will be returned for the list of work items that match the specified value for the attribute. The command will also return, optionally, the total *count* of work items available. If the count is requested and the implementation does not support it, the command will return a pcount value of -1. If pworklist_filter is NULL, then the function, with the corresponding fetch calls will return the list of ALL accessible work items.

```
WMTErrRetType WMOpenWorkList (
        in  WMTPSessionHandle psession_handle,
        in  WMTPFilter pworklist_filter,
        in  WMTBoolean count_flag,
        out WMTPQueryHandle pquery_handle,
        out WMTPInt32 pcount)
```

Argument Name	Description
psession_handle	Pointer to a structure containing information about the context for this action.
pworklist_filter	Pointer to a structure containing the filter information for this request.

`count_flag`	Boolean flag that indicates if the total count of work items should be returned.
`pquery_handle`	Pointer to a structure containing a unique query information returned by this function.
`pcount`	Total number of work items that fulfill the filter condition.

ERROR RETURN VALUE

WM_SUCCESS
WM_INVALID_SESSION_HANDLE
WM_INVALID_FILTER

REQUIREMENTS

None

RATIONALE FOR API

A workflow participant must be able to determine what work has been assigned. A manager must be able to determine who has work and what work is to be done within a department.

4.6.2 WMFetchWorkItem

NAME

WMFetchWorkItem - Returns the next work item from the worklist that met the selection criterion in the corresponding WMOpenWorkList call.

DESCRIPTION

This command returns a work item. This fetch function will return subsequent work items after every call. The fetch process is complete when the function returns the error WM_NO_MORE_DATA.

WMTErrRetType **WMFetchWorkItem** (
    in   WMTPSessionHandle psession_handle,
    in   WMTPQueryHandle pquery_handle,
    out WMTPWorkItem pwork_item)

Argument Name	Description
`psession_handle`	Pointer to a structure containing information about the context for this action.
`pquery_handle`	Identification of the specific query handle returned by the **WMOpenWorkList** query command.
`pwork_item`	Pointer to a buffer area provided by the client application where the set of work item will be placed.

ERROR RETURN VALUE

WM_SUCCESS
WM_INVALID_SESSION_HANDLE
WM_INVALID_QUERY_HANDLE
WM_NO_MORE_DATA

4.6.3 *WMCloseWorkList*

NAME

WMCloseWorkList - Closes the query of work items.

DESCRIPTION

This command will close the query of work items that match the specified query filter, specified in the **WMOpenWorkList** command. The *query handle* can no longer be used.

WMTErrRetType **WMCloseWorkList** (
        in WMTPSessionHandle psession_handle,
        in WMTPQueryHandle pquery_handle)

Argument Name	Description
psession_handle	Pointer to a structure containing information about the context for this action.
pquery_handle	Identification of the specific query handle returned by the **WMOpenWorkList** query command.

ERROR RETURN VALUE

WM_SUCCESS
WM_INVALID_SESSION_HANDLE
WM_INVALID_QUERY_HANDLE

4.6.4 *WMGetWorkItem*

NAME

WMGetWorkItem -   Returns the record of a specific work item

DESCRIPTION

This command allows a workflow participant to designate which piece of work he wishes to do. The viewer may be selecting a work item from a list obtained by the **WMOpenWorkList** command.

This command operates on a single work item basis.   This command execution need not imply that the work item is reserved or locked.

```
WMTErrRetType WMGetWorkItem (
      in  WMTPSessionHandle psession_handle,
      in  WMTPProcInstID pproc_inst_id,
      in  WMTPWorkItemID pwork_item_id,
      out WMTPWorkItem pwork_item )
```

Argument Name	Description
psession_handle	Pointer to a structure containing information about the context for this action.
pproc_inst_id	Pointer to a structure containing the unique process instance ID.
pwork_item_id	Pointer to a structure containing the work item identification for this request.
pwork_item	Pointer to a structure containing the work item being returned by this function.

ERROR RETURN VALUE

WM_SUCCESS
WM_INVALID_SESSION_HANDLE
WM_INVALID_PROCESS_INSTANCE
WM_INVALID_WORKITEM

REQUIREMENTS

The application issuing the command must have sufficient identification information to select the work item desired.

RATIONALE FOR API

A workflow participant must be able to tell the WFM Engine which piece of work is to be selected.

4.6.5 *WMCompleteWorkItem*

NAME

WMCompleteWorkItem - Tell the WFM Engine that this work item has been completed.

DESCRIPTION

This command allows a workflow participant to tell the WFM Engine that a work item has been completed.

To change a work item's attributes, multiple calls to WMAssignWorkItem Attribute.

```
WMTErrRetType WMCompleteWorkItem (
      in  WMTPSessionHandle psession_handle,
      in  WMTPProcInstID pproc_inst_id,
      in  WMTPWorkItemID pwork_item_id)
```

Argument Name	Description
psession_handle	Pointer to a structure containing information about the context for this action.
pproc_inst_id	Pointer to a structure containing the unique process instance ID.
pwork_item_id	Pointer to a structure containing the work item identification for this request.

ERROR RETURN VALUE

WM_SUCCESS
WM_INVALID_SESSION_HANDLE
WM_INVALID_PROCESS_INSTANCE
WM_INVALID_WORKITEM

REQUIREMENTS

None

RATIONALE FOR API

WFM products implement various ways to determine when an activity is complete. The use of the API may range from just a successful/unsuccessful indication to placing values in the completion state which might cause the WFM Engine to select a future model navigation path from among many.

Typically, a work item will correspond to an activity instance. However the API should allow the existence of multiple work items per activity, executed one at a time. So completion of a work item does not necessarily mean that all work for an activity instance is completed. Completion of a work item could trigger the start of the next work item that corresponds to that activity instance. The Workflow Engine will determine the next work item based on the process definition.

4.6.6 WMReassignWorkItem

NAME

WMReassignWorkItem

DESCRIPTION

This command allows a work item from one workflow participant's worklist to be reassigned to another workflow participant's worklist.

(**Note**: Possible future releases of the API specification may provide for an entire worklist to be reassigned in total.)

```
WMTErrRetType WMReassignWorkItem (
    in  WMTPSessionHandle psession_handle,
    in  WMTPWflParticipant psource_user,
    in  WMTPWflParticipant ptarget_user,
    in  WMTPProcInstID pproc_inst_id,
    in  WMTPWorkItemID pwork_item_id)
```

Argument Name	Description
psession_handle	Pointer to a structure containing information about the context for this action.
psource_user	The identification of a workflow participant from which work is to be reassigned.
ptarget_user	The identification of the workflow participant to whom work is to be assigned.
pproc_inst_id	Pointer to a structure containing the unique process instance ID.
pwork_item_id	Pointer to a structure containing the work item identification being reassigned.

ERROR RETURN VALUE

WM_SUCCESS
WM_INVALID_SESSION_HANDLE
WM_INVALID_PROCESS_INSTANCE
WM_INVALID_WORKITEM
WM_INVALID_SOURCE_USER
WM_INVALID_TARGET_USER

REQUIREMENTS

The workflow participant making the reassignment request has the authority to do so.

RATIONALE FOR API

A workflow participant having work assigned may be away from work for various reasons and the work must be given to another workflow participant to get it accomplished. A WFM Engine may direct all work items to a single worklist (departmental worklist for example).

With the reassignment API, workflow participants in that department may reassign work to themselves after they finish a current work item and become available for more work. This creates a possible de facto people load balancing scheme.

4.6.7 *WMOpenWorkItemAttributesList*

NAME

WMOpenWorkItemAttributesList - Specifies and opens the query to produce the list of work item attributes that match the filter criterion.

DESCRIPTION

This command will return a query handle for a list of attributes for a work item. The command will also return, optionally, the total *count* of attributes available. If the count is requested and the implementation does not support it, the command will return a pcount value of -1.

One of the uses of this API, together with the corresponding fetch and close calls is to allow a workflow application to query the Workflow Engine for the available attributes that can be assigned to the work item, in order to offer this list to the application user. Attribute values can be obtained as well provided that a buffer of enough size is passed in the fetch call. Individual attribute values can also be retrieved with the **WMGetWorkItemAttributeValue** call. If `pwork_item_attr_filter` is NULL, then the function, with the corresponding fetch calls will return the list of ALL attributes available for the work item.

```
WMTErrRetType WMOpenWorkItemAttributesList (
    in  WMTPSessionHandle psession_handle,
    in  WMTPProcInstID pproc_inst_id,
    in  WMTPWorkItemID pwork_item_id,
    in  WMTPFilter pwork_item_attr_filter,
    in  WMTBoolean count_flag,
    out WMTPQueryHandle pquery_handle,
    out WMTPInt32 pcount)
```

Argument Name	Description
psession_handle	Pointer to a structure containing information about the context for this action.
pproc_inst_id	Pointer to a structure containing the unique process instance ID.
pwork_item_id	Pointer to a structure containing the unique work item ID.
pwork_item_attr_filter	Filter associated with the work item attributes.
count_flag	Boolean flag that indicates if the total count of work item attributes should be returned.
pquery_handle	Pointer to a structure containing a unique query information.
pcount	Total number of attributes for this work item.

ERROR RETURN VALUE

```
WM_SUCCESS
WM_INVALID_SESSION_HANDLE
WM_INVALID_PROCESS_INSTANCE
WM_INVALID_WORKITEM
```

4.6.8 WMFetchWorkItemAttribute

NAME

WMFetchWorkItemAttribute - Returns the next work item attribute from the list of work item attributes that match the filter criterion.

DESCRIPTION

This command returns a work item attribute. This fetch function will return subsequent work item attributes after every call. The fetch process is complete when the function returns the error WM_NO_MORE_DATA. The fetch function will return the attribute value as well in a buffer specified in the call. If buffer_size is NULL then the attribute value will not be returned. If buffer_size is not large enough to hold the attribute value then the function will return as much of the attribute value as can be fit in the buffer. The proper length of the attribute value is available in the attribute_length field. The application can compare the attribute_length with the buffer_size to determine if the full value was returned.

```
WMTErrRetType WMFetchWorkItemAttribute (
    in   WMTPSessionHandle psession_handle,
    in   WMTPQueryHandle pquery_handle,
    out  WMTPAttrName pattribute_name,
    out  WMTPInt32 pattribute_type,
    out  WMTPInt32 pattribute_length,
    out  WMTPText pattribute_value,
    in   WMTInt32 buffer_size)
```

Argument Name	Description
psession_handle	Pointer to a structure containing information about the context for this action.
pquery_handle	Identification of the specific query handle returned by the **WMOpenWorkItemAttributesList** query command.
pattribute_name	Pointer to the name of the attribute.
pattribute_type	Pointer to the type of the attribute.
pattribute_length	Pointer to the length of the attribute value.
pattribute_value	Pointer to a buffer area provided by the client application where the attribute value will be placed.
buffer_size	Size of the buffer.

ERROR RETURN VALUE

```
WM_SUCCESS
WM_INVALID_SESSION_HANDLE
WM_INVALID_QUERY_HANDLE
WM_NO_MORE_DATA
```

4.6.9 *WMCloseWorkItemAttributesList*

NAME

WMCloseWorkItemAttributesList - Closes the query for work item attributes.

DESCRIPTION

WMTErrRetType **WMCloseWorkItemAttributesList** (
      in WMTPSessionHandle **psession_handle,**
      in WMTPQueryHandle **pquery_handle)**

Argument Name	Description
psession_handle	Pointer to a structure containing information about the context for this action.
pquery_handle	Identification of the specific query handle returned by the **WMOpenWorkItemAttributesList** query command.

ERROR RETURN VALUE

WM_SUCCESS
WM_INVALID_SESSION_HANDLE
WM_INVALID_QUERY_HANDLE

4.6.10 *WMGetWorkItemAttributeValue*

NAME

WMGetWorkItemAttributeValue - Returns the value, type and length of a work item attribute specified by the pwork_item_id parameter.

DESCRIPTION

This command will return the value of a work item attribute in the buffer specified in the call.

WMTErrRetType **WMGetWorkItemAttributeValue** (
      in WMTPSessionHandle psession_handle,
      in WMTPProcInstID pproc_inst_id,
      in WMTPWorkItemID pwork_item_id,
      in WMTPAttrName pattribute_name,
      out WMTPInt32 pattribute_type,
      out WMTPInt32 pattribute_length,
      out WMTPText pattribute_value,
      in WMTInt32 buffer_size)

Argument Name	Description
psession_handle	Pointer to a structure containing information about the context for this action.
pproc_inst_id	Pointer to a structure containing the unique process instance ID.
pwork_item_id	Pointer to a structure containing the unique work item ID.

`pattribute_name`	Pointer to the name of the attribute.
`pattribute_type`	Pointer to the type of the attribute.
`pattribute_length`	Pointer to the length of the attribute value.
`pattribute_value`	Pointer to a buffer area provided by the client application where the attribute value will be placed.
`buffer_size`	Size of the buffer to be filled.

ERROR RETURN VALUE

```
WM_SUCCESS
WM_INVALID_SESSION_HANDLE
WM_INVALID_ATTRIBUTE
WM_INSUFFICIENT_BUFFER_SIZE
```

4.6.11 WMAssignWorkItemAttribute

NAME

WMAssignWorkItemAttribute - Assign the proper attribute to a work item.

DESCRIPTION

This command tells the WFM Engine to assign an attribute, to change an attribute or to change the value of an attribute of a work item.

```
WMTErrRetType WMAssignWorkItemAttribute (
    in   WMTPSessionHandle psession_handle,
    in   WMTPProcInstID pproc_inst_id,
    in   WMTPWorkItemID pwork_item_id,
    in   WMTPAttrName pattribute_name,
    in   WMTInt32 attribute_type,
    in   WMTInt32 attribute_length,
    in   WMTPText pattribute_value)
```

Argument Name	Description
`psession_handle`	Pointer to a structure containing information about the context for this action.
`pproc_inst_id`	Pointer to a structure containing the unique process instance ID.
`pwork_item_id`	Pointer to a structure containing the work item ID for which an attribute will be added or changed.
`pattribute_name`	Pointer to the name of the attribute.
`attribute_type`	Type of the attribute.
`attribute_length`	Length of the attribute value.
`pattribute_value`	Pointer to a buffer area provided by the client application where the attribute value will be placed.

ERROR RETURN VALUE

```
WM_SUCCESS
WM_INVALID_SESSION_HANDLE
WM_INVALID_PROCESS_INSTANCE
WM_INVALID_WORKITEM
WM_INVALID_ATTRIBUTE
WM_ATTRIBUTE_ASSIGNMENT_FAILED
```

4.7 WAPI Administration Functions

The set of administration functions provide the functionality needed to perform administration and maintenance functions of a workflow system. This set includes the minimal services contemplated for this client application interface. The set includes functions to change state of a set of process or activity instances, terminating and aborting process instances, and for assigning attributes to a set of process and activity instances.

4.7.1 WMChangeProcessInstancesState

NAME

WMChangeProcessInstancesState - Change the state of the instances of the named process definition that match the specified filter criterion.

DESCRIPTION

This command is defined to allow a set of process instances in the named process definition to move to a specific new state.

Execution of this command will cause a set of process instances of the named process definition change their state. If the filter pointer `pproc_inst_filter` is NULL, then the command is applied to all process instances. Specific state names and their semantics are dependent upon the particular WFM Engine implementation. This call will be executed when a set of process instances of a process must have a new state, such as *suspended, disabled* or *enabled*. Specific state names and semantics must be included in implementation documentation.

Since this command operates on a set of process instances of a named process definition, it is expected to be issued by a person having the authority to do so. The scope of this operation may be different depending on the vendor's implementation.

```
WMTErrRetType WMChangeProcessInstancesState (
    in  WMTPSessionHandle psession_handle,
    in  WMTPProcDefID pproc_def_id,
    in  WMTPFilter pproc_inst_filter,
    in  WMTPProcInstState pproc_inst_state)
```

Argument Name	Description
psession_handle	Pointer to a structure containing information about the context for this action.
pproc_def_id	Pointer to a structure containing a unique process definition ID.
pproc_inst_filter	Pointer to a structure containing the filter information for this request.
pproc_inst_state	An ID that indicates the process state that you want to change to.

ERROR RETURN VALUE

WM_SUCCESS
WM_INVALID_SESSION_HANDLE
WM_INVALID_PROCESS_DEFINITION
WM_INVALID_FILTER
WM_INVALID_STATE
WM_TRANSITION_NOT_ALLOWED

REQUIREMENTS

Each process instance must have a unique ID within an administrative scope.
Each process definition must have a unique ID within an administrative scope.

RATIONALE FOR API

This API allows the possible intervention of a process administrator in a running process. This might be for the purpose of changing the process definition and having all subsequently created instances reflect the new definition. It provides the capability of halting running process instances while changes in roles, activities, etc. are put into effect. It allows instances to be stopped while problem determination can be done on a malfunctioning process.

4.7.2 *WMChangeActivityInstancesState*

NAME

WMChangeActivityInstancesState - Change the state of the activity instances of a particular name associated to a process definition that match the specified filter criterion.

DESCRIPTION

This command directs a WFM Engine to change the state of the named activity for a set of activity instances. It is assumed that a person who can change the state of the set of activity instances corresponding to a process definition has special authorization to do so. If the implementation supports a state such as *suspended*, and *resumed* or *in-progress*, then the functions for suspend and resume are implemented as state change calls. If the filter pointer pact_inst_filter is NULL, then the command is applied to all activity instances of the given activity definition.

WMTErrRetType **WMChangeActivityInstancesState** (
      in   WMTPSessionHandle psession_handle,
      in   WMTPProcDefID pproc_def_id,
      in   WMTPActivityID pactivity_def_id,
      in   WMTPFilter pact_inst_filter,
      in   WMTPActivityInstState pactivity_inst_state)

Argument Name	Description
`psession_handle`	Pointer to a structure containing information about the context for this action.
`pproc_def_id`	Pointer to a structure containing a unique process definition ID.
`pactivity_def_id`	Pointer to the activity definition ID.
`pact_inst_filter`	Pointer to a structure containing the filter information for this request.
`pactivity_inst_state`	An ID that indicates the activity instance state that you want to change to.

ERROR RETURN VALUE

WM_SUCCESS
WM_INVALID_SESSION_HANDLE
WM_INVALID_PROCESS_DEFINITION
WM_INVALID_ACTIVITY_NAME
WM_INVALID_FILTER
WM_INVALID_STATE
WM_TRANSITION_NOT_ALLOWED

REQUIREMENTS

Each process definition must have a unique ID within an administrative scope.
Each activity must have a unique ID within a process definition.

RATIONALE FOR API

A workflow participant may wish to modify the states of activity instances of a particular activity.   Other situations might involve the malfunctioning of an application associated with an activity. A process containing the activity may be a frequently used one, and it might be issuing dumps each time it is invoked. The use of this API would allow the calling of the application to be stopped while remedial measures were taken.

4.7.3 *WMTerminateProcessInstances*

NAME

WMTerminateProcessInstances - Terminate the process instances of the named process definition that match the specified filter criterion.

DESCRIPTION

This command provides the capability of terminating a set of process instances associated with a process definition. Execution of this command will cause a set of process instances of the named process definition to be terminated. If the filter pointer pproc_inst_filter is NULL, then the command is applied to all process instances.

```
WMTErrRetType      WMTerminateProcessInstances (
     in  WMTPSessionHandle psession_handle,
     in  WMTPProcDefID pproc_def_id,
     in  WMTPFilter pproc_inst_filter)
```

Argument Name	Description
psession_handle	Pointer to a structure containing information about the context for this action.
pproc_def_id	Pointer to a structure containing the process definition for which all process instances are to be terminated.
pproc_inst_filter	Pointer to a structure containing the filter information for this request.

ERROR RETURN VALUE

```
WM_SUCCESS
WM_INVALID_SESSION_HANDLE
WM_INVALID_PROCESS_DEFINITION
WM_INVALID_FILTER
```

4.7.4 *WMAssignProcessInstancesAttribute*

NAME

WMAssignProcessInstancesAttribute -   Assign the proper attribute to a set of process instances within a process definition that match the specific filter criterion.

DESCRIPTION

This command tells the WFM Engine to assign an attribute, or to change an attribute or to change the values of an attribute of a set of process instances within a named process definition.

This command changes the value of the attribute of a process instance. These attributes of process instances are of the kind called *Process Control* or *Process Relevant* Data.

```
WMTErrRetType WMAssignProcessInstancesAttribute (
     in  WMTPSessionHandle psession_handle,
```

```
in  WMTPProcDefID pproc_def_id,
in  WMTPFilter pproc_inst_filter,
in  WMTPAttrName pattribute_name,
in  WMTInt32 attribute_type,
in  WMTInt32 attribute_length,
in  WMTPText pattribute_value)
```

Argument Name	Description
psession_handle	Pointer to a structure containing information about the context for this action.
pproc_def_id	Pointer to a structure containing the process definition ID for which the attribute of all process instances will be changed.
pproc_inst_filter	Pointer to a structure containing the filter information for this request.
ppattribute_name	Pointer to the name of the attribute.
attribute_type	Type of the attribute.
attribute_length	Length of the attribute value.
pattribute_value	Pointer to a buffer area provided by the client application where the attribute value will be placed.

ERROR RETURN VALUE

```
WM_SUCCESS
WM_INVALID_SESSION_HANDLE
WM_INVALID_PROCESS_DEFINITION
WM_INVALID_FILTER
WM_INVALID_ATTRIBUTE
```

4.7.5 *WMAssignActivityInstancesAttribute*

NAME

WMAssignActivityInstancesAttribute - Assign the proper attribute to set of activity instances within a process definition that match the specific filter criterion.

DESCRIPTION

This command tells the WFM Engine to assign an attribute, or to change an attribute or to change the value of an attribute of a set of activity instances within a named process definition. These attributes of activity instances are of the kind called *Process Control* or *Process Relevant* Data. If pact_inst_filter is NULL, then the function is applied to ALL accessible activity instances of the given activity definition.

```
WMTErrRetType WMAssignActivityInstancesAttribute (
    in  WMTPSessionHandle psession_handle,
    in  WMTPProcDefID pproc_def_id,
    in  WMTPActivityID pactivity_def_id,
    in  WMTPFilter pact_inst_filter,
    in  WMTPAttrName pattribute_name,
    in  WMTInt32 attribute_type,
    in  WMTInt32 attribute_length,
    in  WMTPText pattribute_value)
```

Argument Name	Description
psession_handle	Pointer to a structure containing information about the context for this action.
pproc_def_id	Pointer to a structure containing the process definition ID. In the case that the attribute will be changed for all activity instances that correspond to the process definition. This parameter will be NULL otherwise.
pactivity_def_id	Pointer to a structure containing the activity definition identification for which the attribute will be assigned.
pact_inst_filter	Pointer to a structure containing the filter information for this request.
pattribute_name	Pointer to the name of the attribute.
attribute_type	Type of the attribute.
attribute_length	Length of the attribute value.
pattribute_value	Pointer to a buffer area provided by the client application where the attribute value will be placed.

ERROR RETURN VALUE

```
WM_SUCCESS
WM_INVALID_SESSION_HANDLE
WM_INVALID_PROCESS_DEFINITION
WM_INVALID_ACTIVITY_NAME
WM_INVALID_FILTER
WM_INVALID_ATTRIBUTE
```

4.7.6 WMAbortProcessInstances

NAME

WMAbortProcessInstances - Abort the set of process instances that correspond to the named process definition, that match the specific filter criterion, regardless of its state.

DESCRIPTION

This command allows a set of process instances of a process definition to be aborted. All current activities within these process instances will be stopped when possible. The instances will be terminated. If `pproc_inst_filter` is NULL, then the function will be applied to ALL accessible process instances.

```
WMTErrRetType WMAbortProcessInstances (
    in  WMTPSessionHandle psession_handle,
    in  WMTPProcDefID pproc_def_id,
    in  WMTPFilter pproc_inst_filter)
```

Argument Name	Description
psession_handle	Pointer to a structure containing information about the context for this action.
pproc_def_id	Pointer to a structure containing the process definition for who all processes instances is being aborted.
pproc_inst_filter	Pointer to a structure containing the filter information for this request.

ERROR RETURN VALUE

```
WM_SUCCESS
WM_INVALID_SESSION_HANDLE
WM_INVALID_PROCESS_DEFINITION
WM_INVALID_FILTER
```

REQUIREMENTS

None

RATIONALE FOR API

This command is for use in catastrophic circumstances where nothing except clearing the process away can be done.

4.7.7 WMAbortProcessInstance

NAME

WMAbortProcessInstance - Abort the process instance specified regardless of its state.

DESCRIPTION

This command allows a process instance to be aborted. All current activities within the process instance will be stopped when possible. The instance will be terminated.

```
WMTErrRetType WMAbortProcessInstance (
    in  WMTPSessionHandle psession_handle,
    in  WMTPProcInstID pproc_inst_id)
```

Argument Name	**Description**
`psession_handle`	Pointer to a structure containing information about the context for this action.
`pproc_inst_id`	Pointer to a structure containing the process instance being aborted.

ERROR RETURN VALUE

WM_SUCCESS
WM_INVALID_SESSION_HANDLE
WM_INVALID_PROCESS_INSTANCE

REQUIREMENTS

None

RATIONALE FOR API

This command is for use in catastrophic circumstances where nothing except clearing the process away can be done.

5. Future Work

5.1 Additional API Areas

The WfMC API specification work will address the following areas. It will be determined whether API calls should be created for these areas or whether they are the sole domain of particular WFM product implementations.

5.1.1 WFM Data API calls

The types of data that applications need to manipulate through this API specification are process control data, process relevant data, and application data. The current specification addresses the access to these data through the definition and manipulation of attributes of processes, activities and work items. It is currently believed that some additional new API calls or parameter additions to existing API calls will be required for complete data manipulation.

5.1.2 Ad hoc activities

In a future release of API specifications, the API working group will consider the functionality to allow applications to add activities to an instance of a process that are not part of its definition. These ad-hoc additions will be done on an instance basis.

5.1.*3 Administration and Maintenance*

The API working group believes that the functions in this area correspond to interface 5. Services should include functions for:

- Purging
- Backup
- Archiving
- Download and Upload instances (for remote users)

5.1.*4 Names and Roles*

The API working group believes that a Workflow Engine should also provide services for definition, assignment, mapping and maintenance of roles and names (identities). The working group also believes that these services should be provided through interface 5 as well.

5.2 Additional Issues

The WfMC API specification work will be expanded to take care of the following issues for future releases.

5.2.*1 Error reporting and control*

All WAPI function calls have a uniform error return datatype. This data type is shared among all API calls. This specification assumes that the Coalition will specify a subset of the main error return codes, leaving for vendor specific implementation the remaining main error return codes and the set of subcode codes to provide extensibility and specialization of error codes. (See section WAPI Data Types, and WAPI Error Return Codes sections).

5.2.*2 Synchpoint processing*

Synchpoint processing deals with recoverability. The API working group believes that this area is extremely important to WFM exploiters. However, it is also believed that it would be one of the more difficult areas to deal with in terms of member agreement. Work in this area is being deferred to the second release of the API specifications.

5.2.*3 Security*

The current version of the WFM API specification does not include any specific requirements or provisions for security mechanisms, except for the inclusion of user password in the **WMTConnectInfo** structure. Implementation of security mechanisms are left up to the specific implementations.

5.2.4 *Locking*

The current version of the WFM API specification does not include any specific requirements or provisions for locking mechanisms. Implementation of locking mechanisms are left up to the specific implementations.

5.2.5 *Process Integrity*

The current version of the WFM API specification does not include any specific requirements or provisions for mechanisms to guarantee process integrity. Implementation of process integrity mechanisms are left up to the specific implementations.

WAPI Naming Conventions

This section is based on Version 1.1 of *WAPI Naming Conventions*, dated 15th May 1996. Document Reference: WFMC-TC-1013.

1. Guidelines

Successful naming conventions for the WAPI should cover the following points:

- Readability
- Portability
- Usability
- Compile time name space resolution
- Link time name space resolution
- Implementation

1.1 Readability

Naming conventions should be designed to facilitate readability. This can be achieved by a number of simple steps. Using long symbol names that convey the purpose of the symbol in the WAPI facilitates readability. Clearly separating the words in symbol names by using underscores or capitalizing the first letter of each word also improves readability.

The proposed naming convention spells out symbol words fully, and separates different words in the symbol name by capitalizing the first letter of each word.

1.2 Portability

Portability issues usually discourage designers from thinking about readability. Some platforms allow only limited symbol name length, and usage of characters in only one case. This in turn will make symbol names short, encrypted, and discourage the use of underscores or capitalization to separate the words in symbol names.

Most modern environments support symbol names of greater than 32 characters with at least 32 significant characters. These are the environments for which the current API set is most suitable.

The proposed solution should be carefully modified for improved portability. If deemed necessary the API would be modified specifically for those environments where symbol name lengths are restricted. This modification would start by identifying the set of platforms and operating systems supported by the coalition members, and then modifying the naming convention and the APIs to accommodate restrictions of each of those systems, trying to avoid sacrificing readability.

1.3 Usability

The WAPI naming convention should allow WAPI users to write applications that can be linked against any vendor's library with minimal changes to the source code. All WAPI calls are intended to be usable by all the prevalent programming environments currently in use. Although the this convention is biased toward 'C' and 'C++' users, the convention should allow the functions implemented to be called by environments such as Visual Basic, Smalltalk, and various 4GL and other environments.

The proposed solution requires all vendors to name the corresponding symbols with the same name. This will allow users to change WAPI vendor libraries without modifying the application source code.

The proposed solution assumes that the WAPI vendor libraries will be implemented as DLLs (dynamic linked libraries).

1.4 Compile Time Name Space Resolution

Compile time name space issues can be resolved by reserving a prefix for all WAPI symbols. This prefix should be short, and each symbol should start with the prefix. In the case that a particular WAPI vendor or user has a conflict between a WAPI symbol name and an internal symbol name, compile time symbols can be easily re-mapped with the help of C preprocessor or by editing the header files. The naming conventions should be designed so that the need for such interventions is minimized.

This solution chooses 'WM' as a prefix to all WAPI symbol names. Furthermore, different classes of symbol names have an additional letter identifying the class that the symbol belongs to, thus improving readability. For example, all WAPI types start with 'WMT'.

1.5 Link Time Name Space Resolution

Unlike compile time symbols, conflicts between link time symbols, such as multiple defined function names, are not easily correctable. Thus, the major and most important goal of a successfully designed naming convention is to minimize the chance of link time symbol conflicts. A well designed naming convention will not only allow WAPI vendors and users to link WAPI against their internal libraries without conflicts, but it will enable users to link their applications against multiple vendor WAPIs at the same time as well. This ought to be achieved without sacrificing usability. For example, requiring that each vendor uses their own prefix before each WAPI function would facilitate link time name space resolution by elimination of multiple defined symbols between different vendors' functions linked into the same executable, but at the same time it would decrease the usability of the WAPI, since users would have to customize their application source code for each vendor's WAPI separately.

1.6 Implementation

The proposed solution assumes that the Coalition will provide a common header file as a starting point for vendor implementations. This is a crucial step, since the definition of a common WAPI programming vocabulary is essential for usability issues, and at the same time it eliminates many possible misinterpretations among different vendors.

2. Named Entities

In general all of the named entities within the scope of the Workflow Management Coalition specifications should have names which start with the letters 'WM'.
The sections to come will outline specific naming conventions for the following named entities:

Functions	The callable routines specified by the WfMC APIs
Data Type Definitions	The "typedefs" used to declare and create variables for the API
Variables	The necessary variables required to support the APIs, i.e. parameters for those functions.
Structures	The data structures required for passing information to and from the APIs
Files	The files required to support the compilation and linking of programs written with the APIs

2.1 Functions

All functions in the Workflow Management Coalition's API suite should be preceded with the 'WM' prefix. All functions should also return the same return value as specified by the WMTErrRetType typedef. The following is an example of a function declaration:

```
WMTErrRetType WMOpenProcessDefinitionsList (
        in  WMTPSessionHandle psession_handle,
        in  WMTPFilter pproc_def_filter,
        in  WMTBoolean count_flag,
        out WMTPQueryHandle pquery_handle,
        out WMTPInt32 pcount);
```

2.2 Data Type Definitions

There are a few basic data types which must first be defined. The convention will be to create "typedefs" which will then be used to declare variables required by the API. The convention for "typedefs" will be to start their names with the prefix 'WMT' to denote Workflow Management **Types**.

The basic data types from which all other types are derived are defined as follows:

WMTInt8	signed 8 bit value representation
WMTInt16	signed 16 bit value representation
WMTInt32	signed 32 bit value representation
WMTUInt8	unsigned 8 bit value representation
WMTUInt16	unsigned 16 bit value representation
WMTUInt32	unsigned 32 bit value representation

The convention for dealing with pointer "typedefs" will be to use the prefix '**WMTP**'. For example:

```
typedef *WMTConnectInfo WMTPConnectInfo;
```

2.3 Variables

Naming of variables in the API set should be descriptive but are not required to have a special prefix. For variables which are pointers it is recommended that '**p**' be used as a prefix. It is presumed that for those environments that support multiple pointer dimensions that the pointers be defined as the largest supported size, e.g. for Intel based compilers the "FAR" pointer type will be used.

For variables which have a scope outside of a module, those variables should be prefixed with '**WMGV**' to denote Workflow Management Global Variables. For various reasons the use of global variables will be discouraged but this document includes a naming specification for completeness.

2.4 Structures

Naming of structure typedefs should be done following the conventions already given for data type definitions. Naming of the actual structures should follow the conventions for naming variables.

2.5 Static Defines

All static definitions required by the WfMC APIs such as Error Values should have names beginning with '**WM**' and be all caps with underscores where appropriate.

2.6 Files

All files required by the WfMC APIs such as 'C' include files should have names beginning with '**WM**' and be limited to 8 characters with appropriate 3 character extensions.

3. Include Files & Examples

The following sections show the include files as defined to support the Workflow Management Coalition APIs in general and the Interface 2 APIs specifically. These files serve also as examples for the purpose of illustrating the usage of the naming conventions described here in this document.

3.1 Include File - wmbasic.h

File: wmbasic.h

```
1         2         3         4         5         6         7         8
12345678901234567890123456789012345678901234567890123456789012345678901234567890
1234567890
/*
  This file is provided by the vendor for each specific platform
environment.
  It contains definitions of the basic Workflow Management types that
are operating system or platform dependent.
*/

#ifndef WMTBASIC_H
#define WMTBASIC_H

typedef        char   WMTInt8;
```

```
typedef            short WMTInt16;
typedef            long  WMTInt32;
typedef unsigned char   WMTUInt8;
typedef unsigned short WMTUInt16;
typedef unsigned long   WMTUInt32;


/****************
  WMTPointer - generic pointer representation, points to the smallest
  addressable unit of information.
*/

typedef WMTUInt8       *WMTPointer;
#define WMNULL          ((WMTPointer)0)


/****************
  WMTText - since different vendors may represent textual information
in
  different formats for language independence purposes, we treat text
as
  an opaque generic pointer.
*/
typedef WMTInt8     WMTText;
typedef WMTText     *WMTPText;
typedef WMTInt8     *WMTPInt8;
typedef WMTInt16    *WMTPInt16;
typedef WMTInt32    *WMTPInt32;



/*****************
  WMTBoolean - boolean type and value definitions.
*/
typedef WMTInt8     WMTBoolean;
typedef WMTText     *WMTPPrivate;

#define WMFalse     0
#define WMTrue      (!WMFalse)

#define NAME_STRING_SIZE      64
#define UNIQUE_ID_SIZE        64


#endif
```

3.2 Include File - wmapi2.h

File: wmapi2.h

```
1         2         3         4         5         6         7         8
```

```
12345678901234567890123456789012345678901234567890123456789012345678901234567890
1234567890
/*

    WMAPI.H

  This is the file supplied by the Workflow Management Coalition.
  It contains standard parameters, function and value definitions.
*/


#ifndef WMAPI_H
#define WMAPI_H

/****************
  WM* - all global Workflow Management symbols start with WM
  WMT* - all type definitions start with WMT
*/


/****************
  Basic Type Definitions:
  Before including this file, the following types have to be type
defined
  by the vendor according to the current platform definitions.  All
other
  WORKFLOW MANAGEMENT types are derived from these basic types.

  WMTInt8        signed  8 bit value representation
  WMTInt16       signed 16 bit value representation
  WMTInt32       signed 32 bit value representation
  WMTUInt8       unsigned  8 bit value representation
  WMTUInt16      unsigned 16 bit value representation
  WMTUInt32      unsigned 32 bit value representation
  WMTPInt8        8 bit pointer value representation
  WMTPInt16      16 bit pointer value representation
  WMTPInt32      32 bit pointer value representation
*/


#include "wmtbasic.h"


/********************************************************
    This section defines all the structures used by the interface 2
API.
*/


/********************************************************
      WMTErrRetType
*/

typedef struct {
```

```
    WMTInt16     main_code;
    WMTInt16     sub_code;
} WMTErrRetType;

/********************************************************
        WMTConnectInfo
*/

typedef struct
{
  WMTText   user_identification[NAME_STRING_SIZE];
  WMTText   password[NAME_STRING_SIZE];
  WMTText   engine_name[NAME_STRING_SIZE];
  WMTText   scope[NAME_STRING_SIZE];
}WMTConnectInfo;

typedef WMTConnectInfo *WMTPConnectInfo;

/********************************************************
        WMTSessionHandle
*/

typedef struct
{
  WMTUInt32    session_id;
  WMTPPrivate pprivate;
}WMTSessionHandle;

typedef WMTSessionHandle *WMTPSessionHandle;

/********************************************************
        WMTFilter
*/

typedef struct
{
  WMTInt32  filter_type;
  WMTInt32  filter_length;
  WMTText   attribute_name [NAME_STRING_SIZE];
  WMTUInt32 comparison;
  WMTPText  filter_string;
}WMTFilter;

typedef WMTFilter *WMTPFilter;

/** The first 255 filter types (0x00000001 to 0x000000FF) will be
reserved. These will be used for filtering on attributes of process
control data and process relevant data.
*/
```

```
/********************************************************
        WMTQueryHandle
*/

typedef struct
{
  WMTUInt32 query_handle;
}WMTQueryHandle;

typedef WMTQueryHandle *WMTPQueryHandle;

/********************************************************
        WMTWflParticipant
*/

typedef struct
{
  WMTText    wf_participant[NAME_STRING_SIZE];
}WMTWflParticipant;

typedef WMTWflParticipant *WMTPWflParticipant;

/********************************************************
        WMTProcDefID
*/

typedef struct
{
  WMTText   proc_def_id[UNIQUE_ID_SIZE];
}WMTProcDefID;

typedef WMTProcDefID *WMTPProcDefID;

/********************************************************
        WMTActivityID
*/

typedef struct
{
  WMTText   activity_id[NAME_STRING_SIZE];
}WMTActivityID;

typedef WMTActivityID *WMTPActivityID;

/********************************************************
        WMTProcDefState
*/
```

```
typedef struct
{
  WMTText   proc_def_state[NAME_STRING_SIZE];
} WMTProcDefState;

typedef WMTProcDefState *WMTPProcDefState;

/********************************************************
        WMTProcDef
*/

typedef struct
{
        WMTText                 process_name[NAME_STRING_SIZE];
        WMTProcDefID            proc_def_id;
        WMTProcDefState         state;
} WMTProcDef;

typedef WMTProcDef *WMTPProcDef;

/********************************************************
        WMTProcInstID
*/

typedef struct
{
  WMTText   proc_inst_id[UNIQUE_ID_SIZE];
}WMTProcInstID;

typedef WMTProcInstID *WMTPProcInstID;

/********************************************************
        WMTProcInstState
*/

typedef struct
{
  WMTText   proc_inst_state[NAME_STRING_SIZE];
} WMTProcInstState;

typedef WMTProcInstState *WMTPProcInstState;

/********************************************************
        WMTProcInst
*/

typedef struct
```

```
{
  WMTText             process_name[NAME_STRING_SIZE];
  WMTProcInstID       proc_inst_id;
  WMTProcDefID        proc_def_id;
  WMTProcInstState    state;
  WMTInt32            priority;
  WMTWflParticipant   proc_participants[20];
} WMTProcInst;

typedef WMTProcInst *WMTPProcInst;

/***********************************************************
        WMTActivityInstID
*/

typedef struct
{
  WMTText   activity_inst_id[UNIQUE_ID_SIZE];
} WMTActivityInstID;

typedef WMTActivityInstID *WMTPActivityInstID;

/***********************************************************
        WMTActivityInstState
*/

typedef struct
{
  WMTText   activity_inst_state[NAME_STRING_SIZE];
} WMTActivityInstState;

typedef WMTActivityInstState *WMTPActivityInstState;

/***********************************************************
        WMTActivityInst
*/

typedef struct
{
  WMTText              activity_name[NAME_STRING_SIZE];
  WMTActivityInstID    activity_inst_id;
  WMTProcInstID        proc_inst_id;
  WMTActivityInstState state;
  WMTInt32             priority;
  WMTWflParticipant    activity_participants[10];
} WMTActivityInst;

typedef WMTActivityInst *WMTPActivityInst;
```

```
/***********************************************************
        WMTWorkItemID
*/

typedef struct
{
  WMTText     work_item_id[UNIQUE_ID_SIZE];
} WMTWorkItemID;

typedef WMTWorkItemID *WMTPWorkItemID;

/***********************************************************
        WMTWorkItem
*/

typedef struct
{
  WMTText            workitem_name[NAME_STRING_SIZE];
  WMTWorkItemID      workitem_id;
  WMTActivityInstID  activity_inst_id;
  WMTProcInstID      proc_inst_id;
  WMTInt32           priority;
  WMTWflParticipant  participant;
} WMTWorkItem;

typedef WMTWorkItem *WMTPWorkItem;

/***********************************************************
        WMTAttrName
*/
typedef   WMTText WMTAttrName[NAME_STRING_SIZE];
typedef   WMTAttrName *WMTPAttrName;
/*******************
    WAPI - Interface 2 function declarations.

    The definitions include specification of parameters with
indication of the direction of data passing:
in      for parameters with data being passed to the API fuction
out     for parameters with data being passed from the API function
*/

#define in
#define out

WMTErrRetType WMConnect (
    in  WMTPConnectInfo pconnect_info,
    out WMTPSessionHandle psession_handle);
```

```
WMTErrRetType WMDisconnect (
    in  WMTPSessionHandle psession_handle);

WMTErrRetType WMOpenProcessDefinitionsList (
    in  WMTPSessionHandle psession_handle,
    in  WMTPFilter pproc_def_filter,
    in  WMTBoolean count_flag,
    out WMTPQueryHandle pquery_handle,
    out WMTPInt32 pcount);

WMTErrRetType WMFetchProcessDefinition (
    in  WMTPSessionHandle psession_handle,
    in  WMTPQueryHandle pquery_handle,
    out WMTPProcDef pproc_def_buf_ptr);

WMTErrRetType WMCloseProcessDefinitionList(
    in  WMTPSessionHandle psession_handle,
    in  WMTPQueryHandle pquery_handle);

WMTErrRetType WMOpenProcessDefinitionStatesList (
    in  WMTPSessionHandle psession_handle,
    in  WMTPProcDefID pproc_def_id,
    in  WMTPFilter pproc_def_state_filter,
    in  WMTBoolean count_flag,
    out WMTPQueryHandle pquery_handle,
    out WMTUInt32 pcount);

WMTErrRetType WMFetchProcessDefinitionState (
    in  WMTPSessionHandle psession_handle,
    in  WMTPQueryHandle pquery_handle,
    out WMTPProcDefState pproc_def_state);

WMTErrRetType WMCloseProcessDefinitionStatesList (
    in  WMTPSessionHandle psession_handle,
    in  WMTPQueryHandle pquery_handle);

WMTErrRetType WMChangeProcessDefinitionState (
    in  WMTPSessionHandle psession_handle,
    in  WMTPProcDefID pproc_def_id,
    in  WMTPProcDefState pproc_def_state);

WMTErrRetType WMCreateProcessInstance (
    in  WMTPSessionHandle psession_handle,
    in  WMTPProcDefID  pproc_def_id,
    in  WMTPText pproc_inst_name,
    out WMTPProcInstID pproc_inst_id);
```

```
WMTErrRetType WMStartProcess (
     in   WMTPSessionHandle psession_handle,
     in   WMTPProcInstID  pproc_inst_id,
     out WMTPProcInstID  pnew_proc_inst_id );

WMTErrRetType WMTerminateProcessInstance (
     in   WMTPSessionHandle psession_handle,
     in   WMTPProcInstID pproc_inst_id);

WMTErrRetType WMOpenProcessInstanceStatesList (
     in   WMTPSessionHandle psession_handle,
     in   WMTPProcInstID pproc_inst_id,
     in   WMTPFilter pproc_inst_state_filter,
     in   WMTBoolean count_flag,
     out WMTPQueryHandle pquery_handle,
     out WMTPInt32 pcount);

WMTErrRetType WMFetchProcessInstanceState (
     in   WMTPSessionHandle psession_handle,
     in   WMTPQueryHandle pquery_handle,
     out WMTPProcInstState pproc_inst_state);

WMTErrRetType WMCloseProcessInstanceStatesList (
     in   WMTPSessionHandle psession_handle,
     in   WMTPQueryHandle pquery_handle);

WMTErrRetType WMChangeProcessInstanceState (
     in   WMTPSessionHandle psession_handle,
     in   WMTPProcInstID pproc_inst_id,
     in   WMTPProcInstState pproc_inst_state);

WMTErrRetType WMOpenProcessInstanceAttributesList (
     in   WMTPSessionHandle psession_handle,
     in   WMTPProcInstID pproc_inst_id,
     in   WMTPFilter pproc_inst_attr_filter,
     in   WMTBoolean count_flag,
     out WMTPQueryHandle pquery_handle,
     out WMTPInt32 pcount);
WMTErrRetType WMFetchProcessInstanceAttribute (
     in   WMTPSessionHandle psession_handle,
     in   WMTPQueryHandle pquery_handle,
     out WMTPAttrName pattribute_name,
     out WMTPInt32 pattribute_type,
     out WMTPInt32 pattribute_length,
     out WMTPText pattribute_value,
     in   WMTInt32 buffer_size);

WMTErrRetType WMCloseProcessInstanceAttributesList (
     in   WMTPSessionHandle psession_handle,
```

```
    in  WMTPQueryHandle pquery_handle);

WMTErrRetType WMGetProcessInstanceAttributeValue (
    in  WMTPSessionHandle psession_handle,
    in  WMTPProcInstID pproc_inst_id,
    in  WMTPAttrName pattribute_name,
    out WMTPInt32 pattribute_type,
    out WMTPInt32 pattribute_length,
    out WMTPText pattribute_value,
    in  WMTInt32 buffer_size);

WMTErrRetType WMAssignProcessInstanceAttribute (
    in  WMTPSessionHandle psession_handle,
    in  WMTPProcInstID pproc_inst_id,
    in  WMTPAttrName pattribute_name,
    in  WMTInt32 attribute_type,
    in  WMTInt32 attribute_length,
    in  WMTPText pattribute_value);

WMTErrRetType WMOpenActivityInstanceStatesList (
    in  WMTPSessionHandle psession_handle,
    in  WMTPProcInstID pproc_inst_id,
    in  WMTPActivityInstID pactivity_inst_id,
    in  WMTPFilter pact_inst_state_filter,
    in  WMTBoolean count_flag,
    out WMTPQueryHandle pquery_handle,
    out WMTPInt32 pcount);

WMTErrRetType WMFetchActivityInstanceState (
    in  WMTPSessionHandle psession_handle,
    in  WMTPQueryHandle pquery_handle,
    out WMTPActivityInstState pactivity_inst_state);

WMTErrRetType WMCloseActivityInstanceStatesList (
    in  WMTPSessionHandle psession_handle,
    in  WMTPQueryHandle pquery_handle);

WMTErrRetType WMChangeActivityInstanceState (
    in  WMTPSessionHandle psession_handle,
    in  WMTPProcInstID pproc_inst_id,
    in  WMTPActivityInstID pactivity_inst_id,
    in  WMTPActivityInstState pactivity_inst_state);

WMTErrRetType WMOpenActivityInstanceAttributesList (
    in  WMTPSessionHandle psession_handle,
    in  WMTPProcInstID pproc_inst_id,
    in  WMTPActivityInstID pactivity_inst_id,
    in  WMTPFilter pact_inst_attr_filter,
```

```
    in  WMTBoolean count_flag,
    out WMTPQueryHandle pquery_handle,
    out WMTPInt32 pcount);


WMTErrRetType WMFetchActivityInstanceAttribute (
    in  WMTPSessionHandle psession_handle,
    in  WMTPQueryHandle pquery_handle,
    out WMTPAttrName pattribute_name,
    out WMTPInt32 pattribute_type,
    out WMTPInt32 pattribute_length,
    out WMTPText pattribute_value,
    in  WMTInt32 buffer_size);


WMTErrRetType WMCloseActivityInstanceAttributesList (
    in  WMTPSessionHandle psession_handle,
    in  WMTPQueryHandle pquery_handle);


WMTErrRetType WMGetActivityInstanceAttributeValue (
    in  WMTPSessionHandle psession_handle,
    in  WMTPProcInstID pproc_inst_id,
    in  WMTPActivityInstID pactivity_inst_id,
    in  WMTPAttrName pattribute_name,
    out WMTPInt32 pattribute_type,
    out WMTPInt32 pattribute_length,
    out WMTPText pattribute_value,
    in  WMTInt32 buffer_size);


WMTErrRetType WMAssignActivityInstanceAttribute (
    in  WMTPSessionHandle psession_handle,
    in  WMTPProcDefID pproc_def_id,
    in  WMTPActivityInstID pactivity_inst_id,
    in  WMTPAttrName pattribute_name,
    in  WMTInt32 attribute_type,
    in  WMTInt32 attribute_length,
    in  WMTPText pattribute_value);


WMTErrRetType WMOpenProcessInstancesList (
    in  WMTPSessionHandle psession_handle,
    in  WMTPFilter pproc_inst_filter,
    in  WMTBoolean count_flag,
    out WMTPQueryHandle pquery_handle,
    out WMTPInt32 pcount);

WMTErrRetType WMFetchProcessInstance (
    in  WMTPSessionHandle psession_handle,
    in  WMTPQueryHandle pquery_handle,
    out WMTPProcInst pproc_inst_buf_ptr);
```

```
WMTErrRetType WMCloseProcessInstancesList (
    in  WMTPSessionHandle psession_handle,
    in  WMTPQueryHandle pquery_handle);

WMTErrRetType WMGetProcessInstance (
    in  WMTPSessionHandle psession_handle,
    in  WMTPProcInstID pproc_inst_id,
    out WMTPProcInst pproc_inst);

WMTErrRetType WMOpenActivityInstancesList (
    in  WMTPSessionHandle psession_handle,
    in  WMTPFilter pactivity_inst_filter,
    in  WMTBoolean count_flag,
    out WMTPQueryHandle pquery_handle,
    out WMTPInt32 pcount);

WMTErrRetType WMFetchActivityInstance (
    in  WMTPSessionHandle psession_handle,
    in  WMTPQueryHandle pquery_handle,
    out WMTPActivityInst pactivity_inst);

WMTErrRetType WMCloseActivityInstancesList (
    in  WMTPSessionHandle psession_handle,
    in  WMTPQueryHandle pquery_handle);

WMTErrRetType WMGetActivityInstance (
    in  WMTPSessionHandle psession_handle,
    in  WMTPProcInstID pproc_inst_id,
    in  WMTPActivityInstID pactivity_inst_id,
    out WMTPActivityInst pactivity_inst );

WMTErrRetType WMOpenWorkList (
    in  WMTPSessionHandle psession_handle,
    in  WMTPFilter pworklist_filter,
    in  WMTBoolean count_flag,
    out WMTPQueryHandle pquery_handle,
    out WMTPInt32 pcount);

WMTErrRetType WMFetchWorkItem (
    in  WMTPSessionHandle psession_handle,
    in  WMTPQueryHandle pquery_handle,
    out WMTPWorkItem pwork_item);
WMTErrRetType WMCloseWorkList (
    in  WMTPSessionHandle psession_handle,
    in  WMTPQueryHandle pquery_handle);

WMTErrRetType WMGetWorkItem (
    in  WMTPSessionHandle psession_handle,
    in  WMTPProcInstID pproc_inst_id,
    in  WMTPWorkItemID pwork_item_id,
```

```
       out WMTPWorkItem pwork_item );

WMTErrRetType WMCompleteWorkItem (
       in   WMTPSessionHandle psession_handle,
       in   WMTPProcInstID pproc_inst_id,
       in   WMTPWorkItemID pwork_item_id);

WMTErrRetType WMReassignWorkItem (
       in   WMTPSessionHandle psession_handle,
       in   WMTPWflParticipant psource_user,
       in   WMTPWflParticipant ptarget_user,
       in   WMTPProcInstID pproc_inst_id,
       in   WMTPWorkItemID pwork_item_id);

WMTErrRetType WMOpenWorkItemAttributesList (
       in   WMTPSessionHandle psession_handle,
       in   WMTPProcInstID pproc_inst_id,
       in   WMTPWorkItemID pwork_item_id,
       in   WMTPFilter pwork_item_attr_filter,
       in   WMTBoolean count_flag,
       out WMTPQueryHandle pquery_handle,
       out WMTPInt32 pcount);

WMTErrRetType WMFetchWorkItemAttribute (
       in   WMTPSessionHandle psession_handle,
       in   WMTPQueryHandle pquery_handle,
       out WMTPAttrName pattribute_name,
       out WMTPInt32 pattribute_type,
       out WMTPInt32 pattribute_length,
       out WMTPText pattribute_value,
       in   WMTInt32 buffer_size);

WMTErrRetType WMCloseWorkItemAttributesList (
       in   WMTPSessionHandle psession_handle,
       in   WMTPQueryHandle pquery_handle);

WMTErrRetType WMGetWorkItemAttributeValue (
       in   WMTPSessionHandle psession_handle,
       in   WMTPProcInstID pproc_inst_id,
       in   WMTPWorkItemID pwork_item_id,
       in   WMTPAttrName pattribute_name,
       out WMTPInt32 pattribute_type,
       out WMTPInt32 pattribute_length,
       out WMTPText pattribute_value,
       in   WMTInt32 buffer_size);

WMTErrRetType WMAssignWorkItemAttribute (
       in   WMTPSessionHandle psession_handle,
```

```
    in   WMTPProcInstID pproc_inst_id,
    in   WMTPWorkItemID pwork_item_id,
    in   WMTPAttrName pattribute_name,
    in   WMTInt32 attribute_type,
    in   WMTInt32 attribute_length,
    in   WMTPText pattribute_value);

WMTErrRetType WMChangeProcessInstancesState (
    in   WMTPSessionHandle psession_handle,
    in   WMTPProcDefID pproc_def_id,
    in   WMTPFilter pproc_inst_filter,
    in   WMTProcInstState pproc_inst_state);

WMTErrRetType WMChangeActivityInstancesState (
    in   WMTPSessionHandle psession_handle,
    in   WMTPProcDefID pproc_def_id,
    in   WMTPActivityID pactivity_def_id,
    in   WMTPFilter pact_inst_filter,
    in   WMTPActivityInstState pactivity_inst_state);

WMTErrRetType WMTerminateProcessInstances (
    in   WMTPSessionHandle psession_handle,
    in   WMTPProcDefID pproc_def_id,
    in   WMTPFilter pproc_inst_filter);

WMTErrRetType WMAssignProcessInstancesAttribute (
    in   WMTPSessionHandle psession_handle,
    in   WMTPProcDefID pproc_def_id,
    in   WMTPFilter pproc_inst_filter,
    in   WMTAttrName attribute_name,
    in   WMTInt32 attribute_type,
    in   WMTInt32 attribute_length,
    in   WMTPText pattribute_value);

WMTErrRetType WMAssignActivityInstancesAttribute (
    in   WMTPSessionHandle psession_handle,
    in   WMTPProcDefID pproc_def_id,
    in   WMTPActivityID pactivity_def_id,
    in   WMTPFilter pact_inst_filter,
    in   WMTPAttrName pattribute_name,
    in   WMTInt32 attribute_type,
    in   WMTInt32 attribute_length,
    in   WMTPText pattribute_value);

WMTErrRetType WMAbortProcessInstances (
    in   WMTPSessionHandle psession_handle,
    in   WMTPProcDefID pproc_def_id,
    in   WMTPFilter pproc_inst_filter);
```

```
WMTErrRetType WMAbortProcessInstance (
    in   WMTPSessionHandle psession_handle,
    in   WMTPProcInstID pproc_inst_id);

/*********************************************************************
*****
    End of wmAPI.h
*/

#endif
```

3.3 Include File - wmerror.h

File: wmerror.h
```
          1         2         3         4         5         6         7
8
12345678901234567890123456789012345678901234567890123456789012345678901
1234567890
/*
    WMERROR.H

  This is the file supplied by the Workflow Management Coalition.
  It contains defines for the error codes support by the WAPI.
*/

#ifndef WMERR_H
#define WMERR_H

#define WM_MAIN_ERR_MASK          0xFFFF0000
#define WM_SUB_ERR_MASK           0x0000FFFF


#define WM_SUCCESS                            0
#define WM_CONNECT_FAILED                     0x00100000
#define WM_INVALID_PROCESS_DEFINITION         0x00200000
#define WM_INVALID_ACTIVITY_NAME              0x00300000
#define WM_INVALID_PROCESS_INSTANCE           0x00400000
#define WM_INVALID_ACTIVITY_INSTANCE          0x00500000
#define WM_INVALID_WORKITEM                   0x00600000
#define WM_INVALID_ATTRIBUTE                  0x00700000
#define WM_ATTRIBUTE_ASSIGNMENT_FAILED        0x00800000
#define WM_INVALID_STATE                      0x00900000
#define WM_TRANSITION_NOT_ALLOWED             0x00A00000
#define WM_INVALID_SESSION_HANDLE             0x00B00000
#define WM_INVALID_QUERY_HANDLE               0x00C00000
#define WM_INVALID_SOURCE_USER                0x00D00000
```

```
#define WM_INVALID_TARGET_USER              0x00E00000
#define WM_INVALID_FILTER                   0x00F00000
#define WM_LOCKED                           0x00F10000
#define WM_NOT_LOCKED                       0x00F20000
#define WM_NO_MORE_DATA                     0x00F30000
#define WM_INSUFFICIENT_BUFFER_SIZE         0x00F40000


/**********************************************************************
*****
    End of wmerror.h
*/
#endif
```

The W*f*MC Glossary

This section is based on *The Workflow Management Coalition Terminology and Glossary* document dated May 1996.
Document Reference WFMC-TC-1011

An index to terms in this Glossary may be found in the Subject Index under "Glossary".

Within "Definition" paragraphs of this Glossary, other terms which are defined are italicised.

1. Basic Concepts

This section identifies basic concepts and terminology associated with workflow as a general topic.

Workflow

Definition

The automation of a *business process*, in whole or part, during which documents, information or tasks are passed from one participant to another for action, according to a set of procedural rules.

Usage

- The automation of a business process is defined within a process definition, which identifies the various process activities, procedural rules and associated control data used to manage the workflow during process enactment
- Many individual process instances may be operational during process enactment, each associated with a specific set of data relevant to that individual process instance (or workflow "case")

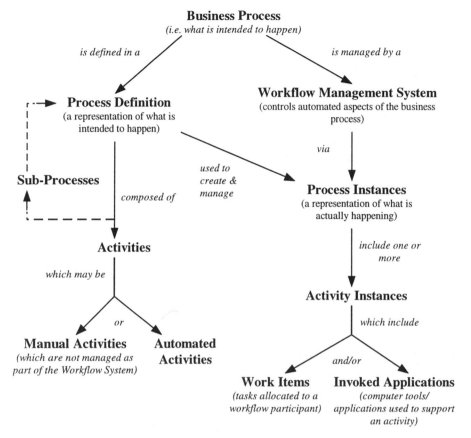

Figure 1   Relationships Among Basic Terminology

- A loose distinction is sometimes drawn between production workflow, in which most of the procedural rules are defined in advance, and ad hoc workflow, in which the procedural rules may be modified or created during the operation of the process.

Synonyms

- Workflow Computing
- Case Management

Workflow Management System

Definition

A system that defines, creates and manages the execution of workflows through the use of software, running on one or more *workflow engines*, which is able to interpret the *process definition*, interact with *workflow participants* and, where required, invoke the use of IT tools and applications.

Usage

- A Workflow Management System consists of software components to store and interpret process definitions, create and manage workflow instances as they are executed, and control their interaction with workflow participants and applications.
- Such systems also typically provide administrative and supervisory functions, for example to allow work reassignment or escalation, plus audit and management information on the system overall or relating to individual process instances.
- The WfMC have published an architectural Workflow Reference Model, describing the structure and interfaces of a workflow management system (see **Section 2–Workflow Reference Model** in this Handbook).

Synonyms

- Workflow automation
- Workflow manager
- Workflow computing system
- Case Management

Business Process

Definition

A set of one or more linked procedures or *activities* which collectively realise a business objective or policy goal, normally within the context of an organizational structure defining functional roles and relationships.

Usage

- A business process is typically associated with operational objectives and business relationships, for example an Insurance Claims Process, or Engineering Development Process. A process may be wholly contained within a single organizational unit or may span several different organizations, such as in a customer-supplier relationship.
- A business process has defined conditions triggering its initiation in each new instance (e.g. the arrival of a claim) and defined outputs at its completion.
- A business process may involve formal or relatively informal interactions between participants; its duration may also vary widely.

- A business process may consist of automated activities, capable of workflow management, and/or manual activities, which lie outside the scope of workflow management.

See also: *Process, Process Definition*

Synonyms

- Process (colloquial)

Process Definition

Definition

The representation of a *business process* in a form which supports automated manipulation, such as modelling, or enactment by a *workflow management system*. The *process definition* consists of a network of *activities* and their relationships, criteria to indicate the start and termination of the *process*, and information about the individual *activities*, such as participants, associated IT applications and data, etc.

Usage

- The process definition results from work during the process definition mode and may include both manual and workflow (automated) activities.
- The process definition may contain references to sub-processes, separately defined, which make up part of the overall process definition
- The Workflow Reference Model includes an interface for the import and export of Process Definitions

Synonyms

- Model definition
- Routing definition
- Flow diagram
- State transition diagram
- Flow schematic
- Workflow script
- Instruction Sheet Definition
- Case type

Activity

Definition

A description of a piece of work that forms one logical step within a *process*. An activity may be a *manual activity*, which does not support computer automation, or a *workflow (automated) activity*. A workflow activity requires human and/or machine resources(s) to support process execution; where human resource is required an activity is allocated to a *workflow participant*.

Usage

- A process definition generally consists of many process activities which are logically related in terms of their contribution to the overall realisation of the business process.
- An activity is typically the smallest unit of work which is scheduled by a workflow engine during process enactment (e.g. using transition and pre/post-conditions), although one activity may result in several work items being assigned (to a workflow participant).
- Wholly manual activities may form part of a business process and be included within its associated process definition, but do not form part of the automated workflow resulting from the computer supported execution of the process.
- An activity may therefore be categorised as "manual", or "automated". Within this document, which is written principally in the context of workflow management, the term is normally used to refer to an automated activity.

Synonyms

- Step
- Node
- Task
- Work Element
- Process Element
- Operation
- Instruction

(Each may be further described as a manual .... , or as an automated ....)

Automated Activity

Definition

An activity which is capable of computer automation using a *workflow management system* to manage the *activity* during execution of the *business process* of which it forms a part.

Usage

During process execution, an automated (or workflow) activity is managed by the workflow management system. This may result in:

- An invoked application being activated directly by the workflow management system (with no workflow participant being involved)
- One or more work items being assigned to a workflow participant, with supporting tools or applications being invoked and managed by the workflow management system
- One or more work items being assigned for a workflow participant to process independently of the workflow management system, with the completion of the work items being notified to the workflow management system by the workflow participant (within a workflow system these may sometimes be described as manually executed work items)

For other aspects of usage see *Activity*

Synonyms

- Workflow Activity
- Activity (colloquial)

Manual Activity

Definition

An activity within a *business process* which is not capable of automation and hence lies outside the scope of a *workflow management system*. Such activities may be included within a *process definition*, for example to support modelling of the process, but do not form part of a resulting *workflow*.

Usage

See *Activity*

Synonyms

- Non-automated Activity
- Manual Step
- Human Task
- Manual Work

Instance (as in Process or Activity Instance)

Definition

The representation of a single enactment of a *process*, or *activity* within a process, including its associated data. Each instance represents a separate thread of execution[1] of the process or activity, which may be controlled independently and will have its own internal state and externally visible identity, which may be used as a handle, for example, to record or retrieve *audit data* relating to the individual enactment.

Usage (Common)

- A process or activity instance is created and managed by a workflow management system for each separate invocation of the process or activity.

Process Instance

Definition

The representation of a single enactment of a *process* (see also general entry on *Instance*).

Usage

- A process instance is created, managed and (eventually) terminated by a workflow management system, in accordance with the process definition.
- Each process instance represents one individual enactment of the process, using its own process instance data, and which is (normally) capable of independent control and audit as it progresses towards completion or termination. It represents the unit of work with respect to a business process which passes through a workflow management system (for example, the processing of one insurance claim, or the production of one engineering design).
- Each process instance exhibits internal state, which represents its progress towards completion and its status with respect to its constituent activities (see *Process State*).
  (Some business processes may never "complete" within a defined timescale in the accepted sense of the word, but achieve a protracted, persistent dormant state,

---

[1]Where a process includes parallel activities, a process instance may include multiple concurrent threads of execution. See *Parallel Routing, And-Split, And-Join*

which may require the process instance to be placed in an archive state, for example to support legal requirements on the maintenance of process data.)

Synonyms

- Process Definition Instance
- Case
- Workflow Definition Instance
- Instruction Sheet Instance

Activity Instance

Definition

The representation of an *activity* within a (single) enactment of a *process*, i.e. within a *process instance* (see also general entry on *Instance*).

Usage

- An activity instance is created and managed by a workflow management system when required within the enactment of process, in accordance with the process definition.
- Each activity instance represents a single invocation of an activity, relates to exactly one process instance and uses the process instance data associated with the process instance. Several activity instances may be associated with one process instance, where parallel activities exist within the process, but one activity instance cannot be associated with more than one process instance.
- Each activity instance is normally capable of independent control and audit and exhibits internal state (see *Activity State*).

Synonyms

- Step Instance
- Node Instance
- Task Instance
- Work Element Instance

Workflow Participant

Definition

A resource which performs the work represented by a workflow *activity instance*. This work is normally manifested as one or more *work items* assigned to the *workflow participant* via the *worklist*.

Usage

- The term workflow participant is normally applied to a human resource but it could conceptually include machine based resources such as an intelligent agent. (Where an activity requires no human resource and is handled automatically by a computer application, the normal terminology for the machine based resource is Invoked Application.)
- A workflow participant may be identified directly within the business process definition, or (more normally) is identified by reference within the process definition to a role, which can then be filled by one or more of the resources available to the workflow system to operate in that role during process enactment.

Synonyms

- Actor
- Agent
- Player
- User
- Role Player
- Work Performer

Work Item

Definition

The representation of the work to be processed (by a *workflow participant*) in the context of an *activity* within a *process instance*.

Usage

- An activity typically generates one or more work items which together constitute the task to be undertaken by the user (a workflow participant) within this activity. (In certain cases an activity may be completely handled by an invoked application which can operate without a workflow participant, in which case there may be no work item assignment.)
- The work item(s) are normally presented to the user via a worklist, which maintains details of the work items allocated to a user, and a worklist handler, which interacts with the worklist on behalf of the user.
- The control and progression of work items rests with the worklist handler and the user, rather than the workflow engine, which is notified of work item status (e.g. completion) via the worklist handler interface. (The *WAPI* interface includes standard API calls for this purpose.)

- Tools or applications may be invoked to support the processing of a work item, or it may be processed independently by a workflow participant, with the workflow management system merely notified of the completion of particular work items

Synonyms

- Work (e.g. document review, fill-in form)
- Work Object
- Work Queue Item
- Element
- Work Pool Item
- Task

Worklist

Definition

A list of *work items* associated with a given *workflow participant* (or in some cases with a group of workflow participants who may share a common *worklist*). The worklist forms part of the interface between a *workflow engine* and the *worklist handler*.

Usage

- Generally, a worklist handler will request work items from a workflow engine in order to create such a list. This is sometimes done via a query mechanism.
- In some workflow management systems work items may be placed in the worklist by a workflow engine for subsequently access and actioning by the worklist handler.

1.1.1 Synonyms

- Work Queue
- In-Tray
- To Do List

Worklist Handler

Definition

A software component that manages the interaction between the user (or group of users) and the *worklist* maintained by a *workflow engine*. It enables *work items* to be passed from the *workflow management system* to users and notifications of completion or other work status conditions to be passed between the user and the workflow management system.

Usage

- A worklist handler may be vendor-supplied as a component of the workflow management software, or may be developed as a standalone custom application. A worklist handler may communicate with several workflow systems, consolidating user work items into a single list of tasks for presentation to the user. This principle may be extended to include other external information sources such as mail in-tray items.
- Possible functions that may be performed by the worklist handler include:
  - Selecting a work item
  - Reassigning a work item
  - Notifying completion of a work item.
  - Invocation of a tool or client application as part of the work item processing
- The WAPI interface includes standard API calls for worklist handler communication with a workflow engine.

Synonyms

- WFM Front End
- WFM Application
- Workflow To-Do List Application
- Task Manager
- Active Work Performer

Workflow Reference Model

Definition

An architectural representation of a *workflow management system*, identifying the most important system interfaces, developed by the Workflow Management Coalition (see ***Section 2–The Workflow Reference Model*** in this Handbook).

Usage

The Workflow Reference Model provides the general architectural framework for the work of the WfMC. It identifies interfaces covering, broadly, five areas of functionality between a workflow management system and its environment.

Overview of Processes and Worklist Structures

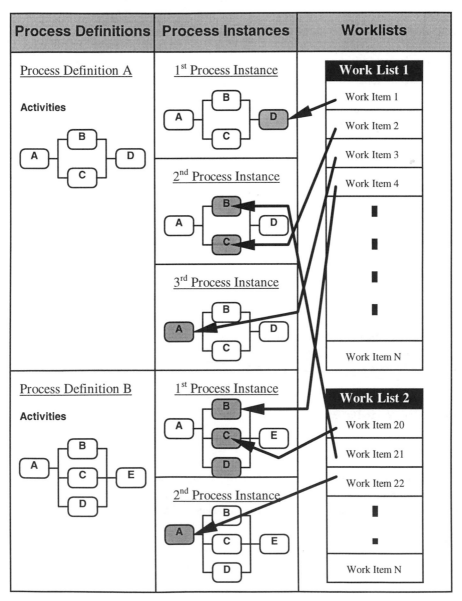

Figure 2   Relationships Between Key Terminology

- The import and export of process definitions
- Interaction with client applications and worklist handler software
- The invocation of software tools or applications
- Interoperability between different workflow management systems
- Administration and monitoring functions

1.1.2 Synonyms

None

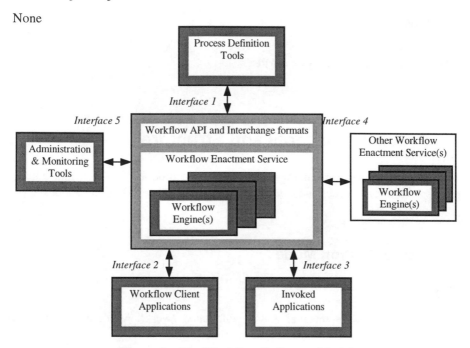

Figure 3   The Workflow Reference Model

WAPI

Definition

WAPI is an abbreviation for **W**orkflow **API**s and **I**nterchange Formats, published by the Workflow Management Coalition, and incorporating specifications to enable interoperability between different components of *workflow management systems* and applications

Usage

WAPI includes

- A range of API calls to support functions between a workflow engine and applications or other system components
- Interchange formats and protocols to support interoperability between different workflow engines
- Formats for the exchange of information such as process definitions and audit data between a workflow engine and other external repositories.

Synonyms

- Workflow APIs
- Workflow Management System APIs

2. Process Concepts and Structure

This section includes terminology used within the process definition and during process execution to describe the nature of the process flow and its interactions.

Process Definition Mode

Definition

The time period when manual and/or automated (workflow) descriptions of a *process* are defined and/or modified electronically.

Usage

Process definitions are initially defined prior to workflow enactment, and may be

- modified at a later date, or
- modified during run time (usually under conditions of privilege or according to a particular user role).

Synonyms

- Process Modelling
- Business Process Modelling
- Build Time

Process

Definition

A formalised view of a *business process,* represented as a coordinated (parallel and/or serial) set of process *activities* that are connected in order to achieve a common goal.

Usage

Example: An eight activity process

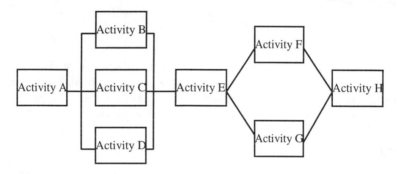

Synonyms

- Activity Network
- Directed Graph
- Petri Net
- Model
- Instruction Sheet

Sub Process

Definition

A *process* that is enacted or called from another (initiating) process (or sub process), and which forms part of the overall (initiating) process. Multiple levels of sub process may be supported.

Usage

- A sub process is useful for defining reusable components within other processes

- A sub-process will have its own process definition
- The WfMC Interoperability scenarios identify various ways in which sub-processes may interact during workflow execution (e.g. nested sub-process, chained)

Synonyms

- Subflow
- Sub Workflow

Activity Block

Definition

A set of *activities* within a *process definition* which share one or more common properties which cause the workflow management software to take certain actions with respect to the block in total. For example a group of activities may be classified as a block if they require a common resource allocation policy.

Usage

- A workflow system may support the concept of an activity block, which then initiates particular action by the workflow management system

Synonyms

- Activity Set

Deadline

Definition

A time based scheduling constraint which requires that a certain *activity* (or *work item*) be completed by a certain time (the "deadline").

Usage

- Activity scheduling by a workflow management system will attempt to meet deadline constraints set against particular activities.
- The deadline may be expressed as an attribute of the process definition or within workflow relevant data.
- Escalation procedures may be invoked if deadlines are not meant.

Synonyms

* Completion Time

Parallel Routing

Definition

A segment of a *process instance* under enactment by a *workflow management system*, where two or more *activity instances* are executing in parallel within the workflow, giving rise to multiple threads of control.

Usage

Example:
> Once the form filling activity is complete the three sections of form X, sections A, B and C, are processed in parallel by the corresponding activities, Process Section A activity, Process Section B activity and Process Section C activity.

Synonyms

* Parallel workflow processing
* Concurrent Processing

Sequential Routing

Definition

A segment of a *process instance* under enactment by a *workflow management system*, in which several *activities* are executed in sequence under a single thread of execution. (No *-Split or -Join* conditions occur during sequential routing.)

Usage

Example: A purchase order is processed in three consecutive activities.

Synonyms

* Serial Routing

AND-Split

Definition

A point within the *workflow* where a single thread of control splits into two or more parallel *activities*.

Usage

Example:

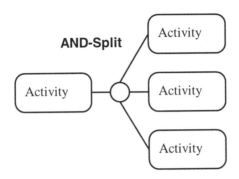

Synonyms

• Split

AND-Join

Definition

A point in the *workflow* where two or more parallel executing *activities* converge into a single common thread of control.

Usage

Example:

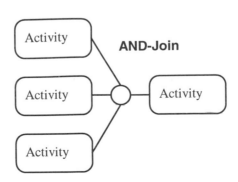

Synonyms

- Join
- Rendezvous
- Synchronisation join

OR-Split

Definition

A point within the *workflow* where a single thread of control makes a decision upon which branch to take when encountered with multiple alternative workflow branches

Usage

Example:

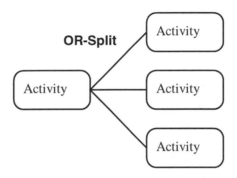

Synonyms

- Conditional Branching
- Conditional Routing
- Switch
- Branch

OR-Join

Definition

A point within the *workflow* where two or more alternative *activity(s)* workflow branches re-converge to a single common activity as the next step within the workflow. (As no parallel activity execution has occurred at the join point, no synchronisation is required.)

Usage

Example:

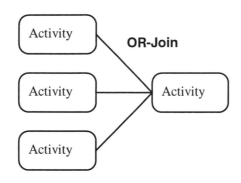

Synonyms

- Join
- Asynchronous join

Iteration

Definition

A workflow activity cycle involving the repetitive execution of one (or more) workflow *activity(s)* until a condition is met.

Usage

Example:

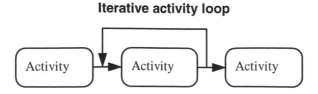

2.1.1 Synonyms

- Workflow Loop
- While Loop
- Activity Block

Pre-Condition

Definition

A logical expression which may be evaluated by a *workflow engine* to decide whether a *process instance* or *activity* within a process instance may be started.

Usage

- One or more pre-conditions may be defined as entry criteria to a particular activity or process instance.
- The pre-condition may refer to workflow relevant data within the expression and may also test system variables such as date or time. It may also refer to an external event of some kind.
- The pre-conditions are defined within the process definition

Synonyms

- Entry criteria
- Activity start rules

Post-Condition

Definition

A logical expression which may be evaluated by a *workflow engine* to decide whether a *process instance* or *activity* within a process instance is completed.

Usage

- One or more post-conditions may be defined as completion criteria for a particular activity or process instance. Such conditions may form part of an iteration, in which one or more activities are repetitively executed until the defined post-condition(s) is/are met.
- The post-condition may refer to workflow relevant data within the expression and may also test system variables such as date or time. It may also refer to an external event of some kind.
- The post-conditions are defined within the process definition

Synonyms

- Exit criteria
- Activity completion rules

Transition Condition

Definition

A logical expression which may be evaluated by a *workflow engine* to decide the sequence of *activity* execution within a *process*.

Usage

- One or more navigation rules may be defined for evaluation at run time after an activity has started or completed, or following an external event of some kind
- The navigation rule may refer to workflow relevant data within the expression and may also test system variables such as date or time.
- Navigation rules are defined within the process definition
- Navigation rules identify the flow relationship between activities and are used to effect the desired sequence of activity execution, which may include parallel or sequential execution conditions.

Note: Some workflow management systems may not define explicit transition conditions but use a combination of pre- and post-conditions to achieve an equivalent effect.

Synonyms

- Navigation Rule
- Routing condition
- Process Rule
- Transition Rule
- Business Process Rule
- Conditional Routing

3. Wider Workflow Concepts and Terminology

This section includes terminology used within the wider context of workflow management systems.

Workflow Application

Definition

A general term for a software program that interacts with a workflow enactment service, handling part of the processing required to support a particular *activity* (or activities).

Generic Workflow Product Structure

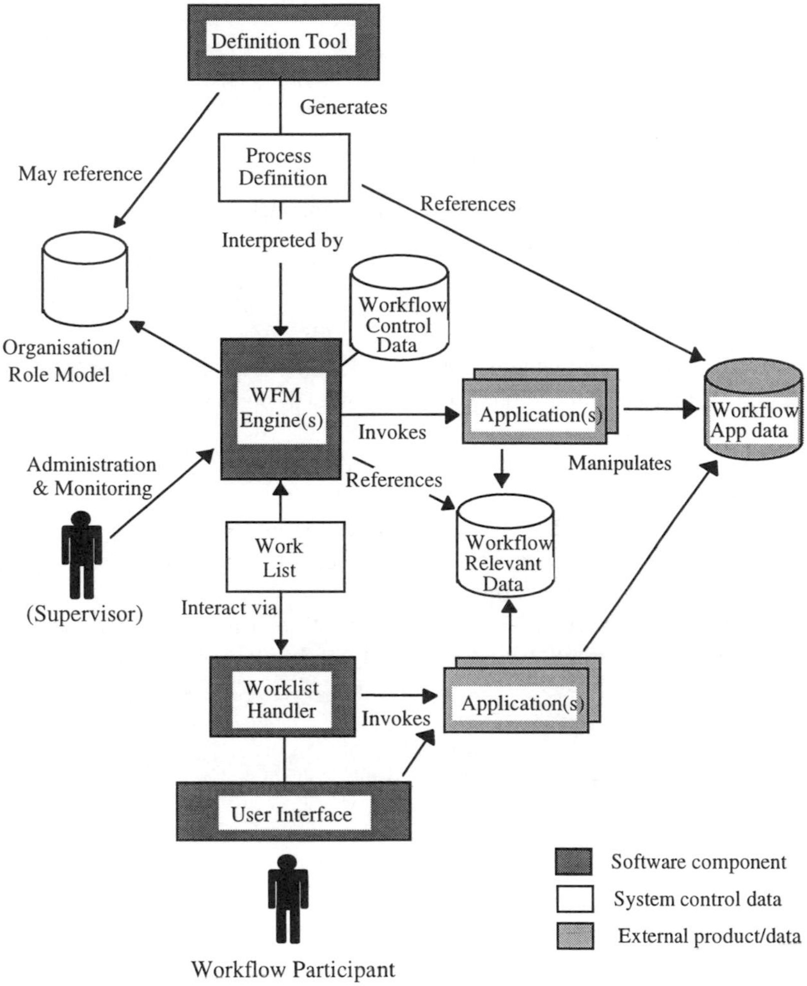

Figure 4 Generic Workflow Product

Usage

The Workflow Reference Model recognises two broad types of workflow application:

- Client Applications, which request facilities and services from a workflow engine
- Invoked Applications, which support the processing of particular activities, or work items, and are initiated by the workflow management system

Synonyms

- Client Application

- Invoked Application
- Tool

Client Application

Definition

A client application is an application which interacts with a *workflow engine*, requesting facilities and services from the engine.

Usage

- Client applications may interact with a workflow engine for a variety of reasons. Common functions which client application may perform are:
    - Worklist handling
    - Process instance initiation and other control functions (e.g. suspend/ resume)
    - Retrieval and manipulation of process definition data
    - Various system administration functions (for example suspending the use of certain process definitions)
- The Workflow Reference Model includes an interface for client application interaction which supports APIs for a variety of the above functions.

Synonyms

- Front-End Application
- Client Program

Invoked Application

Definition

An invoked application is a *workflow application* that is invoked by the *workflow management system* to automate an *activity*, fully or in part, or to support a *workflow participant* in processing a *work item*.

Usage

- Application invocation may be a function of the workflow engine, and/or of the worklist handler.
- The application may be invoked directly by the workflow management system or may be invoked indirectly via an application agent (or "tool agent"). The

application agent provides a general mechanism for application invocation independently from any native workflow management system facilities
- The Workflow Reference Model includes an interface for application invocation functions.

Synonyms

- Tool
- Work Performer
- Application (colloquial)

Application Data

Definition

Data that is application specific and not accessible by the *workflow management system*.

Overview of Workflow Data Structures

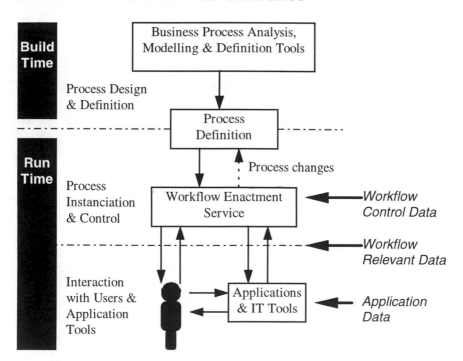

Figure 5 Types of Data in Workflow Management Systems

Usage

- This is data that the workflow management system generally will never see. It is data that is strictly managed by the applications supporting the process instance. (Such data may become process relevant data if it is used by the workflow management system to determine a state change.)

Synonyms

- Application Case Data

Workflow Relevant Data

Definition

Data that is used by a *workflow management system* to determine the state transitions of a workflow *instance*, for example within *pre- and post-conditions*, *transition conditions* or *workflow participant* assignment.

Usage

- Workflow relevant data may be manipulated by workflow applications as well as by the workflow engine
- Workflow relevant data may be made available to a subsequent activity or another process instance and thus may affect the choice of the next activity to be chosen (for example decision data and/or reference values to be passed between activities)
    - Data may be of two broad types
    - Typed - the structure of the data is implied by its type (typically a workflow management system will understand the structure of such data and may be able to process it)
    - Untyped - the workflow management system will not understand the data structure, but may pass the data (or a reference to the data) to workflow applications

Synonyms

- Process flow data
- Case data

Workflow Control Data

Definition

Data that is managed by the *workflow management system* and/or a *workflow engine*. Such data is internal to the workflow management system and is not normally accessible to applications.

Usage

- Workflow control data represents the dynamic state of the workflow system and its process instances.
- Workflow control data examples include:
    - state information about each workflow instance
    - state information about each activity instance (active or inactive)
    - information on recovery and restart points within each process
    - etc.
- The workflow control data may be written to persistent storage periodically to facilitate restart and recovery of the system after failure. It may also be used to derive audit data.

Synonyms

- Workflow system data
- Workflow engine state data
- Workflow enactment service state data

Process State

Definition

A representation of the internal conditions defining the status of a *process instance* at a particular point in time. Most *workflow management systems* maintain such status information as part of their *workflow control data*.

Usage

- The state of each process instance under enactment is maintained by the workflow management system. Different vendor systems have different ways of representing process state and may have their own set of state definitions
- As the execution of a process instance proceeds it follows a series of transitions between the various states which it may take. The complete set of process states

for a process definition fully defines the internal behavior which its process instances may follow.

- The Workflow Reference Model identifies a number of common states which a process instance may take:
    - Initiated - the process instance has been created, but may not yet be running
    - Running - the process instance has started execution and one or more of its activities may be started
    - Active - one or more activities are started and activity instances exist (Further sub-states may be supported by particular implementations to record more detailed information about active activities.)
    - Suspended - the process instance is quiescent; no further activities are started until it is resumed
    - Complete - the process instance has achieved its completion conditions and any post-completion system activities such as audit logging are in progress.
    - Terminated - the execution of the process has been stopped (abnormally) due to error or user request.
    - Archived - the process instance has been placed in an indefinite archive state (but may be retrieved for process resumption - typically supported only for long-lived processes).
- The WAPI interface defines a number of calls to manipulate process state information, for example to interrogate process state or force a transition to a new state

Synonyms

- Workflow state
- Model state

Activity State

Definition

A representation of the internal conditions defining the status of an *activity instance* at a particular point in time. Most *workflow management systems* maintain such status information as part of their *workflow control data*.

Usage

- The state of each process instance under enactment is maintained by the workflow management system. Some systems extend this to maintain state information about each activity instance which has been created. Different vendor systems

have different ways of representing activity state and may have their own set of state definitions
- The Workflow Reference Model identifies a number of common states which an activity instance may take:
    - Inactive - the activity instance has been created, but may not yet been activated; no work item exists for that activity
    - Active - one or more work items have been created and assigned for processing
    - Suspended - the activity instance is quiescent; no further work items are started until it is resumed. (Note that some activities may not be suspendable.)
    - Completed - the process instance has achieved its completion conditions and any post-completion system activities such as audit logging are in progress.

Synonyms

- Step state

State Transition

Definition

A movement from one internal state (of a *Process* or *Activity Instance*) to another within a workflow, reflecting a change in the status of the workflow, for example initiating a particular *activity*. The state transition may be in response to an external event, a user API call, a routing decision taken by the *workflow engine*, etc.

Usage

- A series of state transitions occurs as the workflow progresses its execution. Such transitions can be recorded by the workflow engine and presented as audit data.

Synonyms

None

Event

Definition

An occurrence of a particular condition (which may be internal or external to the workflow system) which causes the *workflow management software* to take one or more actions. For example the arrival of a particular type of email message may cause the workflow system to start an *instance* of a specific *process definition.*

Usage

- A workflow system may react directly to particular events or the event may be monitored and processed by a (client) application, which then initiates action by the workflow system by API call or setting workflow relevant data, etc..

Synonyms

- Trigger

Audit Data

Definition

A historical record of the progress of a *process instance* from start to completion or termination. Such data normally incorporates information on the state transitions of the process instance

Usage

- Example information that may be collected as part of the historical record is date, time and type of work performed per state transition.

Synonyms

- Workflow History
- Case History
- History Repository

Workflow Definition

Definition

That part of the *process definition* which comprises the automatable activities.

Usage

- Where a distinction is drawn between a process definition and those activities within it which are capable of automation, the term workflow definition is used for the latter.

Synonyms

See *Process Definition*

Process Execution

Definition

The time period during which the *process* is operational, with *process instances* being created and managed.

Usage

- The process execution phase may sometimes be differentiated from the process definition phase, during which the process structure and activities are defined. (In some systems, for example where much of the process definition is created dynamically during its execution, this distinction may be irrelevant.)

Synonyms

- Process Enactment
- Run Time Operation
- Workflow Execution (strictly this refers only to the automated parts of process execution)

Organizational Role

Definition

A group of participants exhibiting a specific set of attributes, qualifications and/or skills.

Usage

- Typically any of the participants within a particular organizational role group can undertake an activity or work-item requiring a resource with that set of attributes.
- Examples of an organizational role are:
  - Supervisor role
  - Insurance Underwriter role
  - etc.
- A workflow participant assumes a role given that he or she has the appropriate skill set.

Synonyms

- Role
- User Groups
- Organizational Groups

Organizational Model

Definition

A model which represents organizational entities and their relationships; it may also incorporate a variety of attributes associated with the entities. Such a model may be realised in a directory or other form of database.

Usage

- Such a model normally incorporates concepts such as hierarchy, authority, responsibilities and attributes associated with an organizational role. It may be referenced by a workflow management system as part of the mechanism by which process role is established.

Synonyms

- Role Model
- Organizational Directory

Process Role

Definition

A mechanism that associates *workflow participants* to a collection of workflow *activity(s)*.

Usage

- A workflow participant assumes a role to access and process work from a workflow management system.
- The role defines the context in which the user participates in a particular process or activity. The role often embraces organizational concepts such as structure and relationships, responsibility or authority, but may also refer to other attributes such as skill, location, value data, time or date, etc.

Synonyms

- Role
- Activity Group
- Workflow Performer Definition

Escalation

Definition

A procedure (automated or manual) which is invoked if a particular constraint or condition is not met.

Usage

- Escalation procedures typically involve a higher level of authority *(see Organizational Role).*

Synonyms

None

Constraint

Definition

A condition (typically pertaining to activity/work selection and/or completion) which must be met during work processing; failure to meet a constraint may causes an exception condition or other defined procedure.

Usage

Constraints may be:

- Time based (see *deadline*)
- Resource based (e.g. consumes less than ...)
- Cost based (e.g. costs more than ...)

Synonyms

- Controls

Workflow Monitoring

Definition

The ability to track and report on workflow *events* during workflow execution.

Usage

- Workflow monitoring may be used, for example, by process owners to monitor the performance of a process instance during its execution.

Synonyms

- Workflow Tracking

Workflow Engine

Definition

A software service or "engine" that provides the run time execution environment for a *process instance*.

Usage

- The workflow engine provides operational functions to support the execution of (instances of) business processes, based on the process definitions.. These functions include:
    - Interpretation of the process definition.
    - Creation of process instances and management of their execution, including start / stop / suspend /resume, etc.
    - Navigation between activities and the creation of appropriate work items for their processing
    - Supervisory and management functions
    - etc.
- The workflow engine normally excludes functions such as worklist handling, which are user centred, although these may share a common platform with the engine software.
- One or more workflow engines make up a workflow domain; which provides an homogeneous process execution environment. A workflow enactment service provides support for the execution of specific workflows over one or more workflow engines, which may be in one or more separate domains.
- Two or more workflow engines may cooperate to share the execution of workflows (see *Workflow Interoperability*).

Synonyms

- Workflow Management Engine
- Case Processor

Workflow Interoperability

Definition

The ability for two or more *workflow engines* to communicate and work together to coordinate work.

Usage

Workflow interoperability embraces several important concepts:

- The ability to make two or more workflow engines appear to provide a single workflow enactment service, with process execution shared between engines.
- Several different interoperability scenarios exist, describing alternative ways in which the execution of a process instance is shared between workflow engines.
  - Hierarchic (Nested Subprocess)
  - Connected Discrete (Chained)
  - Connected Indiscrete (Peer-to-Peer)
  - Parallel Synchronised
- Further details can be found in the Workflow Reference Model and Interoperability specifications.
- The ability to interoperate between both homogeneous and heterogeneous workflow engines; possibly with different levels of functional capability.
- The Workflow Reference Model includes a functional interface (Interface 4) to support interoperability between (heterogeneous) workflow engines.

Synonyms

- Interoperability

Workflow Enactment Service

Definition

A software service that may consist of one or more *workflow engines* in order to create, manage and execute particular *workflow instances*. Applications may interface to this service via the Workflow Application Programming Interface (part of *WAPI*).

Usage

- A workflow enactment service consists of one or more workflow engines.
- A workflow enactment service may operate within a single (homogeneous) workflow domain, or using the facilities provided within the W*f*MC interoperability interface enactment may occur across engines within several (heterogeneous) domains.

Synonyms

- Process Execution Environment

Workflow Domain

Definition

A workflow management service that consists of one or more *workflow engines* which are managed as an homogeneous unit, operating to a common administrative model.

Usage

- A single workflow domain will normally exhibit common administrative functions, including:
  - Common workflow naming (processes/activities)
  - Common user naming
  - Common interpretation of process definitions and state transitions
  - A common organizational model and roles
  - A common supervisory interface
  - Common audit data
  - etc.
- Typically a workflow domain is built from a common, homogeneous product set.
- The Workflow Reference Model identifies an interface (Interface 4) to enable workflow interoperability between workflow engines, such that an enactment service for particular processes can span more than one domain, and incorporate heterogeneous products.

Synonyms

- Workflow Service

Work Item Pool

Definition

The representation of all *work items* accessible from a particular *workflow engine*

Usage

- A Worklist Handler may (exceptionally) undertake operations requiring a global view of all available work items. The work item pool can meet this need.

Synonyms

- Total Work Queue

Administrator

Definition

A workflow system user who has special privileges allowing various system set-up, control and management functions to be performed. In some systems these tasks may be shared between several administrators, each taking responsibility for separate areas of administration.

Usage

- Administrative functions may include:
  - Set up and management of user names, passwords and roles
  - Assignment or re-assignment of work items
  - Processing exception conditions
  - Control of process definitions or versions thereof
  - Monitoring of work or process instance progress
  - System audit functions
  - etc.
- Administrators may make use of specialised administrative tools.

Synonyms

- Supervisor

Section 3

The Directory

WfMC Structure and Membership Details

The Coalition is made up of three major committees, the Technical Committee, the External Relations Committee, and the Steering Committee. The Steering Committee sets Coalition policy and oversees the work of the other committees. Small working groups exist within the Technical Committee for the purpose of defining workflow terminology, and interoperability and connectivity standards. The External Relations Committee assists in communicating this information to the workflow user community.

The Coalition's major committees meet four times per calendar year for several days at a time, with meetings currently alternating between a North American location and a European location. The working group meetings are held during those three days and as necessary throughout the year.

Coalition membership is open to all parties involved in the creation, analysis or deployment of workflow software systems. Membership is governed by a Document of Understanding which outlines meeting regulations, voting rights, etc..

There are two types of membership:

1. Funding general members who pay an annual contribution to cover the Coalition yearly operating expenses. These members have voting rights in the Coalition's committees, and vote on the Coalition's policy and budget.
2. Guest members who pay a meeting attendance fee. Guest members have no voting rights but may attend and participate in Coalition meetings.

Funding general members have the following additional benefits:

1. They may use the fact that the member company is a Funding General Member in the member's marketing program. A list of Funding General Members will be provided to any requesting parties including the press. A Funding General Member may use a logo of Funding General Member on the member's marketing materials.
2. Within the Coalition, they may vote on the budget and how Coalition funds are disbursed.
3. They receive full administrative services from the Coalition Secretariat (All mailings, faxing, etc.).
4. They may establish a link from the WfMC Web page to their home page.

Workflow Management Coalition Member Directory

The Workflow Management Coalition has a membership consisting of a wide range of organizations. All members as of June 1996 are listed here. There are two types of membership: Funding General Members, and Guest Members. For details see the *Membership Details* section. Within this Directory, Funding General members are identified by company names in larger emboldened type. Many of these members have included information about their organization or products in this Directory.

Each member has the right to appoint a representative to the Steering Committee and to the Technical Committee. Each member's representative to the Steering Committee is in the left column, and to the Technical Committee in the right column.

Telephone and fax numbers are international numbers. In general, more local callers will need to add the appropriate extra digits (normally a 0).

Steering Committee Representatives   *Technical Committee Representatives*

ABB, Inc.
Mr. Joseph Lee
2 Waterside Crossing
Windsor
CT 06095
USA
1 203 285 6791
1 203 285 6787

Abbott McCarthy, Consulting Associates
Mr. Kenneth Abbott   Mr. Dennis McCarthy
P.O. Box 6262
Holliston
MA 01746
USA
1 508 429 8711
1 508 429 8264
abbott@acm.org

Action Technologies Inc.

Dr. Raul Medina-Mora	Dr. Raul Medina-Mora
1301 Marina Village Parkway,	1301 Marina Village Parkway,
Suite 100	Suite 100
Alameda	Alameda
California 94501	California 94501
USA	USA
1 510 521 6190	1 510 521 6190
1 510 769 0596	1 510 769 0596
RMM@ati.mhs.compuserve.com	RMM@ati.mhs.compuserve.com

Founded in 1983, Action Technologies, Inc. is the leading provider of World Wide Web and client/server-based work co-ordination software for business process design, co-ordination and management. Action's suite of work co-ordination products deliver work management solutions across the extended enterprise to organizations worldwide. Action is a founding member of the Workflow Management Coalition and a leader in establishing key open systems standards for the work management market.

The ActionWorkflow Enterprise Series is a suite of powerful software products that takes a unique real-life approach to business process automation and applies it within enterprises and beyond to suppliers, trading partners and customers via LAN networks and the Internet. The products were designed to simplify and accelerate the development and deployment of robust workflow applications.

The suite offers professional workers a flexible work environment that integrates the Web, messaging, line-of-business and production applications into one collaborative workflow process. The result is dramatic time savings, substantial cost reductions, increased teamwork, new levels of corporate productivity and ultimately, increased customer satisfaction.

Headquartered in Alameda, Calif., Action sells its products worldwide through a direct sales force as well as through OEMs, systems integrators, VARs and distributors in 25 countries. Additional information on Action Technologies is available on Action's home page: http://www.actiontech.com.

Alpha Conseil
Mr. Willy Blanc
26 Rue du Pinail
86210 Vouneuil / Vienne
France
33 49 85 11 26
33 49 85 34 28

Alpharel Inc.

Mr. Gary Stowell
9339 Carroll Park Drive
San Diego
CA 92121
USA
1 619 625 3000 ext. 222
1 619 546 7671
Gary.Stowell@alpharel.com

Mr. Ross Larkin
5153 Camino Ruiz
Camarillo
CA 93012
USA
1 805 482 9815
1 805 482 9818
Ross.Larkin@Alpharel.com

ALVE Software Engineering
Mr. Russell Wilson
8868 Research Blvd.
Suite 403, Austin,
Texas 78158, USA
1 512 467 8868
1 512 467 8888
russ@alve.com

Mr. Russell Wilson
8868 Research Blvd.
Suite 403, Austin,
Texas 78158, USA
1 512 467 8868
1 512 467 8888
russ@alve.com

American Management Systems
Mr. Todd Brunjes
4050 Legato Road
Fairfax, Virginia 22033
USA
1 703 267 8600
1 703 267 2222
todd_brunjes@mail.amsinc.com

Applied Training Resources
Mr. Neil R. Anderson
12337 Jones Rd.
Suite 350
Houston, Texas 77070
USA
1 713 955 0084
1 713 955 0190

Mr. Neil R. Anderson
12337 Jones Rd.
Suite 350
Houston, Texas 77070
USA
1 713 955 0084
1 713 955 0190

Assn. for Information & Image Management

Ms. Marilyn Wright
1100 Wayne Avenue, Suite 1100
Siver Springs, MD 20910
USA
1 301 587 8202
1 301 587 2711
mwright@aiim.mo.md.us

Banctec Inc.

Ms. Katherine Drennan   Ms. Katherine Drennan
P.O. Box 660204   P.O. Box 660204
Dallas   Dallas
TX 75266 - 0204   TX 75266 - 0204
USA   USA
1 214 579 6420   1 214 579 6420
1 214 579 6990   1 214 579 6990
drennan@wpsmtp.dallas.plx.com   drennan@wpsmtp.dallas.plx.com

Headquartered in Sunnyvale, California, the Plexus Software Division of BancTec, Inc. is a leading supplier of client/server-server based imaging and workflow software for automating mission-critical, paper- and data-intensive business processes. With over 1,000 sites and 30,000 seats, Plexus has the largest installed base of open system imaging and workflow software. Plexus software is used in applications such as insurance/medical claims processing, customer services, records management, new application processing, accounts receivable/payable processing.

Plexus products are built on an open architecture and are scaleable from departmental systems to enterprise-wide production environments running transparently across multiple platforms. Interactive workflow is accomplished through Plexus FloWare, a tool that co-ordinates the interaction of documents, data and tasks. FloWare moves work between applications or activities, allowing changes to the workflow without making changes to existing applications.

The MapBuilder tool, a Microsoft Windows-based application, allows workflows to be graphically designed and dynamically changed while work is in process. Automation can be simplified using FloWare Desk software, which provides workflow management to applications without programming.

Work in process is monitored using the FloWare Status Monitor tool, a graphical tool allowing administrators to manage processes by viewing and analysing system workloads. Administrators can redistribute work to other system users. Work audit trails and cycle times are managed using the FloWare Administrator tool and the Exerciser utility allows workflows to be emulated and validated before implementation.

Banyan Systems Inc.
Mr. Eugene Lee
17 New England Executive Park
Burlington
MA 01803
USA
1 617 273 7011
1 617 229 1114

Bet Teseo S.L.
Mr. Enrique Fernandez Bargues
C/Galileo 14 1Dcha
28015 Madrid
Spain
34 1 593 31 60
34 1 447 92 95

Mr. Alfonso Diez Rubio
C/Galileo 14 1Dcha
28015 Madrid
Spain
34 1 593 31 60
34 1 447 92 95

BSG Consulting
Mr. Mike Alsup
11 Greenaway Plaza
Suite 900
Houston, Texas 77046
USA
1 713 965 1138
1 713 993 9249
mike_alsup@notes.bsginc.com

Burlington Northern Santa Fe Railway
Mr. Dave Siemek
777 Main Street, Suite 800
Forth Worth
Texas 76102
USA
1 817 333 7543
1 817 333 7147
david_h_siemek_at_cfw01PO@smtp.bnr.com

Business Concept International
Mr. Jacques Hale
31 Stourcliffe Avenue
Bournemouth BH6 3PU
UK
44 1202 432 752
44 1202 432 752
100112.1272@compuserve.com

Business Review International
Dr. Arabella Seegers
Mosselaan 57
1934 PJ Egmond a/d Hoef
The Netherlands
31 72 506 91 11
31 72 506 58 24
arabella@businessreview.nl

Mr. Ph. Gruslewski
P.O. Box 159
1930 AD Egmond aan Zee
The Netherlands

Cap Gemini Innovation
Mr. Christer Fernström
7 Chemin du Vieux Chene
Zirst 4206
38942 Meylan
France
33 76 76 47 47
33 76 76 47 48

Centre for Information Technology Innovation
Mr. Pierre Desjardins
1575 Chomedey Blvd.
Laval, Quebec
H7V 2X2, Canada
1 514 973 5820
1 514 973 5757
DESJARDINS@CITI.DOC.CA

Chemical Bank
Mr. Robert I. Barocas
Corporate Systems & Architecture
55 Water Street, Room 1804
New York, NY 10041-0199, USA
1 212 638 0730
1 212 638 7977
RobBarocas@AOL.COM

Cimage Corporation
Mr. Michael Weimar
3885 Research Park Drive
Ann Arbor
Michigan 48108, USA
1 313 761 6550
1 313 761 6551

Cimtech Ltd. (UK AIIM)
Mr. Tony Hendley
45 Grosvenor Road St. Albans
Hertfordshire AL1 3AW
United Kingdom
44 1727 813 651
44 1727 813 649
A.Grimshaw@herts.ac.uk

Mr. Tony Hendley
45 Grosvenor Road St. Albans
Hertfordshire AL1 3AW
United Kingdom
44 1727 813 651
44 1727 813 649
A.Grimshaw@herts.ac.uk

Computer Resources International

Mr. David Stewart

Bregnerodvej 144

DK 3460 Birkerod

Denmark

45 45 82 21 00

45 45 82 21 09

ads@csd.cri.dk

Mr. David Stewart

Bregnerodvej 144

DK 3460 Birkerod

Denmark

45 45 82 21 00

45 45 82 21 09

ads@csd.cri.dk

CRI is a Danish systems and software group established in 1978 to provide high quality, innovative, top-notch solutions to the European and international business communities. CRI's expertise as a systems integrator and software development organization is based on a blend of mission critical projects for customers and participation in international research and development projects. This positions CRI to provide customers with competitive solutions using state-of-the-art technology and yielding maximum commercial value. CRI currently provides a team of more than 500 professionals that are committed to working with clients from idea generation to development result.

Although headquartered in Denmark, CRI operates world-wide:

- CRI Inc., Seattle, WA, USA
- CRI Luxembourg
- CRI India Ltd. Madras, India
- CRI Frankfurt, Germany
- CRI Leiden, Netherlands
- CRI Czech, The Czech Republic
- CORENA, Oslo, Norway

CRI provide solutions, products and services to:

1. Airlines
    - Technical Documentation Repository and Publishing Systems
    - Aircraft Maintenance Scheduling and Planning Systems
    - Aircraft Maintenance Production Control Systems
2. Aerospace and Space
    - Technical Compound Document Authoring and Management Systems
    - Advanced Multi-domain Distributed Information Search and Retrieval Systems
    - Space Dynamics and Mathematical Modeling
    - Satellite Checkout Systems
    - Integrated Software Development Environments

3. Banking and Finance
  - Front, Middle and Back Office Systems
4. Industry
  - Process Planning Systems
  - Process Monitoring and Control Systems
  - Airport Information Management Systems
  - ATC Information Support Systems
5. Public and Health-Care Sector
  - Information Management Systems, including imaging and workflow
    management.

Computron Software Inc.
Mr. Richard Bailey
301 Route 17 North
Rutherford
NJ 07070
USA
1 201 935 3400 ext. 311
1 201 935 7678
rfbailey@panix.com

Concordium Software Ltd.
Peter J. Lawrence   Peter J. Lawrence
54 Pondtail Road   54 Pondtail Road
Fleet   Fleet
Hampshire GU13 9JF   Hampshire GU13 9JF
United Kingdom   United Kingdom
44 1252 812 444   44 1252 812 444
44 1252 812 444   44 1252 812 444
plawrence@concordium.co.uk   plawrence@concordium.co.uk

COI GmbH
Mr. Wolfgang Enders   Dr. Michael Amberg
Industriestrasse 1-3   Industriestrasse 1-3
D-91074 Herzogenaurach   D-91074 Herzogenaurach
Germany   Germany
49 9132 82 28 77   49 91 32 82 28 77
49 9132 82 49 59   49 91 32 82 49 59
enderwlf@coi.ina.de

COI GmbH, founded in 1988, is a software house specializing in DMS and
workflow technology and has recently released a toolbox for BPR which generates
workflow runtime code. COI has sold over 200 installations so far (1996) and built
a solid market position in the German manufacturing industry. Customers include
OPEL, BMW RR, MAN, Heidelberger Druck, EDS, Lufthansa.

All COI applications are built in OEL, a JAVA-style language with extensive class libraries. OEL is highly portable and currently available for Win 3.11, NT, OS/2, UNIX (several vendors), with more ports are under consideration. COI offers licensing of the OEL technology as well as technology cooperations. COI is owned by the German INA Group, the 2nd largest manufacturer of rolling bearings worldwide (20,000 employees).

CSE Systems

Dr. Harald Rätzsch	Mr. Kurt Ogris
St. Veiter Strasse 4	St. Veiter Strasse 4
A-9020 Klagenfurt	A-9020 Klagenfurt
Austria	Austria
43 463 50645	43 463 50645
43 463 50677	43 463 50677
hara@csesys.co.at	kuog@csesys.co.at

CSE Systems Computer & Software Engineering GmbH was founded in 1987 by a small group of experienced software specialists with varied professional backgrounds.

Research and development has always been the core of the company. The company first received international acclaim for its product Shortcut, as well as for the software development of several large-scale trade fair and parking, accounting and control systems (Dusseldorf Trade Fair; Munich Airport; Business Center La Defense, Paris).

CSE Systems continues to concentrate its efforts on Workflow Management and therefore has developed WorkFlow - a client/server product that allows organizations to efficiently store, track, retrieve and manage information. WorkFlow was originally built for Austrian government agencies (which work according to very strict rules, similar to ISO9000) but has since broadened out to become a leading provider of workflow management solutions to public and private organizations throughout Europe. It complies with the reference model of the Workflow Management Coalition, which serves as a basic concept for the architecture of workflow systems.

In July 1995, CSE Systems won the world's largest bid for a workflow product. Deutsche Telekom AG (the German telephone conglomerate) chose CSE's WorkFlow from a competitive field of 26 workflow products to be a component of its office communications environment, potentially with 90,000 workstations.

CSE Systems is actively involved in the Workflow Management Coalition, currently holding three elected officer positions, including the position of secretary/treasurer of the Coalition. CSE Systems is also a WfMC country contact, responsible for Austria and Switzerland and in that capacity supports all members and parties interested in the work of the Workflow Management Coalition.

For the future, CSE Systems is already preparing to bring workflow solutions to the U.S. and has plans to strengthen its position in Europe.

CSI - Council for Informatics
Ms. Gloria Nistal   Ms. Gloria Nistal
C/Zurbano 42   C/Zurbano 42
28071 Madrid   28071 Madrid
Spain   Spain
34 1 586 17 26   34 1 586 17 26
34 1 586 19 20   34 1 586 19 20
gloria.nistal@sgci.dgopti.map.es   gloria.nistal@sgci.dgopti.map.es

D&B Software
Mr. Peter Meekin   Mr. Charles Rossi
550 Cochituate Road MS 42D   550 Cochituate Road MS 42D
Framingham   Framingham
MA 01701   MA 01701
USA   USA
1 508 370 6812   1 508 370 5409
1 508 370 6380   1 508 370 6380
                                                     rml@smtpgate.dbsoftware.com

Danet GmbH
Consulting and Software Development
Geschaftsstelle Munich
Hansastrasse 32
80686 Munich
Germany
49 89 54 70 960
49 89 54 70 9699

DCE Nederland BV
Mr. Fred van Leeuwen   Mr. Hans Wierenga
Groenezoom 1   Groenezoom 1
1171 JA Badhoevedorp   1171 JA Badhoevedorp
The Netherlands   The Netherlands
31 20 659 7751   31 20 659 7751
31 20 659 7076   31 20 659 7076
Fred.van.Leeuwen@dce.nl   H.wierenga@dce.nl

DCE Nederland b.v. is an independent management consultancy providing specialist expertise in the areas of information and organisation. The company was founded in 1980 and in September 1991, the management and staff of DCE bought out the company from its previous owners. DCE employs a total of 95 staff, carrying out assignments in Holland as well as in other European countries.

DCE uses new technologies – including DIS, imaging, workflow and groupware, as well as call centres – to make a direct contribution to management objectives, via process improvement and control. Its approach focuses on putting the changes into operation with the people. So for DCE, it is not techniques or standard phases that dominate, but the demands of the change process in the specific client situation. Information technology plays a strong role as a priming pump here.

Typical of DCE's no-nonsense approach are

- *Optimisation of market performance*
  The market demands on a service or product, guide the process improvement scheme
- *Increased potential for flexibility and preparation for continuous change*
  The mobilisation of the existing strengths in the organisation itself are of prime importance here
- *Assurance of measurable improvements, beginning with the short term*
  In the process, DCE can help the IT department of the client greatly strengthen its position, by a drastic improvement in the service it provides internally.

DCE's support can be divided into two categories:

A) Contribution to process improvement pilots and projects.
B) Repositioning of the internal IT service

Along with these DCE also employs her expertise in information economics, which ensures that projects (and the consequent improved processes) will be both manageable and measurable in business economic terms.

Defense Information Systems Agency
Dr. Daniel Wu
10701 Parkridge Blvd.
Reston
VA 22091-43
USA
1 703 735 3569
1 703 735 3257
wud@ncr.disa.mil

Delphi Consulting Group
Mr. Thomas Koulopoulos
Sears' Crescent Building
100 City Hall Plaza
Boston, MA 02108-2106
USA
1 617 247 1511
1 617 247 4957
TK@delphigroup.com

Deutsche Telekom AG

Mr. Clemens Wernsmann
NL Münster / ABISZ
Dahlweg 112
48153 Münster
Germany
49 251 900 95 05
49 251 900 95 49

Mr. Clemens Wernsmann

Dahlweg 112
48153 Münster
Germany
49 251 900 95 05
49 251 900 95 49

Digital Equipment B.v.

Mr. Stan Bosch
European Workflow Expertise Center
P.O. Box 1068
3430 BB Bakenmonde
Nieuwegein, The Netherlands
s.bosch@uto.mts.dec.com

Mr. Manfred Koethe
Vincenz-Priessnitz-Strasse 1
76131 Karlsruhe
Germany

49 721 690 256
49 721 696 816
Koethe@qchan.enet.dec.com

LinkWorks is the award-winning Enterprise Groupware product from Digital Equipment. Based on its open client/server and object-oriented multi-vendor framework, LinkWorks is being deployed to realise complex process management solutions. The framework caters for both document and data intensive environments requiring the highest levels of security and integrity. LinkWorks solutions are based on native LinkWorks workflow and object management roots or are combined with leading workflow systems such as ProMInanD from IABG. The integral workflow functionality of LinkWorks makes it possible to automate standard (workflow) processes to promote efficiency within and across groups and ensure procedural control.

The standard LinkWorks workflow allows for templates to be built in advance and distributed to various sites. LinkWorks accommodates conditional and parallel workflow - the flow of documents can be automatically changed based on criteria defined ahead of time. LinkWorks presents the company's organizational structure in an easily manipulated chart. User profiles maintain information regarding preferred applications, desktop clients and security parameters. This allows for a flexible and secure work environment. Electronic signature authorization and event notification help to streamline and improve the management of business processes. Enhanced workflow provide facilities for pipeline monitoring, blueprint design, workflow rollback and role-based security.

ProMInanD is a registered trademark of IABG mbH.

LinkWorks is a registered trademark of Digital Equipment Corporation.

Digital Tools
Mr. Vinay Deshpande
18900 Stevens Creek Blvd
Cupertino
California 95014
USA
1 408 366 6920
1 408 446 2140
vinay@digit.com

Mr. Sam Uttarwar
18900 Stevens Creek Blvd
Cupertino
California 95014
USA
1 408 366 6920
1 408 446 2140
sam@digit.com

Ditec Ltd.
Mr. Viktor Cingel
Zelezniciarska 16
81104 Bratislava
Slovakia
42 7 49 68 25 or 49 68 35
42 7 49 68 56
viktor@ditec.sk

Mr. Martin Vass
Zelezniciarska 16
81104 Bratislava
Slovakia
42 7 49 68 25 or 49 68 35
42 7 49 68 56

Doculabs
Mr. James Watson
1201 W. Harrison, Suite 205
Chicago
Illinois 60607
USA
1 312 433 7793
1 312 433 7795
U27555@uicvm.uic.edu

Document Access
Mr. Cees Krijgsman
Westersingel 101
3015 Ld. Rotterdam
The Netherlands
31 10 436 66 64
31 10 436 68 44
ceeskrij@docuACCESS.nl

Mr. Bert de Bock
Westersingel 101
3015 Ld. Rotterdam
The Netherlands
31 10 436 66 64
31 10 436 68 44

Docworld B.v.
Mr. Harry Kremers
PO Box 616
2900 AP Capelle aan den Ijsel
The Netherlands
31 10 450 9970
31 10 451 0870

DocWorld is a Netherlands-based company consulting in document management, business process redesign, workflow, and groupware. Established in 1987 we have done many projects in those areas, including the first workflow system in the Netherlands in 1988. We also operate in Benelux, UK, Germany, France and Scandinavia.

DocWorld is a strictly independent consultant with a clear vision of the market for new technologies. Our mission is to educate the end-user in the task of automating their processes and in selecting a vendor or system integrator. We also act as a project leader and as an intermediate between user and vendor. In addition, DocWorld organises trade shows and conferences in Europe on document management, workflow, and groupware.

Dr. Götzer & Co. GmbH
Dr. Klaus Götzer
Am Ganter 34
85635 Höhenkirchen
Germany
49 81 02748 154
49 81 02 748 155
100326.151@compuserve.com

Mr. Klaus Götzer
Am Ganter 34
85635 Höhenkirchen
Germany
49 81 02748 154
49 81 02 748 155
100326.151@compuserve.com

Dresdner Bank AG
Mr. Jürgen Edelmann
KS OR IT-Infrastruktur Software Eng.
Wm. 14 3/F
D-60301 Frankfurt am Main
Germany
49 69 263 6279
49 69 263 10191
edj@dresdnerbank.de

Mr. Jürgen Edelmann
KS OR IT-Infrastruktur Software Eng.
Wm. 14 3/F
D-60301 Frankfurt am Main
Germany
49 69 263 6279
49 69 263 10191
edj@dresdnerbank.de

DST Systems Inc.

Mr. Matt Graver
1055 Broadway
Kansas City
Missouri 64105
USA
1 816 435 3745
1 816 435 4550
MGRAVER@SKY.NET
ELCA Matrix SA

Mr. Ed Rohuer
1055 Broadway
Kansas City
Missouri 64105
USA
1 816 435 8531
1 816 435 4550

Mr. Claude Amiguet
Department Manager
Aveneu de la Harpe 22-24
1000 Lausanne 13
Switzerland
41 21 613 22 41
41 21 613 22 40
Claude.Amiguet@elca-matrix.ch

Electronic Data Systems
Mr. Rick Holman
800 Tower Drive #317
Troy
MI 48098, USA
1 810 265 0206
1 810 265 9275
RHolmanLLC@aol.com

Mr. Chris Wiggins
800 Tower Drive #317
Troy
MI 48098, USA
1 810 265 3406
1 810 265 4275

Elsag Bailey
Mr. Paolo Filauro
Via Puccini 2
16154 Genova-Sestri P.
Italy
39 10 658 2354
39 10 658 2964
pfilauro@elsag.it

Mr. Paolo Filauro
Via Puccini 2
16154 Genova Sestri P.
Italy
39 10 658 2354
39 10 658 2964
pfilauro@elsag.it

Empirica
Mr. Werner Korte
Oxfordstrasse 2
D-53111 Bonn
Germany
49 228 98 530 0
49 228 98 530 12
werner.korte@empirica.de

Mr. Klaur-Dieter Kreplin
Oxfordstrasse 2
D-53111 Bonn
Germany
49 228 98 530 0
49 228 98 530 12
charly@empirica.de

ENIX Ltd.
Mr. Derek Miers
3 The Green
Richmond
Surrey TW9 1PL, UK
44 181 332 0210
44 181 940 7424
miers@enix.co.uk

Ernst & Young LLP

Mr. Joe Gagnon
750 Seventh Avenue
New York
NY 10019
USA
1 214 444 2100
1 214 444 2102

Mr. Rich Barie
104 Decker CT
Irving
Texas 75062-2757
USA
1 214 444 2100
1 214 444 2102

European Enterprise Integration Supportive Services
Mr. Manfred Klittich
Spessartweg 54
D-65760 Eschborn
Germany
49 69 6679 446
49 6196 4845 28
100623.1070@compuserve.com

Mr. Manfred Klittich
Spessartweg 54
D-65760 Eschborn
Germany
49 69 6679 446
49 6196 4845 28
100623.1070@compuserve.com

Excalibur Technologies

Mr. Gerald C. Teudt
9255 Towne Centre Drive, 9th Floor
San Diego
CA 92121-3042
USA
1 619 625 7900
1 619 625 7901

Filenet Corporation

Mrs. Linda Merle
3565 Harbor Blvd
Costa Mesa
California 90274
USA
1 714 966 3982
1 714 966 3490
merle@filenet.com

Mr. Karl Matthews
57-63 Church Road
Wimbledon Village
London SW19 5DQ
UK
44 181 263 6363
44 181 263 6365
Karl_Matthews@filenet.com

FileNet is a worldwide leading provider of client/server software for workflow and document-imaging. FileNet's complete product range offers customers a single-source solution for workflow, document-imaging, document-management, and COLD software (providing management of data in mainframe reports).

Visual WorkFlo is FileNet's flagship production workflow offering. It is designed for use in high-performance workflow scenarios such as the management of claims processing in an insurance company, or the management of customer services processes in a utility company. Its database-based architecture robustly supports high numbers of transactions and high numbers of simultaneous users, whilst its graphical development tools support extensive systems integration and application development activities.

The World Wide Web-based capabilities which FileNet is developing will enhance Visual WorkFlo's ability to exploit Intranet and Internet applications. Users will be able to initiate work, check the status of work, and perform a step in a workflow process over the Internet and Intranet networks.

FileNet Ensemble offers end-users the ability to graphically author work processes at their desktops, without requiring programming effort. Together with its mail-based architecture this enables organisations to take advantage of workflow technology with minimal investment in additional technical infrastructure or software development effort. Ensemble and Visual Workflo can be integrated to support cross-enterprise workflow management.

FileNet is a funding member of the Workflow Management Coalition and participant in the Coalition's efforts. It is actively involved in developing interoperability extensions to its workflow products according to the interface specifications defined by the Coalition.

Fischer International Systems Corp.
Mr. Michael Nordin
4073 Mercantile Avenue
Naples
FL 33942
USA
1 813 643 1500
1 813 643 3772

FormMaker Software, Inc.

Mr. Hsi-Ming Lin
2300 Windy Ridge Parkway
Suite 400 North
Atlanta, Georgia 30339
USA
1 770 858 2282
1 770 859 0252
hlin@formmaker.com

Mr. Robert Steinke
2300 Windy Ridge Parkway
Suite 400 North
Atlanta, Georgia 30339
USA
1 770 859 9900
1 770 859 0252

Forte Software, Inc
Mr. Ken MacKenzie
1800 Harrison Street
Oakland
CA 94612, USA
1 510 869 2105
1 510 834 1508
kmac@forte.com

Fraunhofer - Institut fur Arbeitswirtschaft und Organisation
Mr. Michael Rathgeb   Mr. Sebastian Graf
Nobelstrasse 2   Fraunhoferstrasse 1
D-70176 Stuttgart   76131 Karlsruhe
Germany   Germany
49 711 970 2343   49 721 6091 403
49 711 970 2300   49 721 6091 413
Michael.Rathgeb@iao.fhg.de

Fujitsu
Mr. Rashmi Patel   Mr. Jim Logan
3055 Orchard Drive   3055 Orchard Drive
San Jose   San Jose
California 95134-2022   California 95134-2022
USA   USA
1 408 456 7781   1 408 456 7799
1 408 456 7050   1 408 456 7050
Rashmi@ossi.com   jlogan@ossi.com

Galleymead Ltd.
Mr. Fred Weil
40 Bradmore Way
Brookmans Park
Hatfield, Herts
AL9 7QX England
44 1707 650 961
fredw@fred1.demon.co.uk

Gartner Group
Mr. Jim Bair   Ms. Regina Casonato
5201 Great America Parkway   Corso Garibaldi 49
Suite 219   20121 Milano
Santa Clara, CA 95054   Italy
USA
1 408 450 4524   39 2 864 652 24
1 408 450 4501   39 2 864 654 78
                                             rcasonat@gartner.com

GIGA Information Group
Ms. Connie Moore
One Longwater Circle
Norwell
MA 02061
USA
1 617 982 9500
1 617 878 6650
cmoore@gigasd.com

GLS Conseil
Mr. Gérard Saccone   Mr. Gérard Saccone
8 rue de Varenne   8 rue de Varenne
75007 Paris   75007 Paris
France   France
33 1 42 22 44 00   33 1 42 22 44 00
33 1 45 49 18 92   33 1 45 49 18 92
100143.603@compuserve.com   100143.603@compuserve.com

GUS AG & Co.
Mr. Rolf W. Eckertz   Mr. Volker Birk
Bonner Strasse 211   Bonner Strasse 211
50968 Cologne   50968 Cologne
Germany   Germany
49 221 376 590   49 221 376 590
49 221 3765 949   49 221 3765 949
72660.726@compuserve.com   72660.726@compuserve.com

Hewlett Packard

Mr. Jim Haselmaier   Mr. Ming-Chien Shan
3404 East Harmony Road   1501 Page Mill Road
Fort Collins   Palo Alto
Colorado 80525   California 94304
USA   USA
1 303 229 3345   1 415 857 7158
1 303 229 7182   1 415 852 8137
jimh@fc.hp.com

WorkManager is Hewlett-Packard's highly successful Product Data Management system which has provided benefits to companies world wide in the areas of data and process management. WorkManager provides the capability for companies to manage the creation and revisions of all types of product data such as documentation, product structures, and custom forms. In addition, WorkManager can control the processes which affect the changes to product data by providing notification, routing and concurrency control.

WorkManager version 3.5 will include many features which add to the robustness of the current process management capabilities. Central to this is an object-oriented workflow component which adds the ability to graphically define processes, as well as execute these processes, all within the WorkManager environment. The system allows for varying degrees of freedom of execution to be defined, allowing for portions of the process to be tightly or loosely controlled. This flexibility allows users to define processes where some conditions are not completely determined.

A powerful rules-based decision capability is utilized to control process flow, guarantee that documentation exists or has been modified correctly, or to make decisions on user assignments. The rules are defined using a Basic-like syntax that is both easy to use and has powerful access to data in WorkManager's database.

Timers can be set to monitor elapsed time or at fixed dates, to control process flow and notify appropriate people when required. Managers can easily display the process graphically to determine the status of events and make corrective actions if necessary.

Furthermore, WorkManager has the ability to easily handle exceptions to the process during an execution. This allows for even greater flexibility by allowing the appropriate people to change the defined process flow to address important situations that often can't be predicted. WorkManager's graphical workflow user interface provides a Supervisor mode to allow these users to handle exceptions directly via interaction with the graphical workflow objects.

Hitachi

Dr. Akio Yajima
Software Development Center
Shinamo-cho, Totsuka
Yokohama 244
Japan
81 45 826 8550
81 45 826 7806
yajima@crl.hitachi.co.jp

Mr. Hiroshi Majima
Honmachi Minamisumisei
Shimojima Bldg.
3-8 Kitakyuhozocho.3 chome,
Chuo-ku
Osaka 541
Japan
81 6 281 8350
81 6 281 8392
majimahi@soft.hitachi.co.jp

Hitachi provides various integrated products for groupware, such as email, document information systems, schedule management, etc.. One of these products is Hitachi's Workflow System. Its powerful engines effectively automate office business such as the circulation of documents. It also supports the management of business processes. The introduction of Workflow System brings improvement in work efficiency. The Workflow System circulates a document automatically along with a business process definition chart.

Files created in a variety of application programs can be circulated, because the application layer is independent of the workflow management layer.

To introduce a workflow system into real business, it is necessary to allow for irregular operations which cannot be defined during the initial definition of the business process. The Workflow System supports application processes such as consultation, sending back, taking back, acting, transfer, stop, cancellation, etc..

The Workflow System also provides powerful tools so support all the processes that are necessary for the successful introduction of workflow systems:

(a) The visual status monitor shows a route taken, and the present location of the document on the business process definition

(b) Cooperative functions between servers provide support for a wide area workflow system

Holosofx

Mr. Hassan Khorshid	Dr. Salah Bendifallah
111 N. Sepulveda Blvd, Suite 150	111 N. Sepulveda Blvd, Suite 150
Manhatten Beach	Manhatten Beach
California 90266	California 90266
USA	USA
1 310 798 2425	1 310 798 2425
1 310 798 2365	1 310 798 2365

IA Corporation

Mr. Thierry Leger	Dr. Bernard Pech
Watergate Tower 1	Watergate Tower 1
1900 Powell Street, Suite 600	1900 Powell Street, Suite 600
Emeryville, CA 94608	Emeryville, CA 94608,
USA	USA
1 510 450 6816	1 510 450 6874
1 510 450 7099	1 510 450 7099
Thierry.Leger@ia-us.com	pechgia-us.com

IA Corporation is a provider of high-end, high-performance enterprise applications software products. Focusing currently on the dynamic, multi-billion dollar financial and banking industry, IA has become a major player in this market with its image-enabled cash management application frameworks, CheckVision and RemitVision.

Systems based on IA software products are rarely matched in complexity, performance and reliability. The company boasts such blue chip clients as Merrill Lynch, Fidelity Investments, Federal Express, Sanwa Bank of California, Mellon Bank, Fleet-Shawmut Bank and GE Capital.

WorkVision is an object-oriented work management software platform which includes workflow and document management. WorkVision is a high-performance, geographically distributed product which is highly scaleable. While used primarily for high-end workflow automation in connection with image and document management, this platform can be used with any type of electronic file including text, image, graphics, voice and video.

With the high-performance, open-architecture, WorkVision as the software platform, IA develops new application-specific frameworks incorporating business logic in record time. Solutions built on IA frameworks help customers respond quickly to major industry changes while improving internal efficiencies, enhancing customer service and creating new fee-based offerings.

CheckVision is an application framework for building image-based check processing applications that operates on top of a subset of WorkVision platform components.

RemitVision is a remittance processing application framework for image-based integrated wholesale and retail lockbox functions. Lockbox is a payment processing service offered by commercial banks and service bureaus to large corporations.

IABG

Dr. Klaus Wagner   Dr. Bernhard Karbe
ITV Department   ITV Department
Einsteinstrasse 20   Einsteinstrasse 20
85521 Ottobrunn   85521 Ottobrunn
Germany   Germany
49 89 6088 2394 / 2726   49 89 6088 2480
49 89 6088 3365   49 89 6088 2346
kjwagner@iabg.de

Industrieanlagen-Betriebsgesellschaft mbH (IABG mbH) IABG was originally founded through a German Federal Government initiative in 1961 to oversee and operate the central test facility for the aerospace industry. Today, IABG has successfully expanded its business scope to cover the following areas: Information Technology, organisational consulting (BPR), environmental engineering, space technology, transport and defence. IABG is a leading organisation in the technical services field in Europe, a position strengthened further by the recent addition of BDM International and its subsidiaries.

ProMInanD (Office Process, Migration, Integration and Dispositions) automates, commands and accelerates the distribution and appropriation of co-operative work in an organisation in a flexible manner. Highly advanced electronic circulation folders (ECFs) are used to route data regardless of type. Since organisations change daily and are never stagnant, ProMInanD also allows for exceptions to be effortlessly realised within a functioning system. These exceptions are accomplished by users themselves, and include side-stepping a step or adding one, postponing business processes, cancelling business processes and compensating for such cancellations.

In addition, with over 200 API functions, ProMInanD can easily become the 'engine' for existing interfaces, as was seen in the Dresdner Bank project, or in the integration with the LinkWorks Documentation Management System for Digital Equipment.

IBM

Mr. Dave Shorter   Mr. Marc-Thomas Schmidt
5 W. Kirkwood Blvd   Hans Klemmstr. 45
Roanoke   Boeblingen
Texas 76299-0001   Germany
USA
1 817 962 5066   49 703 116 6118
1 817 962 3470
PAG8@MSNVM1.IINUS1.IBM.COM   mschmidt@vnet.ibm.com

FlowMark is IBM's solution for workflow management that helps organisations define, document, test, control, and improve their business processes whether they are financial services, insurance, telecommunications, transportation, health care, government or other applications.

FlowMark is a state-of-the-art, object-oriented client/server product. It plays a central role in the design, implementation, and execution of distributed applications which may reside on workstations or on mid-range or mainframe computers. The Internet Connection to FlowMark allows organisations to extend business processes even beyond their enterprise through the WWW to include their customers, vendors, and partners.

FlowMark has an extensive list of features including graphical modelling, comprehensive work allocation and monitoring tools, process analysis, audit trails for feedback on performance and productivity, and the ability to use the management reporting application of your choice. The process models defining the workflows are graphically represented as networks of activities. Each activity is described by role assignment, required program or tool to carry out the activity, and the data to be manipulated by the program.

Persons involved in a process see their assigned activities on their personalized work lists on their workstation. When they perform activities from the worklist, they are guided by appropriate help information and supported by seamless invocation of programs. Persons involved in a process or controlling the progress of a process can request status information on a running process which will be displayed in a graphical view.

FlowMark helps organisations to stop battling with uncontrolled processes, to start managing the flow of work, and to focus on their core business activities.

For more information about IBM FlowMark refer to:

http://www.software.ibm.com/ad/flowmark

ICL

Mr. Dave Hollingsworth
ICL Process Solutions Group
Beaumont, Burfield Road
Old Windsor, Berks SL4 2JP
UK
44 1753 868 181 x2166
44 1753 841 775
d.c.hollingsworth@fel0112.wins.icl.co.uk

Mr. Mike Anderson
ICL, Eskdale Road
Winnersh, Workingham
Berks RS44 5TT
UK
44 1734 634 636
44 1734 697 636
M.J.Anderson@fel0107.wins.icl.co.uk

The need for progressive change is one faced by almost all organizations today. An increasing number recognise the key contribution which a focus on their business processes can make to their success. ICL Process Solutions provides a full range of services to help organizations meet these needs with access to the technology and systems integration offerings of ICL as a whole.

Our consultants use and train our clients in the well-tried and practical ProcessWise Guide methodology, with support from ProcessWise WorkBench, one of the most powerful process definition, analysis and simulation tools available. The business process models developed in ProcessWise WorkBench can also be exported to drive the development of workflow and process management systems using the ICL product set:

Role Model - an enterprise scale, production level workflow management system based on CORBA compliant object infrastructure and following the architecture and standards being defined by the WfMC.

Case Manager Desktop - a workflow management product focused on the needs of the knowledge worker operating in an environment of relatively unstructured processes, typically of long duration.

TeamWare Flow - a general purpose workflow management system for use in office system environments and providing tight integration with the other products in the TeamWare office portfolio.

Processwise Integrator - a sophisticated process management product providing support for complex and demanding applications within this emerging class of process driven systems.

A range of pre-built process-enabled applications based on these products is also available.

Our project services staff provide comprehensive support for systems implementation using these and other products. User involvement in the design process, based on the facilitative methods of Process Design Studios, is a key element of our approach.

Identitech Inc.

Mr. Paul Singleton
100 Rialto Place, Suite 800
Melbourne

Mr. David Rocheleau
100 Rialto Place, Suite 800
Melbourne

FL 32901, USA   FL 32901, USA
1 407 951 9503   1 407 951 9503
1 407 951 9505   1 407 951 9505
susan@identitech.com

Identitech's FYI product is an enterprise-wide document management system with built-in workflow and intelligent forms modules. FYI supports the scanning, storing, retrieving, sharing, routing, faxing, and printing of images, as well as documents of any other data type.

FYI is an open architecture, client/server-based application that uses standard SQL database engines, such as Oracie, Sybase, Microsoft SQL Server, and Gupta. FYI consists of may modules that can all be accessed via the application program interface (API) toolkit. These modules can dramatically reduce the programming time to image-enable a legacy system or to create a new application from scratch. These modules include:

- FYIView – an image and document scan, display, and print module
- MassScan – a high-speed document scan engine with integrated bar code recognition
- QA/Import – an image Quality Control and Import module with integrated optical character recognition (OCR) for keyword indexing and full text search
- FYI Object/Server – a mass storage module for filing and storing documents on magnetic or optical disks; includes jukebox drivers
- Workflow – a seamlessly integrated module allowing users to easily automate tasks, set and revise job schedules, integrate workgroups, and control complex projects
- Intelligent Forms – a form designer with electronic signature capture and security control over all data on the form
- Print/Fax Server – FYI's print/fax server allows users to easily print or fax documents within FYI with one command
- Security – FYI provides B-2-type security control over every document and index field in the system

IDS Prof. Scheer GmbH

Dr. Helge Hess   Dr. Helge Hess
Altenkesseler Strasse 20   Altenkesseler Strasse 20
D-66115 Saarbrücken   D-66115 Saarbrücken
Germany   Germany
49 681 9762 772   49 681 9762 772
49 681 9762 762   49 681 9762 762
hess@ids-scheer.de   hess@ids-scheer.de

IDS Prof. Scheer GmbH was founded in 1985 as a consulting and software company. Originally, it was a spin-off from the Institute for Information Systems

(Institut fuer Wirtschaftsinformatik, IWi) at the University of the Saarland in Saarbruecken, Germany (Director: Prof. A.-W. Scheer).

IDS provides effective, high quality consulting services. The 450 employees specialize in different sectors and have profound know-how in business administration and information technology. Additionally, they are experienced in the following sectors: piece-oriented production, car industry and subcontractors, air and space technology, paper, chemical industry, process industry, ceramics, food industry, utility companies, telecommunications, banks, insurance and trade companies.

IDS develops methods, tools and models for reorganizing companies. All products are based on the holistic "Architecture of Integrated Information Systems" (ARIS). For analysing, modelling and optimizing business processes, IDS has equipped the ARIS-Toolset with industry-specific reference models. Full-blown logistics solutions are customized to meet the requirements of individual industries. These logistics solutions allow many companies to work in a more flexible and more decentralised manner.

ARIS-Workflow is the logical result of further developing the ARIS-Toolset. The results of process optimization can be directly used for controlling and monitoring the processes themselves. ARIS-Workflow integrates existing application systems. It also integrates the employees into the process according to their responsibilities, and guarantees a continuous data flow by forwarding documents and records. The workflow system is a client/server system and uses an implementation of the CORBA standard of the Object Management Group (OMG) as a basis for communication.

IMTF, Informatique MTFSA
Mr. Bart Norré   Mr. Salvatore Porfido
Route Du Crochet 7   Route du Crochet 7
1762 Givisiez/Fribourg   1762 Givisiez/Fribourg
Switzerland   Switzerland
41 37 26 66 67   41 37 26 66 67
41 37 26 61 01   41 37 26 61 06

InConcert
Dr. Sunil Sarin   Dr. Sunil Sarin
Four Cambridge Center   Four Cambridge Center
4th Floor   4th Floor
Cambridge   Cambridge
MA 02142   MA 02142
USA   USA
1 617 499 4426   1 617 499 4426
1 617 499 4409   1 617 499 4409
sarin@xait.xerox.com   sarin@xait.xerox.com

Headquartered in Cambridge, Massachusetts, U.S.A., InConcert is dedicated to the development, marketing, and support of its InConcert workflow product, a leading solution for automating and managing enterprise business processes. The company is a member of the Xerox New Enterprises Board, a corporate venture division of Xerox Corporation chartered with the identification, development, and successful commercialization of new technology products.

Released commercially in 1993, InConcert is workflow management software for open systems that scales from the workgroup to the enterprise and adapts to changing organizational requirements and business conditions. InConcert integrates advanced object-oriented technology, document management services, and a dynamic process model that enables organizations to quickly build and tailor superior workflows that match current and evolving organizational needs. InConcert is designed to easily integrate with existing desktop applications and client/server environments delivering improved software applications and data access, repository management, business process knowledge, management inspection and control, and overall ease of use. InConcert's adaptive process model enables users to dynamically modify process instances on-the-fly to allow for exceptions and changes to the processes as they evolve.

InConcert provides multiple options for rapid application development, on Internet/Intranet and other popular client platforms. InConcert also forms the basis for an Engineering Project Management option with additional tools for end-user management of projects and resources, revision control and security for CAD drawings and documents, and auditing of processes associated with distributed and complex engineering activity.

Infodesign Corporation

Mr. David Seaman
130 Albert Street, Suite 1600
K1P5G4 Ottowa
Ontario
Canada
1 609 983 4450
1 609 983 0221
dave@idc.com

Mr. Edward Herl
7700 Leesburg Pike
Suite 204
Falls Church, VA 22043
USA
1 703 822 5541
1 703 519 9715
ed@idc.com

InfoDesign Corporation is a leader in structured information solutions. Our award winning WorkSMART product provides a complete data and work management environment for your corporate needs.

We offer services to help you with SGML. Our training courses and technical services can help you get your application working quickly. We also have full systems integration services that can assist you in a cost effective implementation of a structured information solution.

WorkSMART provides the support and infrastructure to manage the needs of organizations which have an emphasis on structured information, and are utilizing SGML as the standard for structuring that information. These organizations are required to produce and maintain high quality technical information. With the explosion in information delivery options, the job of managing large volumes of data which are subject to ongoing technical, editorial and configuration change, requires a solution that is capable of handling these complexities. WorkSMART is the implementation of choice for this environment.

For further information email: info@idc.com or see us on the World Wide Web at http://www.idc.com.

Infologistik GmbH

Mr. Jim Storm
Budapester Strasse 23
Munich, Germany
49 89 689 3131
49 89 689 3134
100073.2770@compuserve.com

Informix Software
Ms. Marina Buchman
4100 Bohannon Dr.
Menlo Park
CA 94025, USA
1 415 926 6756
1 415 926 6559
marina@informix.com

ING Bank
Dr. Marien Krijger
Postbus 1800
1000 BV Amsterdam
The Netherlands
31 20 565 1625
31 20 565 1609

Mr. Jim Storm
Budapester Strasse 23
Munich, Germany
49 89 689 3131
49 89 689 3134
100073.2770@compuserve.com

Ms. Marina Buchman
4100 Bohannon Dr.
Menlo Park
CA 94025, USA
1 415 926 6756
1 415 926 6559
marina@informix.com

Ing. C. Olivetti & C.

Mr. Bruno Pepino
Via G. Jervis 77
10015 Ivrea (TO), Italy
39 125 523022
39 125 523797

Mr. Patrizio Cavedoni
V. le A. Gramsci 12
56125 Pisa, Italy
39 50 516516
39 50 502664
cavedoni@pvax.ico.olivetti.com

Insiel S.p.A.

Mr. Fulvio Sbroiavacca
Via S. Francesco d'Assisi 43
34133 Trieste
Italy
39 40 3737209 (111)
39 40 3737333

Mr. Marco Giacomello
Via S. Francesco d'Assisi 43
34133 Trieste
Italy
39 40 3737209 (111)
39 40 3737333

Institut für Informatik
Prof Johann Eder
Universität Klagenfurt
Universitätstrasse 65-67
A-9022 Klagenfurt
Austria
43 463 2700 508
43 463 2700 505
eder@ifi.uni-klu.ac.at

Mr. Walter Liebhart
Universität Klagenfurt
Universitätstrasse 65-67
A-9022 Klagenfurt
Austria
43 463 2700 6201
43 463 2700 505
walter@ifi.uni-klu.ac.at

Integrated Work

Mr. John Williams
Black Lion House
45 Whitechapel Road
London E1 1JJ
United Kingdom
44 171 464 4249
44 171 464 4238
jwilliams@intwork.co.uk

Mr. Nigel Smith
Black Lion House
45 Whitechapel Road
London E1 1JJ
United Kingdom
44 171 464 4352
44 171 464 4238
nsmith@intwork.co.uk

Integrated Work is an independent software vendor focused on systems for customer care and business process re-engineering.

Integrated Work's tool-kit for workflow applications, WinWork, provides a robust, scaleable platform for workflow systems able to handle the demands of large scale production environments. WinWork uses low-cost, easily deployable Microsoft technologies such as Windows NT and SQL Server to provide a platform for work flows that integrate document imaging, fax, customer databases, telephony services and existing computer applications, managing sequences of tasks across front-office and back office areas.

WinWork allows users to develop their processes using a graphical workflow designer and common development languages such as Visual Basic and C++ . It provides excellent control centre services to make work visible to management and offers a rich set of interfaces that are being developed in line with the WfMC standards allowing workflows to connect a wide range of user-developed and third party applications such as Microsoft's Exchange.

For customer service applications WinWork can be used in conjunction with CampaignWork. This allows for a workflow that manages the dialogue between staff and customers, supporting customer service over the telephone by integrating computers and telephony. CampaignWork is ideal for call centres and tele-marketing, supporting functions such as call distribution, predictive dialling and intelligent voice response. WinWork's services can then be used to manage the follow up actions resulting from the customer dialogue.

Integrated Work systems are installed in insurance, banking, local government, manufacturing, retail, and telecommunications companies.

Integration Solutions, Inc.

Mr. Herbert M. Stephens
3821 20th Street, Suite 6
San Francisco
CA 94114
USA
1 415 206 9686
1 415 206 9686

Mr. Laurence F. Ryan
3821 20th Street, Suite 6
San Francisco
CA 94114
USA
1 415 206 9686

Intelus Corporation

Ms. Carol Dennis
9210 Corporate Blvd.
Rockville
Maryland 20850
USA
1 301 990 6363
1 301 990 6011
info@intelus.com

Mr. Eric Eisenhouwer
9210 Corporate Blvd.
Rockville
Maryland 20850
USA
1 301 990 6363
1 301 990 6011

Intelus' ProcessFlo is an image-enabled document and workflow system that manages information and business processes throughout an organization. Its object-oriented design and graphic set-up capabilities provide a rich environment to support business process reengineering and rapid system prototyping and deployment. In addition, the system incorporates extensive tools for customisation, extension, and integration with legacy systems and other applications. ProcessFlo manages documents in all forms - images, paper, text, data and voice messages as well as providing complete workflow management. The system's modules may be installed separately, together, or in phases.

Intelus has been providing workflow solutions for thirteen years and imaging-enabling these solutions for the past nine years. Intelus is recognized as an industry leader in providing business process management solutions to the financial services industry, healthcare, government and insurance. supplying out-of-the-box workflow solutions in the United States and abroad.

Intelus is a wholly owned subsidiary, but independently operating subdivision of SunGard Data Systems - a leading provider of disaster recovery for the financial industry. SunGard is a multi-national organization with over 3,000 employees and is publicly traded on the NASDAQ stock exchange. As one of the world's largest and most successful information services companies, we promote a culture of strength, service, innovation and excellence in the way we conduct our business.

Intos Information Service
Mr. Gerald Pitschek
Primoschgasse 3
A-9020 Klagenfurt, Austria
43 463 3875 250
43 463 3875 111

Jetform Corporation

Mr. Andrew Jackson
800 South Street
Watermill Center
Waltham, MA 02154
USA
1 617 647 7700
1 617 647 4121
ajackson@jetform.com

Mr. Andrew Jackson
800 South Street
Watermill Center
Waltham, MA 02154
USA
1 617 647 7700
1 617 647 4121
ajackson@jetform.com

JTS Systems
Mr. Joseph Strul
5090 Orbitor Dr.
Mississauga
Ontario L4W 5B2
Canada
1 905 238 4205
1 905 602 7364
joe@jts.com

JTS Systems is a leading developer of workflow and document management software and services. JTS focuses its direct sales force on the Financial Services market, and is active in cooperative marketing initiatives, together with reseller partnerships in markets and regions not served directly by JTS. JTS Systems develops, markets and implements OPEN IMAGE, a fully integrated document management and workflow automation system designed to operate within an open systems client/server environment. JTS Systems also provides a full suite of consulting services - from feasibility studies and workflow analyses to application development and customized integration.

Open Image is a business process automation system that provides production workflow, document management and document imaging functionality in a distributed, client/server framework. The system operates with client software on a variety of server platforms, and MS Windows desktops, together with multiple specialized software servers including the Sybase SQL Server, the Routing Server and the Document Server. JTS' strategy has been to leverage Sybase fully to make Open Image the product of choice in an enterprise where open integration to legacy data stores, Sybase SQL development facilities, superior user-level functionality and true production scaleability are key.

Jupiter Informatie & Management
Mr. M.A.M. Arens
Erasmusweg 1
2202 CA Noordwijk
The Netherlands
31 1719 47384
31 1719 47396

K.U. Leuven
Mr. Ferdi Put   Mr. Frank Janssens
Dept. TEW   Naamsestraat 69
Naamsestraat 69   3000 Leuven
3000 Leuven   Belgium
Belgium
32 16 32 68 76   32 16 32 68 76
32 16 32 67 32   32 16 32 67 32
Ferdi.Put@econ.Kuleuven.ac.be

Keyfile Corporation
Mr. Roger Sullivan
22 Cotton Road
Nashua NH 03063
USA
1 603 883 3800
1 603 889 9259
marketing@keyfile.com

Lawrence Livermore National Laboratory
Mr. Frank Ploof   Mr. Frank Ploof
Business Process Automation Services   P.O. Box 808, L-304
P.O. Box 808, L-304   7000 East Avenue, Livermore
7000 East Avenue, Livermore, CA 94551   CA 94551
USA   USA
1 510 422 6990   1 510 422 6990
1 510 422 3396   1 510 422 3396

LBMS
Mr. David Redmond-Pyle
Sunny Croft
Tarvin Road, Manley
Cheshire WA6 9EW
United Kingdom
44 1928 740 600
44 1928 740 395

Legent Corporation

Mr. Chistopher G. Slatt
411 108th Avenue NE, Suite 600
Bellevue
WA 98004-5515
USA
1 206 688 2000
1 206 688 2051

Mr. Don Ledford
411 108th Avenue NE, Suite 600
Bellevue
WA 98004-5515
USA
1 206 688 2000
1 206 688 2051
ledford@networx.com

Lion Gesellschaft

Dr. Stefan Wolf
Unitech Center
Universitätstrasse 140
D-44799 Bochum
Germany
49 2 34 97 09 381
49 2 34 97 09 111
wolf@lion.de

Dr. Nikolaos Vlachantonis
Unitech Center
Universitätstrasse 140
D-44799 Bochum
Germany
49 234 9709 336
49 234 9709 111
vlachant@lion.de

LION, established in 1985, belongs to VEBACOM, the German-based telecommunication Company of Veba and Cable & Wireless. LION's strategy is to enter into different markets with its horizontal products and services. LION's products and services have been developed based on a strategy of providing the customer with complete, tailor-made solutions.

LION provides a workflow management tool called LEU that supports business process reengineering and workflow management, including activity, organization and data modelling, business process simulation and analysis, application prototyping and application development. In addition to the workflow management services, LION provides a document management and archive system called MegaMedia which is fully integrated in LEU. The first application realized on the basis of LEU is WIS, an information system for Real Estate Management and Housing Construction and Administration.

Further business areas are business support systems for telecommunication services (e.g. billing and accounting software) and the conceptual planning, installation, support, and maintenance of local area networks. For basic communication support LION provides global messaging services like the EDI-tool TIGER or the e-mail, e-fax and clearing services for X.400. LION's training facilities called CAMPUS and SEAson cover the application and management of DOS, Windows and Unix applications as well as the application of software engineering methods and CASE tools.

In 1995 LION had over 400 full-time staff members, and the LION Group had gross revenues of more than 70 million German Marks.

Logical Software Solutions Corporation
Ms. Mary Collier
7701 Greenbelt Road
Suite 207, Greenbelt
MD 20770, USA
1 301 595 2033
1 301 595 2582
mcollier@lssc.com

Lotus Development Corp
Mrs. Judy Jalbert
1 Charles Park
Cambridge Mass 02172
United Kingdom
44 617 693 5461
44 617 693 2426
judy_jalbert@crd.lotus.com

Mrs. Judy Jalbert
1 Charles Park
Cambridge Mass 02172
United Kingdom
44 617 693 5461
44 617 693 2426
judy_jalbert@crd.com

Lucent Technologies
Mr. Thomas Magg
101 Crawfords Corner Road
Room 212-217
Holmdel, NJ 07733-3030
USA
1 908 949 2812
1 908 949 9650
tmagg@attmail.att.com

Mr. Thomas Magg

Mark V Systems Limited
Mr. Herman Fischer
16400 Ventura Boulevard
Suite 300
Encino
CA 91436-2123, USA
1 818 995 7671
1 818 995 4267
fischer@markv.com

Mr. Herman Fisher
16400 Ventura Boulevard
Suite 300
Encino
CA 91436-2123, USA
1 818 995 7671
1 818 995 4267
fisher@markv.com

Mark V Systems designs, develops and markets tools for the process, workflow, enterprise modelling, business process re-engineering and software engineering markets.

ObjectMaker is a graphical modelling CASE Tool using advanced object modelling techniques to support the development and maintenance of complex applications. *ObjectMaker's* open technology can be extended to fit your process and problem domain. Off the shelf tools for Booch, OMT, FUSION, Coad/Yourdon, Shlaer/Mellor, Colbert, Jacobson, Firesmith, Buhr, ADARTS, Martin/Odell, and Wirfs-Brock can also be extended.

ProcessMaker is a graphical modelling tool using process definition notations to capture business, software, workflow or manufacturing processes. *ProcessMaker* supports many notations to create process models, and documentation. Read only tools allow you to distribute and update process and procedure guidance and documentation on-line at no cost.

MethodMaker Graphical Meta Method Tool is a meta tool for methodologists and other tool builders to graphically rapidly prototype tool support for new object oriented methods for software or process engineering. Tool support for typical notations can be prototyped in hours, providing a tool which can be deployed for user feedback. Tool support includes menus, notation, syntax checking, semantic model, data entry and dictionary views, reporting and publishing interfaces.

ObjectMaker TDK Meta CASE Tool is an open meta technology for methodologists and other expert tool groups seeking to control, evolve and extend methods and method integration into their software engineering process. ObjectMaker is a completely open meta technology offering the possibility of creating or extending any method to create a low cost deliverable tool.

MD&A Business Information Services

Mr. Mark Cooper	Ms. Carina Du Preez
P.O. Box 429	P.O. Box 429
Howard Place 7450	Howard Place 7450
Cape	Cape
South Africa	South Africa
27 21 475 029	27 21 475 029
27 21 448 7544	27 21 448 7544
markc@mda.co.za	carina@mda.co.za

MD&A Business Information Services (MD&A) is one of Cape Town's largest software and services organisations. With extensive experience across diverse industry sectors, it has amassed a great wealth of knowledge, skills and technology in application development, software migration, business process and workflow analysis.

MD&A Complete PME Version 1.5 is a family of computer-based workflow tools facilitating business process design, work monitoring and management.

Aimed at increasing the effectiveness of large-volume/high-value businesses processes, MD&A Complete allows users to design their processes and associated tasks, and guide, monitor and manage the work done. Its considerable success in addressing people-intensive, paper-bound process is attributed to three factors:

- It recognises that items of work flow back and forth between various employees in various roles
- It acknowledges that these employees execute very different tasks against the same item of work and that these tasks must be supervised and managed
- It facilitates the design of well-structured repetitive business processes and provides a managed environment addressing the needs of all role players

The Design Workbench was developed to allow process designers to define the tasks and rules governing the business processes. These are directed to the clerical level, which is empowered by The Case Workbench to execute business cases. The supervisor monitors and manages the business case workload using The Control Workbench. Finally, The Statistical Workbench and The Query Workbench facilitate analysis and interpretation of performance at a managerial level. This information is then relayed to the process designer for fine-tuning.

Organisations using MD&A Complete list the following principal benefits:

- reduced errors and administration costs
- higher staff productivity and simplified staff induction
- improved customer services
- streamlined work management and control and increased insight into processes through comprehensive statistics

Mentor Graphics Corporation
Mr. Phil Kilcoin
8005 S.W. Boeckman Road
Wilsonville
OR 97070 - 7777
USA
1 503 685 7000
1 503 685 1282

Mr. Bill Berg
8005 S.W. Boeckman Road
Wilsonville
OR 97070-7777
USA
1 503 685 7000
1 503 685 1282
bberg@wv.mentorg.com

Meramec Software
Mr. Robert Scott
44058 Gala Circle
Ashburn
Virginia 22011, USA
1 703 729 7240
1 703 729 7241

MetaConcepts Inc.
Ms. Michelle Singh
214 King Street West
Suite 513
Toronto, Ontario M5H 3S6
Canada
1 416 506 1293
1 416 506 0390

Meta Group
Mr. David Yockelson
208 Harbor Drive
Stamford
CT 06912
USA
1 203 973 6744
1 203 359 8066
davidy@metagroup.com
Meta-Generics Ltd.
Mr. Stephen Bull
The Jeffreys Building
St John's Innovation Park
Cowley Road, Cambridge CB4 4WS
United Kingdom
44 1223 420 651
44 1223 420 608

Metaphase Technology Inc.
Mr. Jim Heppelmann
4201 Lexington Avenue North
Arden Hills
MN 55126 - 6198
USA
1 612 482 4600
1 612 482 4348

Mr. Jeff Renfroe
4201 Lexington Avenue North
Arden Hills
MN 55126 - 6198
USA
1 612 482 4600
1 612 482 4348
jeff.renfroe@cdc.com

Microsoft Corporation
Mr. Steve Silverberg
One Microsoft Way
Redmond
Washington 98052-6399
USA
1 206 936 9277
1 206 936 8019
stevesil@microsoft.com

Mr. Andrew Wallace
One Microsoft Way
Redmond
WA 98052-6399
USA
1 206 936 6175
1 206 936 8019
anderwwa@microsoft.com

National Life Of Vermont

Mr. Mark E. Tucker
N-600, One National Life Drive
Montpelier
Vermont 05604-1000
USA
1 802 229 3445
1 802 229 7184
71102.2314@compuserve.com

Mr. Mark E. Tucker
One National Life Drive
Montpellier
Vermont 05604-1000
USA
1 802 229 3445
1 802 229 7184
71102.2314@compuserve.com

Network Imaging Systems Corp.

Mr. Bob Foster
500 Huntmar Park Drive
Herndon, VA 22070
USA
1 703 478 2260
1 703 481 6920
jeffreya@msmailhq.netimage.com

Mr. Brad Clemmens
500 Huntmar Pard Drive
Herndon, VA 22070
USA

Network Imaging Corporation (NIC) is an international developer of object-oriented, client/server software solutions that address the business challenges associated with managing multimedia (graphs, charts, text, audio files, video clips) across distributed networks.

View, which is composed of View:Object Manager, View:Workflow, View:EDM (Engineering Document Management), View:COLD (Computer Output to Laser Disk), and the newly released View:Web Multimedia Object Manager (WebMOM), provides systems integrators and value added resellers with the ability to integrate multimedia data into any existing application. View offers an open solution that supports any database product and provides unlimited scaleability over heterogeneous environments. View:Web Multimedia Object Manager extends the NIC mission to the Web market by providing a technology converging client/server and Web access with multimedia applications.

View:Workflow provides a software structure for logically connecting business tasks into a rules-based relational database workflow system. It provides a graphical representation of business processes, and associates users and tasks to automate the flow of data throughout the enterprise. View:Workflow is designed to operate and control an open systems environment, co-ordinating the flow of work between systems operating on multiple platforms regardless of data storage type, database, or application software. This allows previously incompatible systems to co-ordinate organizational resources without major system overhauls.

View:Workflow operates in conjunction with View:Object Manager to provide an integrated, single view of how your organization conducts business, and provides a comprehensive road map for system integration and access to every type of data you use.

Nihon Unisys
Mr. Tetsu Tada
1-1-1 Toyosu
Koto-ku
Tokyo 135
Japan
81 3 5546 4592
81 3 5546 7808
tetsu.tada@unisys.co.jp

Novell, Inc.

Mr. David Hamson
1555 North Technology Way
Mailstop M334
Orem, UT 84057
USA
1 801 222 3936
1 801 222 4677
dhamson@novell.com

Mr. David Hamson
1555 North Technology Way
Mailstop M334
Orem, UT 84057
USA
1 801 222 3936
1 801 222 4677
dhamson@novell.com

Officeware Ltd
Mr. Alexandre Melo
Av. Brigadeiro Faria Lima 1698 CJ 51
01452-001 Sao Paolo SP
Brazil
55 11 816 3439
55 11 816 3895
officewa@embratel.net.br

Open Text Corporation

Mr. Warren B. Clark
180 Columbia Street West
Waterloo
Ontario, N2L 3L3
Canada
519 888 7111
519 888 0677
wbclark@opentext.com

Mr. David Weinberger
180 Columbia Street West
Waterloo
Ontario, N2L 3L3
Canada

davidw@opentext.com

Open Text Livelink Intranet is the first and most comprehensive intranet application suite, enabling organizations to co-ordinate and control the collaborative work of people no matter where they are located. Livelink Intranet provides robust document management, visual workflow, powerful searching and a productive collaborative project environment that can be accessed by anyone with a standard Web browser and a secure password.

With Livelink, users create workflows using a visual, drag and drop "workflow painter" that supports serial and parallel workflows, conditional routing, rendezvous steps, milestones, and the inclusion of sub-maps so that arbitrarily complex processes can be modelled. Livelink's workflow module is completely integrated with its document management functionality. Documents and any other type of object can be sent through a workflow while simultaneously under the control of the library manager that provides security, versioning, compound document management, and full audit trails.

Because this functionality is accessible through a standard Web browser, Livelink can make workflow and document management available on a far wider scale than has been typical for such systems. And because Livelink is server-based software with no per-user charge, it breaks barriers in the cost per seat so that it becomes feasible as an enterprise-wide tool for collaborative work.

Optika
Mr. A.J. Wand   Mr. Robert Latham
5755 Mark Dabling Blvd.   5755 Mark Dabling Blvd.
Colorado Springs   Colorado Springs
CO 80919   CO 80919
USA   USA
1 719 548 9800   1 719 548 9800
1 719 531 7915   1 719 531 7915
awand@optika.com

Oracle Corporation

Ms Tanya Johnson   Mr. Davor Matic
500 Oracle Parkway   500 Oracle Parkway
Box 659210   Box 659509
Redwood Shores, CA 94065   Redwood Shores, CA 94065
USA   USA
1 415 506 4815   1 415 506 5543
1 415 506 7421   1 415 506 7120
tjohnson@us.oracle.com   dmatic@us.oracle.com

Oracle Workflow is a complete workflow management system that supports business process definition and automation. It is tightly integrated with Oracle database, Developer/2000 tools, and Oracle Applications. It is optimized for the Oracle environment to provide enterprise-wide workflow solutions.

Oracle Workflow supports branching, looping, parallel and sub flows. Each activity is either a PL/SQL function which is automatically executed by the engine, or a human activity that needs to be performed by a user.

The main components of Oracle Workflow are the Workflow Engine, the Notification Service, the Workflow Designer, administrative tools, and the APIs.

The Workflow Engine is a set of tables and PL/SQL stored procedures that manage the execution of workflow processes, execute workflow rules and track work-in-process. It maintains the state information of all the workflow items and generates a complete audit trail.

The Notification Service sends notifications to appropriate users via a form-based connected viewer, as well as via email or WWW. It also interprets responses and delivers response information to the sender.

The Workflow Designer is a Windows 95 program. It allows the user to graphically define a workflow process and its components including activities, users, notifications, etc.. Oracle Workflow stores all workflow objects in Oracle7.

Oracle Workflow includes a comprehensive set of tools that let the user monitor and administer workflow transactions as well as view and analyse transaction history.

Finally, Oracle Workflow provides a complete set of PL/SQL APIs that can be used to workflow-enable Oracle Applications, document management and imaging applications, and other third party applications.

Ovum
Ms. Heather Stark
1 Mortimer Street
London W1N 7RH
UK
44 171 255 26 70
44 171 255 19 95
has@ovum.mhs.compuserve.com

Paradigm Corporation
Mr. Gary Egan
1515 Woodfield Road, Suite 625
Schaumburg
Illinois 60173, USA
1 708 517 8600
1 708 517 8603

Pavone Informationssysteme GmbH

Mr. Peter Vos
Friederich-List-Strasse 67
33100 Paderborn
Germany
49 5251 52 43 10
49 5251 52 43 11
pvos@notes.uni-paderborn.de

Mr. Wolfgang Hilpert
Friederich-List-Strasse 67
33100 Paderborn
Germany
49 5251 52 43 10
49 5251 5243 11
Whilpert@notes.uni-paderborn.de

Pegasystems Inc.

Ms. Terry Driscoll   Mr. Bill Byrn
101 Main Street   101 Main Street
Cambridge   Cambridge
MA 02142-1590   MA 02142-1590
USA   USA
1 617 374 9600 ex. 279   1 617 374 9600   ex. 145
1 617 374 9620   1 617 374 9620
                                            byrn43@aol.com

Pegasystems Inc. is a leading provider of workflow automation solutions to large-scale, information-intensive industries, with special expertise in the financial services sector and related markets. The company was founded in 1983 upon the principle that institutions must deliver high-quality customer service to attain market differentiation and to sustain long-term financial success. Its workflow solutions, using expert-systems principles, provide an enterprise-wide information/communications backbone. This backbone seamlessly connects an institution's service and operations staff to the specialists, information databases, and computer applications - enabling the institution to improve its internal efficiency and heighten its service delivery. Pegasystems' solutions integrate, automate, and manage all customer service processes and labour-intensive work.

Pegasystems Internet-compliant solutions operate within two or three-tier cooperative processing environments. These solutions currently support users across the U.S., Western Europe and in the Asia/Pacific region.

PeopleSoft, Inc.

Mr. Keith Goldberg
4440 Rosewood Dr., Suite 200
Pleasanton
CA 945 88, USA
1 510 227 3880
1 510 227 3505
keith_goldberg@peoplesoft.com

PeopleSoft, Inc. was established in 1987 to provide innovative software solutions that meet the changing business demands of enterprises worldwide. A client/server applications pioneer and market leader, PeopleSoft develops, markets, and supports a complete suite of workflow-enabled enterprise applications for accounting, materials management, distribution, manufacturing, and human resources. PeopleSoft's innovative use of technology empowers individuals to make informed decisions and manage constant change.

With several hundred *Fortune* 1,000 customers around the world, PeopleSoft has been recognized for both its award-winning customer service and remarkable growth.

PeopleSoft product and service information can be located on the World Wide Web at http://www.peoplesoft.com.

Perseo
Mr. Antonio Salvati
Piazza San Babila 3
20122 Milano, Italy
39 2 781 909
39 2 760 217 18
salvati@perseo.it

Portfolio Technologies

Mr. Ernie Moore
5600 Mowry School Road, Suite 100
Newark
California 94560, USA
1 510 226 5627
1 510 226 8182
emoore@officeiq.com

Powersoft Corporation

Mr. David S. Bakin
1111 Bayhill Drive # 125
San Bruno
CA 94066, USA
1 415 872 1543 ext. 5018
1 415 872 3033
dbakin@powersoft.com

Mr. David S. Bakin
1111 Bayhill Drive # 125
San Bruno
CA 94066, USA
1 415 872 1543 ext. 5018
1 415 872 3033
dbakin@powersoft.com

PPP Healthcare
Mr. Simon Tomlinson
Philips House
Crescent Road, Tunbridge Wells
Kent TN1 2PL
United Kingdom
44 1892 503 723
44 1892 503 810
simon.tomlinson@pppgroup.co.uk

Praxis Plc.
Mr. Martyn Ould
20 Manvers Street
Bath BA1 1PX, UK
44 1225 444700
44 1225 465205
mao@praxis.co.uk

Project Consult
Dr. Ulrich Kampffmeyer
Project Consult Unternehmensberatung
Oderfelder Strasse 17
20149 Hamburg
Germany
49 40 46 07 62 20
49 40 46 07 62 29
100422.361@compuserve.com

PROMATIS Informatik
Dr. Frank Schönthaler   Mr. Tibor Németh
Descostr. 10   Descostr. 10
D-76307 Karlsbad   D-76307 Karlsbad
Germany   Germany
49 7248 9145-0
49 7248 9145-19
hq@PROMATIS.DE

Quality Decision Management
Mr. Andrew Jeffrey
200 Sutton Street, Suite 225
North Andover
MA 01845
USA
1 508 688 8266
1 508 688 5181

Rank Xerox Research Centre
Mr. Daniele Pagani
6 Chemin de Maupertuis
38240 Meylan
France
33 7661 5084
33 7661 5099
PAGANI@XEROX.FR

Reach Sofware Corporation
Mr. David Bernstein
872 Hermosa Drive
Sunnyvale
California 94086, USA
1 408 733 8685 x 275
1 408 733 9265
davebern@netcom.com

Riverton Software
Mr. Jerry Katzke
1 Kendall Square
Bldg. 200, Suite 2200
Cambridge, MA 02139
USA
1 617 621 7102
1 617 577 1209
73672.2315@compuserve.com

Mr. David Russell
1 Kendall Square
Bldg. 200, Suite 2200
Cambridge, MA 02139
USA
1 617 621 7102
1 617 577 1209

Royal Bank Of Canada
Mr. Rick Uy
Systems & Technology
315 Front Street W, 15th Floor
Toronto, Ontario M5V 3A4
Canada
1 416 348 5550
1 416 348 5217
carbcfhc@ibmmail.com

SAP AG
Dr. Harald Eckert
Neurottstrasse 16
D-69190 Walldorf
Germany

49 6227 34 2878
49 6227 34 1666
eckert@sap-ag.de

Dr. Harald Eckert
Neurottstrasse 16
D-69190 Walldorf
Germany

49 6227 34 2878
49 6227 34 1666
eckert@sap-ag.de

Founded in 1972, SAP AG has grown to become one of the largest independent software companies in the world and is the market leader in standard business software applications. The company, which is headquartered in Walldorf, Germany, now employs over 7,000 people. In addition to SAP AG in Walldorf the company is globally represented in over 40 countries. With its standard systems, R/2 for mainframes and R/3 for client/server platforms, SAP serves over 6,000 customers in over 50 countries.

With SAP Business Workflow – a part of the R/3 version 3.0 product suite – SAP offers enterprise-wide process automation functionality as a central component of the R/3 System. SAP Business Workflow provides the infrastructure and tools to allow department and application-spanning business processes to be managed, automated and analysed as related entities across the entire company.

SAP Business Workflow views business processes from two perspectives: (1) the processes as they relate to the business, and, (2) the organization as it relates to the processes. R/3 and SAP Business Workflow manage both perspectives and provides the foundation for cross-application process automation and continuous process improvement. SAP Business Workflow capitalizes on the investment made in the R/3 system and exploits the capabilities and benefits of the architecture, services and integrated applications to facilitate the automation and evolution of business processes. SAP Business Workflow is well equipped to assist companies in meeting the challenges presented by evolutionary business processes – today as well as tomorrow.

SAS Institute Inc.

Mr. Steve Jenisch
SAS Campus Drive
Cary
NC 27513, USA
1 919 677 8000 ext. 7956
1 919 677 8123
sassjj@unx.sas.com

Mr. Steve Jenisch
SAS Campus Drive
Cary
NC 27513, USA
1 919 677 8000 ext. 7956
1 919 677 8123
sassjj@unx.sas.com

SEPT
Mr. Hervé Le Corre
42 Rue des Coutures
BP 6243
14066 Caen Cedex
France
33 31 75 91 41
33 31 75 06 31
lecorre@sept.fr

Mr. Patrice Henry
42 Rue des Coutures
BP 6243
14066 Caen Cedex
France
33 31 75 91 11
33 31 75 06 31
patrice.henry@sept.fr

Sema Groq Sae

Mr. Alejandro De Mora-Lozana
Albarracrin 25
28037 Madrid, Spain
34 13 27 28 28
34 17 54 32 52
ademora@sema.es

Mr. Agurtin Gonzalez-Quel
Albarracrin 25
28037 Madrid, Spain
34 13 27 28 28
34 17 54 32 52
agonzalez@sema.es

Siemens Nixdorf Informationssysteme

Mr. Gerhard Wernke
Heinz-Nixdorf-Ring 1
33106 Paderborn
Germany
49 52 518 11618
49 52 518 11926
wernke.pad@sni.de

Mr. Gerhard Wernke
Heinz-Nixdorf-Ring 1
33106 Paderborn
Germany
49 52 518 11618
49 52 518 11926
wernke.pad@sni.de

With annual sales of around DM 12 billion, Siemens Nixdorf is the largest Europe-based information technology (IT) vendor. The global business is divided into three areas: services, solutions and products.

Siemens Nixdorf's product business includes the WorkParty workflow management product. WorkParty provides an open, customizable framework for the management of business cases and related workflows. WorkParty is the strategic product of Siemens Nixdorf in this area. WorkParty comprises a Workflow Manager, a Business Case Manager, and an Organization and Resources Manager.

A business case within WorkParty is represented by related documents, data and workflows. Databases (e.g. Oracle, Informix), document management systems (e.g. DocuLive), archiving systems (e.g. Arcis) and host emulations are options within WorkParty.

The workflow management subset of WorkParty is a toolset for defining workflows and a run-time system for managing workflows. It provides process-oriented handling of data and documents according to a predefined or ad hoc process definition. A graphical workflow editor, an activity editor, an event manager and a worklist handler are the major components.

The Business Case Manager provides information on business cases as well as their administration and operation in accordance with predefined authorizations.

The Organization and Resources Manager - ORM - is a flexible organization modelling tool. Organizations are modelled in terms of employees, roles, positions, resources, organizational units, proxies and tasks.

WorkParty is very strong in defining activity descriptions, managing roles and related organizational behaviour, accessing the functionality via an API, handling events and creating customer-oriented views of worklists and business cases.

Further information on WorkParty is provided at:

http://www.sni.de/public/aswba/offers/workflow/workflow.htm

SINTEF Informatics
Mr. Steinar Carlsen
Information Systems
P.O. Box 124, Blindern
0314 Oslo, Norway
47 2206 7425
47 2206 7350
steinar.carlsen@si.sintef.no

Mr. David Skogan
SINTEF Informatics
P.O. Box 124, Blindern
N-0314 Oslo, Norway
47 2206 7300
47 2206 7350
David.Skogan@si.sintef.no

Sodan
Mr. Keith Hales
20 Mead Road
Uxbridge, Middlesex UB8 1AU
United Kingdom
44 1895 233 194
44 1895 233 194
100322.127@compuserve.com

Softlab GmbH
Mr. Rainer Keser
Zamdorfer Strasse 120
81677 München, Germany
49 89 93001 517
49 89 9302 761
kes@softlab.de

Mr. Gebhard Greiter
Zamdorfer Strasse 120
81677 München, Germany
49 89 9300 10
49 89 9302 761

Softswitch

Mr. Don Fisher
640 Lee Road
Wayne
Pennsylvania 19087
USA
1 215 640 9600
1 215 640 7550

Software 2000

Mr. Jeff Broberg
25 Communications Way
Drawer 6000
Hyannis, MA 02601
USA
1 508 778 20 00 ext. 2809
1 508 778 54 20
Jeff_Broberg@S2K.com

Mr. Jeffrey C. Broberg
25 Communications Way
Drawer 6000
Hyannis, MA 02601
USA
1 508 778 20 00
1 508 778 54 20
Jeff_Broberg@S2K.com

Software AG

Mr. Ralf Meyer
Uhlandstrasse 12
64297 Darmstadt
Germany
49 6151 92 3299
49 6151 92 3220
rme@software-AG.de

Mr. James van Dort
Uhlandstrasse 12
64297 Darmstadt
Germany
49 6151 92 3299
49 6151 92 3220

SOFTWARE AG, Darmstadt (Germany) was founded in 1969 and is still privately owned. Today, it ranks among the world's leading independent software vendors and service providers.

- Revenue: $533 million
- Customers: an estimated 5000 in over 80
  countries

SOFTWARE AG is a member of international associations such as X/Open, the Open Software Foundation (OSF), the Workflow Management Coalition (WfMC), the Object Management Group (OMG), the Message-Oriented Middleware Association (MOMA), and the European Data Warehouse Network.

ENTIRE Workflow is an integrated Workflow Management Product, enabling corporations to model their organisation using IT. The resulting Process Model is thus able to plan, direct and monitor business processes. Using MS Windows Clients, ENTIRE Workflow supports both structured and unstructured processes, with powerful interfaces to the corporate database and a comfortable user interface.

ENTIRE Workflow is database-driven, using modern ODBC technology to achieve database independence. Control-information, reports, graphs, specialist data and documents are stored in the database. A process model is constructed using an intuitive Graphical User Interface. Business activities, application interfaces and flow control can thus be interactively "painted" using state-of-the-art techniques such as drag-and-drop.

ENTIRE Workflow is fully object-oriented, providing functions such as encapsulation, full-fledged inheritance of features, and object reusability, including template reuse. Using version control, the evolution and history of a Process Flow model can be documented.

Across the total range of products in the ENTIRE product line, full integration of various applications on all important platforms can be achieved. SOFTWARE AG's alliance with Microsoft will provide the ability to connect across all platforms via OLE/COM, creating genuine cross platform support. This will enhance the competitive appeal of the product to large corporates.

Software Daten Service GmbH

Mr. Wolfgang Petzl
Aspernbrückengasse 2
1020 Vienna, Austria
43 1 21156 3591
43 1 21156 3590
sdssec@sds.co.at

Mr. Dietmar Auer
Hollandstrasse 11-13
1020 Vienna, Austria
43 1 21156 3501
43 1 21156 3590

Software Engineering Institute
Dr. Alan Christie
Carnegie Mellon University
4500 Fifth Avenue
Pittsburgh, PA 15213-3890, USA
1 412 268 6324
1 412 268 5758

Software Ley GmbH

Mr. Dietmar Ley
Venloerstr. 83-85
50259 Pulheim, Germany
49 2238 96600
49 2238 58330
dl@col.sw-ley.de

Mr. Thomas Basting
Venloerstr. 83-85
50259 Pulheim, Germany
49 2238 96600
49 2238 50842
tb@col.sw-ley.de

Software-Ley GmbH is an early workflow pioneer, and has a competitive workflow product based on sound technology. The German company, based near Cologne, employs over 150 highly qualified professionals working in product development, support, BPR-consulting and training. It is counted as one of the leading European workflow management vendors.

Software-Ley's COSA product-suite is designed to run in a client/server environment as an independent layer used as a service for the modelling, design and control of applications, activities and tasks within business processes.

COSA BPR Toolkit is a tool for the redesign, documentation and simulation of business processes. Designed as a descriptive tool, it provides an intuitive graphical representation and documentation features.

COSA Workflow is a workflow management system offering tools for the modelling, analysis and control of business processes. COSA Workflow acts as a software integration layer for distributed application environments and systems. It is designed to run in heterogeneous environments embedding any major standard SQL database, and it supports the creation of prototypes with subsequent delta analysis as part of an iterative process. COSA Workflow complies with the reference model of the Workflow Management Coalition.

COSA Archive is a system for archiving and retrieving coded and non-coded information on various types of electronic media. A powerful COLD module and a user-friendly scan front-end complement the COSA Archive product.

The product architecture can be extended by three new add-ons: COSA IntraNet, a solution extending COSA Workflow functionality to the Internet; COSA MSA which provides distributed and scaled data management & storage; COSA SoftLink the solution for third-party application integration.

Staffware

Mr. Nick Kingsbury   Mr. Jon Pyke
Halifax House, Halifax Place   Staffware House
The Lace Market   3 The Switchback
Nottingham NG1 1QN, UK   Gardener Road, Maidenhead
44 115 9483088   Berkshire SL6 7RJ, UK
44 115 9483459   44 171 262 1021
nkingsbury@cix.compulink.co.uk   44 171 262 3956
                                                       jpyke@staffware.com

Staffware pioneered Workflow Automation as early as 1984, and currently has more than 100,000 users around the globe.

Applauded by leading industry analysts as being in the vanguard of workflow, the award winning Staffware family offers rich integration facilities with other software products, while protecting investment in existing legacy systems. Operating independently of any specific application development environment, database or DIP system, it integrates with external databases, such as Oracle and Informix, and other software products including email, text and image processing, and general office applications

Staffware places particular emphasis on quality customer support. With its extensive international partner network, the company can deploy some 500 workflow specialists worldwide. This is the largest group of its type in the world, dedicated solely to workflow-based solutions

Staffware's lead in workflow has been recognised by major computer system vendors, and the product has been adopted as part of their strategic client server offerings by IBM, ICL, Unisys, Digital and Data General.

The Staffware software runs on all popular UNIX platforms, with support for character based terminals, Windows NT (client and server), Windows 95, and Apple Mac clients. In a major development programme, Staffware is also being ported to the IBM OS/2 operating environment.

Staffware has offices across Europe, in the USA and Australia. Local support is also provided through authorised distributors in most other countries worldwide.

Standard Life Assurance Company Ltd.
Mr. John Sharp
3 George Street
Edinburgh EH2 2XZ
United Kingdom
44 131 245 1014
44 131 245 1020
100434.3061@compuserve.com

Mr. John Sharp
3 George Street
Edinburgh EH2 2XZ
United Kingdom
44 131 245 1014
44 131 245 1020
100434.3061@compuserve.com

SWT GmbH
Mr. Hans-Josef Homscheid
Auf den Tongruben 3
D-53721 Siegburg
Germany
49 2241 904 502
49 2241 904 509
homscheid@swt-am.com

Sybase, Inc.
Mr. David Dyda
2000 Powell Street
4th Floor, Emeryville
California USA 94608
USA
1 510 922 0198
1 510 922 4747
DDYDA@SYBASE.COM

Synapsis
Mr. Oscar Lopez
Santa Domingo
814 Piso 10, Santiago
Chile
56 2 632 1240
56 2 6965999

Systor AG
Mr. Frank Sauter
Business Unit Manager
Enterprise Workflow Solutions
Baslerstrasse 60
CH-8048 Zurich
41 1 405 32 94
41 1 405 31 13
100560.1217@compuserve.com

Tactica Corporation
Mr. Joe Krisky
10300 SW Greenburg Road #500
Portland
OR 97223
USA
1 503 293 9585
1 503 293 9590

Mr. Ron Parsons
10300 SW Greenburg Road #500
Portland,
OR 97223
USA
1 503 293 9585
1 503 293 9590

Tandem Computers Incorporated
Mr. Johannes Klein
10200 North Tantau Avenue
Cupertino
CA 95014-2543, USA
1 408 285 5094
1 408 285 2227

Mr. Jeri Edwards
10200 North Tantau Avenue
Cupertino
CA 95014-2543, USA
1 408 285 0000
1 408 285 2227

Technical University Of Berlin
Mr. Gérard Derszteler
Informatik/Systemanalyse
Sekr. FR 6-7
Franklinstrasse 28/29
10587 Berlin
Germany
49 30 314 73 135 / 49 30 314 73 260
49 30 314 22 357
gerard@sysana.cs.tu-berlin.de

Mr. Gérard Derszteler
Informatik/Systemanalyse
Sekr. FR 6-7
Franklinstrasse 28/29
10587 Berlin
Germany
49 30 314 73 135
49 30 314 22 357
gerard@sysana.cs.tu-berlin.de

Technical Univ. Of Darmstadt
Ms. Susanne Strahringer
FB 1, BWL 5
Hochschulstr. 1
D-64289 Darmstadt
Germany
49 6151 16 4416
49 6151 16 5162

Technical University of Dresden
Mr. Markus Böhm
Fakultät Informatik
Lehrstuhl DatenBanken
Dürerstrasse 26
01307 Dresden, Germany
49 351 4575 493
boehm@IS2201.inf.tu-dresden.de

Mr. Wolfgang Schulze
Fakultät Informatik
Lehrstuhl DatenBanken
Dürerstrasse 26
01307 Dresden, Germany
49 351 4575 493
schulze@IS2201.inf.tu-dresden.de

Technical University Of Wien

Mr. Harald Stadlbauer
INFA
Gusshausstr. 27-29/361
A-1040 Vienna
Austria
43 1 58801 4040
43 1 505 5983
harald@infa.tuwien.ac.at

Mr. Martin Kollingbaum
INFA
Gusshausstr. 27-29/361
A-1040 Vienna
Austria
43 1 58801 4040
43 1 505 5983

Technology Deployment Inc.
Mr. Nan Xiong
3075 Citrus Circle, Suite 207
Wulnut Creek
CA 94598, USA

Telstra Applied Technologies
Mr. Basil C.P. Borun
Corporate & Government
16-18 Bridge Street, Level 4
Epping NSW 2121
Australia
61 2 868 8562
61 2 869 0261
bborun@wr.com.au   basilb@tulpi.interconnect.com.au (priv)

Ten Ham Informatiesystemen B.V.

Mr. Cor H. Visser
Barneveldseweg 100
Postbus 77
6740 AB Lunteren
The Netherlands
31 342 42 6242
31 342 42 6243

Mr. Cor H. Visser
Barneveldseweg 100
Postbus 77
6740 AB Lunteren
The Netherlands
31 342 42 6242
31 342 42 6243

Tesseract
Ms. Christine Dover
475 Sansome Street
San Francisco
CA 94111
USA
1 415 981 1800
1 415 981 6400

Mr. Mark Barrenechea

The Coca-Cola Company

Mr. William L. Kalahar
P.O. Drawer 1734
Atlanta
GA 30301
USA
1 404 676 4656
1 404 676 2215

Ms. Julie Lawlor
1197 Peach Tree
Atlanta
GA 30309
USA
1 404 676 4656
1 404 676 2215
juliel@ko.com

The CocaCola Company is the global soft drink industry leader. Consumers in nearly 200 countries enjoy the company's products at a rate of more than 800 million servings a day. The CocaCola Company consistently delivers on its stated goals for the business, thereby creating value and wealth for the company's share owners. Since 1980, its share price has grown at an average annual compound rate of 24 percent, creating nearly $89 billion in share owner wealth. During this same period, the Dow Jones Industrial Average and the S&P 500 increased 12 percent and 11 percent per year, respectively.

The CocaCola Company now finds itself faced with a new long-term priority. This long-term priority involves combining state-of-the-art technology to capture information that will serve as the basis of value-added decision-making. In the rapidly changing information environment that is the essence of the communication age, the accessibility of meaningful enterprise-wide information is essential for a global focus. Utilizing state-of-the-art technologies in areas that include client/server processing, global data management, workflow and enterprise-wide integration, The CocaCola Company is positioned to embark on an aggressive journey to evolve its information systems and business processes into an effective global model for doing business in the next century.

The Ohio State University

Mr. Tom D. Sanfilippo
A.R.M.S., J. Leonard Camera Center
5th Floor - Residential Building
2050 Kenny Road, Columbus
OH 43221, USA
1 614 688 3380
1 614 688 3330
sanfilippo.l@osu.edu

Mr. Andrew W. Gray
A.R.M.S., J. Leonard Camera Center
5th Floor - Res. Build.
2050 Kenny Rd., Columbus
OH 43221, USA
1 614 688 4397
1 614 688 3330
laszlo+@osu.edu

TIMS Technology Ltd.

Mr. Oliver Goh
Zollikerstrasse 249
8008 Zürich, Switzerland
41 1 389 16 80
41 1 388 60 11
GO@tims.ch

Mr. Oliver Goh
Zollikerstrasse 249
8008 Zürich, Switzerland
41 1 389 16 80
41 1 388 60 11
GO@tims.ch

T-Kartor Sweden AB
Mr. Sten Ravhed
Box 5097
S-29105 Kristianstad
Sweden
46 44 206 800
46 44 128 256
info@t-kartor.se

Mr. Anders Persson
Box 5097
S-29105 Kristianstad
Sweden
46 44 206 800
46 44 128 256
info@t-kartor.se

Tscheinig & Partner
Mr. Gerhard Tscheinig
Nussdorferstrasse 18
1090 Wien, Austria
43 1 31 999 06
43 1 31 999 07
g.tscheinig@magnet.at

TSI International
Mr. Connie Galley
45 Danbury Road
Wilton
CT 06897-0840, USA
1 203 761 8600
1 203 762 9677
CFG%491-9049@mcimail.com

TT Government Service Ltd.
Mr. Pentti Saastamoinen   Mr. Pentti Saastamoinen
PL 403   PL 403
02101 Espoo   02101 Espoo
Finland   Finland
358 0 4571   358 0 4571
358 0 464 803   358 0 464 803
VTKK.V1PSS@ELVI.VTKK.FI   VTKK.V1PSS@ELVI.VTKK.FI

Twijnstra Gudde
Mr. Aart J. Van Den Berg   Mr. Aart J. Van Den Berg
Postbus 907   Postbus 907
3800 AX Amersfoort   3800 AX Amersfoort
Holland   Holland
31 33 467 77 77   31 33 467 77 77
31 33 467 76 66   31 33 467 76 66
abe@TG.NL   abe@TG.NL

UBIS GmbH
Mr. Josef Michel   Mr. Christoph Herbster
Alt-Moabit 98   Alt-Moabit 98
10559 Berlin   10559 Berlin
Germany   Germany
49 30 39 929 775   49 30 39 929 774
49 30 39 929 900   49 30 39 929 900
hch@ubis.de   mi@ubis.de

UBIS GmbH (Consultants for Integrated Systems Ltd.) was founded in 1988 in Berlin.

Professional Activities

- Management Consulting
- Information management consulting with elaboration regarding suitable IT-strategies
- Business process reengineering including the implementation of complex information and communication systems
- Evaluation and restructuring of work-flow processes and personnel structures
- SAP-integration consulting focusing on process and system optimization
- Implementation of object-oriented technologies
- Support of migration to Host-Client/server architectures
- Information Security consulting including risk analysis
- Security planning and realization for data processing centres, decentralized IS architectures and communication infrastructures

Software development

- Development of integrated, computer-based workplaces
- Implementation of client/server-applications
- Selection and integration of standard software systems (PPS, CAD)
- Development and integration of individual software solutions for production control
- Design and realization of information systems (MIS, EIS) for various business areas, e.g. planning, controlling, finance and accounting
- Development of electronic Business Process Reengineering tools

Software Products

- BONAPART - MS-Windows-based application software for dynamic organization engineering which provides users with graphic PC-tools that allow company-wide communication, system analysis and modelling. These tools support the set-up, analysis and optimization of complex company structures by means of dynamic simulation.

UES-KIC

Mr. Bruce Reed   Mr. Bruce Reed
5162 Blazer Memorial Parkway   5162 Blazer Memorial Parkway
Dublin, Ohio 43017, USA   Dublin, Ohio 43017, USA
1 614 792 9993   1 614 792 9993
1 614 792 0998   1 614 792 0998
breed@columbus.ues.com   breed@columbus.ues.com

UES, Inc., Knowledge Integration Center, supports the WfMC goal of interoperability between workflow tools through its participation as a member of the NIIIP (National Industrial Information Infra-structure Protocols) Project which is developing interoperability standards to enable virtual enterprises to collaborate on the Internet. One of the UES roles in this important DoD/ARPA-sponsored project will be to make the WfMC nominated APIs CORBA compliant. UES is the developer of KI Shell, a generic workflow engine, which is standards-based, 100% open and designed to run in heterogeneous environments.

UES is also a participant, along with several leading aerospace, automotive, and electronics manufacturers in the NCMS-sponsored Project Endeavor which is aimed at developing a cost-effective, business process-driven Information Technology architecture that will encompass concurrent engineering team synchronization, task-oriented data retrieval and application launch, metrics, business process simulation and project management.

UES, with over 20 years of research and development sponsored by the United States Air Force Manufacturing Materials Directorate, NIST, NSF, and such commercial enterprises as IBM, has led the way towards the development of a standards-based, enterprise-wide process infrastucture. KI Shell was one of the first commercial generic workflow engines to be installed. It continues to lead the industry with its Systems Integration Library of over 1,000 APIs that are capable of enabling interoperability between executable process models and applications.

Web Site: http://www.columbus.ues.com

Universal Systems Inc.
Mr. Mike Mikolosko   Mr. Bob Hyer
14585 Avion Parkway   14585 Avion Parkway
Chantilly   Chantilly
Virginia 22021   Virginia 22021
USA   USA
1 703 222 2840   1 703 222 2840
1 703 222 0543   1 703 222 0543
                                           bhyer@USIVA.com

University of Bamberg
Dr. Michel Amberg   Dr. Michael Amberg
Feldkirchenstrasse 21   Feldkirchenstrasse 21
D-96045 Bamberg   D-96045 Bamberg
Germany   Germany
49 951 863 2578   49 951 863 2578
49 951 396 36   49 951 396 36
michael.amberg@sowi.uni-bamberg.de   michael.amberg@sowi.uni-bamberg.de

University of Edinburgh
Prof. Austin Tate
Artificial Intelligence Applications Institute
80 South Bridge
Edinburgh EH1 1HN
United Kingdom
44 131 650 2732
44 131 650 6513
A.tate@ed.ac.uk

University of Erlangen-Nuernberg
Dr. Stefan Jablonski
Lehrstuhl für Datenbanksysteme (Informatik VI)
Martensstrasse 3
D-91508 Erlangen
Germany
49 9131 85 7885
49 9131 32 090
jablonski@informatik.uni-erlangen.de

University of Georgia
Dr. Amit Sheth
Department of Computer Science
415 Graduate Studies
  Research Center
Athens, GA 30602-7404
Greece
30 706 542 2911
30 706 542 2966
amit@cs.uga.edu

Dr. Amit Sheth
415 Graduate Studies
  Research Center
Athens, GA 30602-7404
Greece
30 706 542 2911
30 706 542 2966
amit@cs.uga.edu

University of Hohenheim
Dr. Helmut Kromar
49 711 459 3345 / 3684
49 711 459 3687
kromar@uni.hohenheim.de

Mr. Dietmar Weiss
49 711 459 3345 / 3684
49 711 459 3687
dweiss@uni.hohenheim.de

University of Linz
Dr. Markus Gappmaier
Institut für Wirtschaftsinformatik
Altenbergestrasse 69
A-4040 Linz-Auhof
Austria
43 732 2468 9453
43 732 2468 9452
gappmaier@winie.uni-linz.ac.at

Mr. Markus Gappmaier
Institut für Wirtschaftsinformatik
Altenbergestrasse 69
A-4040 Linz-Auhof
Austria
43 732 2468 9453
43 732 2468 9452
gappmaier@winie.uni-linz.ac.at

University of Manchester
Mr. David Wastell
University of Manchester
Computer Science Department
Oxford Road
Manchester M13 9PL
United Kingdom
44 161 275 6172
44 161 275 6200

University of St. Gallen
Dr. Petra Vogler
Institute for Information Management
Dufourstrasse 50
CH-9000 St. Gallen
Switzerland
41 71 302 420
41 71 228 756
Petra.Vogler@IWI.UNISG.CH

Dr. Petra Vogler
Dufourstrasse 50
CH-9000 St. Gallen
Switzerland

41 71 302 420
41 71 228 756
Petra.Vogler@IWI.UNISG.CH

University of Stuttgart
Mr. Franz Fabian   Mr. Friedemann Schwenkreis
Institute of Parallel and Distributed   IPVR
High-Performance Systems (IPVR)   Breitwiesenstr. 20-22
Breitwiesenstr. 20-22, Stuttgart D-70565 D-70565 Stuttgart
Germany   Germany
49 711 7816 351   49 711 7816 223
49 711 7816 444   49 711 7816 424
franz.fabian@infomatik.uni-stuttgart.de   schwenk@informatik.uni-stuttgart.de

University of Twente

Mr. Stef Joosten
Department of Computer Science
P.O. Box 217
7500 AE Enschede
The Netherlands
31 53 893436
31 53 339605
joosten@cs.utwente.nl

University of Ulm
Dr. Peter Dadam   Dr. Peter Dadam
Oberer Eselsberg   Oberer Eselsberg
D-89081 Ulm   D-89081 Ulm
Germany   Germany
49 731 502 4130   49 731 502 4130
49 731 502 4134   49 731 502 4134
dadam@informatik.uni-ulm.de   dadam@informatik.uni-ulm.de

University of Vienna

Prof Dimitris Karagiannis   Mr. S./ R. Junginger/Strobl
BPMS Research-Group   Bruenner Strasse 72
Bruenner Strasse 72   A-1210 Vienna
A-1210 Vienna   Austria
Austria
43 1 291 28 261   43 1 291 28 262
43 1 291 28 264   43 1 291 28 264
dk@dke.univie.ac.at   sjung/robert@dke.univie.ac.at

Business Objectives Consulting – BOC – helps enterprises to become business process management oriented organizations, and to identify the IT potential in their business. BOC customers receive support from experienced staff to help them successfully implement business-driven as well as technology-driven BPR projects.

To achieve these objectives, BOC offers its customers the *BPMS Business Process Management Systems Methodology* and the Workbench *ADONIS*. The company primarily aims at the financial sector and it specializes in the banking and insurance field. Business Process Models and Libraries for these sectors are available.

ADONIS for OS/2 is a Business Process Reengineering Workbench for multi-user modelling, analysis and evaluation of business processes and their underlying organizational structures.
ADONIS for OS/2 supports:

- Identification of business-based drivers and client information: *Information Acquisition Module*
- Creation of a process management organization: *Modelling Module*
- Delivery of significant values and comparable environments for your business: *Analysis Module*
- Estimation of performance while bringing distributed organizations under control: *Simulation Module*
- Linking architectures and standards with the business: *Transformation Module*
- Delivery of customer satisfaction, auditing and monitoring business processes and services: *Evaluation Module*
- Interoperating by interchange of business models and libraries in organizations, using WfMC standards: *Import/Export Module*
- Facilitation of global business by supporting local languages (German, Greek, English, French, Hungarian, Italian, Portuguese, Spanish): *Multi-Language Module*

Viewstar Corporation

Mr. Shirish Hardikar
1101 Marina Village Parkway
Alameda
California 94501
USA
1 510 337 2000
1 510 337 2222
shirishh@viewstar.com

Mr. Jussi Katonen
1101 Marina Village Parkway
Alameda
California 94501
USA
1 510 337 2000
1 510 337 2222
jussik@viewstar.com

ViewStar Corporation provides an open, object-oriented, network-based business process automation software system encompassing workflow automation and document image and information management. ViewStar's software automates mission-critical business processes such as claims and loan processing, accounts payable and receivable, contract management, and more, across a wide range of client/server platforms. ViewStar's product architecture is open and standards-based, allowing the leverage of existing network infrastructures.

ViewStar Release 4 provides true enterprise support by enabling deployment of multiple system configurations involving Windows NT and UNIX servers; offering scaleability from 10 to more than 1,000 users; capabilities to serve one or many geographic locations; and processing capacities to more than 250,000 pages captured and archived per day, and more than 350,000 workflow transactions daily. With ViewStar, users can capture, convert, index, store, retrieve, annotate, route, track, output and manage compound (multimedia) documents.

ViewStar 4.2 offers the industry's first object-oriented interface for rapid development and deployment of mission-critical workflow applications. ViewStar Release 4.2 features the Business Process Interface (BPI) – a rich, component object interface to the ViewStar System. BPI is a combination of application programming interfaces and Microsoft's OLE 2.0 controls that enable developers to use standard third-party OLE 2.0-compliant application building tools such as Visual Basic or Visual C++ to build ViewStar workflow and document imaging applications, and workflow tasks.

In addition, ViewStar 4.2 extends ViewStar's support for the enterprise by enabling automation of wide-area, multi-site workflows that are intelligently linked by standard Microsoft MAPI messaging and replication services.

Vision

Mr. Gerald Adams
4a Prince's Street South
Dublin 2
Ireland
353 1 6771277
353 1 6771642
100101.512@compuserve.com

Mr. Peter Nichols
4a Prince's Street South
Dublin 2
Ireland

VTT, Information Technology
Dr. Jari Veijalainen
Multimedia Systems
P.B. 1203
Fin - 02044 VTT
Finland
358 0 456 6014
358 0 456 7028
Jari.Veijalainen@Vtt.fi

Mr. Aarno Lehtola
P.B. 1203
Fin - 02044 VTT
Finland

358 0 456 6032
358 0 456 6027
Aarno.Lehtola@Vtt.fi

Wang

Mr. Chris Martins
600 Technology Park Drive
Billerica
MA 01821-4130
USA
1 508 967 5252
1 508 967 2210
chris.martins@wang.com

Wang is a worldwide leader in workflow, integrated imaging, network storage management and document management for client/server open systems, and a major worldwide provider of integration and support services. Through a global network of subsidiaries and distributorships, Wang serves customers in more than 130 countries. Wang's software business is a leading provider of enterprise work management software including workflow, imaging, network storage management, COLD, and document management software. With the largest dedicated R&D operation in this market, Wang continues to deliver industry-leading information management technologies.

Wang's desktop imaging and object controls will be incorporated as standard features in future releases of Windows 95 and NT. In addition, Wang leads the industry with more than 1,500 imaging and workflow systems installed worldwide. Its products provide scaleable, enterprise-wide processing power required by high volume production workflow and imaging systems. Wang provides UNIX-based graphical client/server workflow and imaging products and now also offers workflow and imaging products specifically designed to complement Microsoft's BackOffice suite of server components for Windows NT applications. Wang's product offerings also include industry-leading network storage management software and a cutting edge client/server Computer Output to Laser Disk (COLD) data storage solution.

Wang Software, NY
Mr. John Philpit
622 Third Avenue, 30th Floor
New York
NY 10017, USA
1 212 476 7803
1 212 986 0175
john.philpit@wang.uucp.netcom.com

Mr. John Philpit
622 Third Avenue, 30th Floor
New York
NY 10017, USA
1 212 476 7803
1 212 986 0175
john.philpit@wang.uucp.netcom.com

Workflow & Groupware Strategies
Mr. Martin Ader
37 rue Bouret
75019 Paris, France
33 1 42 380 302
33 1 42 380 302
Ader.M.67M@centraliens.fr

W&GS provides consultancy services in French and English. Its main orientations are:

- To determine strategies to make optimal enterprise wide usage of group technologies for enhanced productivity and quality of services

- To conduct opportunity analysis to detect the most profitable short term opportunities
- To establish 3 year master project plans for technology deployment and results measurements
- To monitor pilot projects and deployment projects in achieving their targeted operational results

W&GS insists on quick identification of the most probable targets, precise analysis of costs and benefits before decisions, a serious project plan for the installation and operation of common facilities (network and servers), and hypothesis validation through short duration pilot projects.

W&GS' approach is participative and implies strong internal commitment to short term goals.

Martin Ader created W&GS. He is one the pioneers of group techniques with more than 12 years experience in Computer Supported Co-operative Work research, developments, strategies and marketing in Europe. He had previous experience mainly concentrated on deployment of databases, transaction processing and networking in the public administrations, banks, and insurance companies.

Workflow Automation Ltd.

Mr. Ian Tong
57 Hallington Close
Woking Surrey GU21 3BW, UK
44 1483 755450
44 1483 720312

Workflow Solutions Group, Inc.

Ms. Susan Bird
3 Church Street, Suite 601
Toronto
Ontario M5E 1M2
Canada
1 416 214 2247
1 416 214 2248
workflow@onramp.ca

Mr. Michael Strenge
3 Church Street, Suite 601
Toronto
Ontario M5E 1M2
Canada
1 416 214 2247
1 416 214 2248
workflow@onramp.ca

Workflow Solutions Group Inc is an international consulting organization, based in Toronto, Canada, specializing in Critical Process Innovation and workflow automation. We are a vendor-independent firm that helps organizations to:

- Effectively and creatively redesign mission critical business processes in response to a compelling business imperative
- Analyse the opportunity and the business case for automated workflow
- Rapidly define business requirements for workflow and related technologies

- Evaluate, select and apply automated workflow and related technologies to support the new business model; and
- Understand and manage the process, people, technology and organizational impact issues that come with a workflow implementation initiative

Our consultants are all experienced professionals with diverse, cross-sector backgrounds, which includes management consulting, workflow vendor experience and corporate business and technology leadership. Our associates and affiliates in Canada, the US and the UK include specialists in workflow implementation and integration, Lotus Notes design and implementation, process documentation automation, project management, client/server technology and education, professional facilitation and GDSS, reskilling the I/S professional, and workflow industry analysis.

We are an active funding member of the Workflow Management Coalition (Conformance Working Group, External Relations Committee, Canadian Country Contact).

WorkPoint Systems Inc.
Mr. Barry Goss
500 Airport Blvd., Suite 100
Burlingame
CA 94010, USA
1 415 579 6660
1 415 347 6660
74552.326@compuserve.com

Mr. David Tanzer
500 Airport Blvd., Suite 100
Burlingame
CA 94010, USA
1 415 579 6660
1 415 347 6660

Wurttembergische Versicherung

Mr. Lutz Doblaski
Gutenbergstrasse 30
70176 Stuttgart
Germany
49 711 662 2201
49 711 662 2208

Mrs. Monika Pfleiderer
Gutenbergstrasse 30
70176 Stuttgart
Germany
49 711 662 2874
49 711 662 1630
dedt9xt9@ibmmail.com

Xedox Software Development Pty Ltd.

Mr. Brett Adam
P.O. Box 3038
Burnley North
VIC 3121 Australia

61 3 214 0111
61 3 214 0102
bpja@xedoc.com.au

Mr. Brett Adam
Alma Unit 11
663 Victoria Street
Abbotsford
VIC 3067 Australia
61 3 214 0111
61 3 214 0102

Zürcher Kantonalbank
Mr. Bruno Baumgartner   Mr. Bruno Baumgartner
Abt. INGK   Abt. INGK
Postfach   Postfach
8010 Zürich   8010 Zürich
Switzerland   Switzerland
41 1 275 79 46   41 1 275 79 46
41 1 275 86 46   41 1 275 86 46

Appendices

Further Reading and Sources of Information

1.1 Bibliography

Assembled by Gérard Saccone

1.1.1 Books

Born G., Process Management to Quality Improvement, 1994
    The Way to Design, Document and Re-Engineer Business Systems
    John Wiley & Sons, Chichester, UK

Brelin, H.K., Davenport K., Jennings L., Murphy P., 1995
    Managing for Results
    John Wiley & Sons, Chichester, UK

Champy J., Reengineering Management, 1995
    The mandate for new leadership
    HarperCollins, New York, USA

Cheryl Currid & Company, Reengineering Toolkit, 1995
    15 tools and technologies for reengineering your organization
    Prima Publishing, Rocklin, CA, USA

Coleman D. and Khanna R., Groupware, 1995
    Technologies and Applications
    Prentice Hall, Upper Saddle River, USA

Davenport T., Process Innovation, 1993
    Reengineering Work through Information Technology
    Harvard Business School Press, USA

Fischer L. et al, The Workflow Paradigm, Second Edition, 1995
    The impact of Information Technology
    Future Strategies, Lighthouse Point, FL, USA

Gouillard F. J. And Kelly J., Transforming the Organization, 1995
          Reframing Corporate Direction, Restructuring the Company,
          Revitalizing the Enterprise, Renewing People
          Mc Graw-Hill, New York, USA

Grover Varub and Kettinger William J., Business Process Change, 1995
          Reengineering concepts, methods and technologies
          Idea Group Publishing, Harrisburg, PA, USA

Halé J., From Concepts to Capabilities, 1995
          Understanding and Exploiting Change as a Competitive Advantage
          John Wiley & Sons, Chichester, UK

Hammer M. and Champy J., Reengineering the Corporation, 1993
          A Manifesto for Business Revolution
          HarperCollins, New York, USA

Hammer M. And Stanton S., The Reengineering Revolution, 1994
          A Handbook
          HarperCollins, New York, USA

Johansson H. McHugh P., Pendlebury A. J. Wheeler III W. A., 1993
          Breakpoint Strategies for Market Dominance
          John Wiley & Sons, Chichester, UK

Keen P. G. And Knapp E.,
          Every Manager's Guide to Business Processes, 1995
          Quality, Learning, Re-engineering, Logistics

Koulopoulos T. M., The Workflow Imperative, 1995
          Building Real World Business Solutions
          Van Nostrand Reinhold, New York, USA

Meyer B., Object Success, 1995
          A Manager's guide to object orientation, its impact on the corporation
          and its use for reengineering the software process
          Prentice Hall International (UK), Hemel Hempstead, UK

Mintzberg H., The structuring of Organisations, 1979
          A Synthesis of the Research
          Prentice Hall International, Englewood Cliffs, USA

Nonaka Ikujiro, Takeuchi Hirotaka, The Knowledge Company, 1995
          How Japanese Companies Create the Dynamics of Innovation
          Oxford University Press, New York, USA

Ould M.A., Business Process, 1995
>   Modelling and Analysis for Re-Engineering and Improvement.
>   John Wiley & Sons Ltd. Chichester, UK

Rummler G.A. and Brache A. P., Improving Performance, 1995
>   How to Manage the White Space on the Organization Chart
>   Jossey-Bass, San Francisco, USA

Scheer A.-W. Business Process Engineering, 1994
>   Reference Models for Industrial Enterprises
>   Springer-Verlag, Berlin, Germany

1.1.2 Conferences and Academic Proceedings

Business Process & Workflow Conference, 1995, 1996
>   Giga Information Group, Norwell, USA

Coleman D., Groupware'95 The Workgroup Solutions Conference, 1995
>   The Conference Group, Scottsdale

The Delphi Report
>   Delphi Consulting Group

The Gilbane Report
>   CAP Ventures

Marshak R. Workflow 95 Business Process Re-Engineering Conference, 1995
>   The Conference Group, Scottsdale

Organizational Computing Systems, 1995
>   ACM SIGOIS, New York, USA

1.1.3 Journals, Newsletters

ACM Transactions on Office Information Systems

Business Process Re-Engineering and Management Journal
>   MCB University Press, Bradford

Lettre du Workflow et du Groupware
>   GLS Conseil, Paris, France

Workflow World
>   Sodan, Uxbridge, UK

1.1.4 Reports

Cory T., Business Process Modelling Tools, 1995
  Sodan, Uxbridge, UK

Hales Keith, Workflow Management Products, Fifth Edition, 1996
  Sodan, Uxbridge, UK

Marshak D., Notes and Workflow, 1994
  Using Lotus Notes to Manage Business Processes
  In-Depth Research Report
  Patricia Seybold Group, Boston, USA

Miers Derek, Process Product Watch, 1995
  Work Management Technologies
  Enix, Richmond, UK

Pyke Jon, Workflow Report, 1995
  Cambridge Market Intelligence, London, UK

Stark H. And Lachal L., Workflow, 1995
  Ovum, London, UK

Whitehead R., Workgroup Computing Strategies, 1995
  Cambridge Market Intelligence, London, UK

1.2 Other Sources of Information

1.2.1 Associations

In addition to the Workflow Management Coalition, a number of international industry associations exist.

AIIM - Association for Information and Image Management International
1100 Wayne Avenue
Suite 1100, Silver Spring
MD 20910-5603
USA
1 301 587 8202
1 301 587 5129
aiim@aiim.org
http://www.aiim.org

AIIM International
Boulevard St. Michel 15
1040 Brussels, Belgium
32 2 743 15 43
32.2.743.15.50

As well as organising a regular conference and exhibition (see below), AIIM, who are a W*f*MC member, are a standards development organization in the document management arena. They publish a magazine: *Inform*, and a comprehensive catalogue of books, reports, and tapes: *AIIM InfoShop*.

WARIA - Workflow and Reengineering International Association
3640 North Federal Highway
Lighthouse Point
Florida 33064
USA
1 305 782 3376
1 305 782 6365
waria@gate.net
http://www.waria.com/waria

WARIA is a professional association for those working in the areas of workflow and BPR. Their charter is to identify and clarify issues that are common to all users of workflow and those who are in the process of reengineering their organizations.

1.2.2 International Events

A number of conferences and exhibitions which relate to workflow run on a regular basis. Contact the organisers for up to date information. In some cases the Workflow Management Coalition are a supporting organisation.

AIIM Show and Conference - USA
A major annual event in the imaging industry's calendar.
1100 Wayne Avenue,
Suite 1100, Silver Spring
MD 20910-5603
USA
1 301 587 8202
1 301 587 5129
aiim@aiim.org
http://www.aiim.org

Business Process and Workflow Conference - Europe and USA
Conferences focused on workflow and business process issues, with tutorials and
product test labs.
Giga Information Group
One Longwater Circle
Norwell, MA 02061-1620
USA
1 617 982 9500
1 617 982 1724
conferences@gigasd.com
http://www.gigasd.com

Documation
Conferences on document management held in various locations around the world.
78, Rue des Grands-Champs
75020 PARIS
FRANCE
33 1 4348 3841
33 1 4348 5543
documation@argos.rio.org

IMC
Various document management-related events around the world, including Europe,
Asia and the Far East.
IMC World Headquarters
1650 38th St., Suite 205W
Boulder, CO 80301
USA
1 303 440 7085
1 303 440 7234

1.2.3 World Wide Web

Many product vendors and other suppliers have their own Web pages, of course.
Here are some sites which are "product-neutral".

Workflow Management Coalition
The Coalition's own pages include information on the latest state of standards
documents, copies of press releases, and the member directory.
The pages are mirrored on each side of the Atlantic:

> http://www.aiai.ed.ac.uk/WfMC/
> http://www.arms.ohio-state.edu/WfMC/

Workflow on the Web
A site provided by consultancy Concordium, including various workflow-related resources, such as a product directory, monthly workflow news summaries, and a diary of relevant events. There are links to many other Web sites, too.

http://www.concordium.co.uk/concordium

WARIA
The Workflow and Reengineering International Association (see Associations above) maintain a comprehensive Web site on workflow and business process reengineering topics, including a useful book list of books they can supply.

http://www.waria.com/waria

University of Twente
Lots of research-orientated workflow information.

http://www_is.cs.utwente.nl:8080/~joosten/workflow.html

Product Index

Note: This index excludes products which provide underlying enabling technologies, such as operating systems, programming languages and environments, and databases

Organization Index

Note: This index excludes references to *Section 3–The Directory*. Consult the *Workflow Management Coalition Member Directory* in that section for a list of member organizations.

Subject Index